A HISTORY OF JEWISH LITERATURE
VOLUME VII

Israel Zinberg's *History of Jewish Literature*

An Analytic Index to the *History of Jewish Literature* will appear in Volume XII.

Israel Zinberg

A HISTORY OF
JEWISH
LITERATURE

TRANSLATED AND EDITED BY BERNARD MARTIN

*Old Yiddish Literature from Its
Origins to the Haskalah Period*

HEBREW UNION COLLEGE PRESS
CINCINNATI, OHIO

KTAV PUBLISHING HOUSE, INC.
NEW YORK, NEW YORK

1975

The full translation into English of Israel Zinberg's
HISTORY OF JEWISH LITERATURE, compris-
ing twelve volumes, is being brought to publication
by the generous and continuing support of the
Memorial Foundation for Jewish Culture.

Library of Congress Cataloging in Publication Data

Zinberg, Israel, 1873–1938.
  Old Yiddish literature from its origins to the
Haskalah period.

  (His A history of Jewish literature ; v. 7)
  Translation of Alt-yidishe literatur fun di eltste
tsaytn biz der haskole-tkufe, which was published as v. 6
of the author's Di geshikhte fun der literatur bay Yidn.
  Includes bibliographical references and index.
  1. Yiddish literature—History and criticism.
I. Title.
PJ5008.Z5313 vol. 7 [PJ5120] 839'.09'09 75–11545
ISBN 0–87068–465–5

Printed in the United States of America.

Contents

PART VIII: OLD YIDDISH LITERATURE FROM ITS ORIGINS TO THE HASKALAH PERIOD

Chapter One: LANGUAGES AMONG JEWS; THE ORIGINS OF YIDDISH   /   3

National literature and popular creativity; national language and colloquial language—The scarcity and high cost of books in the Middle Ages; the consequent role of patrons—The vernacular of the German Jews in the Middle Ages—The Judeo-German dialect—German Jewish scholars on the "despised jargon"—Hebrew and foreign language elements in Judeo-German—Colloquial and literary languages—Prayers in a mixture of languages among the French Jews and prayers in Judeo-German—*Firzogerins* (women's precentresses), *generins* (benefactors), and patronesses—Translators and expository preachers—Transformations of aggadic material—From Midrash to heroic epic—*Spielmänner* (minstrels) *badḥanim* (jesters) and *Gesellekeit-Leute* (entertainers).

Chapter Two: BIBLE GLOSSARIES AND THE BEGIN-
NINGS OF YIDDISH LITERATURE / 29

The handwritten glossaries—*Derush* elements in the glossar-
ies—The medieval translations of books of the Bible and of
the Festival Prayerbook—"Godly songs" in Yiddish—Old-
Yiddish secular literature—The translation of *Ben Ha-Melech
Veha-Nazir*—Menaḥem Oldendorf's collection of poems—
Didactic-satirical poems and controversy or debate poems—
Medieval love-songs—The Polish-Jewish community and its
vernacular—The social-cultural changes at the end of the
Middle Ages—The strengthening of the urban bourgeosie—
The folk language as cultural language—The printing press
and its cultural role—Oral folklore and folk literature—The
popular books and their anonymous editors and publishers
—The cultural significance of the printed book.

Chapter Three: ROMANCES AND EPICS / 49

The oldest printed popular books in Yiddish—German
works in Hebrew characters—Rabbi Anshel's *Mirkevet Ha-
Mishneh*—The *Spielmann* repertoire—The Arthur-romance
and its versions—Its publisher Josef Witzenhausen—The
significance of the Hamburg manuscripts—From *Spielmann*
poetry to popular book—Elijah Baḥur (Levita) and his *Spielmann* poems—His *Ha-Mavdil* and his Purim poem on the
conflagration in Venice—His knightly romance *Bove-Bukh*—
The style of the romance—The stanza meter—The Jewish
fashion in chivalrous romance—Levita's romance *Paris un
Viene*—Its unique style.

Chapter Four: BIBLE TRANSLATIONS AND MIDRA-
SHIM IN YIDDISH / 87

The battle against the "foolish books"—Isaac Wallich's collection of poems—Dance songs and love songs—The Pentateuch translations in the Augsburg and Constance editions
—Elijah Baḥur's translation of the Psalms—Cornelius
Adelkind as publisher—Joseph bar Yakar and his translation
of the Prayerbook—Jewish publishers and their advertisements—Judeo-German poetic reworkings of Midrashic
material—The *Shire Fun Yitzḥok* and *Der Yidisher Shtam*—
The Yiddish *Midrash Va-Yosha* and the Esther poems—Epics

Contents

of Biblical heroes—*Shmuel-Bukh* and its significance—The
Melokhim-Bukh—"Adam and Eve" poem—Two types of
Spielmänner.

Chapter Five: POPULAR LITERATURE; *TZE'ENAH
U-RE'ENAH* / 119

Literal and homiletic translations of the Bible—Jehudah
Leib Bresch and the Cremona edition of The Pentateuch—
Isaac Sulkes and his translation of the Song of Songs—Isaac
Sulkes as a man of the people—Midrashic material as "reading material"—*Di Lange Megile*—Women's literature and
folk literature—Isaac Prossnitz on the cultural importance
of the woman—The style of *Di Lange Megile*—Stories as
material for moral instruction—The prose preaching style—
Rabbi Isaac ben Samson and his *Taytsh-Khumesh*—Jacob ben
Isaac Ashkenazi of Yanov—The *Tze'enah U-Re'enah* as "the
women's Torah"—Its cultural-historical significance—The
battle against the homiletic way in the educational system—
Be'er Mosheh—The Bible translations of Yekutiel Blitz and
Josef Witzenhausen—Their unsuccessful battle against the
homiletic style of the *Tze'enah U-Re'enah.*

Chapter Six: MORALITY BOOKS / 141

Morality books in Yiddish—*Ein schön Frauen Buchlein (Seder
Nashim)*—The Yiddish translation of *Sefer Ha-Yirah* (1546
and 1583) and the rhymed paraphrase *Hayyei Olam (Das Buch
des ewigen Lebens)*—The Hebrew *Sefer Middot* and its Yiddish
translation—*Roizn-Gortn (Sefer Ha-Gan)* and Abraham Ashkenazi's *Sam Hayyim*—The ethnographic interest of Ashkenazi's *Divrei Musar*—Moses Altschuler's *Brantshpigl*—Altschuler on the Jewish woman—Isaac ben Eliakum and his
Lev Tov—The style of *Lev Tov*—Issac ben Eliakum on
prayers in Yiddish and on the education of children—To an
impasse—Solomon Zalman ben Eliezer Ufenhausen and his
Yidisher Teryak—The significance of the work.

Transliteration of Yiddish Terms

Hebrew	Translit.		Hebrew	Translit.
א	not transliterated		יי	ey
אַ	a		ײַ	ay
אָ	o		כ	k
ב	b		כ,ך	kh
בֿ	v		ל	l
ג	g		מ,ם	m
ד	d		נ,ן	n
ה	h		ס	s
ו,וּ	u		ע	e
וו	v		פּ	p
וי	oy		פֿ,ף	f
ז	z		צ,ץ	ts
זש	zh		ק	k
ח	kh		ר	r
ט	t		ש	sh
טש	tsh. ch		שׂ	s
י	(consonant) y		ת	t
י	(vowel) i		ת	s

Abbreviations

JQR	*Jewish Quarterly Review*
JQR, n.s.	*Jewish Quarterly Review*, new series
MGWJ	*Monatsschrift für die Geschichte und Wissenschaft des Judentums*
PAAJR	*Proceedings of the American Academy for Jewish Research*
REJ	*Revue des Études Juives*
ZHB	*Zeitschrift für hebräische Bibliographie*

This volume is dedicated
to
S. H. Scheuer
Patron of Learning
Proud American and Jew

OLD YIDDISH LITERATURE FROM ITS ORIGINS TO THE HASKALAH PERIOD

CHAPTER ONE

Languages Among Jews:
THE ORIGINS OF YIDDISH

National literature and popular creativity; national language and colloquial language - The scarcity and high cost of books in the Middle Ages; the consequent role of patrons - The vernacular of the German Jews in the Middle Ages - The Judeo-German dialect - German Jewish scholars on the "despised jargon" - Hebrew and foreign language elements in Judeo-German - Colloquial and literary languages - Prayers in a mixture of languages among the French Jews and prayers in Judeo-German - *Firzogerins* (women's precentresses), *generins* (benefactors), and patronesses - Translators and expository preachers - Transformations of aggadic material - From Midrash to heroic epic - *Spielmänner* (minstrels) *baḍḥanim* (jesters) and *Gesellekeit-Leute* (entertainers).

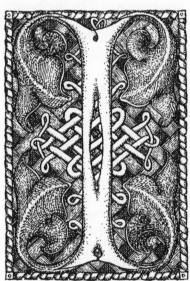

N THE introduction to our work[1] we dwelt at some length on a highly unique phenomenon in the literary productivity of the Jewish people in ancient times, namely, that even at the higher stages of cultural evolution, creativity among the Jews still remained anonymous. The individual, the divinely blessed writer, was still subordinate to the community and literally lost in it; everything he created, everything about which he dreamed and hoped and for which his soul yearned, belonged exclusively to the community, the people. For centuries the collective creativity of the people remains closely associated with the national literature. All the spiritual and intellectual treasures produced and gathered among the people belong to the entire community,

1. Volume I, pp. 4ff.

and bear its name alone. They acknowledge only one creator
—and that is the whole nation, the congregation of Israel. To
be sure, in the final redaction of the spiritual treasures of the
Biblical era that have come down to us, no small role was
played by the world view and the intellectual and social interests of a definite group. Many important monuments of national culture and brilliant originality were lost (condemned to
be "hidden" in a *genizah*) under the strict censorship of these
editors. But all this was done in the name of the community,
with a concern only for the needs of the people, as understood
by the group in question which functioned as its spiritual
leaders and protectors.

Indeed, this in very significant measure brought it about that
when, in the era of the Second Temple, the Jewish people lost
its language and, in the Mishnaic period, the vernacular of the
Jewish community was no longer Hebrew but the Aramaic
dialect interspersed with a certain number of Hebrew, Greek
and Latin words, Aramaic was promptly raised to the level of
a highly important cultural-national factor. In it, the *leshon
hedyot* (language of the common people), as it was called by the
men of the Mishnah, the Torah was expounded to the people
in the synagogues and houses of study and at public assemblies.
It became the great cultural factor, the spiritual sentry that
aroused national sentiments in the masses and strengthened
the bond uniting the elements of the "trinity"—Israel, God,
and the Torah. Aramaic, the vernacular and language of creation of the broad strata of the population, was interwoven with
Hebrew, the national language of the Bible. They became twin
sisters for all generations. Both hallowed in the consciousness
of the people, they continued together to spin the golden
thread of national culture, even in later times when the language of the Targum (Aramaic) also died in the mouth of the
people and, along with Hebrew, became solely a literary language. Throughout the Diaspora the Torah was read in both
together (twice in Hebrew and once in the Targum each week),
and prayers were composed in both. In Aramaic the great
national treasures that were hallowed and revered by the people were produced and collected—not only the Talmud but
even the *Zohar* of the Middle Ages. "Because the Talmud," we
noted in our introduction,

is the result of many generations of collective effort, because the
entire community built this mighty structure, there had to be in it
all types of folk creativity—religious laws, philosophical ideas, and

speculative doubts, together with popular stories, legends, magical incantations, proverbs, jokes, dancing songs, and the like. The Talmud also is, by its very nature, an anonymous work; its author is the entire people of Israel, from the greatest scholar to the meanest ignoramus. This great anthology is a monument of popular creativity as well as of national literature. The folkloristic and the national, the personal and the communal, the individual and the collective—all are fraternally braided together in it.[2]

A quite different phenomenon is to be observed in the later Arabic-Moslem period, when the majority of the Jewish people once again lost its language and, under the influence of the newly awakened Arabic civilization, exchanged its vernacular, Aramaic, for the language of the colossal new Arab world-empire. But the new vernacular, despite the fact that it is cognate with the language of the Bible, just as Aramaic is, could no longer obtain such an honored place in the national Jewish culture as Aramaic had in its day. Arabic did not become the twin sister of Hebrew, but its proud rival. "For centuries the Arabic language became, for the major part of the Jewish people, the most significant factor of general culture but not of national creativity." This was the consequence of some extremely important cultural-historical factors. First of all, it was precisely under the enormous influence of Arabic civilization that the unique and specific quality whereby the ancient Hebrew-Aramaic literature was so sharply differentiated from its sisters disappeared; from the Arabic period on the creative individual in Jewish literature, too, spiritually overcame the community. Not the group, but the individual—the poet, the thinker, the scholar, who is culturally superior to the group—now creates on his own account and responsibility and collects under his own name national treasures upon which he places his own stamp and his individual creative spirit.[3]

Since the Arabic period, national literature has been separated from popular, from the collective creativity of the people, among Jews also. These two golden threads of culture are no longer woven together in one skein, as in the Biblical-Talmudic era, but are spun individually, each by itself. The national literature is produced by individuals who are, indeed, under the powerful influence of their environment but nevertheless stand above the people intellectually and spiritually.

2. *Ibid.*, p. 10.
3. *Ibid.*, p. 11.

And the people, the masses, create independently for themselves. One generation transmits to another treasures of legends, tales, songs, and proverbs orally. These are not noted down in books and are not collected in the national treasury; they abide only in the memory of the living generation. Much is thereby lost. Much obtains in time a different form and undergoes improvement; it is utilized by superior individuals, the creators of the national treasures.

We noted in our introduction another highly important phenomenon which again distinguishes the Jews from many other peoples of the world. Among most peoples both branches of cultural creativity are developed in the same language, but among Jews this has occurred in different tongues. The national literature evolves in the old vernaculars, Hebrew and Aramaic; the popular literature, so-called folklore, however, develops in the current language of the environment.

In the first part of our work[4] we dwelt at some length on the significant point that it was precisely under the influence of Arabic civilization that Jewish national creativity in the language of the Bible also burgeoned. The new Moslem world of ideas, which burst so impetuously into the Jewish community that had lapsed into intellectual somnolence after the writing down of the Talmud, sharply posed before Judaism the alternative: either to be deluged by the triumphant stream of Arabic civilization, or to exercise its own national powers and, through struggle, obtain its right to independent national-cultural existence. As we know, the Jewish community chose the second way.

Under the government of the highly cultured caliphs, the two related civilizations, the Jewish and the Arabic, established fraternal bonds. They influenced each other, and this influence produced magnificent results. One cannot speak here of assimilation or of self-annihilation, but only of stimulus, of spiritual and intellectual influence. Arabic culture worked on the somnolent Jewish powers like a catalyst, eliciting the strongest life processes, and the material deeply sunk in sleep was thereby transformed into energy and spirit that could not rest but strove ever upward.[5]

Because of national self-consciousness, of the drive for national-cultural existence, Arabic, the revered language of the Ko-

4. *Ibid.*, Chapters 1–3, 5.
5. *Ibid.*, pp. 14–15.

ran, did not become the sister of Hebrew but remained its proud rival, a mirror-image of Sarah and Hagar.

The efflorescence of the language of the Koran, held sacred by the Arabs, provoked, as we observed in the first volume of our work, a feeling of envy among the Jews. It aroused in them the national will to strengthen and develop the language of their own shrine—the Bible.[6] It is therefore quite characteristic that the first great Jewish poet who grew up under the powerful influence of Arabic civilization, Solomon Ibn Gabirol, regarded himself as the redeemer of the holy tongue and its faithful guardian sent by Providence to arouse love for the language of Scripture in the hearts of his brethren through his flaming word.[7] The poet's proud verses, however, suggest another very important point. Arabic poetry bloomed magnificently in Spain, arousing envy in the Jewish intelligentsia, among whom was born the desire to attempt the creation in Hebrew not only of religious poems but of secular poetry as well. We have seen that Solomon Ibn Gabirol and the poets who followed him enriched national Jewish literature and raised secular poetry in Hebrew to a high level. Their poems, however, were not accessible to the broad strata of the Jewish people, for not only women but a very significant part of the male population understood neither the language of the Bible nor that of the Talmud. When Ibn Gabirol complains that "the eye of his people has become blind," that the people has forgotten its holy book and its language has become foreign to it, that it can no longer even read the script, he is not indulging in poetic exaggeration. As reliable a witness as the renowned Spanish rabbi of the fourteenth century, Rabbi Isaac bar Sheshet (Ribash), relates that the majority of the common people could not read the prayers and it was therefore necessary to be content with having the *hazzan* or precentor chant them, with the congregation repeating them after him.[8] One must also take into consideration in this connection that even in the fourteenth century a significant percentage of the Spanish Jews were common laborers—peasants and artisans. Virtually

6. *Ibid.*, p. 15.
7. *Ibid.*, p. 50.
8. Rabbi Isaac bar Sheshet Perfet, *Responsa*, No. 37. An authority on the Ashkenazic communities, the author of *Lev Tov*, also notes: "In former times frequently in many synagogues there was not more than one *mahzor*, or two or three, at most. Also there were not many *selihot*. So no one recited. Hence, the precentor (*hazzan*) had to know it well" (p. 105).

whole communities were engaged in weaving and dyeing.[9]
However, there is no doubt that an incessant process of unique
popular creativity was going on at the same time in the depths
of the people. Works were produced not only especially *for* the
people but *by* the people. Not only would *ḥazzanim* and
preachers read in the synagogues certain passages from the
Bible in the vernacular—e.g., on the Seventh Day of Passover
the "Shirat Ha-Yam" (Song of the Sea), on Shavuot the Decalogue, on the Sabbath the blessings before the lection from the
Prophets,[10] on Purim the Scroll of Esther,[11] and on Passover
the Haggadah—but the mass of the people itself created in its
colloquial language legends, tales, and songs with which mothers would rock their children to sleep and young people accompany their dancing, or in which the woes and joys of love were
expressed. But all this, as has been noted, was oral, for in the
Middle Ages the common people had no books.

At that time, before printing and rag paper were invented,
books were among the most expensive of items and something
only a very wealthy person could afford. "Writing is an art,"
declares Jehudah Ibn Tibbon, the "chief of the translators."[12]
"In writing," says the author of *Iggeret Musar*, Solomon Alami,
"one must be extremely careful." A precise and beautiful manuscript in those times was actually a significant cultural factor.
The value of a manuscript depended on the care and expertise
of the copyist. Men of extensive knowledge[13] frequently engaged in the "art" of copying manuscripts, and their work was
extremely well paid.[14] A parchment Pentateuch or Bible was
bequeathed to one's posterity, together with pearls, diamonds,
and other jewels. And when it happened that an heir's fortunes
declined and he was compelled to sell his inherited parchment
books to pay his debts, this was done in the courthouse; on the
book itself, on the last page on which there was no writing, a
formal bill of sale subscribed by no less than three witnesses
was placed.[15] And so that no one should venture to take the

9. See Graetz, *Geschichte der Juden*, Vol. VIII, p. 194, for the decree of King John II.
See also Jean Régné, *Catalogue des actes*, etc., Nos. 1289, 1946, 1953, 2054.
10. See Isaac bar Sheshet Perfet, *Responsa*, No., 25; Rabbi Simeon ben Tzemaḥ Duran,
Responsa, III, 121; and also *Ha-Palit*, 38.
11. Rabbi Isaac bar Sheshet Perfet, *Responsa*, No. 38: "It is a custom to read the *megillah*
to women in the vernacular, and also the *ketubah* in the vernacular."
12. See our *History*, Vol. Two, p. 90ff.
13. For a list of names of copyists in Spain and Portugal, see *ZHB*, XIV, 105–112.
14. On the prices of books in the Middle Ages, see Zunz, *Zur Geschichte und Literatur*,
pp. 211–213; *JQR* n.s., IV, 530.
15. Several old parchment sheets of the 11th–13th centuries with such inscriptions,

book without the knowledge of its owner, the bill of sale warned against such action with the severest excommunications and with the curses of the Biblical list of anathemas.

In the Middle Ages trials concerning manuscripts appraised at considerable sums of money used to take place, with each party eager to gain possession of the book.[16] Students in *yeshivot* or Talmudic academies, when unable to borrow the books required for their study, not infrequently violated the commandment "Thou shalt not steal" and returned the purloined manuscript only after copying it in full.[17] Even in the schools of the wealthy Spanish-Arabic communities instruction was carried on without books, for those who had their own could not trust small children with such expensive objects. The teacher would write out the *sidrah* or weekly reading from the Pentateuch on a large tablet and drill the children in it.[18] It is therefore not surprising that when Rabbi Abraham Ibn Daud in his *Sefer Ha-Kabbalah* sings the praises of the famous Jewish scholar and statesman, Samuel Ha-Nagid, he stresses that Samuel had at his court a whole corps of scribes who copied the books of the Bible and the tractates of the Talmud and provided the *yeshivot* and houses of study with them.

Thus we see that even for *yeshivot* to be supplied with the necessary religious books, wealthy philanthropists and patrons were required. All the more was this the case with scholarly works and secular literature in general. If a scholar or poet was himself not wealthy, he could engage in the sciences and poetry only with the support of some patron or philanthropist. We noted in the first volume of our work[19] that it was, in fact, only because of Jewish philanthropists and nobles that secular Hebrew literature could bloom in Arabic Spain. Jehudah Ibn Tibbon executed his famous translations at the commission of

---

which are extremely interesting from the cultural-ethnographic point of view, are to be found in the library in Leningrad of the Society for the Promotion of Enlightenment Among Jews. In these are also noted the very high prices for which these books were sold.

16. See Rabbi Isaac ben Jacob Alfasi (Rif), *Responsa*, No. 84: "Reuben argued that Simeon gave him a Bible as pledge for five hundred dinars, and wishes to take it for this money, but Simeon says: This never happened; it was loaned to you."

17. *Ibid.*, No. 133. "One of the pupils stole some books of commentaries from his colleague, and when they demanded them of him, he swore a grievous oath that he would not return them until he had copied them; and there is he who teaches that it is permitted to steal them."

18. Rabbi Simeon ben Tzemah Duran, *Responsa*, I, No. 2.

19. P. 181. See also our work "Der Kamf Far Yidish In Der Alt-Yidisher Literatur" (*Filologishe Shriftn*, II, 76–78).

cultured patrons. It was thanks to patrons, philanthropists, and wealthy pupils that Abraham Ibn Ezra wrote his scholarly works. There is virtually not a single significant poetic work of the Judeo-Arabic Middle Ages which does not carry on its title-page a song of praise dedicated to the Jewish "prince" who gave the author the support he required. When the great Solomon Ibn Gabirol praises the philanthropist Samuel Ha-Nagid, he emphasizes that, as a result of the latter's graciousness and generosity, the poet's purse was filled with money. The Jewish troubador, the wandering minstrel Jehudah Alḥarizi, derived his livelihood from the fact that various Jewish lords and officials supported him and paid him in gold coin for his witty verses and exercises. We observed[20] that the young poet Isaac dedicated his poem *Ezrat Nashim* to a Jewish philanthropist. He explains his motives in the poem itself in quite prosaic fashion. He addresses the following wish to his poems: "O hasten, my songs, to the gracious lord. Under his shelter seek help and protection; broad is his heart and generous. There you will find prepared the table, the stool, and the candelabrum [a Biblical expression]. Serve him faithfully like slaves; he will watch over you and protect you."

It is readily comprehensible that the products of popular creativity—what served as spiritual sustenance for the common people, for women and simple peasants, in the vernacular—could obtain very few patrons and supporters among the Jewish officials and nobility. Even in the scholarly works of that era we find extremely little, even of a general nature, about the intellectual nourishment of the common people that might provide us with some conception of the songs the Jewish masses sang or the legends they spun. We do not even have precise information about what language the Spanish Jews spoke in various eras, nor do we know clearly and distinctly when the Castilian dialect displaced Arabic among the Jewish masses in Spain. There is, of course, no doubt that popular productivity in the vernacular found a certain response in the national literature. But this was already in altered form—in the reflection of the poet's individual creation in Hebrew. Since popular creativity remained oral, it was largely lost in its original form.

The same thing, although under different cultural conditions, occurred in the most important Jewish community of Christian Europe, namely, in Franco-German Jewry. We

20. Vol. I, p. 181.

noted in the second volume[21] that, as merchants, both the German and French Jews came into close association with the local populace. The result of this intercourse, however, was completely different from what it was in highly cultured Arabic Spain. The Arabs, we observed in the first chapter of our work,

were blessed with something not to be found at that time among any people of Christian Europe: their spiritual and intellectual life was harmoniously integral, and their culture unitary and seamless . . . The Koran, the sacred book of Islam, grew out of Arabic soil and was created out of the living vernacular of the people. The religious enthusiasm and cultural reawakening of the Arabs in that period, when Islam revealed itself to the world, had a remarkably powerful influence on the development of the popular language, for a whole universe of new concepts and ideas was required to embrace it. The living speech of the people, when it became a sacred language, was also raised to the level of a flourishing cultural language, the language of science and literature.

But the Christian peoples of Europe did not know this harmonious wholeness. They, we noted,

had received their religion, then the sole bearer of culture, from an external source. The only cultural language of medieval Europe was also a foreign one, the dead Latin language. The tongues and dialects which the European peoples then spoke served only as vernaculars and were not employed for cultural purposes. Under such circumstances the vernaculars did not have the possibility of developing normally and attaining the status of cultural languages. Religion and science, in their alien Latin garments, were separated as by a solid wall from the people and its language. Given such a partition, there could be no question either of normal development of religion and science or of genuine national culture.

The Franco-German Jews therefore had nothing for which to "envy" their Christian neighbors. The Christian populace in Germany and northern France at that time was at a very low level of civilization. Virtually the only persons of knowledge in that era were the higher clergy and the monks in the cloisters, and even their knowledge was extremely one-sided, strictly limited to the realm of Christian dogmatics. Even this very restricted discipline was studied in the only language of culture in medieval Christian Europe—Latin.

We noted in the second volume of our history how the Jews

21. P. 5.

reacted to the "language of the priests."[22] As far as the other strata of the Christian populace is concerned, even in the world of knighthood, not to speak of the common people, literate persons were extremely rare. It is therefore quite understandable that medieval knightly poetry, which was intimately associated with the nobility and the feudal way of life, was essentially oral poetry. Generally speaking, the knight could neither read nor write; his power was based on the sword and the spear, not on the pen. The knight and his household did not read poems and songs but listened to the jongleur and *Spielmann* or gleeman declaim them, generally to musical accompaniment. Highly characteristic in this respect is the famous poet of the twelfth century, Wolfram of Eschenbach, who glories in his knightly status and his weapons. Proudly he declares: *"Zum Schildesamt bin Ich geboren* (I was born into the class that bears shields)." But as far as reading books and the art of writing are concerned, he was, as we have noted,[23] not well-versed.

It is quite understandable that Franco-German Jewry, living in such a culturally retarded environment, had very slight knowledge of scientific and philosophical matters. Intellectually isolated, the Jews of these lands devoted all their mental powers to religious questions associated with Judaism and its laws and precepts. The Jewish scholars of Germany and France naturally wrote their works not in the crude vernacular but in the "holy" language—to be more precise, in a mixture of both the ancient languages, Hebrew and Aramaic. Books were even more rare and expensive in the Franco-German Jewish community than they were in highly civilized Arabic Spain. It is worthy of note that a contemporary of Rabbenu Gershom's, the great scholar Rabbi Eliezer Ha-Gadol, never studied the Talmudic tractate *Avodah Zarah* "because he never saw it with his own eyes."[24] The renowned commentator Rashi indicates in his responsa that in many communities only the *ḥazzanim* (cantors or precentors) had prayer books while the congregation listened to the prayers without books in their hands.[25] And when a religious question was asked of the famous Rabbenu Tam, he was not embarrassed to reply: "If you will send me parchment, I shall have wherewith to write my

22. *Ibid.*
23. *Ibid.*
24. *Teshuvot Hachmei Tzarefat Ve-Lotir*, 84.
25. See also *Maḥzor Vitry*, 323.

reply." It was because of the extreme costliness and scarcity of books that the *Sefer Ḥasidim* frequently stresses what a great good deed it is to lend another a book.[26]

To the very high price of parchment, the major raw material for manuscripts in those times, the special character of numerous old Hebrew manuscripts of the Middle Ages presents clear testimony: many pages are deeply cut at the bottom "to the flesh," i.e., close to the written text. In the Middle Ages all kinds of receipts and promissory notes, not to mention *mezuzot*, amulets, and the like, were written on parchment. Since this material was very expensive, people would frequently, in time of need, utilize the uninscribed margins of the parchment pages in the handwritten books of that time, books that were bequeathed from generation to generation. If a long strip of parchment was required, they would cut out the clean, uninscribed margin along the entire length or width of the manuscript; if a smaller strip was needed, they would cut out from the page only a part of the margin that had no writing on it.

The Hebrew-Aramaic dialect, the cultural language of Franco-German Jewry, was comprehensible only to scholars. The common people, not to speak of women, had very limited knowledge of it. For them the vernacular or colloquial language had to fulfill the functions of a cultural language as well.

It must first of all be clearly established what this vernacular which the Jews of medieval Christian Europe spoke looked like. For our subject, naturally, it is important only to dwell on the vernacular of the German Jews, the creators of the so-called *Leshon Ashkenaz* and Old-Yiddish literature. We noted at the beginning of the second volume that the majority of German Jewry in the tenth to the thirteenth centuries was constituted by the communities of the Rhine region, the closest neighbor of the French provinces. The Jews who settled in the Rhine area immigrated there from the Roman lands and their route passed through France. Furthermore, it is also very probable that they brought with them from France the local vernacular —the Romance dialect. Even considerably later, in the twelfth century, when the German Jews had already adopted the German dialect, they still spoke fluent French as a result of their close connection with their French coreligionists and the extensive trade they carried on with France. Because the oldest Jewish settlements arose mainly in south Germany, where the High German dialect predominated, it is clear that this dialect

26. *Sefer Ḥasidim*, Nos. 861–875, 911, 927, etc.

was adopted by the Jews who immigrated thence from the Roman countries. For our purposes only the Middle High German[27] dialect can be of substantial interest, for independent cultural creativity, even in the rabbinic language, began among the German Jews only at the threshold of the eleventh century.

But the question arises whether the dialect that the Jews of Worms and Regensburg in the days of Jehudah Ḥasid and Eleazar of Worms spoke was different from the Middle High German their Christian neighbors spoke. Were there already at that time noticeable signs of a unique "Judeo-German" dialect? As is known, the founders of *die Wissenschaft des Judentums*, the German Jewish scholars of the nineteenth century, sought, out of patriotic motives, to demonstrate that Jews always spoke the same language as the inhabitants of the country from the time they first came to Germany; only at the end of the Middle Ages, more correctly in the sixteenth century, did the "Pollaks," i.e., the Polish Jews who had immigrated in large numbers, corrupt the vernacular of the German Jews and transform it into a "despicable jargon," about which the German Jewish scholars speak with the profoundest hostility and contempt.

The historian Heinrich Graetz brands the Yiddish "jargon" as a "half bestial language." Moritz Steinschneider, who accomplished so much in the field of Old-Yiddish bibliography, frankly admits that "the jargon is something repulsive to me."[28] And the brilliant Abraham Geiger judges that Judeo-German literature "is a model of tastelessness."[29] Leopold Zunz believes that the first discernible signs of a Judeo-German dialect appear no earlier than the sixteenth century;[30] Steinschneider concludes that it was much later, only in the seventeenth century, when, after the great persecutions of 1648, the German-Jewish settlements were deluged by refugees

27. As is known, the history of the evolution of the German language is divided into the following three eras: (1) Old High German, from 750 to 1100 A.D.; (2) Middle High German, from c. 1100 to 1500, and (3) New High German, from 1500 to the present day.

28. *Purim und Parodie,* 89.

29. *Gesammelte Schriften,* II, 221. Geiger further adds: "Wie schon in den Volksbüchern von den Sagen, Anekdoten u.s.w. ab, so ist die religiöse Literatur nicht bloss inhaltlich, sondern auch sprachlich das *erbärmlichste Kauderwälsch*; ein deutscher Jossiphon, ein Zeenah Urenah, ein Tam we'Jaschar und dergleichen wahrhaft den Geschmack vergiftend . . ."

30. *Die gottesdienstlichen Vorträge der Juden,* Second Edition, p. 253.

from the Ukraine and Poland. Of the German-Jewish scholars of the nineteenth century, only Isaac Marcus Jost believed that the Judeo-German dialect is already in evidence at the end of the thirteenth century, when the Jews driven out of Provence settled in large numbers in south Germany. Jost declares that "French coloration is to be observed in the Judeo-German dialect to the present day."[31]

It is beyond doubt that Jost is, indeed, closer to the truth, notwithstanding the fact that he gives too partial a portrait, since he dwells only on a single factor, namely, the French influence. "No people," remarks the founder of modern philology Wilhelm von Humboldt, "can vivify and fructify a foreign tongue with its own spirit, save by reworking it and creating a new language out of it." This insight is confirmed in the development of *Leshon Ashkenaz*, the Judeo-German language which the Jewish community in Germany created. Unfortunately, the investigation of the first stages of this evolution is bound up, as we shall presently see, with enormous difficulties. But this is not sufficient reason to abandon the problem entirely or to leave it untouched.

When Zunz dwells in his *Die gottesdienstlichen Vorträge der Juden* (pp. 438–441)[32] on the function of the Hebrew elements in Yiddish he notes that Hebrew words are utilized (1) for objects related to Judaism, e.g., *tallit, huppah, mitzvah, averah,* etc. and to the Jewish way of life, e.g., *yeshivah, kahal, dayyan, baal ha-bayyit, borer,* and the like; (2) for concepts associated with study in the *yeshivot* and schools, e.g., *davka, baki, harif, aderabah, peshita,* and similar terms; (3) for various expressions of daily life (*achilah, gedulah, da'agah, mazzal, tachlit,* etc.; and (4) for entities and objects which Jews deliberately did not wish to call by German terms (*bilbul, gezerah, meshummad,* etc.).

Historically, however, this definition is not quite correct, for an extremely important group of objects is missing from it. We noted in the previous volume the significant economic role which the Jewish wholesale merchants, the Radanites, "who knew the routes," played in consequence of their trade with

---

31. See Ersch and Gruber, *Allgemeine Enzyklopädie der Wissenschaften und Künste*, Second Section, 2, 27, 323: "Sichtbar und deutlich ist die französische Färbung der jüdisch-deutscher Konstruktion." A similar view was expressed as early as the sixteenth century by Elijah Levita who notes in his *Tishbi* at the word *krovetz*, that "we German Jews come from the stock of the French; for when we were expelled from France . . . we were spread over Germany, and many words of their language remained in our mouth."

32. Second Edition, 453, 455.

the Far East across the German and Slavic lands. On the threshold of the second millenium according to the Christian reckoning, the major shipping points of the Radanite trade were the Rhine cities of Mainz and Regensburg. The Jewish merchants on their long and difficult journeys everywhere felt at home, for in every country they encountered brethren of the same origin and religion in whose homes they found assured protection and rest. However, a characteristic feature on which a writer of the twelfth century already dwelt must be noted here. Jehudah Halevi's pupil, the Spanish grammarian Solomon Parḥon,[33] writes at the end of his *Maḥberet He-Aruch:*

I strongly beg that if my readers find in my work inappropriate and unsuccessful expressions, they will judge me in the scale of merit. In our country [Spain] people are not so proficient in Hebrew, for in all the Moslem lands one language is prevalent, and wherever our Spanish Jews come, their language is understood and they can easily converse with their brethren. It is otherwise, however, in the Christian lands; in every country a different tongue is spoken, and when a Jew comes from one country to another, his language is not understood and he cannot converse with his brethren there except in the holy tongue. As a result, they are more accustomed to think and speak in Hebrew.

The route over which the Jewish international wholesale merchants of the Rhine region conducted their trade with the rich Moslem lands of anterior Asia lay over countries and kingdoms in which Jews spoke the most varied languages, and the only universal language through which the merchants who had come from abroad could make themselves more or less understood by their brethren who spoke different tongues was Hebrew. Hebrew trade terms and commercial designations undoubtedly played the most important role in the frequent intercourse which the Jews of various countries had with one another. It is, therefore, highly probably that Hebrew trade terms and expressions were introduced into the vernacular of the German Jews even before the designations of entities that have some relationship to Judaism and its sacred objects.

Besides Hebrew, Romance elements were also generously represented in the vernacular of the Jews of south Germany who, at the beginning of the second millenium, were still in close relationships with the Jews of France. Present day Yiddish preserves many of these elements. It suffices to note

33. Vol. II, p. 165ff.

such words as *alker,*[34] *almer,*[35] *impet,*[36] *farumert,*[37] *farvogelt,*[38] *plet,*[39] *goyder,*[40] *bentshen,*[41] *davenen,*[42] *nitol,*[43] *sarver,*[44] and many others.[45]

Since, however, the Jewish environment was a singular one and in it concepts unknown to the Christian population were prevalent, verbal forms of which Christians knew nothing also had to be created in the Jewish vernacular. So, for example, the teachers instructing the children in the schools had, when translating the weekly lections from the Pentateuch verbatim, to create expressions which simply are not found in the German vernacular. Some of these new words are preserved in the Old-Yiddish translations of the Pentateuch. For example: *hare'a = ibeln; ve-erastich = ich soll dich antshpoizen* (from the Romance *sposare*); *mohar maher = morgengob soll er morgengeben; maloch = kinigin; yalad = kindlen; shever = broch, onshikenish; haloch elech = geyn gey ich; karo ekra = rufn ruf ich; kedeshah = bereiterin; tifletzet = shturdishkeit;* etc.[46] However, it was not only through a certain number of foreign (Hebrew and Romance) words that the Jewish *Leshon Ashkenaz* in the Middle Ages was distinguished from Middle High German. It must be borne in mind that it is not only the way of life but the unique spiritual essence and psyche of a people that is mirrored in its language. It is beyond doubt that the vernacular of the German Jews in the Middle Ages was distinguished from the German dialect that their Christian neighbors spoke not only in a special pronunciation and nuances of certain vowels, but also in its unique syntax, in the construction of whole sentences and expressions. To illustrate this with living examples, however, is impossible, considering the fact that the simple vernacular in the mouth of the people was significantly different from the

34. alcove
35. armoire
36. impété
37. humeur
38. vagué
39. billet
40. goitre
41. benéz
42. divinisser
43. natalis (from the Latin)
44. serviteur
45. The influence of French is also discernible in the spelling of many words with the silent *alef* in the old manuscripts and printed editions.
46. See Grünbaum, *Jüdisch-deutsche Chrestomathie*, p. 143; Eleazar Schulmann, *Ha-Shiloah*, V, 42–43.

literary and official language in which the oldest Yiddish documents that have come down to us are written.[47]

Zunz endeavors to show in his previously cited work that all the old (to the end of the Middle Ages) Yiddish documents that have survived provide the best evidence that the Jews in Germany "spoke no other language than their Christian countrymen" and "were the same in language as the German Christians" (*Die gottesdienstlichen Vorträge*, p. 452). To be sure, the old Jewish documents that have been preserved are distinguished linguistically in very slight measure from the German documents of that age. Nevertheless, Zunz's argument is hardly convincing. One of the oldest dated Yiddish documents that has come down to us in full is the solemn oath to refrain from vengeance *(Urfehde)* of the famous Rabbi Meir ben Baruch Ha-Levi[48] which he issued in 1392 after his release from prison. This official document, subscribed with nine rabbinic signatures, cannot, however, give us any notion of the vernacular of the Jews in the Middle Ages, because it is written in the official chancellery style of that era; it is in fact, a German official document written in Hebrew letters.[49] Another solemn official declaration[50] of a Polish Jew named Yekutiel, written in Breslau in 1435, is couched in the same manner. How far removed the style of these declarations was from the customary epistolary style prevalent among the Jews at that time is attested by a letter written by a Jew of Frankfurt to a relative of his in 1454

47. We have already spoken of this incidentally in our work "Der Kamf Far Yidish" (*Filologishe Shriftn*, II, 82).

48. See our *History*, Vol. Three, pp. 145ff.

49. This document was first published by A. Freimann in *ZHB*, 1907, 107–111. We present here the first lines:

„איך מאיר בון ערפורט יוד ערקינן מיך מיט דיזם בריף בור מיך אליין הירן אונד
אירבן אלזו אז מיך די אירזמן פורזיהטיגן (vürsichtigen) אונד וויזן לויטא די בורגער־
מיישטער אונד רוט (rat) צו ורנקבורט אן גורטיגס (angefertigt) אונד גואנגן
(gefangen) האטן פון ברוך וועגן"‏. . .

50. This document, which has been greatly damaged by mice, was first published in Marcus Brann's *Geschichte der Juden in Schlesien* (1896), Supplement, IV, 683, and reprinted in Schipper's *Kultur-Geshikhte*, 272. We present here the first lines of this statement:

„איך יקותיאל יודא איטוון־בינוש יודן־זונא (Etwan Beinusch's Judensohn)
בקינא מיט דיזם בריבא אללן די אין זעהן הורן (הערן) אודר לעזן, דז איך גלובט
האבא אונ' גלובא אין קראפט דיש. . . אונ' אונא בטוונגן (אן צוואנג) ביי מיינעם
יודישן רעכט אונ' איידא" (שבועה)‏.

which has been preserved. This Jew was named Naftali ben Mosheh and he writes to his brother-in-law as follows:

„ר״ד (ראשית דבר) ליבר יעקב וויש דאס איך ערשט היום אויף די לילה בין בון שפייער קומן אונ׳ האָב געהוירט (געהערט) דו בישט ניט אויף דר ברײַלפט (חתונה) צי וואָרמז גיוועזן. זיין מיר דרשרוקן (דערשראָקן) אוב דו ח״ו (חס ושלום) ניט וואָל אויף בישט. ע״ז (על זאת) האָבן מיר ניט קונין אונטר לושן אונ׳ שיקן דיר דיזן שליח מיוחד דו וועלשט אונז כ״ד (כל דבר) באריכות מודיע זיין. . . עוד ליבר ורויינד (פריינד) שרייבט מיר על ידי מוקדם וויא לאַנג איר נאָך הבט בדעה צו האַניו (Hanau) צו בלייבן אודר אין וועלכם אופן איר אלדאָ זייט״.

(First of all, dear Jacob, know that I have just come from Speyer tonight and heard that you were not at the wedding in Worms. We were afraid that you are—God forbid—not well. Therefore we could not restrain ourselves and send you this special messenger so that you will let us know everything at length . . . Also, dear friend, write me in the near future how long you intend to remain in Hanau and how all of you are.)

Not only the considerable number of Hebrew words in the original fragment but the whole style and sentence construction provide evidence that we have before us not *Leshon Ashkenaz* but genuinely *Jewish* German. An even clearer notion of the oral speech of the German Jews of the Middle Ages might be provided for us by the testimony of the rabbinic responsa. Unfortunately, we first encounter such testimony (and mainly in brief sentences) only in the responsa of the end of the Middle Ages, as, for example, in Israel Isserlein and Jacob Weil.[51]

Thus, we have seen that Judeo-German is much older than the German-Jewish scholars wished to prove and that, already in the generations when the *Sefer Ḥasidim* was produced, the *Leshon Ashkenaz* which the Jews spoke was distinguished in a certain measure from the Middle High German that their Christian neighbors employed.[52] Now, the question arises: To what extent did the people create in this language? Certainly, the masses of the people produced in their vernacular legends, tales, and songs with which the mother would rock her child to sleep and young people accompanied their dances, or in

51. See H. Lunski, "Isserleins Yidish" (*Yidishe Filologye,* 288–295) and "Yidish Bay R. Yaakov Weiln" (*Landau-Bukh,* 286–288).
52. Dr. Schipper attempts to demonstrate this, basing himself on anonymous sources (*Yidishe Filologye,* 101–112, 272–287).

which people expressed their sorrows and joys in love. But all this was oral, for we have already noted that in view of the great costliness and scarcity of books in the Middle Ages the common people owned none. Some notion of the rich Jewish folklore of that time can be provided by the well known *Sefer Ḥasidim.*[53] But there were some folkloristic elements that were preserved orally but also had to be written down on parchment or paper to be remembered. These are certain adjurations, incantations, and popular remedies. It was considered extremely important to preserve the exact text, and so men did not rely on their memory but wrote these things down verbatim. As a result some very old Judeo-German exorcisms[54] and rhymed formulas and remedies written in the thirteenth century in the French dialect with Hebrew characters have been preserved.[55] Two badly damaged pages with medical prescriptions in Judeo-German regarding blood-letting and dated 1364 are to be found in the library at Cologne.[56] The dialects which the German and French Jews in the twelfth and thirteenth centuries spoke were, however, not merely the vernacular of the Jewish home and marketplace but also the language of instruction in the schools and, in a certain measure, the language of prayer in the synagogues. Certain passages of the Bible, the Scroll of Esther, the Passover Haggadah,[57] and various prayers were translated into the vernacular for "women and children" and read aloud. As early as the thirteenth century the Italian Jews already utilized an Italian translation of the Scroll of Esther and of other Biblical books.[58]

Here we must dwell on a characteristic feature. We have noted[59] how the efflorescence of the language of the Koran,

53. See our *History*, Vol. Two, Part One, Chapter Three.
54. Published by Güdemann (*MGWJ*, 185) and Perles (*Graetz Festschrift*).
55. See Steinschneider, *Verzeichniss der hebräischen Handschriften der königlichen Bibliothek zu Berlin*, II, 154–156.
56. The fragment that has been preserved concludes with this addendum in Hebrew: "In the year 5124 I completed this document about the powers of blood-letting and veins as the physicians have written." See *ZHB*, 1904, 113–14.
57. See *Maḥzor Vitry*, Part Two, 295, *Hilchot Haggadah Shel Pesaḥ*: " 'This is the bread of affliction . . .' in the vernacular"; and " 'Why is this night different . . .' in the vernacular." On the island of Crete it was a long-established custom that on the Day of Atonement at the afternoon service only the first three verses of the Book of Jonah were read in the original. The remainder was read in Greek, the vernacular of the Jews dwelling there.
58. On translations of Biblical books among the Italian Jews, see Vogelstein and Rieger, *Geschichte der Juden in Rom*, I, 339, 370, 372.
59. See above, p. 7.

considered sacred by the Arabs, aroused a feeling of envy among the Jews in Arabic Spain. The national will to strengthen and develop *their* holy language, the language of the Bible, was awakened in them. As a result of national self-consciousness, of the drive for national-cultural existence and survival, Arabic became, among the Spanish Jews, not the sister of the language of the Bible, as Aramaic had in its day, but remained its proud opponent. Because of the motives mentioned above, there were among the Sephardic scholars purists who agreed with Naḥmanides in his conclusion that "it is permitted to write the holy books only in the holy language (Hebrew), not in any dialect or other language whatsoever." The Spanish Rabbi Isaac bar Sheshet, for example, complains strongly of the fact that the Scroll of Esther is read for women not in the original but in translation. In the medieval Franco-German as well as in the Italian Jewish communities, the kind of envy that had been aroused among the Spanish Jews could naturally not emerge toward the colloquial languages of the Christian milieu. For these were still plain, everyday vernaculars; the language of religion and culture was an altogether different one—"the language of the priestly class," the ancient Latin. The Jewish ghetto at that time lacked any real ground for a "controversy over languages." For this reason the severely pious and orthodox Rabbi Jonah Gerondi declares in his *Sefer Ha-Yirah* that if one does not have a Torah with the Targum, he should read it "twice in Hebrew and once in the vernacular." A contemporary of his, the Italian Jehudah ben Benjamin, goes even further. He points out that "our present-day vernacular occupies the same place as the Targum once held," for the entire purpose of the Targum in ancient times was, after all, merely to explain the Torah to women and unlettered persons who do not understand Hebrew.[60] The author of *Shibbolei Ha-Leket* stresses that it is a *mitzvah* (commandment or good deed) that, when the Torah is read, translators or interpreters should be present to translate and explain ev-

60. "And the whole purpose of the Targum is nothing but to explain the words of the Torah to women and ignorant persons who do not understand the holy language." Further on we read in *Sefer Ha-Yirah:* "And he shall go through the weekly lections of the Torah with the congregation every week twice in Hebrew and once in the Targum. And if he has no Targum, he shall read twice in Hebrew and once in the vernacular." In an old Yiddish translation that will be discussed further on we read the following statement: "Every week you shall read the *sidrah* with other people twice in Hebrew and once in the Targum. This would be well for you, but if you do not have a Targum, be prepared to read once in German."

erything that is read in order that women and ignorant persons may also understand, and thereby the Biblical verse be fulfilled: "So they read in the book in the law of God distinctly, and gave the sense, and caused them to understand the reading" (Nehemiah 8:8).[61] And the *Sefer Ḥasidim* teaches:

If a Jew who does not understand Hebrew but is a pious man and wishes to pray with devotion *(kavvanah)* comes to you, or a Jewess who certainly does not understand Hebrew comes, you shall tell them to pray in the language they understand, for prayer is the petition of the heart, and if the heart does not know what the lips say, of what avail can such a prayer be? Hence it is better that every man should pray in the language that he understands.[62]

These scholars in fact practiced what they preached. Liturgical poems and penitential prayers have been preserved from the thirteenth century in which, along with the Hebrew original, the French translation is written in Hebrew characters.[63] We quote here the first stanza of the well known *piyyut* for the evening of Rosh Ha-Shanah "Emunah Nevonim" in such a translation:

Les anfanz des abat sages i apris, bian ansenez
A tocher do chofar ce sétén mais cheke an sont penez
Roi de rainçon, remanbra l'amor d'ancianz, ver soi eteiant
   adonez
Les anfanz si acrésse come ételes de ciel, plus ne seiant mal
   menez.

Especially interesting is a wedding song preserved in a manuscript copy of the *Maḥzor Vitry* from the second half of the thirteenth century.[64] We have observed that among the Hebrew poets in the Arabic countries bilingual poems in which Hebrew lines and entire verses were braided together with Arabic were extremely popular. Such "macaroni" poems also existed among the French Jews of the thirteenth century. The *Maḥzor Vitry* notes that at weddings it was customary to place

61. *Shibbolei Ha-Leket*, No. 78; see also *ibid.*, No, 19.
62. *Op. cit.*, Nos. 588 and 785.
63. See *REJ*, 1881, 211–201; *ibid.*, 1927, 36–51, 146–62; *Romania*, II, 443–486.
64. Located in the Jewish Theological Seminary in New York City. The author's name was Eliezer ben Samuel (see *REJ*, 1926, 379–393).

the bride and groom on high stools and young and old would entertain them with dancing and singing. One of these dance-songs is in fact given in the manuscript *Maḥzor Vitry.* This is a bilingual poem, in which every Hebrew line is followed by one in French.[65] The poem begins with the following lines:

שטו גלובאייש ליבריר	אל גבעת הלבונה —
(Si tu ne li vais livrer)	נוטרא חתן איט אריביץ
נוש נטנפורייט שאביר	(Notre hatan et arivez)
(Nus te t'an poreit saver)	אור חמה ולבנה —
לא ישוב אל נדנה —	טון קטיאיי פאיי דליבריר
איינץ איפורייש טאוט מיקביר	(Ton chatie fai delivrer)
(Ainz i poreis tet mechewer)	כי בידי חרב יונה —

The German Jews of the Middle Ages also had prayers and liturgical poems in their vernacular. We know quite definitely that in the fourteenth century there were among the Jews of Germany not only translations of prayers but specially rhymed religious poems composed according to the model of the hymns "Adon Olam" and "Yigdal." The famous Rabbi Jacob ben Moses Mölln (Maharil), who tells about these, complains strongly of them.[66]

There is no doubt, however, that such prayers existed much earlier. The Kabbalist Rabbi Eleazar ben Jehudah of Worms, when mourning the tragic death of his wife Dolca, who was killed in 1196,[67] says in praise of her: "A singer of hymns and prayers, and a speaker of supplications *(taḥanunim)*, a declarer of 'Pittum Ha-Ketoret' and the Ten Commandments." The phrase "and a speaker of supplications" shows most clearly that what is meant here are supplications and prayers in the vernacular which the knowledgeable *firzogerin* or "fore-sayer" (precentress for women) used to read aloud or sing for the female congregation.[68] There is no doubt that the congregation

65. Published in *REJ*, 1926, 22–32.
66. *Minhagim*, No. 112: "The rhymes and metrical verses that they make in *Leshon Ashkenaz* on the unity of God and on the Thirteen Principles—would that they did not make them, for most ignorant persons think that on this hang all the command-ments, and they abandon many positive and negative precepts. In those verses are noted only the principles of the religion of Israel, but not one of the six hundred and thirteen commandments that Israel is obliged to perform."
67. See Vol. II, p. 71.
68. The name of another *firzogerin* of the Middle Ages has been preserved—Marat Guta bat R. Nathan (died 1308) of whom it is related that "she prayed for the women in her lovely prayer."

listened to these prayer translations orally, but the *firzogerin* certainly had them written down.

The translations of all the sections of the Bible that were read aloud in the synagogue before the congregation in the vernacular, such as the Ten Commandments, the Song at the Sea, the Scroll of Esther, the Book of Jonah, and the like, were also written down. This is stressed by the rabbi of the fourteenth century mentioned above, Isaac bar Sheshet. He notes that "they used to read the Scroll of Esther to the women in the vernacular, and it was written down in the vernacular," i.e., it was read from a *written* text of the translation.

We have already noted that what served as spiritual and intellectual nourishment for the common people, for women and simple peasants, in the vernacular could not find any patrons or philanthropists. But there were, even though in very limited numbers, some wealthy women who played the role of "patronesses," who allowed themselves the luxury of ordering for their use from copyists written translations of the prayers, of the Psalms, and certain other Biblical works such as the Scroll of Esther, or accounts of the *mitzvot nashim*, all the commandments which a Jewish woman must know, as well as descriptions of other customs of Jewish religious life, braided together with ethical instruction. A parchment manuscript containing a collection of prayer translations in Italian that was written in 1383 for such a "patroness" by the name of Rebecca has been preserved.[69]

It was not, however, translations of supplications and prayers alone that were copied for the Jewish patronesses and *firzogerins.* We have quoted the view of the author of *Shibbolei Ha-Leket* that it is a commandment and religious duty for a translator to be present at the reading of the Torah to translate and explain everything that is read. But it was not the text of the Torah alone that the translators and interpreters explained. We know that already in the era of the Second Temple complete sermons filled with moral lessons and directions for proper conduct were gradually produced out of the "explanation" of the Torah.[70] Such sermons were given by the teachers and guides of the people on the Sabbath and festivals in the synagogues and houses of study. The verse from the weekly *sidrah* or lection on which the preacher based himself was only the introduction, the framework into which he would weave

69. See Steinschneider, *MGWJ*, 1898, 319.
70. Vol. I, p. 15.

his artful tapestry of heartfelt instruction, earnest words of reproof, and lovely legends and parables, on which both the aggadic part of the Talmud and the ancient Midrashim were later constructed. We have already observed[71] that after the Talmud and the old Midrashim were written down, the well of Aggadah was not thereby stopped up. The national tales and legends occupied a very honored place in the public religious cult in the later period also. They merely changed their dress; the preacher was transformed into the liturgical poet or *paytan*, and the material of the sermons was reforged into the *piyyut* or liturgical poem. Under the influence of Christian religious poetry among the Syrians, Greeks, and others, the Jewish liturgical poem was born. The *paytan*, who generally was also the precentor of the congregation,[72] played the same role that the preacher had in the earlier period. He also utilized for his poems the ancient material of the Aggadah. The content remained the same; only the form, the dress, was changed.

But the liturgical poet did not push the preacher out of Jewish cultural life; he merely transformed the preacher's role to a certain degree. In the earlier period the sermon was an organic part of the synagogue ritual, of divine worship. But in later generations, after the order of the prayers and liturgical poems had grown greatly and the *hazzan* or precentor and the *paytan* or liturgical poet (who were generally combined in one person) had come to play the chief role in the religious cult, the prayer service had to be interrupted for the people to listen to the preacher's sermon. Because of lack of time, the preacher would now give a sermon only on certain Sabbaths during the morning service before the reading of the Torah; on the other Sabbaths, the congregation would hear the address in the synagogue later in the day, before the afternoon service.

In the European Jewish communities the golden thread of Aggadah was spun further. These communities no longer spoke the dialect that Asiatic Jewry had spoken during the time when the ancient material of the Midrash was produced. Hence the Midrashim also (not only the Torah) now required interpreters who might explain and, indeed, thereby rework the new aggadic material created by the people. Near the expository preacher stood the *paytan* who no longer produced his work according to the pattern of the Syrians but according to

71 See our *History*, Vol, 1, p. 16.
72. It is also not impossible that for his liturgical hymns he would frequently borrow melodies from the Christian milieu.

that of the Arabs, and later also of Christian European models. The *Sefer Yuḥasin* of Aḥimaaz bar Paltiel[73] gives us a vivid picture of how in the ninth century a preacher from Palestine gave a sermon every day in the community of Venosa in Italy. He would always begin with a midrash and, on the basis of the midrashic text, construct his sermon. His language was the Hebrew-Aramaic dialect, and since most of his auditors did not understand it, an interpreter was present—the local *paytan* Silano, who would at once explain every sentence of the preacher in the vernacular. This Silano was himself a liturgical poet and composed lovely *seliḥot* or penitential poems which the *ḥazzanim* or precentors would sing in the synagogue with a touching melody.

However, the aggadic material was not only rewritten into moving liturgical poems but also not infrequently utilized for purely secular purposes, reworked as interesting entertainment material. It will suffice to dwell on the following characteristic example. The *Akedah*-motif, the story of how the primal ancestor of the Jewish people, Abraham, was prepared to sacrifice his only son out of love and devotion to God is very richly employed in the Midrash literature and adorned with a colorful crown of imaginative and beautiful legends. This midrashic material was also rewritten in poetic form in lovely, moving liturgical poems. It is enough to mention the splendid poem "Et Shaarei Ratzon" which a Spanish poet of the twelfth century, Jehudah ben Samuel Ibn Abbas, composed in Arabic meter.[74] The poet leaves entirely untouched the motif which is so thoroughly worked over in the Midrashim (*Midrash Tanḥuma, Yalkut Shimeoni):* the struggle of Abraham with Satan, who will not allow him to fulfill God's will. The poet concentrates all his attention on the drama which the father, the mother, and the son designated as a victim live through. With great literary power he portrays how the son regrets not so much losing his own young life, which is to be offered up as a sacrifice, as the enormous suffering of his mother at the loss of her only son. Trembling, the angels beg mercy from the Creator of the world:

> O give ransom and bring indemnity!
> Let not the world be without a moon.

73. See our *History*, Vol. II, p. 159ff.
74. The poem is reprinted in the journal *Ha-Safah*, I, 1912, 15–16.

The same *Akedah*-motif, however, is also utilized in *Sefer Ha-Yashar*,[75] which even bears the title *Midrash Benei Yaakov*. But *Sefer Ha-Yashar* is already in fact a hero-epic in which, as we have shown, the influence of the old Romance ballads and poems about the marvelous exploits of the famous knights is very strongly discernible, and exclusively Jewish motifs are mingled with pagan and Christian European themes. The religious material obtains a secular-belletristic vestment.

The same thing happened again in the folk creativity in the vernacular. Following the pattern of *Sefer Ha-Yashar*, all kinds of hero-epics and poems in which Jewish *Spielmänner* or minstrels reworked Judaic as well as alien materials were produced in the vernacular. And just as the Jewish poets of Arabic Spain utilized Arabic forms and meter, so the Jewish *Spielmänner* of the Rhine provinces wrote their works in the meter and according to the poetic forms of their environment. To be sure, these creations of the Jewish *Spielmann* circulated very little in book form, for his epic works were—as medieval knightly poetry generally was—in essence purely *oral*. We have noted that the knight and his household did not *read* songs and poems but *listened* to them as the jongleur and *Spielmann* declaimed them in a singing recitative, mainly to the accompaniment of music. Nevertheless, it is beyond doubt that the *Spielmänner* themselves, as well as ordinary lovers of their works, collected and wrote down certain songs and poems in order to be able to use them at the appropriate moment,[76] just as the preachers and female "fore-sayers," in their sermons and ethical instruction, would certainly make use of notes and written jottings in the vernacular.

It was not, however, serious works alone that were produced in the vernacular. We know that even in Hebrew literature it was not only the passionately earnest Solomon Ibn Gabirol and Jehudah Halevi who wrote poems but also such life-loving troubadors and wandering minstrels as Jehudah Alḥarizi, who

75. See Vol. I, pp. 186–188.
76. L. Landau (and after him, Weinreich and Erik) cites, as evidence that Jews already in the time of Jehudah Ḥasid certainly read romances in the vernacular, the following passage in *Sefer Ḥasidim*: "And so he should not cover his book with parchments on which a romance is written. And there is a story of one who covered his Pentateuch with skin and on it were written in a foreign language vain things about the wars of the kings of the nations, and a righteous man came and tore it and removed it" (see *Arthurian Legends*, 21, in *Landau-Bukh*, 129). This passage, however, does not demonstrate what Landau wishes to show, for it speaks only of romances and various stories *written in German and French*.

derived a livelihood from reciting his lusty epigrams and witty *makamas*. A still larger role was played by the life-loving element in the creativity of the masses of the people. We know very well that, despite all persecutions and afflictions which the Jews had to endure in the Middle Ages, the common folk bubbled with love of life. Of course, the rabbis and leaders of the people tried to carry through in daily Jewish life with rigorous consistency the principle "Jews may not rejoice like the other peoples," but the common folk would not surrender. This stubborn battle is certainly one of the most interesting but, regrettably, still unwritten pages of our cultural history. The Jewish masses, especially the Jewish youth, had their dance and love songs, derived—to be sure—mainly from foreign peoples. The Jewish woman had her cradle songs and children's tales. The Jewish *Gesellekeit-Leute*—the wedding jesters *(badhanim)*, entertainers, and *Spielmänner*—would declaim merry songs, witty sayings, and epigrams at Jewish occasions of rejoicing and gatherings: weddings, engagement feasts, Saturday night banquets, and the like. We have observed[77] that Kalonymos ben Kalonymos produced a merry Purim parody in Hebrew. Such parodies and clever pieces were undoubtedly recited in great measure in the vernacular as well at the happy Purim holiday, on which "to increase rejoicing" was considered a *mitzvah*, a religious commandment. Certainly all this took place orally; all these things were *listened to*, not *read*. Nevertheless it is beyond doubt that there were also aficionados, not to speak of professional craftsmen, such as *badhanim* and *Gesellekeit-Leute*, who used to collect such songs and write them down.

Thus we conclude that, despite the fact that the majority of the common people did without books, there existed already in the Middle Ages—even though in very limited numbers—writings in the vernacular of the Jewish community. In the chapter that follows we shall see what has actually been preserved of these writings.

77. See Vol. II, pp. 223ff.

CHAPTER TWO

Bible Glossaries and the Beginnings of Yiddish Literature

The handwritten glossaries—*Derush* elements in the glossaries—The medieval translations of books of the Bible and of the Festival Prayerbook—"Godly songs" in Yiddish—Old-Yiddish secular literature—The translation of *Ben Ha-Melech Veha-Nazir*—Menaḥem Oldendorf's collection of poems—Didactic-satirical poems and controversy or debate poems—Medieval love-songs—The Polish-Jewish community and its vernacular—The social-cultural changes at the end of the Middle Ages—The strengthening of the urban bourgeoisie—The folk language as cultural language—The printing press and its cultural role—Oral folklore and folk literature—The popular books and their anonymous editors and publishers—The cultural significance of the printed book.

E NOTED in the previous chapter that, even though the common people ordinarily received their spiritual and intellectual nourishment not by way of the book but orally, a certain part of this oral literature undoubtedly also existed in writing. It must not surprise us, however, that no dated Old-Yiddish manuscripts of the thirteenth and fourteenth centuries have been preserved, and that the number of manuscripts of the fifteenth century that have come down to us is also extremely limited. The Jewish people, after all, was a wandering people. With the frequent persecutions, expulsions, and catastrophes that their communities had to endure in medieval Christian Europe, the exiles and refugees considered it necessary to preserve, first of all, the cultural riches that were *held sacred* in the popular consciousness—the Holy Writings, the folios of the Gemara, and the rabbinic books. Books in the everyday vernacular were too profane in their estimation, too slight in value, to be saved in a time of trouble and to be devotedly taken along in their homelessness. It is therefore quite understandable that the oldest manuscripts that have been preserved in which there are remnants of Old-Yiddish are works having some relationship to "studying Torah"—the so-called "glossaries," i.e., dictionaries in which the meaning of difficult words in the Bible are noted.[1] Glossaries such as these were in those times essential "helping books" that were utilized by the teachers in instructing the children. Such a Biblical glossary which was put together by a pupil of the well-known Moses Ha-Darshan in the thirteenth century and is now located in the library of Munich was described by J. Perles.[2] In this library there is also another glossary (from the 14th-15th centuries) to the Book of Joshua and the Book of the Twelve.[3] To give the reader some notion of the old "translations" in the spelling of the time, we present here several extracts from this glossary:[4]

(1 גדלתי – צוכאיך (איך האָב אויפדערצויגן), 2) התבונן – ווש גפרובט,
3) תוסיפו – זולטיר מירן, 4) רכבה – ווש גווייכט; 5) כמלונה – אַזא הירבירירגא
(ווי אַ הערבערג); 6) הותיר – לש אובר בלובן; 7) יאמר – דש זעייט (דאַס זאַגט
ער); 8) מריאים – וועיישט (פייסט – פעט); 9) מעלליכם – אוור ווערקא (אייער
ווערק); 10) ילבינו – זולנווישן (זאַלן וויַס ווערן); 11) כבור – אַזא זעייפא
(ווי זייף); 12) ישפיקו – זולן קלופן; 13) במה נחשב הוא – אומוש אישט

---

1. Hebrew-French glossaries have also been preserved. On this see *Romania*, I, 146–176; *Roman. Studien*, 163–220; Steinschneider, *Verzeichniss der hebräischen Handschriften der Königlichen Bibliothek zu Berlin*; I, 7; *REJ*, II; *Literaturblatt des Orients*, 1844, p. 738; *Ibid.*, 1845, p. 90. Staerk and Leitzmann even believed that Bible glossaries appeared among the French Jews before they did among the German.

2. See his *Beiträge zur Geschichte der hebräischen und aramäischen Studien*, 1884, pp. 145–153. See also Staerk-Leitzmann, *Die jüdisch-deutschen Bibelübersetzungen von den Anfängen bis zum Ausgang des 18. Jahrhunderts*, pp. 9–15.

3. See M. Grünbaum, *Jüdisch-deutsche Chrestomathie*, 25–53; Staerk-Leitzmann, *op. cit.*, 15–22.

4. According to Grünbaum, *op. cit.*

גפרייזט; (14 ענתה — גצוגדא (געצײַגט); (15 והצערות — ארם בוגן; (16 והחריטים — מלבש־שוש (מאַלשלאַס); (17 ברוח משפט — בן מוט ונרעכט; (18 מקראה — אונגפרײדן (אָנגעפרײדן) שטאַמט וואָרשײַנלעך פונעם פראַנצײזישן prier; (19 ולסעדה — אונצוליינן; (20 ראש וזנב — קונינק און׳ גריבא (קיניג און גראָף; (21 כפה ואגמון — בשוף און׳ אירצבישוף; (22 חומר חוצות — מורטער בון גשן; (23 צפעוני — איגדעש (אן עקדיש); (24 ברושים — בושבוום (בוקסבוים; (25 הברכה — די ביבר; (26 קרא — לייא (דער אימפערֿאטיוו פון לייענען; (27 חובליך — דינמערנר (דײַנע שיפֿרודערער); (28 חרמי — מיין אורוגא (מײן קריג; (29 כובס — וועלקרא; (30 נשמה ורוח — אדם און׳ מוט (אָטעם און מוט; (31 אסיר בזיקים — געבישרט אין וועשלן (געפֿעסֿלט אין פֿעסֿעלן; (32 כשריון — אזא הלשפֿערק; (33 צרפת — בון ורנקריכא; (34 ספרד — שפֿנגן לנט.[5]

Not all the glossaries, however, are satisfied simply to translate single words. At times translations of whole sentences and phrases are provided. Furthermore, the translation is not always content merely with explaining the literal meaning of the text but passes over into homiletical interpretation *(derush)*. For example, in a glossary of the 14th-15th centuries to the Book of Samuel, the words *metzukei aretz,* "the pillars of the earth," in Hannah's prayer are explained thus: "The righteous *(tzaddikim)*—these are the pillars of the earth."[6] In another glossary to the Book of Psalms, the words "Why do the heathen rage?" are translated: "Why do peoples storm against the King Messiah?" In a glossary to the Book of Job the words "Now there was a day" (Job 1:6) are accompanied by the words: "And it was the day of Rosh Ha-Shanah."[7]

Glossaries such as these form a transitional stage to complete translations of Biblical books. We noted in the first chapter that such translations in *Leshon Ashkenaz* undoubtedly existed even in the Middle Ages—above all, translations of those Biblical books that are intimately associated with the synagogue and the Jewish way of life, such as the Pentateuch, the prophetic lections, the five Scrolls, the Book of Job. Most of these manu-

---

5. On other glossaries of the 13–15th centuries that have come down to us, see Staerk-Leitzmann, *op. cit.,* pp. 22–60.
6. See Staerk-Leitzmann, p. 26.
7. *Ibid.,* p. 50.

scripts have been lost, but certain remnants have been preserved. The manuscripts that have come down to us show that the Judeo-German translations were of two kinds. In one the translation holds strictly to the text and slavishly translates word by word, not taking account of the fact that the construction of the sentences thereby becomes cumbersome and stilted and that the content also is not infrequently obscured and made incomprehensible.[8] Here the considerable affinity to the glossaries that were produced as helping books for the teacher in instructing children in the elementary schools is discernible. Other translations, however, are not content merely with a literal rendering of the words. They often enter into the ways of homiletical explanation *(derush)*, and in them the echo of the expository preacher is heard. As illustrations we present here segments from two translations of the Ninetieth Psalm.[9] Both translations come from the fifteenth century, but the first follows the system of literal translation, while the second is more inclined to the method of homiletical interpretation.

A (From the manuscript in the Royal Library of Berlin described by Steinschneider):[10] Prayer for Moses, man of God. God, a dwelling have You been for us in generation and generation *(be-dor va-dor).* even before mountains were created and land and world founded, from eternity to eternity *(ume-olam ad olam)* You are God. You return man to contrition *(tashev enosh ad dakka)* and You say: Return, children of men *(shuvu venei adam).* Because a thousand years in Your eyes are as yesterday when it is past, and a watch in the night *(ve-ashmurah va-la'ilah).* You streamed them away, they are sleep *(zeramtam shenah yih'yu),* in the morning like vegetation *(ke-hatzir)* that passes away. In the morning it sprouts and passes away, in the evening it is cut down and is dried out, for we are consumed in Your anger, and in Your wrath are we terrified. You have placed our sins before Yourself, our hidden deeds in light before Yourself. For all our days are laden with Your wrath, we have consumed our years like an utterance *(killinu shanenu kemo hegeh)* . . .

B (From the manuscript in the Hamburg library): A prayer of Moses, a man of God's ways. O God, a dwelling have You been for us; so may You still be for generation and generation. Before the

---

8. The problem of these Old-Yiddish secular Bible translations is treated especially by Nehamah Leibowitz in her German work *Die Übersetzungstechnik der jüdisch-deutschen Bibelübersetzungen des 15. und 16. Jahrhunderts dargestellt an den Psalmen* (Marburg, 1931).

9. We take these extracts from Staerk-Leitzmann's transcribed text *(op. cit.,* 92, 93).

10. This is the oldest *dated* manuscript (1490) known to us till now of a literary work in Yiddish.

mountains were created and the land of Israel and outside the land were created, forevermore You are God. You speak to men: Repent before you come to the great sin—this is murder and apostasy and adultery—and that you may not be cast off with afflictions. And when You send them afflictions, this is just as if You had spoken: Repent, children of men. More than a thousand years in Your eyes are like yesterday when it is past, and like a watch, a constituent part of the night. You have stormed away the same thousand years like a sleep. They became like a grass that grows at night and in the morning passes away. Now though it grows in the morning and passes away, at evening it is cut down and becomes dried out. Because they have disappeared in Your anger, in Your wrath we are terrified. You set our sins that we have committed in our youth in the light of Your *Shechinah*. Because all our days have melted away in Your anger, our days have disappeared like a blink of an eye.

The segment quoted from the Berlin manuscript gives the reader a clear notion of the type of Bible translation that set itself the same task as the glossaries: to be a helping book for the elementary school teacher or for the unlettered person and simple countryman not familiar with the meaning of the words. Naturally, such a translation can provide no notion whatever of the contemporary vernacular, the speech that lived at that time in the *mouth* of the Jewish people. In this connection it is interesting to compare this Psalm translation with the handwritten translation of the *Maḥzor* or Festival Prayer Book of the fifteenth century located in the Munich library.[11] We quoted earlier the well known statement of the *Sefer Ḥasidim:* "If one does not understand any Hebrew and is pious and would like to comprehend what he prays, it is better that he recite his prayer in the language that he knows, for prayer requires that the heart shall understand what he says." In accordance with this attitude, the prayers from this Festival Prayer Book were written in the language that the common people and the Jewish woman spoke:[12]

Our God and God of our fathers, be with the prayer-representatives *(Mundboten)* of Your people, the household of Israel, who are the precentors *(ḥazzanim)* who rise to beseech You for the good of Your people Israel. Show them what to say. Make them understand what they should speak. Respond to what they ask. Let them know how they should glorify You, so that they may walk before You in the light of Your *Shechinah*, bend the knee before You, and bless Your

11. This translation is described in Grünbaum's *Chrestomathie*, pp. 289–296.
12. In any case, it is very close to the *spoken* vernacular.

people Israel with their mouth, so that they may be blessed always with the benediction of Your mouth . . . That their mouth may not speak anything that is not in accordance with Your will, when they beseech You, O God, and when they study Your teaching, for we know well, O God, that him to whom You are gracious is favored and him to whom You are merciful is dealt with mercifully, for it is written in Your Torah: 'And I will be gracious to whom I will be gracious, and I will have mercy on whom I will have mercy.'

Slight remnants of the so-called "divine songs" or "godly songs" have survived in manuscripts of the fifteenth century. We noted above how the Maharil complained of the fact that Jews were singing Yiddish songs about God's unity and the Thirteen Principles of Faith. There were also songs about the Decalogue and the giving of the Torah, as well as Pesaḥ and Ḥannukah songs that were sung on the festivals in question. In the well-known and richly illustrated Haggadah manuscript of Paris, which undoubtedly comes from the first half of the fifteenth century, the Judeo-German translation of the well known poem *Addir Hu* is preserved. This translation also follows the alphabet:

אײניגר גוט (גאָט)	זענפטיגר גוט
נון בױא דײן טעמפיל שירי (גיך, באלד)	טרודיטר (געטרײער) גוט
אלזוי שיר, אלזוי שיר אין אָנזרין טאגין שירי	יודן גוט
נון בױיא, נון בױיא, נון בױיא	כרפטיגר גוט
נון בױיא, נון בױיא דײן טעמפיל	לעבדיגר גוט
שירי, יא שירי.	מעכטיגר גוט
ברם הערציגר גוט	נאָהטער גוט
גרעכטר גוט	עויגר גוט
דממויטיגר גוט	פארכטצומר גוט
הוך גילבטר גוט	צימליכר גוט
ווירדיגר גאָט	קעניגליכר גוט
	רײכר גוט
	שטרקר גוט.

Dr. Schipper quite correctly noted[13] that the original version of this poem is older than the fifteenth century. The best proof of this is the fact that in the Paris Haggadah three lines (on the letters *ḥet, samech,* and *tav*) are missing, while in the printed Haggadahs, e.g., the first one published (Prague, 1526), the poem is given in full. This is to be explained simply by the impreci-

13. *Yidishe Velt*, 1928, I, 123–124.

sion of the copyist who, through oversight, omitted these lines.

A small number of manuscripts of secular Old-Yiddish literature have also been preserved. In the Public Library of Munich there is a collection, under number 347, from around the sixteenth century, and in it are copies of two Old-Yiddish poems which undoubtedly come from the fourteenth century. One is a rhymed paraphrase of the Scroll of Esther in which the aggadic *Targum Sheni* material is used in rich measure,[14] and the other is a translation of Abraham Ibn Ḥasdai's work *Ben Ha-Melech Veha-Nazir*.[15] The anonymous translator was undoubtedly a talented poet. With great skill he renders Ḥasdai's ingenious *makamas* in rhymed lines. The poems with which the *makamas* are interwoven are given by the translator in a meter that is completely different from the Hebrew original. Instead of Ḥasdai's Arabic meter, the translator employs the intimate form of the medieval German folk-song. To be sure, even such a skilled versifier as our translator is unable to reproduce poetically in Judeo-German verse all of Ḥasdai's poems that were composed in such unique, complicated, and ingenious forms. In such instances he simply omits parts of Ḥasdai's poems—indeed, of the loveliest and most intimate of them.

To give the reader some notion of this rendering, we quote here several passages along with the Hebrew original:

פון דער 16טער מאַקאַמע:

העברעישער טעקסט	יידיש־דײַטשע איבערזעצונג
בלילה ההוא נדדה שנת המלך ויאמר	דא איינער נאכט דאס גישאך (גישאא)
למשנה כפעם בפעם, הבא נא ונלך שנינו	דעש קעניגס שלאף אויף אים בראך,
על העיר בטח ונשמע מה בפי העם,	ער שפראך צו דעם מרשלק גוט:
ונראה מנהגיהם, ומה מעשיהם, בחדרי	מיך באטריבט מיין זין אויך מיין מוט
משכביהם. וילכו וישוטטו בכל המדינה	דאס וויר ערגאנגן די שטאט הין
לארכה ולרחבה עד אשר באו אל רחוב	און׳ הער
אחד אשר נקרא שער האשפות, כי שם	און׳ היימליכן פארנעמן וואָס מאן
היו כל אנשי המדינה משליכין ומקבצין	זאג מער,
הדומן והאשפה אשר בתוכם עד אשר	און׳ ווי זיך די נאכט האלטן
נעשה מהם מקום גבוה מאוד. ויהי הם	די יונגען און׳ אויך די אלטן
הולכים ומביטים אל המקום ההוא ויראו	און׳ וואס לעכש זי טרייבן
בתוכו כדמות להב אש מאיר ומתנוצץ.	אין אירן קאמער מיט אירן ווייבן.

14. Extracts from the poem are presented by Staerk and Leitzmann in their work cited above, p. 235.
15. See our *History*, Vol. I, pp. 189–193.

דא גינגען זי ביידע אן דער צייט
די שטאט די לענגע אונ׳ די ווייט;
דא קאמען זי אין איין גאסע די וואס
(וואר) די מיסטשטאט גינאנט
ווען (וויל) דער יעדער מאן זאגט
אלי מישט אונ׳ אלי אונזוייבערקייט
מאן שיטעט אין די גרוב
ביז זיך דא איין גרויס הויפן הוב.
אז זי דעם הויפן בעגונדען נאהען
פיל באלד זי דא איין פלאמע ערזאאן
די גאב שיין אונ׳ פונקען פיל.

פון דער 18טער מאַקאַמע:

העברעישער טעקסט	יידיש־איבערזעצונג
מה תסגרי, יעלה, דלת לפני, הלא —	וואס בעשליסטו דערריין
די שומרים לך בצפעוני לחייך:	פאר מיר אליין,
או תחפצו לי בתוך שער לדבר דבר —	אין איינעם וואלד וואר זי וואל בעהיט:
יואב לאבנר וצור חרבו בעיניך.	איזט נור איר גיר
	דאס זי רייד מיט מיר
	אז יואב הינטער דער טיר
	מיט אבנר פארגאס זיין בליט.
תגזול לבבי בעין גוזל ואיך תאמר —	בערויבט איך בין
עפרה בשרי לאהבתך מאוד סמר.	אל מיינער זין
תתאב צבי חן למטעמות ידידות כ —	דיין זיסע שפראך וועלט ליבשאפט זוכן
אמנון באות לביבות מידי תמר.	דו פירסט איין וווייז
	ווי דיר געליסט דער שפייז
	אלס אמנון געליסט תמרס קוכן.

פון דער 20סטער מאַקאַמע:

עולם כמו מכלא והימים כמו —	דיז וועלט איבער אל
רועה ואדם צאן ובהמות יער:	די איזט דער שטאל
מות ככר נרחב ושם ירעה ושם —.	די צייט איין הירט, די לויט דאס פיך זינט.
ירבץ אנוש, ישיש, ושב ונער.	דער טויט די הער
קבר כמו שער ובא בו כל אנוש	די אין וועלכער וועד
מי ידע מה אחרי השער?	קליין, גרויס, ווייב, אלט און קינט —
	דאס גראב זיין פארט.
	האט אימאנט געהאָרט
	ווי אלדע וואס מאן דא הינטער פינט?

This translation is undoubtedly one of the major poetic creations of Old-Yiddish literature, and it is regrettable that such

an important work remained hidden and forgotten in a German library and was never published.[16]

Up to this point we have dealt exclusively with translations. However, a certain number of didactic and satirical poems from the fifteenth century which form a transitional stage from translations to original works have also been preserved. Especially interesting in this respect is a Hebrew-Yiddish collection of poems which the *sofer* or scribe Menaḥem ben Naphtali Oldendorf completed at the end of the year 1516. Born in Frankfurt-am-Main in 1449, he apparently spent his mature years in Italy. In any case, in 1504 in the small Italian town of Mestre near Venice he wrote for the patroness "Marat Hanlein" a Festival Prayer Book—a collection of *yotzerot* for the Great Sabbath *(Shabbat Ha-Gadol)* and the festivals, along with *kinot, seliḥot,* etc. He also wrote some original works, e.g., "*Gedanken Vegn Toyt*" (Thoughts on Death).[17] Especially interesting, however, is the collection of poems mentioned above which he completed in his old age when he was already a man of sixty-seven. In the manuscript forty-three numbers were written down, but the first pages are missing and the manuscript begins at the end of No. 18. The poems come from various authors. Only four of them (two Sabbath poems, a satirical poem about the futility of money, and a poem describing the debate between the "good impulse" and the "evil impulse") were composed by Oldendorf himself in his youth, i.e., in the second half of the fifteenth century.[18] Most of the poems are Hebrew; only five of them have, aside from the Hebrew, a Yiddish text as well. Before we proceed to the content of these poems it is important to note the following interesting point. We observed previously[19] that many Hebrew poets—Solomon ben Mazzal Tov, Israel Najara, and others—frequently composed their poems (even those of religious content) according to the meter and melody of foreign folksongs. The same thing

16. Only in modern times did Erik *(Vegn Alt-Yidishn Roman,* pp. 223–229) and Staerk *(Landau-Bukh,* pp. 58–62) publish considerable fragments of this translation.
17. Preserved at the end of a handwritten collection located in the library of Cambridge University (see Weinreich, *Bilder Fun Der Yidisher Literatur,* 1928, pp. 145–148). At the close of Oldendorf's *Toyt-Gedanken* is the following epilogue: "God Blessed Be He is truthful and does injustice to no one. This his servant Menaḥem Oldendorf can well acknowledge. Therefore let every man reflect behind him and before him and not be frivolous. The last thing is death. This the living person should take to his heart. Monday, the fourth of Av 1504."
18. The collection was described by L. Loewenstein in Hildesheimer's *Jubelschrift* (1890), 126–144, and in MGWJ, 1894, 79–84.
19. Vol. V, pp. 89ff.

is to be noted in Oldendorf's collection. In it is given a "scholarly" Hebrew poem containing principles for studying the Gemara, *"Hilchata Ke-Man"* which the nephew of the renowned Maharil, Jacob ben Yekutiel of Gleinhausen composed. The poem is preceded by the anthologist's remark that *"Hilchata Ke-Man* was composed *be-nigun Herzog Ernst,"* i.e., according to the rhyme key and verse structure of the then very popular German song. Also according to "the melody of *Herzog Ernst"* is another poem in Oldendorf's collection, a Sabbath song of Solomon Zelmeln ben Yakar of Erfurt who lived in the first half of the fifteenth century. This poem is composed in two languages (Hebrew and Yiddish), and we present here the first stanza:[20]

גוטס ליב אוב׳ אל זיין וונדר	זייטן שפיל אוב׳ אלן לושט
די אי גשאך אוב׳ נאך גשיכט (געשעט)	דיא קוניג דוד ניע גויושט.
	אוב׳ אנדער פרופיטן מער,
דיא ער דא קור (ערקארן) בזונדרס	אוב׳ וועם דיא אל ווירן קינד
זיפציג פירזאן אין ייפטן (מצרים) קאמן	אוב׳ וועד דר בולט (דערפולט) זיינס
קיניג פרעה יוסף פערגס	הערצן גרונד
אוב׳ פייניגט זיינער קינדר זאמן.	זיין בוטשאפט אוב׳ לער.
	דאך מיכט ער דרצייילן ניכט

(Harp playing and lusty songs which neither King David, nor the other prophets, nor he before whom all this was revealed and who fulfilled with his whole heart God's message and His teaching, knew—but all these are not able to relate God's praise and all His wonders that once occurred and still occur now. Those whom He especially chose, seventy souls in number, came to Egypt. King Pharoah forgot Joseph and greatly oppressed the seed of his children).

The bilingual poem "Al Ahavat Ha-Kesef" (On the Love of Money) mentioned above, which Oldendorf composed in his youth, was also written "in the melody" of a popular German folksong, "Hoch Rief der Wächter." The satirical morality-poem begins with the following verse:

> May God will that unpunished
> Be the world of fools,
> Who with all their senses,
> Their sitting, their standing,
> Their thinking with which they go about,

20. According to Loewenstein's transcribed text.

Make money their love.
To gain money,
Low and high—
All the world—are eager.
Chasing and straining after a livelihood—
That you [can] observe the whole day through.

The moral of the entire poem, which consists of ten stanzas, is given in the seventh stanza:

To what purpose all this running and worry?
Naked must one return
To the earth from which he is taken.
Repent strongly
For your evil deeds.
A mountain of silver is of no avail
In *that* world to which we shall come.

Especially interesting is another satiric poem (also bilingual) which is in Oldendorf's collection, "Al Ha-Sehok" (On Play) by Samuel ben Moses Hogerlin.[21] We noted[22] that Leo de Modena, who wrote a satire on gambling, was himself an ardent card-player all his life; this, undoubtedly, was also the case with the author of the satire in question, Samuel Hogerlin. He himself, when speaking of card-players and the social harm they perpetrate, adds: "It happened to my hurt; I was also in this situation." With great skill the author presents all the details about card and dice-playing, and he portrays the pastime of those who are intoxicated with card-playing in the following vivid colors:

Morning and evening without interruption,
They have no other pastime,
Except to sit long;
Hungry and thirsty and fainting,
Both days and nights,
They play as they grow warm.
They swear, weep, and bite,

21. The acrostic of this poem—"Samuel the Little the son of Rabbi Moses Uri, may his memory be for a blessing; be strong and of good courage"—is put together so that the first letter of every Hebrew stanza is connected with the first letter of the corresponding Yiddish stanza.
22. Vol. IV, p. 133.

They know of no good to say.
They hardly take the trouble to worship
At night and by day,
They hardly observe God's commandment.
Each one covets his neighbor's good;
Hence, they never become contented or good.

One not skilled at play
Who knows not the ways of dice—
Such a one is completely lost;
I say this of a truth.
Young and old attach themselves to him;
Long and short they cheat him.
Ah, the enormous frauds
Practiced by those intent on it.
With quicksilver and with lead
They [the dice] are sticky and dipped.
They have eyes, yet are blind—
May their makers become like them,
As all who stick up for them.

What can he boast of his winnings?
Very soon they depart from him,
Like the grass before the sun;
They take them away from him,
More quickly than a little bird.
His gain runs away from him;
Though the money bag be heavily laden,
It very soon becomes light and thin.
It is said: Gamblers are
Only each other's purse-carriers.
As he wins it, so it goes away again;
He is left standing naked and bare,
And, in addition, harm, shame, and mockery
    remain to him.

In the closing stanza the author declares that he wishes *Ur-lupe gebn* (to take leave of) both kinds of play, dice-throwing and card-playing, in order that they *sein Laster nit mern* (not increase his vice). He wishes to repent, to give himself over

Entirely into God's care
So I can remain well protected;
May God give me this for a benefit.

Less interesting are the two other poems that are written down in Oldendorf's collection in both languages, the poem of Zalman Sofer[23] "Zera Gefen," describing the controversy between wine and water, and Oldendorf's own poem "Maḥaloket Ve-Ta'anat Yetzer Tov Al Yetzer Ha-Ra" (The Controversy and the Complaint of the Good Impulse Against the Evil Impulse). These are typical "controversy" or "debate" poems, hundreds of examples of which have been preserved in medieval Hebrew literature.[24] We shall content ourselves with giving here only the first stanzas of the two poems in both versions, Hebrew and Yiddish:

I. From Zalman Sofer's "Maḥaloket Yayin Veha-Mayyim:"[25]

> *Hebrew Text*
> The seed of the vine am I called,
> That is—wine.
> To one who drinks me
> I am like a gem,
> And so also to warriors bearing weapons.
> Man is stupefied by me,
> And I dim his vision.
> Wine rejoices the heart of man.

> *Yiddish Version*
> And after the vine am I named—
> So said wine to itself.
> They drink me quite eagerly;
> For this I am very fine.
> I can make merriment and frolic,
> I can drive away great pains,
> And rejoice the heart of man.

II. From Menaḥem Oldendorf's "Maḥaloket Ve-Ta'anat"

> *Hebrew Text*
> Lift up your eyes on high.
> For the sake of my brethren I will speak;
> Rend your hearts and not your garments
> . . . who rebel against the Lord.

23. Lived in the first half of the fifteenth century.
24. See, for instance, Vol. I, p. 160, Note 26.
25. In both texts the acrostic "Zalman Sofer" is woven.

Wash yourselves, make yourselves clean,
Walk after the Lord your God,
Bless Him, all you servants of the Lord.

Yiddish Version
Be diligent toward God in heaven—
I say this to my brethren.
Rend your hearts in penitence,
Fear God the whole year through.
Purify and wash yourselves properly,
Run after God and fight [i.e., His battles];
Praise God, all you His servants.

The pious scribe Menaḥem Oldendorf collected only religious and didactic poems, or satirical poems that had a certain moral. He included in his collection neither love nor dancing poems, nor even wedding songs. We shall see further on how another anthologist, who lived less than a hundred years after Oldendorf, did preserve for us a whole series of such poems. However, in a parchment manuscript of the fifteenth century, a commentary of Rashi on the Prophets and the Hagiographa that was in the collection of Pope Leo X's secretary Pietro Bembo (born in 1470), an old Yiddish love song was written down. We here reprint it from Moshe Bassin's anthology (page 27).

Whither shall I go,
Whither shall I turn?
I am an inflamed [with love] tinder, my heart is
   burning;
I cannot be free of it.
This is felt by the one dearest to my heart
That I have on earth.

That the medieval Yiddish love-lyric was comparatively rich is attested by the fact that even presentday folksongs, as Dr. Schipper and Y.L. Cohen[26] have shown, still carry quite prominent signs of their medieval origin. Such songs as "Es Sitzn Meydlekh Dray" ("Three Little Girls Sit," in the Ginsburg-Marek collection, No. 166), "Vi Es Kumt Der Liber Zumer" ("As the Delightful Summer Comes," *ibid.*, No. 171), "Muter, Libste Muter" ("Mother, Beloved Mother," *ibid.*, No. 365) were

26. *Amerikaner Pinkes*, 1927, 65–77; Schipper, *Yidishe Folks-Dramatik*, 1928, 75–79.

already sung—naturally, with certain changes—by our great-great-grandmothers in the medieval German ghettos.

As we see, relatively few remnants of the Old-Yiddish literature have been preserved in the medieval manuscripts that have come down to us. An incomparably larger part, however, was saved—even though in more or less altered form—as a result of the enormous changes that took place at the end of the Middle Ages and that had a very extensive influence on the cultural life of the Ashkenazic Jews and on the development of Old-Yiddish literature. We noted earlier that already in the twelfth and thirteenth centuries the dialect which the German Jews of the Rhine provinces spoke had its own coloration to a definite degree. Already at that time *Leshon Ashkenaz* or *Jüdisch-Deutsch* (Judeo-German) was distinguished from Christian German. This singularity became even more prominent in the fourteenth century, when the Jewish community of France was banished (England had become *judenrein* even earlier) and many of the exiled French Jews moved to the other side of the Rhine. In Germany persecutions of Jews became ever more severe[27] and, gradually, under the pressure of constant oppression and forced migrations from the western provinces to the eastern, Slavic lands (first to Moravia and Silesia, later to the Polish provinces), the *Franco-German* Jewish community was transformed, at the end of the Middle Ages, into the *German-Polish* community which spoke one language—*Leshon Ashkenaz.* At that same time, and closely connected therewith, the long process which lasted for many successive generations came, in a certain sense, to an end: in the course of the long wanderings from the German southern provinces to the Slavic eastern lands, and under the definite influence of the new and alien environment, the Middle High German dialect which the Jews of the Rhine provinces spoke in the twelfth century was transformed into a unique *Judeo-German* language with a quite unique style. It is beyond doubt that, until the middle of the thirteenth century, the Jewish community of the Belorussian Polish areas consisted mainly of immigrants who came from the Far and Near East, as well as from various lands of the south—Arabia, Asia Minor, Egypt, Greece, the Caucasus, and, above all, the Volga regions, where the powerful Chazar state flourished until the end of the tenth century.[28] From the middle of the thirteenth century, however, the main stream of the

27. See our *History*, Vol. III, pp. 145ff.
28. Our *History*, Vol. VI, Chapter One.

Jewish immigrants who came in masses from the neighboring western and southern lands, such as Germany, Czechia, Silesia, and Hungary, obtained dominance.[29] The new immigrants soon gained hegemony culturally over the old inhabitants, and in a relatively brief time *Leshon Ashkenaz* became, with a few exceptions, the sole vernacular of the largest part of Polish Jewry.[30] Naturally in the new environment *Leshon Ashkenaz* adopted a marked quantity of Slavic elements,[31] and this removed it even further from its original Middle High German source.

It must also not be forgotten that, given the vast power which the rabbinic-pilpulistic spirit and world outlook had over the communal as well as the private life of the German-Polish Jews, their vernacular became increasingly saturated with words and concepts from the rabbinic literature. Not only the morphology of the language, but also its syntax and structure were changed. As early as the beginning of the sixteenth century the Jewish vernacular had taken on, in very significant measure, the unique "Judaic" forms which later so enraged the German scholar of the seventeenth century Wagenseil, who could not forgive the German Jews for their "blasphemous" use of the German language, inasmuch as they "corrupted" it and made it an alien monstrosity.[32]

At the end of the Middle Ages, however, tremendous changes also took place in the external world, in the environment in which the large Jewish community lived—changes

29. See Dr. Schipper, *Kultur-Geshikhte*, pp. 262–270.
30. There has been much debate about the vernacular of the Jews in the Polish provinces in various periods. On this question see A. Harkavy, *Sefat Ha-Yehudim* (1868); S. Dubnow's well known article in *Yevreyskaya Starina*, 1909, 1–30, and *Der Pinkes*, 1913, 36–38; B. Rubstein, "Di Amolike Shprakh Fun Yidn in Rusland" (*ibid.*, 21–36); B. Borochov, "Di Biblioteik Fun Yidishn Farlag" (*ibid.*, 56); R. Centnersz-werowa, *O języku Żydów* (Warsaw 1907); Y. Willer, *Filologishe Shriftn*, II, 118–120; I. Schipper, *Kultur-Geshikhte*, 262–268, 277–280; J. Lurie, *Tsaytshrift*, II, 747.
31. On Slavic elements in Yiddish see A. Landau in *Filologishe Shriftn*, II, 200–204; Dr. Schipper, *op. cit.*, 277–278; *ibid.*, *MGWJ*, 1929, 475; J. A. Joffe, *Amerikaner Pinkes*, 1928, 235–256, 296–312; E. Schulmann, "Imkei Safah," *Ha-Shiloah*, IV.
32. J. C. Wagenseil, *Belehrung der jüdisch-teutschen Red-und Schreibart*, Introduction, 7: "Mit keiner Sprach sind die Juden jemals so wie man zu reden pflegt lästerlich als mit unserer Teutschen umgegangen, denn sie haben solcher einen gantz fremden Thon und Laut gegeben, die guten teutshen Worten gestümmelt, gerad brecht, verkehrt, neue uns unbekante erdacht wie auch unzählich viel Hebreische Wörter und Redarten in das Teutsche gemischt dass soicher gestalt wer sie teutsch rede höret nit anderst glaubt, als sie reden pur lauter Hebreisch in den fast kein einzige Wort verständlich fürkommet."

which effected a revolution in the whole order of European life and also had a great influence on the development of Old-Yiddish literature.

The centuries-long Crusades which familiarized the European peoples with the culturally rich and colorful world of the Orient had a very considerable influence on the civilization of western Europe. The importance of the urban populace became ever greater, and gradually urban civilization revived and began to develop once more. Through the economic changes that occurred, as well as the political developments closely associated with them, the scope and significance of the knightly class was weakened and the urban bourgeoisie rose at its expense. The merchants' guilds and the artisans' guilds began to play a significant role in social life. The urban citizen class in Germany gradually became the bearer of culture. Knightly poetry yielded its honored place to bourgeois-urban poetry, and the wandering troubadors and *Spielmänner*, or minstrels, were gradually replaced by the calm, pedantic, serious *Minnesinger*.

We have noted that the ability to read and write was rare even among the nobility. What the knight required chiefly was the sword, not the pen, and the previously mentioned poet Wolfram of Eschenbach, who himself relates that he did not learn the art of writing, nevertheless stresses with great pride as a knight that his vocation is to bear weaponry *(Zum Schildesamt bin Ich geboren)*. It was different, however, in the case of the bourgeoisie. The merchant, the storekeeper, and even the artisan had to be able to write, read, and figure arithmetical sums in order to earn a livelihood, and this not in the ancient tongue of the Romans but in the language of everyday life. In the high Middle Ages there existed even in Germany only Latin schools. Gradually, with the development of bourgeois citizen life, however, there appeared also plain *German* folk-schools, in which the sons of merchants and artisans learned reading, writing, and the basic principles of arithmetic. At first the learned elements regarded these "vulgar" folk-schools with great contempt, and as late as the fifteenth century the rule prevailed in these circles that one who wishes to give his son culture is obliged to send him to a *recht*, i.e., a Latin, school—not one where instruction is presented in the common vernacular.[33] The supervisors in the Latin schools were obliged to

33. ". . . in die *rechte* schul schicke, un nit in tütsch lere."

note on the black penalty-tablet those pupils "who talk German or do other indecent things."[34] It was feared that speaking German can only corrupt the student's pure Latin speech. German itself was not something to be studied; it was merely to be used to communicate with "the crude public."

In time, however, as the importance and role of the "crude public," i.e., of the urban bourgeoisie, increased and as its cultural needs developed, the role of the vernacular also grew. The language of the masses of the people gradually pushed Latin out of the urban chancellories and government offices. Anyone who wished to influence the urban bourgeoisie, which had become a significant social force, had to address it in its colloquial language. The renowned humanist and battler for culture Ulrich von Hutten himself relates: "At first I wrote in Latin, but very few understood it. Now I address the fatherland, the German people, in its own language, and call it to battle to take vengeance for all the evil that has been done to it."

Hence, it is readily understandable that when a whole chain of cultural, social, and political factors called forth the broad movement of the Reformation, it ended with Germany seceding not only from the foreign, papal, Catholic church but also from the *Latin* church. The culturally matured bourgeois citizen class demanded that its spiritual-religious sustenance, the Bible, be made accessible to it in its mother tongue. The celebrated German translation of the Bible was not a brilliant invention of Martin Luther's; it was the necessary result of a long and significant cultural process—the transformation of the dialect of serfs and peasants, the common undeveloped vernacular of the marketplace and everyday life, into an extraordinarily ingenious instrument for rich and variegated culture. And, indeed, closely associated with this, also as an inevitable result, as a necessity, Gutenberg came forth with his marvelous invention, the printing press, just as at the same time the invention of gunpowder, with whose aid the bourgeoisie first obtained the possibility of destroying the castles of the marauding knights on the sloping crags and high-peaked mountains, occurred.

The invention of book-printing had an enormous influence on the cultural evolution of the peoples of Europe. The printing press democratized the book immensely, all at once making it available to the masses. The entire Luther translation of the

34. ". . . die deutsch reden oder sust unzüchtig sein."

Bible could be obtained for one and a half gulden. In place of the patron, the generous "prince" who used to support literature and its servants and priests, appeared the people itself—not, however, as a philanthropist but as a plain buyer. From being an expensive luxury item the book became the cheapest merchandise.

Previously not only knightly poetry but bourgeois poetry as well was closely associated with music and song. The printing press, however, managed to separate the poem from the melody, to erect a barrier between lyrical creativity and music, between the word and singing. It was the printing press alone which first provided the possibility of raising the ordinary vernacular with its oral folklore to the level of folk-*literature*, which becomes an important factor of national civilization. A new period in the history of culture is inaugurated. At the end of the fifteenth century and in the first half of the sixteenth an enormous number of popular books appeared in Germany. It would, however, be erroneous to suppose that these were first created at that time. Their material had been collected through the course of generations in the depths of the society. As soon as the book became a current and cheap item that penetrated into the broad strata of the people, entrepreneurs with a practical sense appeared and collected the masses of tales, legends, anecdotes, and jests with which the imagination of the people had, with special partiality, embellished certain heroes, such as the knights of King Arthur's court, Faust, the wandering Ahasuerus, Till Eulenspiegel, and many others. In this connection it is highly characteristic that the best loved and most popular books of that age have no author; they are anonymous works. The anthologists, editors, and publishers of the popular books which first appeared at that time represent a veritable cross-section of society: priests, storekeepers, monks, students, copyists, archivists. Whoever could hold pen in hand became an anthologist and publisher. The people received back in book form what they had elaborated and produced in the course of generations. The masses ceased to be merely the foundation of the national structure, the fertilizing soil, the humus of national culture; they became themselves co-workers in the production and collection of national cultural treasures.

All this, of course, had to find the sharpest resonance in the Jewish milieu, where the percentage of literate persons was relatively larger than in the German Christian populace. It is, however, not enough to say "sharpest resonance." The fact that the printing press first provided the possibility that the vernacular, with its oral folklore, be raised to the level of folk-*literature* which becomes an important factor in national culture called forth a complete revolution in Jewish cultural life. Gutenberg's brilliant invention brought it about in significant measure that *Leshon Ashkenaz*, the Judeo-German dialect, among all the vernaculars which the wandering people employed in its long homelessness, became, as we shall presently see, the only justified heir of the old Aramaic-Hebrew dialect and, together with it, formed the two major links in the cultural history of the Jewish people.

The rapid flowering of the Judeo-German literature is also closely associated with the efflorescence of German popular literature.

CHAPTER THREE

Romances and Epics

The oldest printed popular books in Yiddish—German works in Hebrew characters—Rabbi Anshel's *Mirkevet Ha-Mishneh*—The *Spielmann* repertoire—The Arthur-romance and its versions—Its publisher Josef Witzenhausen—The significance of the Hamburg manuscripts—From *Spielmann* poetry to popular book—Elijah Baḥur (Levita) and his *Spielmann* poems—His *Ha-Mavdil* and his Purim poem on the conflagration in Venice—His knightly romance *Bove-Bukh*—The style of the romance—The stanza meter—The Jewish fashion in chivalrous romance—Levita's romance *Paris un Viene*—Its unique style.

HE OLDEST printed poem in Yiddish that has come down to us is the translation of *Addir Hu* in the Prague edition of the Haggadah of 1526 mentioned above. The oldest printed book in Yiddish which has been preserved is Rabbi Anshel's *Mirkevet Ha-Mishneh* (Cracow, 1534)—a kind of concordance in which the Hebrew words are set forth according to the alphabet, with an indication where the word is employed in the Bible, and afterward a translation of the word into "*Leshon Ashkenaz* that is customary among us Ashkenazim."[1] However, there is no doubt that considerably earlier in Germany (and perhaps also in North Italy, where a relatively important community of German Jews lived at that time) many books appeared in Judeo-German, but as chapbooks that passed from hand to hand—and this among a reading public which was not accustomed to saving books, in consequence of which they were soon lost. Indeed, in the introduction to *Mirkevet Ha-Mishneh* it is stressed that it has now become a "customary" thing "to bring to light" [i.e., publish] all "hidden things" and all kinds of books, to the end "that every common man should be able to obtain knowledge."[2] Already in the oldest printed Yiddish books that have come down to us, about which we shall speak later, it is strongly deplored that the common people pass their time with "foolish books" such as *Dietrich von Bern, Meister Hildebrant, Der schönen Glück*, and the like, "whose number is so large."

Some of these works have come down to us in later editions or copies, and from them it is apparent that we have to do here not at all with Yiddish translations or reworkings. To satisfy the newly risen and considerable Jewish reading public, the majority of those German popular books of which we spoke at the end of the previous chapter were simply reprinted in Hebrew letters. Only the passages which carried an exclusively Christian coloration were altered. Typical in this respect is the Cracow edition (1597) of *Dietrich von Bern* which J. Perles described.[3] While the German original says "Accept my Chris-

---

1. According to the title-page of the first edition: *"Mirkevet Ha-Mishneh,* a concordance, put together from two languages, Hebrew and the Ashkenazic language which is the tongue that is customary among us Ashkenazim and is used to teach the words of the Torah, the Prophets, and the Writings, all the twenty-four [books of the Bible]." On the polemical tendency of Rabbi Anshel's book, see Perles, *op. cit.,* 117; M. Weinreich, *Shtaplen,* 124. See also our *History,* Vol. III, pp. 243ff.

2. The preface to Rabbi Anshel's book begins as follows: "Since it has become customary that all hidden things and books are brought to light [i.e., published] in German, so that every common man should be able to obtain knowledge, it seems to me well to publish a useful little book, so that one may study all the twenty-four [books of the Bible] out of this little book. Whether difficult words or easy words, you will find all of them written in Hebrew and the German placed alongside, and in the case of each word it is noted where it is found in all the twenty-four [books], in what book, in what chapter, and in what verse." (We quote according to the second edition, 1584).

3. *MGWJ,* 1876, 354–361. We quote here the title-page of this edition: "This is the gate of the Lord; the righteous shall enter into it. A beautiful poem and great chivalry will you find in it, very entertaining to read for women and maidens, translated very clearly into German, entitled *Herr Dietreich,* for rich and poor to buy. If you spend your good money for it, God blessed be He will keep you from all fast-

tian faithfulness," we read in the Jewish edition, "Accept my godly faithfulness." In the same manner further changes were also made:

In the German Text	In the Yiddish Edition
1) O Mary, most pure virgin	1) Almighty, holy God
2) That in Christendom	2) That in the whole wide world
3) Help me, you are a Christian	3) Help me, you are an upright man
4) Then the chaste virgin sublime from heaven and her dear child	4) For the Almighty sublime and his dear host
5) O heavenly queen	5) O heavenly Lord
6) O kind mother, pure virgin, let it be your child's will	6) O Almighty, kind God, You do this of your own will

Similar alterations were also made in other editions and copies. For example, in the German poem "Warum betrübst du dich, mein Herz" which was also popular among Jews, the line "I thank thee, Christ, O Son of God" appears. This was changed to the phrase, "I thank Thee, God, on the exalted throne." The expression "Jesus, the little lamb" was reworked into "the almighty God alone," and the expression "swine-roast," so uncongenial to the Jewish ear, was changed to "fat roast."[4]

It would be erroneous, however, to think that the wide circle of readers produced by the invention of printing was nourished exclusively by simple reprints of German chapbooks in Hebrew transcription. There also appeared reworkings and poetic pieces newly created according to foreign models which earlier had circulated only orally. We have already mentioned the hero poems and hero epics that the Jewish *Spielmänner* used to sing and declaim publicly in the Middle Ages. It is not at all surprising that not a single manuscript has been preserved from this *Spielmann* repertoire, even from the fifteenth century which closes the medieval era. Judeo-German manuscripts of religious or ethical content were in the hands of more or less

---

coming afflictions. Printed in the renowned city of Cracow under the mighty king Sigismund, may his glory be exalted, in the year 5357 (1597) through Isaac the son of Rabbi Aaron of Prosstitz."

4. See Rosenberg's work in *Zeitschrift für die Geschichte der Juden*, II, 218, 269–270, 294; Schipper, *Teater-Geshikhte*, I, 113. Such changes were also made in prose works. See Steinschneider, *Serapeum*, 1864, 74–76.

wealthy owners, established country people, or rich *generins* (benefactors) and patronesses. But the knightly poems and hero poems in the Middle Ages had no *generins*, for, as we noted, these poetic works were not read but *listened to*. Only the itinerant *Spielmänner*, or minstrels, would occasionally write down for themselves the text of the poems which they used to read and declaim in public. With the wandering life that the *Spielmänner* led, these copies were mainly lost in their own lifetimes and most certainly following their death. But after the invention of printing greatly democratized the book, separated the poem from the melody, and created a barrier between word and singing, the earlier *Spielmann* poem that had been sung was transformed into a popular book belonging to the category of desirable reading material. Even for the poems that were not printed, there were also among the *generins* people interested in reading them. The copyists provided transcripts for these persons, and, indeed, the copies and printed editions of the sixteenth and seventeenth centuries provide us the possibility of gaining familiarity with the *Spielmann* repertoire of the end of the Middle Ages.[5]

We know from medieval Hebrew literature how popular foreign literary motifs were among Jews, how favored among Jewish readers were translations of works imported from the distant East, such as *Kalilah Ve-Dimnah, Mishlei Sendebar, Ben Ha-Melech Veha-Nazir*, and the like. The Alexander of Macedon romance was so popular that it was even included in *Josippon*. The author of *Shesh Kenafayim*, Immanuel Bonfils, as we know,[6] translated the Latin version of the Alexander-romance into Hebrew, and considered it necessary to note in the introduction: "Let the reader not think that I intend herewith to win glory and praise. My intention is simply to provide myself and others a little pleasure. I only think that when I shall be in a company of cultured persons or a gathering of common people, and I shall tell them interesting events from this work, they will have great pleasure therefrom and it will be sweeter than honey."[7]

However, it was not only oriental but also west European

5. Eleazar Schulmann (*Sefat Yehudit Ashkenazit*, VIII), L. Landau (in the introduction to his *Arthurian Legends*), and others pointed in their time to the role of the *Spielmann* in Old-Yiddish literature. This conjecture was firmly established through a critical-analytic examination of a whole mass of literary monuments of Old-Yiddish literature by M. Erik in his *Vegn Alt-Yidishn Roman* and in his *Geshikhte*.

6. See our *History*, Vol. III, 151–52 (Note No. 31).

7. *REJ*, VI, 279.

motifs that were introduced into Hebrew literature. We have observed[8] that the author of *Sefer Ha-Yashar* utilized numerous stories and legends of the European peoples. From approximately that time (1297) a Hebrew translation of the Arthur-romance *Lancelot du Lac (Sefer Ha-Shemad Ha-Tavlah Ha-Agulah)* has been preserved. It should occasion no surprise, therefore, that many works of the German *Spielmann* poetry were also reworked into Judeo-German. We know that these German works were produced not to be read but to be sung or declaimed before listeners who did not hold a book in their hands. The Judeo-German reworkings were also produced by the Jewish *Spielmann* with the definite purpose of singing and declaiming them before a Jewish audience.

The foremost place in this material imported from the German *Spielmann* poetry was occupied, apparently, by one of the knightly romances, composed in rhymed verses, that was closely associated with the rich treasure of imaginative stories and legends concerning the heroes and mighty men who sat at the round table of the great Celtic King Arthur (Artus).

We noted that as early as the thirteenth century one Arthur-romance (about the knight Lancelot) was already translated into Hebrew. The translator's explanation of why he undertook this work is interesting. The first motive was that he had occasion in his personal life to suffer great afflictions and misfortunes; apprehensive that he might fall into melancholia, he occupied himself with the Arthur-romance to distract himself. The second and, as the author stresses, the most important, was that he hoped that the book would make many sinners repent and return to God.[9] Only a fragment of the Hebrew translation has been preserved.[10] Much more fortunate was the Yiddish Artus-romance. This romance is the only Judeo-German knightly epic taken from foreign sources which has come down to us in full. Several printed editions[11] as well as three manuscripts have been preserved.[12] This romance has considerable cultural-historical significance, for it gives us a clear

8. See Vol. I, 187–88.
9. "For, through the aim of this book, sinners will learn the ways of penitence, will remember their latter end, and will return to God blessed be He."
10. In Rome at the Vatican library. Printed in *Magazin für die Wissenschaft des Judentums*, 1885, Hebrew section, 1–11.
11. In two versions: in rhymed couplets, several times reprinted, and in stanzas. Printed in Prague between 1652–1679.
12. Two manuscripts are in the State Library of Hamburg, a third in England in the library of Cambridge University.

notion of the poetic creativity of the medieval Jewish *Spielmann* —not only how he would employ the foreign material but the manner in which he would declaim his poetry before the public. In addition, we obtain indications of how the knightly romance, which was intended to be sung and declaimed with a special melody was, in time, transformed into a popular book for reading. We shall therefore dwell at some length on the Yiddish Arthur-romance.

The Arthur legends were extremely popular in medieval Germany and served as poetic material for numerous hero and chivalry epics. As early as the beginning of the thirteenth century the renowned Wolfram of Eschenbach appeared with his romance *Parzival.* Contemporaneously with him, Hartmann von Aue produced his romances *Erec* and *Iwain*, and Wirnt of Gravenberg his *Wigalois*, The last mentioned romance must be considered the source which a Jewish *Spielmann* of the fourteenth century utilized for his Arthur-romance. Dr. Leo Landau, the worthy editor of the version in rhymed couplets (according to the printed text and the two Hamburg manuscripts)[13] and, after him, M. Erik[14] concluded that the original Yiddish version was made directly from Wirnt's romance. We, however, doubt this and believe that in the genesis of the Yiddish Arthur-romance another work which appeared later than *Wigalois* apparently played the role of a connecting link. Only so are the differences in the plot and the confusion and incomprehensible inconsistencies in the Yiddish reworking explicable.

The first printed version of the Yiddish Arthur-romance is that of Prague of the years 1652–1679, which is composed in stanzas, i.e., in verses of eight lines with the rhyme scheme: *ab, ab, ab, cc.* Of this edition only a single copy is known (located in the library of Oxford University). The title-page begins with the following lines: "King Artus' Court *(Kenig Artus Hof)* is this book called—Great signs and wonders are recounted therein—How they allowed eating on no day—Until they received new tidings."[15] Because this edition is extremely rare, we present here the translation of an extract according to Landau's facsimile (from folio 11a):

13. *Arthurian Legends*, 1912.
14. *Vegn Alt-Yidishn Roman*, 94.
15. We quote according to Leo Landau, *op. cit.*

Now every year at Easter time
It was the custom in King Artus' reign
That on the greensward three miles long and wide
They set up a tent with beautiful adornments.
And fifty kings, each with a large escort,
Came to promenade before him
And remained four weeks on the greensward.
Many feats were there performed.
When Easter arrived
They would set up on the broad greensward
Many gold and silver furnishings
And provide numerous field kitchens on it.
Each king who came there
Arrived with no less than fifty thousand horsemen,
And King Artus rode out to meet each one,
And received each according to the usual custom.

The first publisher of the version in rhymed couplets[16] was the printer and proofreader of Amsterdam, Josef Witzenhausen, who acquired renown, as we shall presently see, as the translator of the entire Bible into Yiddish. From Witzenhausen's introduction it might be thought that he had before him an Arthur-romance written in prose and that he "set the book in verse." However, Müller long ago showed in his thorough work "Der Artushof und Josef Witzenhausen"[17] that Witzenhausen was merely the editor of an Arthur-romance which came to his hand ("I found one written out in my father's house").

According to Wagenseil's reprint, this edition of the Arthur-romance has the following title: "A beautiful story of King Artus' court, [describing] how he conducted himself in his kingdom, and what his customs were, and of the renowned knight Widuwilt, the valiant hero, composed very beautifully in rhyme. If you read it, your heart will rejoice."

Before the story itself comes a pious introduction:

To God alone reverence,
For He is Lord of all the world;
He created heaven and earth,
Therefore He is worthy of laudation, praise, and awe.

16. Published before 1680; reprinted in 1699 in Wagenseil, *op. cit.*
17. *ZHB*, VIII, 1904.

Such pious sentences were part of the established style of *Spielmann* poetry. Every *Spielmann* would begin his "prescribed text" with them.

Afterwards the story itself begins:

In the court of King Artus it was the custom not to sit down at table to dine before hearing something new on that day. It once happened that they waited a whole day and nothing new occurred, so that all had to go to sleep hungry. The next day they waited with great impatience for something new to happen, and vast was the joy when the news was heard that before the wall of the king's castle an unknown knight on a horse was waiting and wished to speak with the queen. When she went out to him, he asked her to accept a marvelously beautiful girdle as a gift. The queen inquired of her husband King Artus whether she should accept the gift. The king called together all his associates, the renowned knights, and took counsel with them whether he should allow the queen to accept the gift from the foreign knight. All agreed that she should, except one knight—and he the mightiest one, Gawain (according to the stanza version, Gawin), who contended that the queen ought not to accept the gift because it is proper for a queen to give presents but not to receive them from others. The king agreed with Gawain, and the queen refused the foreign knight's gift. The knight felt highly insulted and challenged Gawain to combat. Thereupon he vanquished the mighty hero in battle, and Gawain had to go with him as his captive. They travelled many days and nights until they arrived in a marvelously rich land such as Gawain had never in his life seen. Everything was of gold and silver. This land belonged to the foreign knight. Gawain learned that his conqueror was a powerful king who had come especially to the celebrated court of Artus in order there to obtain the mighty knight Gawain as a husband for his only daughter. When they entered his magnificent palace Gawain was overcome by the princess' marvelous beauty, and he at once consented to the match. He married her and they lived very happily. Several months later, however, Gawain began to long for Artus' court. Despite the fact that his wife was already pregnant, he decided to travel there to learn what was happening at court. The woman was beside herself and asked him what name she should give the child to which she would give birth. *Wie du willt* (Whatever you wish), Gawain answered distractedly. The next day Gawain set out on the way without his wife's knowledge, but he could not find the right road to King Artus' land. He wandered about for ten years until he finally arrived at Artus' court, but he could no longer return to his wife. He had forgotten the way.

Gawain's wife gave birth to a boy and named him Widuwilt, following the father's reply before he set out on his way. The boy grew up tremendously large and strong. He was always hearing people tell of his father and his great might, and learned from his mother that his father was at King Artus' court. When Widuwilt was thirteen years old he declared that he was setting out to seek his father. The mother was not willing to let him go. His grandfather thereupon intervened, and Widuwilt set out on the way. Before his departure his mother gave him the wondrous magical girdle that prevents anyone who wears it from losing his way, and in the course of four weeks Widuwilt came to the most distant place to which he wished to go. At his first riding forth he already showed his great heroism, and upon arriving at King Artus' court he was received with the greatest affection and obtained Gawain as his educator and trainer.

One morning a young woman arrives, riding on a horse, with a little dwarf. She announces that she has come as an emissary of the queen of Hungary, seeking protection and help from King Artus. The king of Hungary has perished. The whole land is in flames; all that has remained is the single castle "Zum Wachsenstein" where the queen has fled with her marvelously beautiful daughter Lorel. The misfortune that has befallen the land came from a terrible witch or sorceress who is as tall as a mountain. Because the king of Hungary refused to give his lovely Lorel in marriage to her son, a fearful giant, she placed him and the whole land under an enchantment. Now the young woman has come to King Artus' court to request that one of his gallant knights, whose fame resounds over the whole world, come to her aid. She tells him that the one who vanquishes the witch and her son will obtain the beautiful Lorel for a wife as reward and, after the queen's death, will inherit the entire kingdom. However, none of Artus' knights has any desire to fight with a witch. The young woman from abroad becomes very angry, mocks King Artus and his pusillanimous knights, and forthwith departs with her dwarf, the wise counselor. The young Widuwilt champions the honor of Artus' court and declares that he will go save the enchanted land of Hungary. King Artus agrees, and at his departure Widuwilt explains to Gawain that he is his son. Widuwilt pursues the young woman from Hungary on his horse. She is terribly angry that out of all of Artus' knights, she has been given a still not grown-up boy to do battle against the terrible witch and her son, the enormous giant. However, she is soon mollified, for she becomes persuaded that she was mistaken: the youthful Widuwilt quickly demonstrates what a mighty and fearless hero he is.

The heroic deeds Widuwilt performs are adorned with many imaginative details. There is a description of how on the way they meet a young girl with flowing hair who laments and mourns. She relates that at a tournament she was acknowledged the most beautiful and therefore received three precious objects as prizes—a marvelously beautiful horse, a bird that speaks like a man, and a gilded cage. Along came a wicked knight and took away from her all the gifts, out of anger that his own daughter had not been given the prize for excellence. The heroic Widuwilt takes up the cause of the wronged girl, pursues the robbing knight, and promptly overcomes him in a duel. As was the custom among knights, the young Widuwilt spares the defeated knight's life on condition that the latter, with all his four hundred men, go to the court of King Artus and there declare themselves his captives. Widuwilt returns the precious objects to the robbed maiden, but the latter is so touched that she refuses to take them back. Finally they come to the agreement that the girl will take back the horse, while the bird with the gilded cage is awarded by Widuwilt to his companion, the young woman from Hungary.

After many such heroic exploits, Widuwilt finally arrives at the magnificent castle in which the queen and the lovely Lorel dwell. The young knight is smitten by her beauty and falls in love with her. But first he must battle against the sorceress and free the enchanted land. Every day around noon a deer comes running to the castle with tears running from its eyes. It knocks with its horns three times on the gate of the castle and immediately runs away. Widuwilt decides to pursue the deer in order to learn what it means by its visits. The next day he runs after the deer. The latter, at first, flees into a meadow. There stands a well into which the deer hastily jumps, and when Widuwilt comes to the well an old, naked man with a beard coming down over his breast rises out of it. He tells the young knight that he is the enchanted king of the land, Lorel's father, and only for a brief time each day can he assume human form. He warns Widuwilt not to enter into the dangerous battle, for the power of the sorceress and her servants is fearfully great. The knight, however, remains firm in his intention. The enchanted king then gives him all the details on how to conduct himself in the battle with his powerful opponents. In the middle of his speech the king suddenly breaks off, for the allotted time has passed and he is again transformed into a deer. Widuwilt must therefore wait for the next day. Then he again pursues the deer. The king rises from the well and tells him more about the dangers that lie before him: that he will have to rush through the ruined land burning with fire, that he will then enter a forest where he will have to struggle with a terrible dragon, and then five hundred wild women will attack him. The latter are the sorceress's servants. Only thereupon will he have his encounter with the sorceress and her son.

Widuwilt sets out across the ruined, enchanted land where he has many trials to suffer. Later he comes to a large forest and there hears the terrible cry of a woman. The dragon has just eaten up her husband, the king of a neighboring land, together with her son. Widuwilt pursues the dragon and soon sees the monster holding the king in its mouth and the son clamped in its tail. The brave Widuwilt attacks the dragon with his naked sword. An obdurate struggle breaks out. The dragon drops its victim from its mouth. It must also straighten out its tail during the battle, and in this way the king's son is saved as well. The dragon spits fire at the heroic battler, but Widuwilt manages to kill it. In its last convulsions, however, the mortally wounded dragon, with its gigantic body, hurls its gallant opponent far away to the bank of a river and Widuwilt remains lying there in a deep faint, half dead of his wounds. A fisherman and his wife pass by and see the young knight lying in his rich clothing and expensive armor. They strip him naked. The fisherman even intends to kill him, but his wife has pity on the fainted warrior and does not allow it. They depart with their spoils. However, one of the queen's servants notices them and the queen ascertains from the fisherman that the rescuer of her husband and son is alive. Widuwilt is soon found and comes out of his faint. He is brought with great honor into the palace. The rescued king sets before the young hero half of his kingdom and wishes to give him his daughter to wife. But Widuwilt declines and sets out further to save the enchanted land of Hungary.

Deep in the forest he encounters at a large fire four hundred wild women—the sorceress's servants. They attack him with a great din. He sets himself courageously against them, and they flee in clamour and alarm to their mistress, the fearful sorceress, who runs toward the unwished-for visitor. The heroic Widuwilt tries to fight her but is powerless in the face of her sorcery. She takes him captive, splits a great tree, places him in a vise so that he cannot move, and wishes to kill him with his own sword. Suddenly a noise is heard from the forest. It is Widuwilt's horse running about. The sorceress, however, believes that it is the sound of the approach of her strongest enemy, the only one of whom she has any fear, the terrible dragon, and so she quickly flees. She did not know that the dragon was dead. For two days and three nights Widuwilt remains in the vise, but finally manages to free himself from the tree and sets out for the castle of the sorceress. He has occasion to perform many great deeds. He must battle with two giants. The first of these he kills, but he spares the life of the second, who warns him not to enter the castle, for the power of the sorceress and her gigantic son is fearful. Widuwilt, however, knows nothing of fear and bravely rushes into the palace. Again the sorceress steps before him. Once more a terrible battle between her and Widuwilt takes place, and this time again the knight is unable to vanquish the sorceress. She runs him through with his own spear, and the broken point remains lodged in his shoulder. Death hovers over the gallant fighter. To his good fortune, however, the women of the forest come running and inform the sorceress that Widuwilt has slain her terrible enemy, the dragon. Out of great joy, the sorceress spares his life and tells him that the wound in his shoulder will be healed if his bride, the lovely Lorel, will pull out the point of the broken spear after he has spent three days in silence, not saying a single word, despite the fact that Lorel will come to him every day and speak to him hour after hour. She will beg him and inquire of him, but he must remain silent if he wishes to be healed. The wounded Widuwilt leaves the castle and then meets the sorceress's son, the enormous giant. Here Widuwilt first demonstrates all his power. Wounded and weak, he nevertheless overcomes the sorceress's son, and as soon as he slays him, the power of her magic is broken and the enchanted land of Hungary is liberated, along with its king. Widuwilt had fulfilled his mission and proved the greatness of Artus' heroic knights.

At the end, however, the story of our Arthur-romance becomes somewhat confused. When one compares the Judeo-German version of this knightly romance with its prototype *Wigalois*, it is easy to discern the attempt of the Jewish *Spielmann* to simplify and shorten the action, to concentrate it and make it less complex through various omissions and abbreviations.[18] At the end of the romance, however the Jewish *Spielmann* introduces new episodes which are not present in Wirnt's romance and consequently arrives at certain inconsistencies. At first it is indicated that Widuwilt can be healed only on condition that the beautiful Lorel pulls the spear out of his wound after he remains dumb for three days. The *Spielmann*, however, later forgets this condition. Widuwilt, after slaying the sorceress's son, returns to the king whom he had rescued from the dragon. He is welcomed with great honor but remains dumb and does not speak a word. The people wish to heal his wound, but he does not allow this. Nevertheless, the king's daughter manages, without his knowledge and will, to remove the spear from his wound. Even now, however, Widuwilt continues to play dumb and speaks not a word. The king proclaims to all lands that in a short time the marriage of his daughter with the knight will take place. The invited guests, many kings and knights, assemble. Lorel comes with her saved father, the erstwhile deer. Artus himself arrives with Gawain, and so does Widuwilt's mother with her aged father, the king. Widuwilt remains silent. Three days successively Lorel comes and speaks to him hour after hour, but he does not reply. Only on the fourth day does he begin to speak and declares to all the assembled guests that Lorel is his beloved bride. Gawain learns that his wife is among the guests. General rejoicing ensues. The wedding of Lorel and Widuwilt is celebrated with great pomp and circumstance. The other daughter of the king is also not put to shame. King Artus marries her off to the "great duke of Tuscany."

The contradictions that have been noted at the close of the romance are perhaps explicable by the fact that the Jewish *Spielmann* did not employ Wirnt's romance directly but a later version into which many new episodes were interwoven. The reworker into Yiddish who endeavored to simplify the action, however, omitted numerous details and, in this way, several points of the story remained unresolved and are even, to a degree, inconsistent.

Max Erik has[19] rightly evaluated the Yiddish Arthur-romance from its literary and artistic aspects. Wirnt's romance, Erik notes, is an organic product of a definite age, harmoniously grown together with the feudal environment,

18. See M. Erik, *Vegn Alt-Yidishn Roman*, 115.
19. *Op. cit.*, 113–121.

with the unique world of chivalry. The characteristic feature
of *Wigalois* is

its knightly and religious spirit; at every step the author offers instructions on how knights and noblewomen ought to conduct themselves in the most varied circumstances, and comments in moralistic
verses and postscripts on the course of the action. The charm of
Wirnt's romance consists, in fact, in the mingling of lyric and epic,
of objective and subjective poetic elements . . . The Christian knightly
poet's seriousness and solemnity rest on a world-view, on the consciousness of the important mission that is fulfilled through the recitation of the romance; this recitation is also a knightly deed. What
could it be in the case of the Jewish *Spielmann* who was unable to base
himself on this foundation of the chivalrous world outlook? . . . How
did he, the Jew, operate with this material so alien to the ghetto? He
simply omitted the purely Christian motifs. He also calmly set aside
Wirnt's poetic-lyric and moralizing verses . . . If the Yiddish Arthur-
romance, because of understandable factors, could not breathe that
exalted atmosphere which is the major charm of Wirnt's romance,
then the Yiddish romance was from the outset condemned to remain
only a story, an intriguing work in which confusion and tangle are
everything and fill out everything, leaving no place for other motives.
Chivalry is already a fantastic entity, the heroes are wooden mannequins of intrigue . . . it is a knightly romance without knights and
without knightlihood, a romance built on the tangle of intrigue and
yet remaining thoroughly monotonous."[20]

From the cultural-historical point of view it is also interesting to compare the text of the manuscripts of the Arthur-
romance that have been preserved from the sixteenth century
with the printed editions that Witzenhausen published on the
threshold of the 1680's. Here the phenonoma that we encounter
in the two versions of the *Sefer Ḥasidim* that have come down
to us are repeated.[21] Because the manuscript version preserved
in Parma was written at a considerably earlier time, one obtains through it a more or less clear concept of how this collective work was produced, whereas in the second, later version,
these indications are no longer so clear and it therefore became
impossible to recognize the links that bind together the various
parts of the work. A similar picture is obtained in exploring the
text of the Yiddish Arthur-romance. The text of the Hamburg
manuscripts still carries quite clearly its original character as
a *Spielmann* composition, while in the printed edition all these

20. *Ibid.*, 119–120.
21. See our *History*, Vol. II, pp. 36ff.

typical signs have already largely disappeared and one notices altogether new features that indicate how the *Spielmann* poem was transformed into a popular book that was *read*, not declaimed.

Max Erik has quite rightly noted[22] that from the Hamburg manuscripts it is not difficult to see that the original was divided into songs or chants. The division was really made not so much according to the content but to provide a natural pause for the singer, so that he might rest a bit. In both manuscripts, the beginning of a new "song" is marked by a new line in which the first word is written in large letters and by the following address to the audience: "If you will now be still, I will continue." In the printed edition, no sign of these pauses has generally remained. For example, where the marble chair that stands before King Artus' castle is described, we read in the manuscript:

> Here stood a marble stone,
> As we have heard.

At this point the *Spielmann* apparently paused, then resumed:

> If you will now be still,
> I will tell you many wonders about this chair.

In the printed edition this passage obtains a completely different form:

> There stood a marble chair very well made,
> As we know *from this book;*
> Of this chair I will now tell you
> Many great wonders.[23]

The manuscripts refer only once to the text of a book:

> He rode through many lands,
> As the book tells us.[24]

The printed text, however, refers to the book at every turn. We present here a few examples. In the manuscript we read, "I did

22. *Vegn Alt-Yidishn Roman*, p. 96.
23. We quote according to Wagenseil, *op. cit.*, 184.
24. L. Landau, *op. cit.*, 22.

not know what was in the little house, and this I will explain to you here"; in the printed text, "Now everything that was in the house, *as we have read in this book.*"[25] In the manuscript it is related, "And he was here four weeks, I tell you this in truth"; in the printed text the corresponding passage reads, "And he was here four weeks, as we understood *in reading.*"[26] When Widuwilt catches up with the dragon, the printed text declares, "Now the book tells us for a truth";[27] in the manuscript not a word is said of the book. When King Artus orders Gawain to be Widuwilt's trainer and says to him, "And do the best you can with him, and quickly teach him everything you know," the manuscript lists: "to joust, to storm, or engage in tournaments, to fence, to ride, or be a courtier."[28] However, in the printed text, which already appeared as a popular book for *reading*, King Artus tells Gawain:

> To fence, to storm and fight
> To engage in tournaments, joust, and ride;
> You shall also be for him a teacher of virtue,
> And tutor him to write and *read well.*

Also characteristic is another passage. We noted that the Arthur-romance was divided into "songs" which were actually only notations for pauses, when the *Spielmann* would cease reciting, refresh his throat with a glass of beer or wine, and then continue his recitation. Where the *Spielmann* passes from one subject to another, he employs the typical formula: "Now let us leave the giant, and we shall tell how things went with Widuwilt."[29] To enliven the audience, to enhance the attentiveness of his hearers, the *Spielmann* calls out from time to time, "Listen to me"; "Listen, dear people"; "In truth I tell you this." But where the attention was sufficiently strong and the audience listened with bated breath, the *Spielmann* knew quite well how to exploit the mood that had been produced. Approaching the episode where the sorceress splits a tree and sets the knight Widuwilt into the vise so that he cannot move, the *Spielmann* suddenly

25. Wagenseil, 174.
26. *Ibid.*, 178.
27. *Ibid.*, 244.
28. Landau, *op. cit.*, 30. Only later does the manuscript incidentally mention that Gawain also taught Widuwilt "writing or riding."
29. In the printed text the expression "we shall tell" is exchanged for "we will *write* further."

stops. He will not tell anything more, and Widuwilt will remain stuck in the tree until a full glass of wine is brought him:

> Now Widuwilt must remain caught
> Until you give me good wine to drink;
> I will help him well,
> If you give me a large glass full.[30]

In the printed edition this whole passage is missing. This, after all, is already a book only for reading; hence, the *Spielmann's* trick became superfluous and, in fact, not even comprehensible. On the other hand, in the printed editions there are details not present in the manuscripts. In the introduction to the Amsterdam Arthur-edition of 1683, the publisher Joseph Witzenhausen writes: "Listen, dear people—For the time has come—When people do not gladly read the holy tongue—And enjoy German more—And so I could not fail—to print such a happy and edifying book—So that people might find joy in it —And not waste their time with babbling and idle talk.—Here ends the introduction.—May God soon send the Messiah— Speedily, in our day—To which we shall say, Amen." Witzenhausen did, indeed, endeavor to make his book "pious" and as "happy" as possible, so that "people might find joy in it." According to the manuscript, Widuwilt declares:

> I help you out of your distress,
> Even though I lie dead on account thereof.

In Witzenhausen, however, the heroic knight becomes more "God-fearing" and asserts with a pious mien:

> I help you in all your distress,
> If the almighty God stands at my side.[31]

In the manuscript the battle of Widuwilt with the giant, the sorceress's son, is described:

> Widuwilt, the worthy warrior
> With one jump . . .

---

30. Landau, *op. cit.*, p. 100.
31. Wagenseil, *op. cit.*, 222.

In the Witzenhausen edition, however, it is told:

> Widuwilt evaded his stroke,
> And called to God in heaven.

To make the narration more interesting and arresting, Witzenhausen intensifies its fantastic and supernatural aspects. According to the Hamburg manuscript, the maiden of the castle Falkenstein tells King Artus of the sorceress's son: "A strong giant is he called." In the Witzenhausen edition, however, the young woman declares "A strong giant Lucifer is he called." The giant is transformed into a demon. In the manuscript there is a story about the sorceress's four hundred servants: "They were measurelessly black, they were of the devil's form." In the Witzenhausen edition even darker colors are employed: "Four hundred monstrous women sat around here, and were horrible and black as the Moors; they looked like diabolical whores; I tell you assuredly and of a truth and do not lie as much as by a hair; they looked undoubtedly like the living devil."[32] While in the manuscript it is related that the women met the hero "with a great noise," the Witzenhausen edition adds, "with a very great and monstrous noise." Whereas the manuscript says, "The she-devil rode fast," the Witzenhausen edition relates, "The large and monstrous she-devil ran here." So it is at every turn.

Finally, one other small detail which shows the false conclusions at which one can arrive when one wishes to make conjectures, on the basis of poetic reworkings of foreign material, about the *spoken* language of that time. In the hand-written text of the Yiddish Arthur-romance, there are only a few Hebraisms, but even these were removed by Witzenhausen from the printed edition. In the Hamburg manuscript, for instance, doctors are called *rofanim;* in the printed edition, *Ärzte.* Only at the conclusion of the romance do we have the customary pious sentence: "Herewith ends this book; may God send us the Messiah speedily, Amen."

The Jewish *Spielmann* who reworked the text of the Arthur-romance for the Jewish audience has remained anonymous. However, we do know the name of another poet who reworked two popular chivalrous romances for the Jewish quarter and achieved great success with them. This is the philologist Elijah Baḥur, or Elijah Levita, of whom we spoke at length in the

32. Wagenseil, *op. cit.,* 260.

fourth volume of our *History*. As a philologist Baḥur had certain merits not merely in Hebrew but in Old-Yiddish philology as well—not only in his interesting little Judeo-German dictionary *Shemot Devarim* (Isny, 1542) but also in his *Tishbi* (1541), where many words that occur in the Talmud and the Midrashim are also explained in *Leshon Ashkenaz*, the vernacular of the Ashkenazic Jews.[33] Baḥur also wrote some special Yiddish works[34] in the first period of his literary productivity before becoming acquainted with his patron Cardinal Egidio da Viterbo. In this first period Elijah Baḥur lived under extremely difficult material circumstances. In a manuscript of the year 1503 that has been preserved he signs himself, "the young versifier, humble grammarian, and teacher of children."[35] He apparently instructed youngsters, wrote poems, and occupied himself with philological investigations; yet, with all these occupations, it seems he had a very meager livelihood. Testimony to this is provided by his bitter and somewhat obscene lampoon *Ha-Mavdil*,[36] in which he settles accounts in a very cynical way with a competitor of his in Venice, a teacher by the name of Hillel Ha-Kohen. From another libelous lampoon of his, a Purim-poem (about the conflagration in Venice) which begins with the lines

> Now I will sing to you a bit
> With my bad voice,
> Tell of new happenings
> That everyone should know[37]

it may be conjectured that Elijah Baḥur also used to sing poems before an assembly as a *Spielmann*. These two lampoons have a certain importance for Elijah Baḥur's biography; they show that in the first period of his activity he lived in dire financial circumstances and was involved in the muck of petty gossip and dirty slander. Their literary value, however, is very slight. Of a completely different character, however, are his reworkings of two knightly romances, *Bove-Bukh* and *Paris un Viene*.

33. On the significance of these works for the study of Yiddish, see M. Weinreich, *Shtaplen*, 77–86.
34. "My German books," as Elijah Baḥur calls them in his introduction to the first edition of the *Bove-Bukh*.
35. See M. Erik, *Geshikhte Fun Der Yidisher Literatur*, 179.
36. Published by N. Shtif according to two manuscripts, *Tsaytshrift*, I, 150–158; *Shriftn*, 148–179.
37. For a discussion of this poem, see M. Erik, in *Tsaytshrift*, I, 177–178.

The confused and complex love story of the young Bove and the lovely Druzane was extremely popular in medieval Europe. The oldest English-Norman versions of the knightly romance *Sir Bevis of Hampton* derive from the twelfth century, the era of the Crusades, when the Moslem world with its variegated culture and treasures of imaginative legends and marvelous stories was disclosed to the deeply pious Christian knights. For the Yiddish Bove-romance, the Italian version about the knight Buovo d'Antona, more precisely, the later Tuscan version which was produced around 1400 and which, shortly after the invention of printing, appeared among the first published editions, served as source. It was one of these editions that Elijah Baḥur employed.[38]

The Italian Tuscan version, which was produced in the Renaissance era, bears a character quite different from that of the older medieval versions. In the Italian epic poetry of the Renaissance, knightly romanticism had already lost its erstwhile naive faith, its orthodox and pietistic world outlook. Among the knights who are celebrated in this poetry, the old religious pathos and genuine romantic love are lacking. The powerful interest of that age in the classic culture of the Greeks and Romans contributed not a little to the fact that, in the Italian epic poems of the Renaissance, the Christian and the pagan, the emotive and the comical, are all so extraordinarily intermingled. In addition, there is a skeptical irony regarding the clergy that not infrequently amounts to atheistic sarcasm. It suffices to note Ludovico Ariosto's famous knightly epic *Orlando Furioso* with its graceful humor and skeptical smile, an epic that is a harbinger of the caustic sarcasm with which the brilliant Spaniard Miguel de Cervantes issued forth less than a hundred years later against the fantastic romanticism of the knightly romances.

It was this ironic smile, naturally, that was especially congenial to the Jewish poet, for whom the sentiment of reverence for the world of chivalry was generally alien. Like the Tuscan version, so Elijah Baḥur's *Bove-Bukh* was written in the unique meter known as *ottava rima*, or, as it is called in Yiddish, *raym in akht-gezets*, in which the eight lines of each stanza are set in a system of three rhymes, following the schema: *ab ab, abcc*.

The time when the *Bove-Bukh* was written is noted by Elijah Baḥur quite precisely in the last verses of his work:

38. In the period from 1480 to 1500 six editions appeared.

But I wish to indicate
Who made and wrote this book;
He is called Elijah Baḥur.
A whole year he spent on it
And made it in the year
That is numbered 5267 (1507).
He finished it in Nissan and began it in Iyyar.
May God protect us from all evil beasts.

However, until quite recently, aside from two manuscripts,[39] no printed editions of the *Bove-Bukh* earlier than the
second half of the seventeenth century—the Prague edition of
1660 and the Amsterdam edition of 1661—were known. Nevertheless, Steinschneider and, following him, Benjacob conjectured that the Prague edition was certainly not the first and
that Elijah Baḥur's *Bove-Bukh* was undoubtedly printed while
the author was still alive. Only in 1931 was Dr. Max Weinreich
fortunate enough to find in the Zentral-Bibliotek of Zurich a
remarkably well-preserved copy of this first printing, which
appeared in Isny in 1541.[40]

Extremely interesting is Elijah Baḥur's explanation in the
preface of the reasons for which he decided in his old age to
publish his "Toytsh Bikher:"

I, Elijah Halevi the writer,
The servant of all good women
With honor and good breeding.
And I let this thought prevail—
And it ought to be believed—
That some women take it ill of me
Because I do not publish for them, too,
A sum of my German books,
So that they might pleasantly pass the time with them
And read them on Sabbaths and festivals.
Now I wish to tell the truth:
This seems to me also just and fair.
Since I have written eight or nine books in Hebrew,
And wanted to bring them into the world in print,

39. One in the Bibliotheque Nationale in Paris, the other in a private collection in
Berlin.
40. *YIVO-Bleter*, II, 280–284. The date of the edition is noted on the title-page: "It was
printed in the town of Isny, and "Elijah the author" *(Eliabu Ha-Meḥabber)* is equal
to the date." Also at the end of the book: "Printed at Isny in the year that is counted
5301 (1541)."

So I decided
That because I have come to an advanced age,
And today or tomorrow go the way of all flesh,
All my books and poems
Will be forgotten and laid aside.
So, let none of them disappear from me;
I will publish all of them one after another.
Even if there were ever so many books,
And if some other thing would not shorten my life's term,
And I will commence in a favorable hour
With this book called *Bove*.
And it is true and correct
That it is now thirty-four years
Since I wrote it out of a foreign [i.e., Italian] book,
But I added much of my own thereto.

In the first edition the work is still called *Buovo d'Antona*;[41] only in the later editions was it changed to *Bove-Bukh*. That this work was written, like all the other *Spielmann* poems, to be sung or recited with a special melody is attested by the author himself in the previously quoted introduction:

But the melody that goes with it—
This I cannot give to you to understand.
One who knows music or musical notation
I would fain have helped,
But I sing it with a foreign [i.e., Italian] tune.
If one can make a better melody—he will have my thanks.

That the octaves of the *Bove-Bukh* were sung is also frequently indicated in the text itself. So, for example, the author declares:

> Now we will let Bove ride many a mile
> And traverse a long road.
> Meanwhile I will *sing* to you
> How things went with the lovely Druzane.

Like all the *Spielmann* poems, the *Bove-Bukh* begins with a pious, God-fearing mien:

41. At the end of the work it is noted: "Conclusion of the treatise "Buovo d'Antona."

God is to be eternally praised
And His wonders proclaimed,
Because He is revered and exalted
In the mouths of good and pious men.
He is all-powerful above and below;
His praise is not to be fathomed,
No one can exhaust it,
For it has neither limit nor end.
May His holy name strengthen me
That I may not fail
To complete this work,
To translate a foreign book into German,
And that I pay close attention
And not make any mistakes,
And that people should not laugh at me.
Now commence listening; my story is about to begin.

Then the narrative itself begins:

They say that in Lombardy
There lived for a long time
A duke of exalted character.
His like was not to be found far and wide.
The noble man was called Duke Guidon.
A mighty warrior in all battles,
With great honor he wore the crown
In a city called Antona.

In his old age Duke Guidon married the beautiful princess Brandonia, who bore him a son named Bove. The young Brandonia hated her aged husband and thought of ways to get rid of him. She secretly dispatched a letter to the duke Dodon of Mayence (Mainz) with a criminal plan, proposing that he subjugate Antona and offering to help see to it that her husband fall into his hands. The plan is carried through, Guidon falls at Dodon's hands, and the murderer occupies the land and marries Brandonia. Brandonia also wished to poison her son; by accident, however, the young Bove managed to escape death and fled. Here the thrilling story of Bove's wandering life begins. Passing merchants find him asleep on the shore of the sea. He delights them with his fine appearance, and they take him along on their ship and sell him as a stable-slave to the king of Flanders, Arminion. With his marvelous handsomeness Bove wins the heart of the eighteen-year-old princess Druzane.

But the princess' beauty resounds in all lands; hence, the son of a powerful king, the brave knight Macabron, comes and requests Druzane's hand. To honor him King Arminion arranges a tournament of knights, and Macabron defeats all his opponents in the competition. Witnessing the tournament, the stable-boy Bove feels awakening in himself the valiant knight and battler. Armed only with a crooked bar, he rides out into the tournament and vanquishes the proud Macabron. Druzane is enchanted by Bove's heroism. She kisses and embraces him and declares herself in love. While the loving pair carry on an amiable conversation, a tumult erupts in the city. The sultan of Babylonia has surrounded the city with ten thousand brave warriors. He wishes to force King Arminion to give the lovely Druzane as wife to his son Lucifer, who is as ugly and terrible as the devil himself. Arminion places himself against the sultan's army, but the sultan triumphs and Arminion is taken captive, along with Macabron. As soon as he learns of the defeat, Bove tells Druzane that he is ready to fight against the sultan's army. The princess, who knows that her beloved is not a common stable-boy but a prince, brings him an enchanted horse Pumele and a magic sword Rondele that belonged to her deceased brother. Like an arrow out of a bow, Bove flies on his magic horse to the battlefield:

> Bove the brave warrior rushed there,
> Placed the bridle on Rondele's ears,
> And rode toward the heathen.
> They thought he had gone completely mad.
> Rondele whinnied and snorted and grumbled
> And bit and struck out backward and forward
> . . . .
> And Bove with his sharp lance
> Troubled many a man.
> No shield remained unbroken before him;
> He shattered all of them into little pieces.
> He was the first to ride into the dance,
> The others followed without hesitation.

Bove slays Lucifer, smashes the sultan's army, and liberates the king and Macabron.

Only now does the intricate plot of the romance unfold, and one confused situation follows another. Through the treachery of an envious person Bove is dispatched to the sultan of Babylonia with a sealed letter in which it is indicated that he is the murderer of the sultan's son Lucifer. The sultan wishes to have Bove executed at once, but the sultan's daughter Margaretta sees the prince, falls in love with him, and saves him from death. After numerous trials and heroic exploits, Bove manages to escape. He boards a ship, travels over the sea, and arrives in the capital city of Macabron's country precisely on the day when the wedding of Macabron and Druzane, both of whom thought he was already long dead, is scheduled to take place. Bove reveals himself to Druzane. She gives Macabron a sleeping potion and runs away on the bridal night with Bove. A wild creature, half-man and half-dog, named Plekun, is sent out to pursue the lovers. Plekun, however, enters into a close fraternal relationship with Bove and becomes his faithful servant. But the trials of Bove and Druzane do not end with this. The loving couple live together for a year and Druzane bears a set of twins. Then they must run away before an enemy. By accident they are separated, and the confusion continues. Bove manages to capture Antona. He avenges his father's murder and locks up his criminal mother in a cloister. Druzane, who believes that Bove has perished, arrives with her children at her father's house. Bove, for his part, thinks that Druzane is dead. Then he receives a letter from the sultan's daughter Margaretta, begging him to come to her aid, for an enemy has attacked her land. Bove arrives with his strong army and drives away the enemy. Margaretta again declares herself in love, and Bove agrees to marry her. Druzane learns of this and comes with both her children on the very day that Margaretta's marriage to Bove is to be celebrated. She disguises herself as a beggar and sings a song about Bove and Druzane. Bove recognizes her. The joy that supervenes is indescribable. Margaretta marries Bove's friend Tritz, and Bove goes off, with wife and children, home to Antona.

> He was a king immeasurably great,
> He reigned over three kingdoms.
> His two sons both grew up
> And became two valorous warriors.
> And he gave to each in his land a fief;
> In the whole world there was not its like.
> They had much land in their possession.
> With this the book comes to an end.
>   (according to the Amsterdam edition)

Like the anonymous reworker of the Yiddish Arthur-romance, Elijah Baḥur also greatly condensed the foreign material which served him as his model. While the Tuscan version of the Bovo-romance runs to approximately 1400 octaves, the Yiddish version contains only about 650. On the other hand, in numerous other respects Elijah Baḥur followed a way quite different from that of the anonymous *Spielmann*-poet of the Yiddish Arthur-romance. The latter is deadly serious; he never smiles; his language is emotive and exalted; he does not permit himself to use any simple, popular expression; and the *Jew* is discernible in the *Spielmann* only in so far as he removes or alters all expressions of a distinctly Christian coloration. The *Bove-Bukh* is written in a very different style. In Elijah Baḥur we feel at every point that we have before us a *Jewish* author. Already in the first song, where it is related that the duke Guidon in his old age married the young Brandonia, the Biblical motif of King David and the Shunamite maiden Abishag is interwoven; Guidon also "came into his old age, when the more they covered him, the colder he grew," and his associates counsel him: "Send to seek in all corners some young, ardent lady, who will warm and cherish you." And when the treacherous Brandonia destroys her aged husband, the first song concludes with a rather Jewish moral:

> Therefore, dear gentlemen, consider
> What misfortune comes from wicked women:
> How one would like to hew her husband in pieces,
> So that she may carry on her indecencies.
> All misfortune comes from evil women.
> See how King Solomon writes
> That he sought a pure woman
> And found none in his day.

Druzane's father, when it is pointed out to him that marriage with the stable boy Bove is not suitable for the daughter of a king, responds like a scholarly Jew with a dictum of the sages who said that "one should examine a kernel well; of what avail is the distinguished ancestry of father and mother, when a person himself is not good?" His daughter Druzane also speaks at times like a learned Jewess. She knows the expression "May his name and memory be blotted out," and she declares to the disguised Bove:

Shall this ill form be likened
To that of the noble lord?
Ah, as the difference between the holy and profane,
So is that between his dear face and yours.

Her intimate friend the countess, as soon as she sees Druzane through the window, calls out: "By the Creator of the world, it is my friend Druzane; I will go and give her *shalom* (greetings)." Druzane laments to her father that in her wandering life she has not had the opportunity to circumcise her children, and the father consoles her: "Do not worry; tomorrow I will arrange a great circumcision feast." Margaretta's wedding is set "with *mazzal tov* (good luck) immediately now for *Rosh Ḥodesh Nissan*, and to this wedding came "many *letzanim* (jesters) and about fifty strange *minyanim* (prayer quorums)." These Yiddishisms are an organic part of the living, popular style in which the Jewish Bove-romance is written.

We noted earlier that in the Tuscan version of the Buovo-romance, which was produced in the Renaissance era, a skeptical irony toward the world of knighthood as well as toward the clergy is already noticeable.[42] The light, mocking tone toward the heroes described and the events related appears more prominently in the Yiddish reworking. The ironic smile of the Renaissance, however, is exchanged in Elijah Baḥur for the grimace of the common man of the people. In the Yiddish *Bove-Bukh* is felt not the representative figure of the Renaissance but one of the clever jesters of the Jewish ghetto who, in a popular and frequently quite crude fashion, mocks the foreign world of chivalry with its behavior.

Another point must be especially noted. Elijah Baḥur was the first to introduce *ottava rima* into Yiddish literature, and it is literally astonishing to see the mastery with which the author of the *Bove-Bukh* commanded this complicated stanza form. The verses are rich, resonant, and often overwhelm one with their unexpected assonances. An example or two is worth giving:

אורלב נאם דער ריצרד אונ׳ פֿון איר שׁ י ד ער
אונ׳ נאם דען בריף אונ׳ צוך (צאג) זײן שטרושן
דוך גידוכט ער זײן הערין אלזו ב י ד ר
אונ׳ ער טריב מיט אים זעלבסט אײן ימאר גרושן.

---

42. Highly characteristic in this respect is the comical scene in which Plekun attacks the monastery and in which the idleness and pusillanimity of the gluttonous and drunken monks is especially stressed.

or

וואָש גרושי ורייד (פריד) טריב נון זיין פּאָטער
דאָן מעכט איר נון וואָל גלאָבן
נון הט ער איין בורג גרובן, דען בּאָט ער
דש ער אים זולט היטן דען קנאָבן.

The mastery of this form, however, is manifested by Elijah
Baḥur in its true glory only in his other romance, *Paris un Viene*.

Habent sua fata libelli, "Books have their special fate," says an
ancient Latin proverb, and the truth of the proverb may be
seen most clearly in this work of Elijah Baḥur's. The author
wrote two romances. Both of them are chivalrous romances
and both are composed in *ottava rima*, following Italian patterns. *Paris un Viene* is incomparably superior to, and more
mature than, the *Bove-Bukh*. The Bove-romance, with its vulgar, mischievous grotesqueries, is a popular work for whiling
away the time pleasantly, while *Paris un Viene*, with its clearly
stamped individualism, its fine, delicate maxims and reflections
on the world, is a work of art. But how different was their fate.
The *Bove-Bukh* became one of the most beloved of books among
Jewish readers. It was reprinted for centuries, and when the
taste of the Jewish reading public was greatly changed—and
changed for the worse, to the point that the knightly romance
produced in Italy was in overly sharp contrast with the Polish
ghetto of the eighteenth century—the *Bove-Bukh*, which had
been composed in verse, was transformed into the prosaic,
fantastic *Bove-Maaseh*. In this altered form it went through a
great number of editions[43] and became so popular that the
expression *bove-maaseh* became a household word, a symbol of
unbelievable, fantastic stories.

Elijah Baḥur's other romance, *Paris un Viene*, had a completely different fate. It was erased from the memory of the
people and fell into complete oblivion. Relying only on the
report of an Italian priest Guiseppe Ventori, several bibliographers, such as Benjacob and Steinschneider, reported drily that
in 1594 in Verona a romance *Paris un Viene*, translated from
Latin(?), was printed with lovely illustrations, and that the

43. It is worth mentioning as a curiosity that the czarist "Commission for Jews"
(1744–1800), which used to censor Jewish books imported from abroad, proscribed
the importation into Russia of the Lemberg *Bove-Maaseh* edition of 1789, because
in it magic is spoken of in very ugly and profligate expressions, and it is related
how a king is murdered and his queen falls in love with the murderer of her
husband. See Julius Isidorovich Hessen, *Yevrei v Rosii*, p. 428.

translator apparently was Elijah Baḥur. Only in recent years, thanks to the scholars J. Shatzky[44] and especially M. Weinreich,[45] was this forgotten romance resurrected. A single copy of the work was located[46] (unfortunately a defective one; the first twenty-four pages, approximately a third of the entire work, are missing), and it is Weinreich's great merit that he was the first to make us aware of this splendid monument of secular Old-Yiddish literature.

The *Paris un Viene* romance, which derives from the Provençal circle, was extremely popular in medieval Europe. It was reworked into various languages[47] and was especially loved in Italy. In Elijah Baḥur's time alone the romance appeared in nine editions, and one of these apparently served him as the source for his Yiddish version. The story was taken from the world of chivalry and is constructed on the same family-pedigree motif as the well-known novella *Beriah Ve-Zimrah*. It portrays the love of a knight named Paris, a son of the duke Joachimus, for the lovely Viene, the daughter of his king. The proud king Dolphin, however, does not consent to the match; the groom, after all, is merely his vassal, and he desires as a son-in-law his own like—a king or a prince. The love-stricken pair attempt to run away secretly, but they are pursued. To save his life, Paris must leave his beloved. The poor knight wanders over the whole world. He comes finally to the sultan in the distant East and becomes highly popular at his court as a skilled physician. Viene allows her father to propose various matches, but nothing comes of these; the beautiful princess remains true to her beloved and drives away all prospective bridegrooms. The enraged king orders her locked up in a prison chamber; she remains unmoved. In the meantime King Dolphin involves himself with other Christian kings in a war against the sultan. Dolphin is captured in the sultan's land as a spy. He is incarcerated, and certain death, preceded by horrible tortures, awaits him. Paris learns of this, manages through his cleverness to free the king, and flees with him on a hired ship back to their country. Dolphin, however, does not know who his rescuer is; he does not recognize Paris in his oriental dress, and Paris gives himself out to be a Moslem who does not

---

44. *Landau-Bukh*, 187–196.
45. *Bilder Fun Der Yidisher Literatur*, 172–191.
46. Now in the library of Trinity College at Cambridge University. We have employed a photographic copy that was in the possession of the well known scholar of Yiddish Naḥum Shtif.
47. For the literature, see Shatzky, *op. cit.*, 193–194.

understand the "Welsh" language. When Dolphin returns home in peace he wishes to express his gratitude by making his rescuer his son-in-law. Viene, however, refuses to hear of this new groom. The king is beside himself with rage. Paris then proposes that he be given the opportunity personally to persuade the recalcitrant bride. He immediately reveals himself to Viene. Boundless joy supervenes. Now when Dolphin begs his daughter to have mercy on his aged head and agree to the match, she promptly assents and declares with a mischievous smile: "For your sake I will take this man." Only then does Paris disclose himself to King Dolphin. All are delighted and a joyous wedding feast is conducted.

The romance is written in a highly realistic fashion. Everything occurs naturally. There are no sorcerers or giants in it; no great exploits are performed. The major motif is simply the true love that is stronger than death and overcomes everything. There is no doubt that *Paris un Viene* was written by Elijah Baḥur after the *Bove-Bukh*. Testimony to this is provided by the high technical level which is first disclosed in this work. In the *Bove-Bukh* the irony is still quite crude and umpolished; the "Ashkenazi," the cumbersome spirit of Levita's native land, is more discernible in it. Only in *Paris un Viene* does the piquant, ironic smile of the Renaissance, of which we have spoken in the previous volumes of our work, manifest itself in all its loveliness.[48]

48. *Paris un Viene* was apparently composed by Elijah Baḥur in the years 1509–1513 in Venice. For the time being it is not clear whether Levita published this work during his lifetime and whether the Verona edition is merely a reprint. On the last two pages of the Verona edition it is only noted clearly, and this in both Italian and Judeo-German, that the edition was printed in 1594 in Verona at the press of Messer Francesco dalle Donne. Aside from the rhymed epilogue that is quoted from the Italian priest Ventori and from there reprinted by J. Shatzky in his abovementioned article, there is on the penultimate page (72a) another epilogue in the following lines in verse: "Printed at the firm of Messer Francesco dalle Donne by hand—Of your servant, good friend of all—Both men and women.—Believe me —I wrote it—That you might not be idle—And let it be printed in this size—Not too small and not too large.—Though it may be difficult for some—They will soon understand it—When they come to it.—You have understood well—What I have come for here.—Herewith I shall close.—Those who buy it will not be disappointed—For you will certainly say in truth—That you have not seen anything like it all your days—Through the hands of your servant, as I began to say.— Herewith we will beg God—To send to us—The anointed, Messiah son of David —And may he lead us into the holy land—Where we shall have rest—To which we will all say Amen—Amen. Selah." We learn the name of the twice-mentioned "servant" through whose "hand" the book was printed from the final illustration

Elijah Levita himself notes that he greatly abbreviated the Welsh, i.e., the Italian, text:

This book in a foreign language
That is everywhere written at such length,
I do not wish to draw out still more;
Many words I leave out.
Otherwise, my little book will be too large,
And I shall not have enough time for it.
Hence, let one who has read it before in the foreign tongue
Not think that I wish to be faithless to it. (44b)

However, Elijah Baḥur not only abbreviated the text but rewrote it in a completely different style—a Jewish style. In *Paris un Viene* the poet does not exceed proper measure, as in the *Bove-Bukh* where the princess Druzane, for instance, indicates to the king that her children are not circumcised and the king at once calms her and tells her not to worry: "A great circumcision feast will I arrange tomorrow." In the second romance Levita clearly shows that the heroes are Christian; in it figure monks, priests, and a bishop as well. But the poet deliberately rejects the emotive, exalted tone of the knightly poems. With an ironic smile he weaves around the Christian environment a Jewish atmosphere, with the world view of the Jewish ghetto. In *Paris un Viene* we encounter at every step such Hebrew expressions as *mitah meshunah* (bizarre death), *gan eden* (garden of Eden; heaven), *meḥilah* (forgiveness), *raḥamanut* (mercy), *ḥanifut* (flattery), *le-ma'an ha-Shem* (for God's sake), and *shemuah* (report). In it are rhymed the words *simanim* and *panim; ḥavvayot* and *ḥayyot; tekufah* and *terufah; keniah* and *de'ah; seder* and *ḥeder; sakanah* and *kavvanah,* etc. It is also noted in it that "thus our sages said that necessity frequently breaks stone and iron." Of the friendship of Odoardus for Paris it is said that "the love was not dependent on anything, like that of Amnon for his sister" but "it was the love between David and his brother-in-law (Jonathan)" (53a). Of the heavy sleep of the drunken Mamelukes it is related:

---

which concludes the whole work. In this typical Italian woodcut the following words are inscribed: "Through the hand and in the name of your servant Abraham, son of my lord my father, the scholar—may his name be honored—Mattathias of the stock of Bathsheba, may God keep him." This Abraham Bathsheba apparently attended to the Verona edition of *Paris un Viene.*

They were lame, they were deaf,
They never moved by a hair.
I let them sleep there on that ground
Till they, by God's will, become *bar mitzvah* [i.e., for a very
  long time].

(63b)

The son of the duke of Burgundy who wishes to marry
Viene and of whom it is told that "the groom rummages like
a cat after a mouse," on becoming convinced that nothing will
come of the match, arrives at a very Jewish moral:

What pertains to the marriage of men and women
Comes from Heaven; there is the Writer [of the decree].

(48a)

King Dolphin tells "from *alef* to *tav*" ("A" to "Z"), and as
soon as the match between Paris and Viene is concluded, the
king sent "to fetch a golden ring and had *mazzal tov* (good luck)
inscribed on it." Paris immediately betroths *(tut antshpoizen)*
Viene, and when the city learns that Viene's groom is the
returned Paris, it is related that

The greetings *(shalom aleichem)* and good wishes *(mazzal tov)*
Would have no end.

(70b)

Viene prays in a very Jewish fashion:

O Lord of the whole world's foundations,
Remove not now your grace,
And keep my Paris fresh and hale . . .
So, Lord God, hasten now the hour
That I may hear something from him.

(67a)

The encounter of Paris with his aged father, who believed
his son had long since departed from the world, forcibly reminds one of the Biblical scene in which the patriarch Jacob
once again sees his son Joseph:

The father wept, as much he could,
And then he spoke: O son Paris!

I did not think to see your face again,
And now God has shown me your wife also!
Blessed be God who brought you here
That I may see you this day.
Now will I die, and I am content,
Seeing that I have lived to see your face.

(70b)

Whereas in the *Bove-Bukh* the characters are merely schematic figures, wooden mannequins, in the major figures of the other romance the breath of real life, the forcefulness of temperamental personalities, is felt. The dialogues are highly dynamic. The events are portrayed in clear, sharp forms, and the octaves very frequently overwhelm one with their poetic resonance and high level of technical achievement. Here are some brief examples.

The son of the Duke of Burgundy comes to King Dolphin to arrange a match with the latter's daughter, but Viene is obstinate and utterly refuses to appear before the groom. The king is beside himself with anger and shame, but the people outside know nothing of this. They rejoice and give tumultuous ovations to the welcomed guest:

The king burned with wrath
With intense pain, with great dread;
He saw before him the disgrace and shame
And did not know how to cover it.
And as he stood in this condition,
In all corners was loudly heard
Exultation, shouting, roaring with great joy:
He comes, the king's son-in-law comes!

(47a)

The joyous welcome that the people of the city accord King Dolphin on his homecoming after his long captivity is portrayed as follows:

So a shooting and a ringing,
With great guns and with bells.
One heard only: tip-top, ging-gong.
Whoever did not know of it was frightened.
There were great crowds of small and large.

Every man rejoiced to see the good king released from
  captivity.
Every man wished to accompany him to his home.

(64b)

In *Paris un Viene*, however, the narration itself is not as important as the long and frequent "Not this do I intend" with
which the poet appears in his own person. The trick that we
already encounter in the author of *Minḥat Yehudah*, who suddenly himself leaps into the middle of the narration,[49] is employed by Elijah Levita in highly unusual fashion. The poet is
not content merely to narrate the details of the medieval
"Welsh" love story. He himself comes forth before the reader
with his own maxims and reflections on the world. He everywhere ironically shreds the romantic texture of the novel, with
its old-fashioned heroes, and appears with his own world view,
his opinions and conclusions in regard to real life and the
practical demands of the new times. The sarcastic, skeptical
smile of the Renaissance is harmoniously forged in the Yiddish
Paris un Viene with the moralism and shrewd insights into life
of the Jewish books of ethical instruction—and also of the
Jewish jesters. This adds a special grace and unique coloration
to the entire work. We present here as illustrations a couple of
such digressions in which the author comes forward with his
own sayings and moral maxims.

The sixth canto which relates that Viene's father rejects
Paris because he does not consider him a suitable son-in-law
begins with the following lines:

Cursed be gold and wealth,
And also he who puts his trust in them.
On their account a man rests neither day nor night.
Often he gains them justly, and often through robbery.
Frequently one sells flesh and blood
Only because he wishes to have a great treasure.
The devil lures on here, like sulphur lures fire,
And like a great wind leads the cloud.
If one wishes to marry off his daughter
Or give his sons wives,
They never ask whether perchance he knows anything,
Whether he is a man of learning or a writer.
Only money is the crucial question.

49. See our *History*, Vol. I, p. 180.

Elijah Baḥur's Paris un Viene

Even if he be a donkey-driver
A dwarf, a fool, an idiot, a good-for-nothing—
If only he has money, they snatch him up.

A boy, a girl, go to them without slickness(?),
And take counsel with them on the matter.
The first question, the first utterance:
"Has she much money? Has he ducats?"
They inquire no more about sense or wit,
About piety or good breeding.
Money covers up every bad trait,
Even if he be the worst kind of bastard.

When the poet relates how faithful Viene was in her love, he
immediately notes with a sigh that at present such faithful
women are no longer to be found:

Who is the woman, who the girl,
Who is the maiden or young lady,
Who will endure suffering?
This I cannot conceive.
Say, who will give up a dress,
Who will be willing to lose a dance?
Who will be willing to try out and wait
A single year, a month, or even two weeks?

The first unknown young man who comes along
And only smiles at her—
If he has a velvet cape
And a fancy coat and trousers,
Even if he be a damned fool
And unskilled in everything,
He is still very dear to her and desirable
And she acts as if she would laud him to the skies.

And if now a third should come along
With a large gold chain,
I tell you that she will take him
And cast off the previous one.
She will show all affection to this one—
On this I will gladly wager my head!
They have the same constancy as leaves
On the tree during wind and weather.

With a jesting smile, the poet, already at that time the father of a family, concludes:

Praised be God, I am still free and single!

Another interesting point is worth noting. Following the established *Spielmann* or gleeman fashion, Levita ends each song in *Paris un Viene* with the statement that he—and certainly the public, along with him—is already very tired of long singing and recitation. So, for instance, the fourth canto concludes:

And if you wish to hear more about these goings-on,
Wait, I must go wet my throat.

(26b)

At the end of the sixth canto the poet calls out:

I have sung long and much
And had forgotten to stop.
Now that I think of it, I would say
That I cannot go on longer.

In the penultimate verse of the ninth canto, going to sleep is mentioned. The poet uses this to conclude as follows:

Now this story
That tells of sleeping reminds me
That over this canto
A dizziness comes before my eyes.
I have continued long—
You cannot complain of me.
Let me now stretch, as those in the story do
Then will I say more, if only I am able. (61a)

At the beginning of the tenth (final) canto, however, the poet finds it necessary to note:

Now we have all become wearied
Of this book, I will wager—
You are tired of listening to these lines,
And I am tired and bored with reciting to you.

But this is not merely pretense, conventional style. Levita, who lived in abject poverty until he became acquainted with Cardinal Egidio da Viterbo, very probably earned some money from publicly declaiming his knightly poems. Apparently the recitation of the ten cantos of *Paris un Viene* used to take two whole evenings. This is indicated by the closing lines of the fifth canto:

> I cannot sing more of him,
> Because I pity him so,
> Hence I will now sit down,
> And if you wish to hear me—come back again.

Evidently the first evening concluded with the fifth canto, and the other half of the poem was declaimed by the author the second evening.

Following the established style, Elijah Baḥur ended his two romances with the pious wish that the Messiah might come as quickly as possible. But this stock closing formula is expressed in a very unique and playful fashion.

The *Bove-Bukh* concludes with the following octave:

> And may we be redeemed from our affliction,
> And may we be given grace,
> That all of us may be privileged
> To live to see the times of the Messiah.
> May he lead us to Jerusalem,
> Or somewhere in a little village near by,
> And may he rebuild for us the Temple.
> Amen, so may it be God's will. Amen.

Paris un Viene ends as following:

> My hope and my stronghold
> Is that one may come riding
> On a gray he-goat with long ears,
> And blow a terrible horn.
> And may he bring us to the city
> That God long ago chose,
> So that here may be settled
> All our bodies and our souls.
> There we will talk our fill
> And recount God's help,

And not tell of Paris and Viene nor of Isabella.
May this come true in God's name. Amen, Selah.

Another work of Old Yiddish literature is associated with Elijah Baḥur's name, but this work—his translation of the Psalms—belongs to a very different realm.

CHAPTER FOUR

Bible Translations and Midrashim in Yiddish

The battle against the "foolish books"—Issac Wallich's collection of poems—Dance songs and love songs—The Pentateuch translations in the Augsburg and Constance editions—Elijah Baḥur's translation of the Psalms—Cornelius Adelkind as publisher—Joseph bar Yakar and his translation of the Prayerbook—Jewish publishers and their advertisements—Judeo-German poetic reworkings of Midrashic material—The *Shire Fun Yitzkhok* and *Der Yidisher Shtam*—The Yiddish *Midrash Va-Yosha* and the Esther poems—Epics of Biblical heroes—The *Shmuel-Bukh* and its significance—The *Melokhim-Bukh*—The "Adam and Eve" poem—Two types of *Spielmänner*.

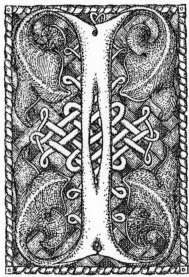

N THE introduction to the translation of the Pentateuch that was published in Constance in 1544, and of which we shall speak later at length, it is incidentally noted: "This book also has another virtue. For the women and maidens, all of whom can usually read German well, spend their time with foolish books like *Dietrich von Bern, Hildebrant,* and the like, which are nothing but lies and fantasies. These same women and maidens may now have their pastime in this Pentateuch that is nothing other than the pure, clear truth." A year later, in 1545, a similar complaint was expressed by the well-known publisher and printer Cornelius Adelkind in the preface to Elijah Baḥur's translation of the Psalms which he issued. Adelkind stresses that the pious women and those householders who had no time to study in their younger years "would be glad to spend their time on the Sabbath or on festivals in reading godly stories, and not those of *Dietrich von Bern* or *Der*

schönen Glück."[1] A certain Isaac Sulkes, who in 1579 published in Cracow a Yiddish translation of the Song of Songs, also finds it necessary to note in his long preface: "I believe it is pleasing to Almighty God that such German books as are useful and godly be written, but not *Dietrich von Bern* and *Hildebrant* and all the others, and not [just] a few, but many whose names I do not know. Those who spend their time with them certainly commit a sin."

Such attacks on "foolish books" of secular content are to be encountered in numerous authors of that era. This demonstrates most clearly how intense at the time was the indignation of the rabbis and religious leaders toward the new secular literature imported from the external world which was literally flooding the Jewish quarter. We know quite well how strongly the rabbis in Germany endeavored to isolate the Jewish people as sharply as possible from the outside environment in cultural respects. However, they did not easily succeed in doing so. We have observed the enormous popularity that was obtained in the Jewish quarter by such typical German songs as "Herzog Ernst" and the "Hildebrant"—poem. Especially interesting in this respect is a collection of poems of the sixteenth century which is to be found in manuscript in the renowned library of Oxford University and which was critically reworked by Felix Rosenberg.[2] The collector of these poems, Isaac ben Moses Wallich of Worms was the scion of a prominent family and was himself, Rosenberg conjectured, a *parnass* in Worms. This communal official of Worms apparently was a great lover of folksongs and himself the author of poems.[3] Thus in the last years of the sixteenth century he

---

1. However, the following piquant feature is worth noting: Precisely this "foolish" *Buch von der schönen Glück*, which Adelkind intended to displace by Elijah Baḥur's translation of the Psalms, was apparently printed by none other than Elijah Baḥur himself. Testimony to this is provided by the following note on the last page of the first edition of the *Bove-Bukh* which Baḥur published at Isny in 1541: "And the God who has done us the favor that we have printed *Bove*, may He also help us to print *Der schönen Glück* and other German books besides. So may it be God's will. Amen" (*YIVO-Bleter*, II, 282). The romance *Der schönen Glück* apparently was still very popular in the second half of the seventeenth century, for at the end of the Prague edition of the *Bove-Bukh* (1661) the printer announces: "And now will I first properly devote myself to printing many lovely pieces and the book *Der schönen Glück.*"
2. *Über eine Sammlung deutscher Volks- und Gesellschafts-liedern in hebräische Lettern*, first published in *Zeitschrift für die Geschichte der Juden in Deutschland*, II–III (1888–89).
3. The last poem of the collection ends with the following stanza:

wrote down very diligently, in a special collection, many poems that were especially popular in the Jewish quarter of his day. Characteristic is the following point: of the fifty-five numbers included in the collection, only twelve derive from Jewish authors. All the others are German folksongs that were also loved by Jews. The most honored place is occupied by song- and dance-poems.

The rabbis and leaders of the people did, indeed, attempt to carry through with strict consistency in daily Jewish life the basic principle that Jews "may not rejoice like other peoples." But the people refused to surrender. The Jewish masses, especially the youth, did not lose their love of life even in the dark and narrow alleys of the ghetto and the merry verses of the dance-songs resounded loudly and joyously in the *Tanzhäuser:*

> Young maiden, will you not
> Do a little dance with me?
> I beg that you do not think it ill of me;
> I must be happy,
> I must be happy,
> As long as I can have it.
>
> Your delicate young body
> Has wounded me with love;
> So also your clear little eye,
> As well as your red mouth.
> Link your arm,
> Dear love, with mine.
> Then will my heart be healed.

Turning in the circle of the waltz, the dancing couples sing:

> Now dance we the pretty circles
> And will be hale and joyous with each other,
> While it goes on
> And as long as it is honorable.
> Who wishes to forbid us a cheerful spirit,

I would gladly show myself quite wild,
However I am forced to be quiet;
No blustering will avail me.
All men must, alas, depart
When the Almighty God wishes.—
So speaks Eisik Wallich of Worms.

As long as our luck vouchsafes it to us?
Lovely maiden, lovely maiden,
Take it for good.

"Who wishes to forbid us a cheerful spirit?," ask the dancing youth. The religious leaders of the people wished to "forbid" this. One of the most esteemed rabbis of that age Rabbi Solomon Luria, as we know, considered joy and laughter sinful and branded the dance in which young men and young women take part together a criminal transgression. He even asserted that when men sit together with women at a wedding, God's favor does not rest on that house.[4] To this harsh verdict the life-loving youth responded with the playful verses of a dance-song:

Singing and jumping,
Cheerfulness at all times,
Is certainly permitted.
Promenading, courting,
Embracing and playing,
Turn all my suffering to joy.
As long as it takes place in honor
No one can forbid it,
Right here at this time and this place.

Lovesongs also resounded in the streets of the ghetto. Amorous young people expressed the pangs of their love in sad, despairing verses:

Extinguish, extinguish the fire in my burning heart.
My beautiful love has kindled it in me.
O noble crown, dweller in my heart,
How I love you,
If you will believe me.
For you my heart yearns
Bears great pains,
Caused by your lovely form.

Maidens suffering from unrequited love pour out their longing in elegiac verses:

4. See Vol. VI, p. 44.

> Once when I desired
> To court a young man,
> To become a married woman,
> It first occurred to me
> What kind of joy awaits a maiden
> On this earth.

One poem in which the beloved complains to her lover that he has forgotten her has a special interest, for this lovesong was so strongly rooted in the ghetto in the course of many generations that its echo is still quite clearly detectable in a folksong included in the well known Ginsburg-Marek collection, *Di Yidishe Folkslider in Rusland,* that appeared in 1901 (No. 178). One can easily persuade himself of this by comparing the two texts:

(In the Wallich collection):

> O why do you wish to go away,
> My heart, my inmost solace?
> And when will you come here again,
> To redeem and rejoice my soul?
>
> And even if I do come here again,
> What good will it do you?
> I shall certainly love you,
> But marry you I will not!

(In the Ginsburg-Marek collection):

> O, lonely have I remained,
> Lonely as a stone!
> I beg you, my dear one,
> Come to me, come!
>
> I will certainly come to you,
> But I cannot comfort you.
> I love you with all my heart,
> But marry, dear little soul, we cannot!

German poems of a frivolous and mocking character also entered the ghetto—for instance, this poem about old women which has been preserved thanks to Wallich:

I am cross with old women
And I well know why.
They are stiff in their joints
And they grow crooked.

Old women and ducks
Belong on the water.
They should preferably be drowned,
So that they quack no more.

Typical in Wallich's collection are the poems deriving from Jewish authors. The anthologist wrote down two bride-and-groom-songs. One of them with dual texts (Hebrew and Yiddish) begins as follows:

I open my mouth with sweet song
In honor of the groom, in gratitude for the bride.
I will not expatiate before you:
Let fear of God be the beginning of all.

The other epithalamion begins with lines of praise in which the loveliness of the bride is celebrated:

Pure gold certainly pales
Before the gentle bride;
She is so modest,
So chaste and pure,
Beyond all [precious] stones.

The *parnass* of Worms, however, deemed it necessary to write down in his collection not only bridal songs, satiric poems of the talented Shelomoh Singer, and joyous Purim poems of which we will have occasion to speak later, but also an erotic and profligate lampoon composed by one Eizik Kitul in collaboration with a friend of his. This poem, which consists of twenty-seven stanzas, is written in the meter of the very popular "Akeydas Yitzkhok" and even begins with the first line of this pious *Spielmann*-poem: "Jewish stock of a genuine kind." "Jewish stock"—these are the wealthy and debauched young playboys who serve Venus, the goddess of love, in a dirty and cynical way. The authors dwell extensively and happily on all the details of their unchastity and unclean eroticism, and conclude the lampoon with the following lines:

Now I will close this song.
We fellows are very annoyed
That they make it [i.e., sex] so expensive for us.
Let falling-sickness seize them, let their hearts crack.
Now I will read you the title.
It greatly annoys us young men,
Both me and Eizik Kitul,
Who are no fools in this matter,
And also gladly ride on such wheelbarrows.

The religious leaders of the people, the rabbis, were unable to drive out from the ghetto, through their bans and prohibitions, the secular folk literature with its fantastic heroes and gay, "amusing" songs that had been imported from abroad and written following alien patterns. Indeed some of the rabbis themselves understood this quite well; these more farsighted leaders soon realized that the books that were so popular could not be displaced by prohibitions, but only by giving the masses of the people, the reading public newly created by the printing press, another kind of reading material more suited to the Jewish tradition and the Jewish world of ideas. And this, in fact, happened. At the same time that the Jewish quarter was flooded with German knightly poems and romances, there was also gradually produced a unique popular literature deeply permeated with one definite, basic motif: to lead its readers on the "right way" of proper conduct, piety, and good deeds.

We have noted[5] that even in the Middle Ages there already existed Judeo-German translations of certain Biblical books that are closely associated with the school and the Jewish way of life—first of all, the Pentateuch, then the weekly prophetic readings in the synagogue, the Scrolls, Psalms, etc. Many of these translations were lost. After the printing press appeared in the Jewish quarter, Judeo-German translations of the Pentateuch soon found suitable publishers. The oldest of these editions of the Pentateuch in Yiddish (together with the prophetic readings and the five Scrolls) that have come down to us are those that appeared in the same year (1544) in Augsburg and Constance.

The Augsburg edition was published by the convert to Christianity Paulus Emilius. Emilius himself notes on the

5. See above.

title-page,[6] as well as in a special letter,[7] that the translation is not his own but by someone else, and that it was written many years previously. This is also the case with the translation of the Pentateuch that appeared the same year in Constance; its editor, the convert Michael Adam, considers it necessary to note that he made use of older translations.[8] He indicates in the preface that the translation has as its aim to be a helping-book in instructing children. Indeed, this is why it is so slavishly bound to the Hebrew text. To familiarize the pupil with the literal meaning of the sacred text, the teachers faithfully followed the word-order of the Hebrew original, were afraid to add or remove a word, and took no account of the spirit and character of the language into which they were translating. In this way a firmly established, traditional style that was transmitted from generation to generation without any changes was produced. For example: *Vayedabber Adonai* is translated "And He said, God"; *al penei ha-mayyim*, "on face the water"; *me'al ha-rakia*, "from above the firmament"; *yom eḥad*, "day one"; *tov me'od*, "good very"; etc. As an illustration of its style, we present here the first verses of the Constance translation:[9]

בראשית, אי דען ער האט דר שאפן גוט (גאָט) די הימל אונ׳ די ערד, אונ׳ די
ערד וש וואישט אונ׳ לער אונ׳ וינשטרניש אויף אן גזיכט דש אבגרונדש: אונ׳ ווינד
גוטש שוועבט אויף גזיכט דער וואשרן. אונ׳ ער שפראך גוט עש זול זיין ליכט אונ׳
עש וואר ליכט, אונ׳ ער זאך (זא) גוט דש עש גאט וואש אונ׳ ער מאכט שיידן גוט
צווישן דעם ליכט אונ׳ צווישן דר וינשטרניש, אונ׳ ער רופט גוט צום ליכט — טאג
אונ׳ צו דער וינשטרניש האָט ער גרופט נאכט; אונ׳ עש וואר אבנט אונ׳ עש וואר
מארגן.

6. "The Pentateuch in German and what pertains to it, the whole with the lection for each week, and the Prophetic lessons of the festivals, also the five Scrolls. . . . All this rightly and well translated from an old Pentateuch written a long time ago, now printed at Augsburg."

7. "For I did not add and I did not take away, and I did not change a word of it, but the translation which was made from the holy tongue into *Leshon Ashkenaz* many years ago I printed word for word." (See Perles, *Beiträge*, 169; Nash, *Sendschreiben an Professor Zarncke*, 14).

8. "Hence we were moved to print the Pentateuch in German, as several learned Jews and rabbis translated it from the holy tongue into *Leshon Ashkenaz*. Hence, we also used translations that we had before us that were rendered from the holy tongue word for word, so that the householders and the plain, simple Jews might all the more easily teach the children the Pentateuch and the other books."

9. Only in the form of marginal notes does Michael Adam permit himself in places to interpret the text, to explain it with the aid of the Aggadah, Midrash, and older commentators.

("Before He created, God, the heaven and the earth, and the earth was waste and empty and darkness on face of the abyss; and wind God's hovered over face of the waters. And He spoke, God: Let there be light, and there was light. And He saw, God, that it good was, and He made a separation, God, between the light and between the darkness. And He called, God, to the light—day, and to the darkness He called—night; and it was evening and it was morning.")

It is quite understandable that such a slavishly faithful translation can give us no conception of the state of the actual speech of the people at the time. Indeed, this is demonstrated most clearly by Michael Adam's previously mentioned preface. Here, where the editor is not bound to the Hebrew text, we have before us not the cumbersome "Daytshmerish" with its bizarre syntax, but a living and flowing Judeo-German. Adam writes:

„זינטמאל מיר זעהן דאז זיך די הערצן בון (פון) טאג צו טאג מינדרן אין דעם
ורשטאנד אונ׳ אין דער וייסהייט . . . צו דעם דאז וויר זעהן די קהלות בעונות
הרבים אויך אימר־דר אבנעמען אונ׳ צרשטערט ווערדן דורך וילפפאלטיג גירושים,
דז וואו מאן בור צייטן הט צעהן קהילות גיבונדן (געפונדן) גיפונט מן אצונדר קום
איינ׳ בעו״ה, אונ׳ דורך זאלכי גרושים ווערדן די בעלי בתים גינויטיגט אויף דען
דורפרן (דערפער) צו זיצן, אונ׳ איז אבר ניט אין איינש איטליכן ור מיגן דז ער קאן
איין מלמד האלטן דער אים זייני קינדר לערנט, דא דורך דען גרושי עם הארצים
דר־וואקסן"․

(Since we see that from day to day hearts grow lesser in understanding and wisdom . . . since we also see that the communities, because of our many sins, also constantly decline and are destroyed through many expulsions, so that where formerly ten communities could be found we now find barely one, and through such expulsions the householders are compelled to dwell in the villages, and it is not possible for each individual to keep a tutor to teach his children; thereby great ignoramuses grow up.")[10]

The same pedagogical motif is also to be noted in the preface to the well-known translation of the Psalms[11] by Elijah Baḥur which Cornelius Adelkind issued in Venice in 1545:

10. For the rest of the preface, see Staerk and Leitzmann, *Die jüdisch-deutsche Bibelüber-setzungen*, 126–129.
11. It is really not an entirely new translation but a reworking of older translations. On this, see Staerk and Leitzmann, *op. cit.*, p. 148.

Therefore the teachers who drill the young,
And wish to translate the Psalms rightly,
Will be instructed by this edition of the Psalms,
So that they will no longer make mistakes in translating.

The most interesting thing in this connection, however, is that the publisher himself, the well-known printer Adelkind, is not content with this statement. He issues forth with his own explanation: what is involved here is the payment of an old debt to the masses of the people. This explanation undoubtedly has a definite cultural-historical interest, and we therefore quote it in full:

Cornelius Adelkind writes this for the pious maidens and householders who have not had time to study. In my youth I helped print many precious and large books and directed all my endeavors thereto, as one may easily see in all the books that have been published at Daniel Bomberg's press in which my signature is to be found in the front or at the back. Now that I have come to old age, I reflected that I had done nothing for the pious maidens and for all the householders who did not have time to study in their youth or thereafter. These would gladly spend their time on the Sabbath or on festivals in reading godly stories and not *Dietrich von Bern* or *Der schönen Glück*. And for the sake of these who would eagerly read of God's word, but few books are to be found in the German language that are well and accurately translated, I went to Rabbi Elijah Baḥur and contracted with him to translate several books for me, and first the Book of Psalms according to the grammar. Soon, God willing, I will also print the Books of Proverbs, Job, and Daniel, well translated. And if God lets me live for a time longer, I will bring it about that small and great will be able to know thoroughly what is written in the twenty-four [books of the Hebrew Bible] which now, because of our sins, every man knows more of than we. Therefore, I beg you, dear pious maidens and householders, cheerfully and with good heart buy the Psalms and give us money so that we many soon be able to begin to print the Book of Proverbs.[12] Amen.

Thus Adelkind in his old age conceived the idea that one ought to be concerned for the spiritual and intellectual needs of the masses of the people also. However, as a result of the revolution which the printing press called forth in cultural life, there appeared among the masses of the people themselves

12. From this it may be conjectured that Elijah Baḥur at that time already had his translation of Proverbs completed. On Baḥur's unpublished translation of Job, see M. Weinreich, *Shtaplen*, 77.

interesting representatives of culture who even had the courage to manifest a certain contempt for the scholars and recognized spiritual leaders. Especially interesting in this respect is the publisher and editor of the first printed translation of the *Siddur* or Prayerbook, Joseph bar Yakar.

We observed previously[13] that already in the Middle Ages there existed not only translations of the Pentateuch but also renditions of the prayers in Yiddish. Indeed, in the very year that the Yiddish translations of the Pentateuch appeared in Constance and in Augsburg, there also came off the press a Prayerbook in Yiddish[14] in the small town of Ichenhausen in Bavaria. The publisher, Joseph bar Yakar,[15] himself notes that he used for his edition older translations ("I have not translated the prayers for you from my own head, but read some that seem to me to have been the best"). This publisher and editor of the oldest Prayerbook in Judeo-German that has come down to us is an extremely interesting personality. Apparently he was not much of a scholar and he himself attests to this: "For I am an ignorant fool *(am ha-aretz).*" He was a partner as well as a typesetter in the press of his father-in-law, the well known printer Ḥayyim Schwartz (Shaḥor). He not only edited the translation of the prayers but also set the type, as is noted on the last page of the edition, where his name is mentioned among the three typesetters of the work.[16]

Before the printing press was invented, when books were to be found only in the hands of scholars, such persons as Joseph bar Yakar never dreamed of becoming authors or editors of books. As a result, however, of the cultural revolution called forth by the printing press, when the book penetrated the broad strata of the people, common persons with powerful sense and natural gifts came to the foreground and had the courage to laugh at what was so revered and sanctified among

13. See above, pp. 23ff.

14. Only a single copy of this edition has been preserved (located in the State Library in Munich). See *Israelitische Wochenschrift*, 1872, 271–272; *Hebräische Bibliographie*, XII, 125–27; *MGWJ*, 1876, 355; and especially in Grünbaum, *op. cit.*, 296–319. The prayerbook, which consisted of forty-two printer's sheets, cost a crown. "For one crown it is yours."

15. Because after the name Yakar comes the acronym He-Yod-Dalet (an abbreviation for "May the Lord avenge his blood"), it must be concluded that his father died as a martyr.

16. The other two typesetters were the printer Ḥayyim Schwartz himself and his son Isaac.

the scholars and "leaders" of the people. Sarcastically Joseph bar Yakar asks an ostensibly naive and simple question: Of what use are so many liturgical hymns with such difficult language in the Prayerbook—hymns that no mortal can understand? To be sure, every one knows that "the holy language is the wheaten flour, the cream of the crop," but since the "common rabble" are not very familiar with the holy tongue, our sages of ancient times composed the prayers "briefly and well" in an easily comprehensible language. However, people were not content with this and "added thereto every day": "And they made in the prayers extremely difficult expressions, so that, on account of our sins, barely one in a thousand who knows what they mean is to be found."[17] Hence Joseph bar Yakar openly declares: "I consider those who wish to pray in the holy tongue and do not understand a word of it empty fools. I would be glad to know merely what kind of *kavvanah* (inner intention, or devotion) they can have. Hence, we have decided to print the Prayerbook, and more books besides later."[18]

Joseph bar Yakar, however, does not aim merely at piety and fear of God. The printed book had, after all, become an article of merchandise, and Joseph is not at all ashamed to note that he intends to derive a bit of income from his edition. He seeks purchasers for his wares, and since advertisements were still

17. To be sure, some of the great Sephardic scholars were also opposed to the *piyyutim*, but for different reasons. Abraham Ibn Ezra attacks the *paytanim* because they sin quite frequently, in his view, against the laws and principles of the Hebrew language (in his *Safah Berurah* he writes, "Poets arose and made liturgical hymns without end; they did not know how to compose properly"). Maimonides cannot forgive the *paytanim* because they permit themselves anthropomorphisms (see our *History*, Vol. I, p. 144. The rationalist Jacob Anatoli believes that one ought not to spend so much time on prayers and praises ("The worshipper ought to shorten them and diminish them, and he should recite of them only what the Men of the Great Synagogue ordained"). The same view is also held by the author of *Ha-Mevakkesh*, Shem Tov Falaquera, who declares that one completely fulfills his duty simply with King David's prayers ("It is proper to have only a few of their *piyyutim* sung, not all of them; and with the songs of David alone is it proper to praise God and to laud Him").

18. It is virtually beyond doubt that it was, indeed, thanks to Joseph bar Yakar that the renowned *Shmuel-Bukh* appeared that same year from Hayyim Schwartz's press. Testimony to this is provided by Joseph bar Yakar's closing lines in the introduction to the translation of the Prayerbook: "Now we would thank God who has helped us to this point, that He may further strengthen us like the lions for the *Shmuel-Bukh* that we begin, so that we may complete it quickly, and may He send us the Messiah this year."

unknown at that time he employs the title-page for this purpose:

> Come here, you pious women;
> Here you will see beautiful things.
> You will see it—
> A Prayerbook for the whole year
> Well and clearly translated.
> Therefore, come and buy joyfully.
> Otherwise you will miss it,
> For they do not grow on trees.
> Also, the book is not too expensive;
> It is yours for one crown.

Joseph ben Yakar is not content with this. At the end of the book he again reminds the reader:

> I have set the price at one crown,
> But I swear by my head
> That it is well worth ten.
> You will easily realize this yourself
> When you compare other Prayerbooks with it.
> It can freely be said
> That there is as great a difference between them
> As between an old woman and a young maid.

Such a comparison on the pages of a Prayerbook was something altogether new; it necessarily sounded very odd to the ears of the scholars who had grown up on rabbinic literature. Joseph bar Yakar, however, was not at all exceptional. His manner and style is typical of the Judeo-German literature of that era. The book which addressed itself to the masses of the people reckoned with the taste of these people, breathed their air and world-view. The Hebrew books were provided with *haskamot* or approbations from rabbis and scholars, but the Judeo-German books that were produced for the common people had no need whatever for *haskamot*. Their publishers, mainly themselves common people, would turn directly to the public and in jester-like rhymes praise their merchandise and invite purchasers. On the title-pages of their editions they address the public,[19] urging them to buy this most interesting

19. "For women and girls to read with joy, for young men and householders both";
   "In honor of all men, young girls, and women"; etc.

book as quickly as possible, lest they miss out.[20] Others assert
that if one does not purchase the book promptly, it will be too
late; the book will be dispatched to foreign countries.[21] There
were also publishers who candidly admitted that they had in
mind only a bit of income in issuing their book: "I am pressed
(es drikt mikh), therefore I publish *(drum drik ikh)*; what presses
me is known to God; Zanvil Papers is my name."[22] These
announcements and title-page advertisements were mainly
written in the customary form of the German *Knittel*-verses,
i.e., doggerel without a unitary rhythm. At times, however, our
publishers were not satisfied with this common form and employed the old Arabic meter in which Dunash ben Labrat
wrote his polemic poems and Solomon Ibn Gabirol and other
liturgical poets produced their *azharot*. In this complicated
meter, for example, is Jehudah Bresch's address to the reader
on the title-page of the Cremona edition of the Pentateuch
(1560):

איך דער שרייבער — אלע ווייבער — און פרום לייבער — טו איך רופן. . .

איז עס ניט שיין — דאָס בוך זיי פיין — דאָס דא אלס דריין — איז געשלאפן
(געשליפן). . .

אלס דער ספיר — איז דאָס פאפיר — און אך טאפפיר — אָנצוגרייפן. . .

איטליכי מאד — זיי עס ניט לאַד (לייד) — איר איגן קלאַד (קלייד) — צו פארקאפין

איר אַל זאכין — געלט צו מאכין — זייא מיט באכין (באַקן) — און גענז שטאָפפן. . .

און באַדי (ביידע) וועלט — גאָט עס פר געלט — ווער מיט דעם געלט דאָס ווערט
קאָפין. . . אאז״ו.

It is not simply a matter of accident that Joseph bar Yakar,
to whom we are indebted for the first printed Prayerbook in
Yiddish, also set himself the task of publishing, immediately
after the Prayerbook, the famous *Shmuel-Bukh* epic. We noted
earlier[23] the role of the *firzogers* (foresayers or synagogue precentors) and expository preachers. In that context we observed
that in the post-Talmudic era, when the Talmud and the ancient Midrashim were edited and written down, the source of
Aggadah was not thereby stopped up. The national legends in
the later era also occupied a highly honored place in the public
religious cult, even though in altered form and though the
sermon was reforged into the *piyyut* or liturgical poem. In the

20. "Therefore come quickly running, to buy this beautiful story, for not many were
printed; hence, they will soon be exhausted."
21. "Come running and buy quickly. Not many were printed, so they will soon be
exhausted. Buy them quickly before they come to strange lands."
22. See Schulmann, *op. cit.*, VIII.
23. See above, pp. 23ff.

European Jewish communities the golden material of *Aggadah* was spun further. These communities no longer spoke the dialect which Asiatic Jewry had spoken at the time when the old Midrashic material was produced. Hence the Midrashim also, not merely the Torah, required translators and interpreters who might explain and also poetically rework the aggadic material produced by previous generations. Once again near the expository preacher stood the *paytan* or liturgical poet; however, he no longer wrote, as in the post-Talmudic era, following the pattern of the Syrians and Greeks, but according to medieval European models. Not merely the prayers were translated into the vernacular of the people, not only sermons were given to the public in French *(be-la'az)* or in Judeo-German *(Leshon Ashkenaz);* poetic reworkings of the Midrashic material were also recited in the *lingua franca* of the community. Like the *paytanim* and *hazzanim* in Hebrew, so also the *firzogers* would declaim liturgical creations in the vernacular before the people in the synagogue.

Highly interesting in this respect is the elegy for the Ninth of Av produced around the end of the thirteenth century[24] in the Judeo-Italian dialect of the Italian Jews of that era. In this elegy, which very movingly laments the troubles that the people of Israel endure in exile, the well-known Midrashic legend of the two children (a son and daughter) of the High Priest Ishmael ben Elisha, who were captured and sold as slaves after the destruction of the Temple,[25] is poetically reworked in powerful stanzas. The elegy ends with the customary pious wish: May God send redemption as quickly as possible and may we be privileged to live to see the advent of the Messiah. The well known scholar Immanuel Cassuto, who treats this elegy in a special work,[26] emphasizes that along with its national content, its external form and the construction of its verses reflect the sharp influence of the Christian jongleurs, the wandering Italian singers and minstrels of that age. Apparently this elegy was produced by a Jewish *Spielmann* who utilized the forms of his Christian colleagues in his national liturgical poem.

The same thing, in perhaps even broader measure, took place in the German-Jewish communities. In the era of the Second Temple, as we know, it was customary to read before

24. Preserved in two old manuscripts of the fourteenth century, published in 1913.
25. *Gittin,* fol. 55.
26. "Un antichissima elegia in dialecto guideo-italiano" (1929). For a discussion of this work, see *Kiryat Sefer,* VIII, 499–501.

the people on every Sabbath the prescribed lection for the week and immediately, along with the reading, to explain it in *Targum*-language, i.e., the contemporary vernacular of the people. In the communities of the European lands where the *Targum*-language was already incomprehensible to the masses, it became the custom, therefore, to read only the Hebrew text, without the Aramaic translation but also without the translation into the vernacular. Only in special cases were certain lections from the Bible read aloud in the vernacular. We previously cited the testimony of Rabbi Isaac bar Sheshet that on Purim it was customary to read the Scroll of Esther before the people *be-la'az*, i.e., in the colloquial language. This translation, however, was not a verbatim one, but interwoven with homiletic interpretation. We know that even the old Greek translation [Septuagint] which, according to legend, was made by seventy elders, already contains in the Scroll of Esther a certain amount of Midrashic material. In the medieval collections of religious laws we also find quite clear indications that certain *parashot* or lections of the Pentateuch were explained homiletically to the people in the synagogue service. In the *Kol-Bo*[27] and in Aaron Ha-Kohen's *Orehot Hayyim* it is noted that on the first day of Shavuot the Ten Commandments were explained to the people homiletically in the vernacular, "in order that women and unlettered persons might also be able to understand."[28] Also on the Seventh Day of Passover and *Shabbat Shirah* it was customary to preach on the exodus from Egypt and the Song of the Sea (Exodus 14:30–15:19) and to relate "in the language that all can understand the wonders that God did with us." It was also customary to preach "about the redemptive acts that God Blessed Be He will perform for us."

Indeed, the text of the Midrashim that were preached during the Middle Ages in the European communities on these festi-

27. First edition, 57b.
28. We quote this interesting passage here in full: "There was a custom on the seventh day of Pesach and on the first day of Sukkot in many places to translate the whole lection in order that women and unlettered persons should understand all the miracles and wondrous things, and to explain them to them so that they might give praise to God. For at the time that it was ordained, all spoke the Aramaic language, and at that time the custom did not change; but they added to it by expounding from "And he saved" *(Va-Yosha)* to the end of the song *in the vernacular* and telling of the wondrous deeds God did for us and for our ancestors *in the language that all understand,* and *they also expounded* what God would do in the time to come when He will bring us out from exile" *(Orehot Hayyim,* Florence, 1750, 57–58).

val days has been preserved. The first is called *Midrash Aseret Ha-Dibberot* or also *Haggadah Shel Shavuot*, and the second is called *Midrash Va-Yosha* (written around the tenth-eleventh centuries and first printed in 1519 in Constantinople). To be sure, these Midrashim were preserved in Hebrew, but Zunz already noted quite correctly that these Hebrew Midrashim preserved from the Middle Ages are either extracts of older Midrashim or a translation of the oral address that was given in the vernacular.[29]

Especially interesting for the history of Old-Yiddish writing is the *Midrash Va-Yosha*. Here are forged together two distinct midrashic motifs, the story of the binding of Isaac and the story of the exodus from Egypt. In fact a Judeo-German reworking[30] of the legend of the binding of Isaac in precisely the version in which it is transmitted in *Midrash Va-Yosha*,[31] has been preserved in an old manuscript. This *Shire Fun Yitzkhok* (Poem of Isaac) is written in simple, tender prose. It is beyond doubt that it was in this version that the binding of Isaac was portrayed in the synagogue before the people. But this is not only the prose reworking that has survived. The Midrash was also reforged into a liturgical poem, into a *Judeo-German* liturgical poem. We know how eagerly the *paytanim* in the Middle Ages reworked this legend poetically in special hymns, and how the Sephardic Jew Jehudah ben Samuel Ibn Abbas in his day wrote his splendid *Et Shaarei Ratzon*.[32] A later poet, a religiously-minded *Spielmann*, reworked the same material into a Judeo-German poem and produced his lovely *Der Yidisher Shtam*. This poem, which was extremely popular in former times, has been preserved in two manuscripts. One, located in the library of Hamburg and consisting of sixty-three verses, was written in 1574 by a certain Isaac Kutens.[33] The second, which contains eighty verses, is to be found at the University of Paris and was written in 1579 by a certain Anshel Levi for a *generin* named Pessl bat Shmuel Favisha.[34] Both copies agree in general; only at the end of the Paris manuscript is added the episode about

---

29. See *Die gottesdienstlichen Vorträge der Juden*, second edition, p. 371. "A large part, finally, of the Hebrew Aggadah—the more recent, of course—is either the professional work of the anthologist or a translation from the living speech of the oral addresses."
30. Published by M. Weinreich in his *Bilder*, 134–138.
31. Also in the Talmud (*Sanhedrin*, fol. 89), in *Midrash Tanhuma*, and in *Yalkut Shimeoni*.
32. See above, Chapter I, p. 26.
33. We have employed an autograph copy that Nahum Shtif provided us with.
34. We have employed a photographic copy that M. Erik kindly provided us with.

Sarah's death, followed by another epilogue which is lacking in the Hamburg manuscript and in which are enthusiastically blessed "Abraham and Isaac, the upright men," as well as the knife and the ram, the mountain and the thornbush, and even the skin, flesh and horns of the sacrificial victim.

The style of the poem is serious, exalted, and emotive, as in the ancient *piyyutim* and *azharot*. In the first verse the earnest pathos of the God-fearing poet is already felt in all its power:

> Jewish stock of a genuine kind,[35]
> Who was born of our father Abraham
> And of our noble mother Sarah,
> Both of whom did not spare themselves in God's service.

In contradistinction to the Hebrew *paytan* of the twelfth century Jehudah Ibn Abbas who, in his previously mentioned poem, leaves out the accusatory role of Satan, the anonymous poet of *Akeydas Yitzkhok* faithfully follows all the episodes of the Midrash. As illustration we present here a fragment of the abovementioned, virtually verbatim Midrash translation in prose, followed by the corresponding verses of the *Akeydas Yitzkhok* poem:

The Prose Translation *(Shire Fun Yitskhok):*

Then Abraham went to the place and made an altar, and Isaac himself arranged the stones and the wood. Then [Isaac] said: "Dear father, bind my hands and my feet, for I am a young man vigorous at the age of thirty, and you are old, and when I see the slaughtering knife I may not easily hold myself still. Take care also that you burn me and pulverize me well, and bring the ashes to my mother Sarah." Then Isaac spoke further: "Dear father, when you have slaughtered me and burned me and go to my mother, what will you say to her as to where you left me? And what will you do in the days of your old age?" Then Abraham spoke: "Dear son, "We know well that we shall not live long after you. The same One who has comforted us since the day you were born, may He comfort us."

The *Akeydas Yitzkhok* verses:

> Father and son comforted each other
> In their grief and painful suffering.
> Isaac himself prepared the wood on the altar,
> Like a bridegroom who rejoices at his marriage
>   canopy.

35. In the Paris manuscript: "Jewish stock of worthy kind".

"Roll up your sleeve and bind all my four
  [limbs] properly
That I may not be terrified and tremble,
When I see the knife wherewith I shall be
  slaughtered,
And not be spoiled for a sacrifice."

"And when you will have burned me to ashes,
You shall take them up
And bring them to my mother Sarah,
That they may remain a memorial to her."[36]

Isaac was awash with hot tears.
"Dear father, what will you say to my mother,
When she sees me not coming with you?"
"Dear son, I will tell what will happen to us
after your death:

I and Sarah your mother
Will not be on earth long after your death.
Who shall now comfort my misery
And your mother's grievous pain?"

Isaac again said to Abraham:
"He who has comforted you both
Even before I was created and placed on earth,
May He also comfort your sorrow."

This extremely popular poem which had its own melody
(*akeyde-nign*)[37] was undoubtedly declaimed in the synagogue
before the people on the Sabbath when the *parashah* "*Vayyera*"
was read, or on the first day of Rosh Ha-Shanah when the same
parashah is also read. On *Shabbat Shirah* or the Seventh Day of
Passover, it was customary to read another poem also written
in *Spielmann*-verses. This is the poetic reworking of the second,
larger part of the *Midrash Va-Yosha,* in which the theme of the
exodus from Egypt is treated. The Judeo-German poetic com-

36. In Jehudah Ibn Abbas' *Akedah:*
          Before the knife I moaned;
          Now, father, sharpen it, and my bonds
          Tighten; And when the fire has consumed my flesh,
          Take with you the remnant of my ashes
          And say to Sarah: This is the odor of Isaac.
37. In the poem itself the poet notes: "Now we will leave Satan and will *sing* more
    of Abraham and Isaac."

position, in which an anonymous Jewish *Spielmann*-poet reworked the midrashic material, also bears the name *Midrash
Va-Yosha*[38] and consists of ninety-two seven-line verses with
the rhyme structure *ab aba dg*. That this poem came after
Akeydas Yitzkbok may be conjectured from the fourth verse,
where "the holy Abraham" is mentioned with the indication,
"Of him people still speak and sing today." That the Yiddish
Midrash Va-Yosha was also recited with a special melody is
attested by the introductory stanza:

> I will sing you a good story
> Such as is rarely heard.
> Let it not be child's-play to you;
> You will not reproach me because of it.
> The story that I wish to begin—
> Let it not be too hard for you.
> We sing it to honor Almighty God.

The poem concludes in the accepted fashion with the wish
for the speedy coming of the Messiah:

> Amen and Amen, may it become true,
> This we beg You from the heart,
> Amen, that it happen this year,
> That the exile no more grieve us,
> So that we may praise You eternally
> And all the better keep your Torah and commandments.
> Say Amen, you young and you old.[39]

We noted previously that on Purim it was customary to read
the Scroll of Esther with aggadic ornamentation in the vernacular to the congregation. The midrashic material that was
presented to the people in ancient times when the *lingua franca*
of the major Jewish communities was Aramaic is preserved in

38. Testimony to the fact that this poem used to be read in the synagogue is provided
by the notation in the Paris manuscript No. 335: "To the reader: finish the reading
according to the usual order till 'your healers' " (See M. Erik, *Geshibkte*, p. 126). The
poem *Midrash Va-Yosba* was first printed in the 1680's, reprinted by L. Landau in
Filologisbe Shriftn, II, and with a German transcription in *MGWJ*, 1929, 601–621.
39. The corresponding Midrash ends with the same motif: "May he who performed
miracles and wonders in those days at that season perform miracles and wonders
in these days and in this season, and may He gather us from the four corners of
the earth, and lead us to Jerusalem, and make us rejoice in it, and let us say Amen.
Selah."

the celebrated *Targum Sheni*. The midrashic material recited in the synagogue in later generations is preserved in the medieval Midrashim entitled *Abba Guryon, Midrash Megillat Ester, Halom Mordecai*, etc. The latter midrashic material was also worked over into Judeo-German in *Spielmann* verses, and it is virtually beyond doubt that in the German communities of the Middle Ages these poetic reworkings were declaimed or sung on Purim.[40] It is highly probable that the midrashic material of the *Haggadah Shel Shavuot (Midrash Aseret Ha-Dibberot)* was also reworked into *Spielmann* verses. This poem, however, has not been preserved; merely an allusion to it is found in the fragments that N. Prylucki published in his first volume, *Yidishe Folks-Lider* (pp. 99–109).

The poetic reworkings of which we have spoken here— *Akeydas Yitzkhok, Midrash Va-Yosha*, the Esther poems—had a definite connection with the Sabbath and festival prayers. They were a kind of popular liturgical poetry, a midrash poetically reworked and set in German *Spielmann* verse-forms. We know,[41] however, that it was not always only a change of dress that was involved here. We have already observed in the case of *Sefer Ha-Yashar* how the religious material also obtains a secular, belletristic content and the midrashic material is transformed into a hero-poem of the knightly type. This phenomenon may be observed in greater measure in Old-Yiddish literature. Virtually all the narrative parts of the Bible—Joshua, Judges, Samuel, Kings, Jonah—were poetically worked over into hero-epics and set in the classic form and meter of the major Old-German popular poem, the *Niebelungenlied*.[42] The crown of the Old-Yiddish Bible-poems is the celebrated *Shmuel-Bukh*.

On this masterpiece we have a rather rich literature.[43] Nev-

---

40. A whole series of such Esther paraphrases deriving from the 14–15th centuries have been preserved in manuscript. One of them which was rewritten by a certain Koppelmann in 1590 is composed in eight-line stanzas (in the so-called "Berner Ton"). For fragments of this poem, see Staerk-Leitzmann, *op. cit.*, 229–235. Bruno Korman wrote a special dissertation on the "rhyme technique" of this paraphrase (Hamburg, 1930).

41. See above, pp. 26ff.

42. M. Weinreich notes that there is, nevertheless, a small difference between the meter of the Jewish epics and the meter of the *Niebelungenlied*. The stanza in which the *Shmuel-Bukh* is composed is known among the Germans as the *Hildebrand-Strophe* (see *Bilder*, 98).

43. A report on this literature is given by Falk in his excellent but unfortunately uncompleted work *(Mitteilungen für jüdische Volkskunde*, 1908, 129–149). See also M. Weinreich, *Bilder*, 68–111; M. Erik, *Geshikhte*, 112–120; Staerk-Leitzmann, *op. cit.*, 241.

ertheless, it remains to the present day wrapped in a veil of mystery, and the name of the author and the time when the work was produced are still unknown. The manuscripts of the *Shmuel-Bukh* that have been preserved are no older than the first printed editions[44] and, indeed, have only magnified the confusion surrounding the name of the epic poet. In the defective manuscript now located in the library of Hamburg the name of the copyist is noted on the last page:

> This book I wrote with my hand,
> Liva of Regenspuk is my name.
> My dear *generin's* name is Breidlen.
> May she use and read it in joy—this I desire.

However, the bibliographer Johann Christoph Wolf, who first described this manuscript, was mistaken in the name and read Lita of Regensburg. Furthermore, he conjectured that this woman was, in fact, a composer of the work. His report was uncritically accepted by later bibliographers, and in this way the legend about the "famous woman" Lita of Regensburg who wrote the Samuel-epic was created. Only in modern times did Karpeles and, following him, Kohut, Falk, and Borochov lay the legend to rest and demonstrate that old Wolf was mistaken.

A bit of confusion was also contributed by the other manuscript located in the library of Paris. The penultimate verse ends with the following lines:

> Moses Esrim Ve-Arba is my name;
> I made this book with my hand.

From this a modern scholar Zalman Rubashov[45] [later Zalman Shazar, third president of the State of Israel] wishes to conclude that this was certainly the Palestinian emissary Moses Esrim Ve-Arba who took part in the sharp conflict which broke out in the second half of the fifteenth century between the two great rabbis of that time, Moses Capsali and

---

44. It was printed for the first time in Augsburg in 1544 at the press of Joseph bar Yakar's father-in-law, Hayyim Schwartz. It is possible that a participant in this edition was Paulus Emilius who, in 1526, reprinted the *Shmuel-Bukh* with a German transcription for the German public (*"Die zway ersten Buecher der Künig zu reimen weise verfast aus den hebraischen Buchstaben mit Fleiss in unser Hochdeutsch gebracht"*).

45. In *Zukunft*, July 1927.

Joseph Colon,[46] and that apparently he is the author of the *Shmuel-Bukh*. Rubashov's conjecture, however, is quite weak. The family name Esrim Ve-Arba was by no means rare in the fifteenth century, and the fact that this emissary was called by the surname Ashkenazi is no proof whatever that he himself came from Germany. In any case even if both men named Moses Esrim Ve-Arba should be the same person, it is indubitable that the emissary from Jerusalem could only be the copyist, not the clever and witty *Spielmann* who wrote the *Shmuel-Bukh*.

The time when the poem was written has also not been established. It is beyond doubt, however, that the work was known *before* the sixteenth century. An indication of this is to be found at the end of the Augsburg edition of 1544, where it is noted that "all Jews know the melody of the Book of Samuel." Evidently the *Shmuel-Bukh* had already long been familiar in all the dispersions of Israel. This "melody of the Book of Samuel" was so popular that it served as the prototype and pattern of numerous other poetic reworkings of Biblical books. "It was made according to the melody of the *Shmuel-Bukh*"—this was the best possible advertisement, since the reputation of the work was so great. And, indeed, it fully deserved its renown; it is undoubtedly one of the most splendid monuments of Old-Yiddish literature.

The *Shmuel-Bukh* is described by many scholars as a poetic paraphrase of the Bible,[47] but this is not altogether correct. In point of fact, the Midrash literature served as the major source of the hero-epic.[48] We have repeatedly referred to the role of the *paytanim*, or writers of liturgical hymns, who worked the midrashic material over into poetic form. The poet of the *Shmuel-Bukh* also relied on the rich aggadic material collected in the Midrash literature. It was not necessary for him to obtain this material from the ancient books, for it lived in the mouth of the people and was an organic part of the cultural environment in which he dwelled. We have also noted the role of the expository preachers (*maggidim*) and precentors (*firzogers*). Given the high cost of books in the Middle Ages, the common man had no possibility of individually owning a Pen-

---

46. See our *History*, Vol. V, p. 13, Note 31.
47. See, for instance, Staerk and Leitzmann, *op. cit.*, 241.
48. Grünbaum in his *Chrestomathie*, 15–16, already pointed to this in his day. See also Noah Prylucki's informative article in *Der Yidisher Velt*, 1930, VII–VIII.

tateuch with the translation and a commentary in the vernacular. "Previously, relates *Lev Tov* (first published in 1620), "in many synagogues there was frequently no more than one *maḥzor* or two or three at most . . . so no one recited, and the *ḥazzan* had to know it well."[49] The renowned author of the *Tze'enah U-Re'enah*, Jacob Ashkenazi of Yanov, also notes this in his introduction to *Sefer Ha-Maggid:* "So that all the people of the land, both small and great, might themselves know and understand how to read all of the twenty-four books [of the Bible], since previously only one from a city and two from a family had a name and memorial [i.e., a book] out of which to exposit, and now the earth is filled with knowledge and there is no need to exposit." Indeed, he at once explains the same thought in Yiddish as well: "Hence, the whole twenty-four books were translated completely, so that a person will not have to seek an expositor or interpreter who will tell him the twenty-four, for even if people already conclude and ordain that classes should sit down to hear the twenty-four, it happens many times that one must miss the lesson."[50] The preachers and expositors used to explain the readings from the Pentateuch and the Prophets for the Sabbath and festivals before the people, not according to the literal meaning but woven together with the aggadic, homiletic tapestry of the ancient Hebrew exegesis. Many elements of this preaching material were already familiar to the Jewish youth from their years of study in elementary schools where the teacher used to drill the Biblical text into them according to a definite, traditional, homiletic style.[51]

The anonymous author of the *Shmuel-Bukh* absorbed this rich midrashic material from childhood on.[52] He also gained a close familiarity with German epic poetry, obtained empathy into its world, and breathed its atmosphere. And he set himself the task of harmoniously merging these two worlds. Thanks to his considerable poetic talent, the author of the *Shmuel-Bukh*

---

49. *Ibid.*, 10a. See also Zunz, *Die gottesdienstlichen Vorträge der Juden*, Second Edition, 400.
50. We quote according to the Prague edition of 1657.
51. We shall have occasion to speak of this further below.
52. In this connection it would be interesting to compare the first stanzas of the *Shmuel-Bukh* with the translation of the prophetic readings for Rosh Ha-Shanah in the Augsburg or Cremona editions of the Pentateuch. It would also be worthwhile to make parallel comparisons with the *Midrash Shmuel* composed in the eleventh century.

succeeded brilliantly in this by no means easy task and managed to produce a true national hero-poem. He was inspired by the rich material with its dramatic elements. Already in the introductory verses his ardent pathos is discernible:

Whoever with his whole heart has turned his mind
To our dear Lord, how frequently He saves him;
His grace and His protection have never failed,
He helps His servants, be it night or day.

His praise no one, neither man nor woman, can exhaust.
Since it cannot be fully expressed, let there be silence about
    it.
He has often helped us out of our distress
And has forgiven us our sins and misdeeds.

We have frequently angered Him and rebelled against Him.
So He has, for a while, given us into the hands of our
    enemies.
But when we called to Him again and performed his
    precepts,
He helped us, saved us from our distress.

Of this I will be silent; there would be much to sing.
From the Book of Samuel I would sing to you,
How God, through His goodness, has done great wonders,
May He, in the exile, not leave us in any trouble.

Beginning with the first verses, the poet is not content with the dry notation in the Biblical text that Peninah "provoked her rival" Hannah, and in this context he ingeniously utilizes an appropriate *aggadah* of the Midrash.

Here her rival mocked and said: You should tell me,
Hannah, my dear rival, what you have bought for your
    boys—
The big and the little one. Let me understand this!
You should also show your children's gifts.

Do you see how my children carry their gifts?
You know of no joy to express.
When you die, you will be brought completely to an end.

Your name will be forgotten and remembered never
  more.

This angered Hannah but she remained silent:
"My husband Elkanah—I will not tell him . . ."

Hannah expresses her despondent mood in a tender prayer
to Almighty God:[53]

She lifted up her eyes and looked at the heavens:
Help me, O God, so that I can bear children!
In Your Grace You have created on the earth
People to bear children: such let me also be.

You have in Your holy heavenly kingdom
Angels who bear no children and live eternally;
If I cannot have a child, my dear Lord,
Let me live eternally like your angels.

If I am to die and be buried,
Let me, dear Lord God, first bear children . . ."

Like the author of *Sefer Ha-Yashar*, the poet of the *Shmuel-
Bukh* eagerly portrays battle-scenes and the heroic exploits of
the Biblical heroes. Here the influence of the German hero-
epics and knightly romances is probably at work. The heroes
of the *Shmuel-Bukh*, however, are *Jewish* heroes, God-fearing
and pious, who hold the Torah sacred. When the youthful
David son of Jesse appears before Goliath, the giant is beside
himself with rage:

You are only a child and recently still nursed.
If you wish to fight with me, you betray yourself.
You think perhaps, O child, that I am a little dog;
You come with a stick, and wish to wound me . . .

Your flesh will I tear apart; so will I take your life;
To the beasts on the field and the birds will I give it.

To this the bold young hero David replies:

53. The content of this prayer, which is taken from a Midrash, is given in Rashi's
    commentary to Samuel I.

··❁[*112*]❀··

God will deliver you into my hands today.
Your swords and your weapons I will make like clay.
I hear your words; you are a stupid man.
You say I shall be eaten by animals that cannot eat.

You say that you will give me to the beasts of the field,
The cow and the oxen—your mention of these have assured
     me.
You confused heathen, even today I will give your life
To the beasts of the field; them will I give your carcass.

To the wolves and to the bears, the lions and other wild
     beasts,
That they should tear you apart, when I take away your
     shield.
You come encased in steel armor;
Nevertheless God will deliver you into my hand.

He on whom I have relied with my whole heart
Will soon deprive you of your life.
You have reproached my Lord, to whom no one can be like.
Therefore He will teach me to kill you.

You have greatly angered God in Heaven;
Therefore your sword and all your armor will fail you.
My God will stop your wicked mockery.
In the name of God the Lord I will slay you.

And when David had overcome all his enemies and opponents and everyone trembled before his great heroism, he rev-
erently and humbly sings a praise and laudation to Almighty
God:

The Song of David[54]

I praise You, God, with joy; gone is my suffering.
My enemies have disappeared; Your grace has made me
     glad.
You have not given me over to my lord King Saul;
You help me, Lord God, always; my enemies had to
     disappear.

54. We quote from the rather long poem only a few fragments. On various versions
    of this song, see Staerk and Leitzmann, *op. cit.*, 274–279.

Sole God of Israel, who can fully express Your praise?
Your enemies come to Hell; Your friends You quickly
    help.
You aid me with great wonders on the rock so high;
You sent an angel especially to join me.

I was unburdened; I praise You, my Lord;
You helped me in the forest wherein Saul came,
My fortress and my stronghold, with all my help so
    great.
You are God the best, on Whom I rely.

You are my shield, my sword; You slay my enemies.
Whoever desires Your help need suffer no distress.
I praise God my Lord with my thinking;
My throat that must resound—may You hear it.

I call to Him in all my suffering, God my Lord.
He hears me from His sanctuary, He accepts my
    petition.
Men rightly praise God by day and night.
He aids His servants; His help has never failed us.

God gave us the Torah on Mount Sinai
With signs and with fear and with great strength.
Living God, my Creator, my eternal Helper,
Sole God and sovereign in the holy kingdom.

God has avenged me on my adversaries.
My enemies are broken; they must be my slaves.
From all my enemies—whoever brought me into
    distress
Has always fallen—God has helped me.

All the wicked on earth—their evil has availed them
    not;
They had to drop dead—these false wretches.
God can well save me, I praise Him justly;
He helps His servant David from all evil.

Publicly will I praise You, before all the peoples.
In Your heaven above, I praise You, God aloud.
Be gracious to me, dear Lord—for this I come to You;
Instruct my heart that I may serve You.

With great emotive power the poet portrays how the prophet Gad fulfills his mission and obliges King David to choose one of three punishments. When the Angel of Death has stretched forth his naked sword over the tents of Israel and the terrible plague has broken out

> King David saw the angel smiting the people.
> His heart was terrified; it grieved him greatly.
> He cried with all his heart to Almighty God:
> O Glorious God in heaven, slay me first!
>
> Take your judgment seat in Your heaven,
> Lord God, I am the intercessor for the people Israel.
> Let Your poor lambs live;
> Take vengeance on me; I have committed the sin.

Despite the serious emotive tone, the author does not avoid frivolous, erotic episodes—for instance, the scene in which Amnon's servants make crude jokes while their master locks himself up in a room with his sister Tamar. This, however, does not at all mar the harmonious integrity of the work; it is, after all, not a religious-didactic poem but a secular-national epic.

The Christian scholar Franz Delitzsch[55] quite justly designated the *Shmuel-Bukh* a "Davidida," i.e., an epic about the heroic King David. David is, indeed, the central figure of the entire poem, and with his death the work ends.

Closely associated thematically with the *Shmuel-Bukh* is another work composed in the same verse-meter. This is the *Melokhim-Bukh* which was published by the same press, but a year before the *Shmuel-Bukh*.[56] The publishers considered these two poems two parts of one work. On the title-page of the Augsburg *Shmuel-Bukh* it is noted: "*Shmuel* is the first part of the book *Melokhim*, for it is all related. Before you had the book *Melokhim*, and now I have printed *Shmuel* also as one writing." In the epilogue to the *Shmuel-Bukh*, immediately after the notation that "the melody of the *Shmuel-Bukh* is known to all Israel," it is once again stated: "It and the book *Melokhim* are as one." So it was also regarded in later generations. The author

---

55. *Zur Geschichte der jüdischen Poesie*, 1836, p. 81.
56. "The Book of Kings in the German language, beautiful and clear and very entertaining to read. Printed in the imperial city of Augsburg in the year that is counted 303 in the abbreviated notation (1543)."

of *Kehillat Yaakov*, Jacob ben Isaac Siegel, notes in the introduction: "This *Shmuel* book and *Melokhim* book were made into one poem." However, it is beyond doubt, as Staerk and Leitzmann demonstrated,[57] that these are two quite different works and were very probably written by two different poets. The *Melokhim-Buch* also begins with emotive lines of praise to Almighty God:

I praise You, O God, from my heart. You who are
    deserving of praise,
With Your powers You created heaven and earth,
And many wonders and signs besides, that no one can
    count,
Plants and wild beasts, women and men.

Therefore it is better to be silent; one cannot express it
    fully.
Because You are so powerful—You can do all things—
Therefore You should be feared. This is just and right.
All crooked things You can make straight.

You have frequently performed signs for the children of
    Israel;
Therefore they are obliged to have You for their Lord,
And to fear Your name—that is useful and good for them.
That man is foolish who acts contrary to Your word.

The children of Israel were in Egypt,
Where You showed them many signs through Your mighty
    hand,
And led them out of exile into the wild desert,
And gave them the Torah on Mount Sinai.

You fed them forty years with the heavenly bread
Until Moses our teacher had to lie down and die.
Then Your servant Joshua led them into the Holy Land;
He conquered it by force, through Your powerful hand.

The poets of the *Shmuel-Bukh* and the *Melokhim-Bukh* were undoubtedly *Spielmänner* who used to declaim their works to the people. Allusions to this are still discernible in many verses. For example, in the *Shmuel-Bukh* we read:

57. *Op. cit.*, 42.

Eli the high priest looked at the woman.
Now would you gladly *hear* how he spoke to her.

These poems, however, were no longer bound up, like the *Midrash Va-Yosha* or *Akeydas Yitzkhok*, with the synagogue, with the order of worship. They were secular productions, Jewish hero-poems that were recited by *Spielmänner* at evenings of entertainment. Such long poems would be read with intermissions, and perhaps also divided for presentation on separate evenings. But briefer poems, no longer than a common popular song or ballad, were also written on Biblical themes. One such poem was preserved in a quite singular way. It was transmitted orally for generations and, after long metamorphoses, was woven together with a clown's welcome-formula in a play for the theater that was published only in modern times.[58] After the address of the clown to the public, requesting that "it be patient and quiet a while, for we shall present the reign of King Saul, "there immediately begins, without any connection, the following poem which probably bore the name *"Adam Ve-Havah Lid"* (Adam and Eve Poem):

Now we will sing the song
Of Adam and Eve in Paradise.
It greatly pleased God
To fashion Adam in His image.
Here Adam lived for a long time,
And he had no companion at his side.
Here he was quite alone,
And so the Eternal took Eve from his bone.
The Eternal bethought Himself
And brought a sleep on Adam,
And made Eve out of His rib.
The Eternal went walking in Paradise
And adjured them not to touch the apple.
Eve, Eve was not lazy;
She took the apple and stuffed it into her mouth.
The Eternal went loudly into the garden,
Knowing well what had happened there.
O Adam, O Adam, what have you done?
Adam replied: What is it to me?—
The woman You gave me did it.

58. *Meluchat Sha'ul Gam Akedat Yitzḥak*, Vilna, 1875. For more about this edition, see below, Chapter Twelve.

O Eve, O Eve, what have you done?
Eve said: What is it to me?—
The evil serpent enticed me thereto.
He is much cleverer, and he is the one.
O serpent, O serpent, what are you doing here?
On your naked belly must you swim on the earth.[59]
And also regarding Eve, God swore
That she should bear children in pain and sorrow.
He also decreed concerning Adam
That he should not prolong his years.[60]

The question remains: What is the relationship between the *Spielmänner* who wrote the Bible epics to those who reworked such knightly romances as *Artus Hof* and the like? It is difficult to give a definitive answer at present. There were probably two types of *Spielmänner*. There were those who, in their way of life, were assimilated to a certain degree;[61] we know, after all, that among the Jewish *Spielmänner* there were some who sang before German nobles and kings.[62] Such *Spielmänner*, who became used to living in a foreign environment, devoted their attention to foreign materials. Those, however, who were more rooted in the Jewish way of life and whose imagination was dominated by the world of Jewish ideas and legends, chose for their productions Jewish national themes.[63] It is clear, however, that in the repertoire of the Jewish *Spielmann* there were poems and songs of both types, and the same *Spielmann* would recite before the public both national Biblical poems and knightly romances in Yiddish.

59. The word "swim" obviously has no sense. In the original text, apparently, the double line in question looked different. It may be that the rhyme there was *gefinden-vinden*.
60. In later times this poem was completely reworked stylistically. The *Daytshmerish* vestment was exchanged for a popular Yiddish one. It also received a new mane: "Beginning of the Story of Adam, the First Man." The new version was also published together with a *Meluchat Sha'ul* text.
61. One of these, Susskind of Trimberg, was so assimilated that his poetic creativity belongs exclusively to the history of German *Spielmann* poetry.
62. L. Landau, *Arthurian Legends*, XXV.
63. It may also be imagined that such a *Spielmann* would at times fulfill the functions of a *ḥazzan* and precentor in the synagogue.

CHAPTER FIVE

Popular Literature;
TZE'ENAH U-RE'ENAH

Literal and homiletic translations of the Bible—Jehudah Leib Bresch and the Cremona edition of the Pentateuch—Isaac Sulkes and his translation of the Song of Songs—Isaac Sulkes as a man of the people—Midrashic material as "reading material"—*Di Lange Megile* —Women's literature and folk literature—Isaac Prossnitz on the cultural importance of the woman—The style of *Di Lange Megile*—Stories as material for moral instruction—The prose preaching style—Rabbi Isaac ben Samson and his *Taytsh-Khumesh*—Jacob ben Isaac Ashkenazi of Yanov—The *Tze'enah U-Re'enah* as a continuation of the old midrashic literature—The *Tze'enah U-Re'enah* as "the women's Torah"—Its cultural-historical significance—The battle against the homiletic way in the educational system—*Be'er Mosheh*—The Bible translations of Yekutiel Blitz and Josef Witzenhausen—Their unsuccessful battle against the homiletic style of the *Tze'enah U-Re'enah.*

S WE noted previously, the medieval Judeo-Germa translations of the Bible were of two types: one, a literal translation that would remain quite close to the original and slavishly translate word for word; and the second, a homiletic type in which the text was not merely translated but also explained and interpreted on the basis of the Midrash and aggadic literature, at times employing these sources directly but more frequently indirectly, with the aid of the medieval exegesis, chiefly Rashi's beloved commentary. Richly ornamented with midrashic material to a special degree were the translations of the Song of Songs and the Scroll of Esther.

Given the high cost and scarcity of books before printing was invented, both types of Bible translations existed mainly orally. In time a fixed style was worked out which was transmitted from generation to generation, and which the teacher would follow in drilling the children in school and the *maggid* in preaching to the people. After the invention of printing, when the reading of books penetrated among the broad strata of the populace, and, as the pious author of the *Tze'enah U-Re'enah* puts it, "the earth was filled with knowledge," the two types of translations of the Pentateuch and the Five Scrolls which had been worked out in the course of generations were transformed from an "oral Torah" into a "written Torah"— a printed text censored by various editors.

The oldest printed translations of the Pentateuch that have come down to us (the editions of Augsburg and Constance), both issued by converts to Christianity, belong generally to the first type of translation. The editor of the Constance edition allows himself merely to provide special explanations for the text on the margin of the page in the form of glosses. However, the Cremona edition of the Pentateuch of 1560, which had a Jewish editor Jehudah Leib Bresch, bears a different character.

Bresch himself notes in the introduction that he does not here present a new translation but an improved edition of the "first Pentateuchs," i.e., of the Augsburg and Constance editions.[1] The publisher complains:

For our many sins we do not have much learning, and the women and maidens who observe that the men do not study also refrain from it. But some householders would gladly learn. These are men who in their youth were not willing to study or could not do so, but now in their older years they are eager to learn but are ashamed to study the weekly lection of the Torah with an explanation given by a teacher. I saw all this and thought to benefit many and to print this Pentateuch in the German language with the greatest possible fidelity . . . Thus every woman and maiden would be able to know of the

1. Bresch mainly used the Augsburg edition of Paulus Emilius.

Torah of God Blessed Be He, and what piety is, if they will read
herein on all the Sabbaths and festivals.[2]

In order, however, to interest the "women, young women, and
maidens," Bresch wove into his translation legends and sayings
of the Midrash, mainly in the form in which these are presented in the classic Bible commentator Rashi. In fact, fragments of Rashi's commentary are also presented at the side of
the page in Yiddish.[3]

Bresch's edition was reprinted in Basel in 1583, but four years
earlier, in 1579, at the well known press of Isaac ben Aaron of
Prossnitz in Cracow an interesting edition appeared—a Yiddish translation of the Song of Songs by a certain Isaac Sulkes.

Who this Sulkes was is not known. However, when we read
his interesting introduction, we are forcibly reminded of Joseph bar Yakar. Sulkes also apparently belonged to that group
of common but capable men of the people whom Gutenberg's
great invention associated with the book in an unexpected
fashion, and whose names were thereby inscribed on the pages
of the history of Jewish literature. We quoted above the passage
in his introduction in which he warns against the sinful "German books," such as *Dietrich von Bern, Hildebrant,* and "all the
others."[4] In Sulkes we become incidentally aware of another
interesting point. We noted that the rabbis and scholars were
highly displeased with the old knightly romances and fantastic
stories that penetrated in hosts into the Jewish quarter through
the printing-press and book-peddlers. These men understood
very well that to wrest the interesting and "amusing" books
from the hands of the people was an extremely difficult task.
Instead, care had to be taken to provide other spiritual nourishment for the masses. Books had to be produced in the language
of the people that would be both Jewish, permeated with the
Jewish tradition, and attract the common reader and be congenial to him. Among the rabbis and scholars, however, there
were also some rigorous interpreters of the law who were

2. We quote according to Grünbaum, *op. cit.,* 550–551.
3. It is very possible that in this realm Bresch had predecessors. The well-known
    bibliographer Samuel Wiener had preserved a single page of an old handwritten
    Taytsh-Khumesh or Yiddish translation of the Pentateuch (certainly not later than
    the sixteenth century). This page, which came from Lublin, consisted of two parts.
    Above was written the Yiddish translation of the *parashah "Va-Yishlah,"* and under
    the text were fragments of Rashi's commentary in Yiddish. These fragments begin
    with the initials *Pe-Yod,* standing for *Perush Yitzhaki* (Commentary of Yitzhaki).
4. Above, Chapter IV.

highly displeased not only with the secular literature, all the knightly romances and old wives' tales in Yiddish, but even with the religious book written in Judeo-German—with the *popular book* in general.[5] The demands and needs of the common people, the artisan and the worker, very frequently came into conflict with the conceptions and also, as we shall see later on, the *interests* of the scholars. Hence they had to come into collision. The previously mentioned Joseph bar Yakar, with his popular manner and ironic attitude to the *yotzerot* and liturgical hymns, could also not be particularly acceptable to the rabbis and scholars. Moreover, the very fact of "Is Saul also among the prophets?," the fact that ordinary people ventured to become authors and write on religious subjects, was displeasing to certain rabbis of the type, for example, of Maharam of Lublin.[6] Indeed, Isaac Sulkes complains in his introduction that the scholars look with contempt on the religious books that are written in Judeo-German and aim to teach morality and awaken piety among the people. "But I believe that it is pleasing to the Almighty God that such German books as are useful and godly be written." Let the rabbis not complain, he adds, that he, a common, everyday Jew, betakes himself to writing books—an occupation in which the rabbis, the great scholars, engage. "My dear masters," he says, defending himself before them:

I see that I have failed,
And my folly has drawn me
To trespass into your domain,
That of the great masters, who are filled with Torah,
Who sit whole days and nights over their books.
But as for poor me, only on occasion do I look into them.
They can make books from which much is achieved,
But I hardly know how to recite the benediction for bread.
Hence, I should be ashamed
To take on such things.
But in truth, this is certain, you must believe me;
Such things must be had in the world.
For not everyone can run to rich shops
To buy gold and silver, velvet and silk.

5. For a further discussion of this see our special work, *"Der Kamf Far Yidish in Der Alt-Yidisher Literatur"* (*Filologishe Shriftn*, II, 69–106) and also the subsequent chapters.
6. On the Maharam of Lublin, see our *History*, Vol. VI, Chapter III, pp. 63ff.

One must rather have in the house other things.
There are many more peasants than nobles—so I can make
it [the book].
Therefore, we must also have small shopkeepers
Who can serve the common people for their money;
And the little storekeepers have everything people ask for—
Elijah the shopkeeper[7] can attest to this.
They sell everyone what he wishes to have.
If the nobleman comes to buy,
He can easily pick up in the little store
A mirror for his wife, a whistle for his child.
The common man connot do this.
When he comes to the rich merchant,
He can buy nothing for his money,
Even if something there pleases him;
Everything is too expensive and high-priced.
At the little shopkeepers, however, he finds all that he
  needs.
Therefore I have also ventured to do this:
I have set up my little shop
For common people and for women.
Let them come inspect the store.
They will find all kinds of things that are written in our
  holy books.
All this have I patched together in the Song of Songs.[8]

Sulkes' translation of the Song of Songs is indeed "patched together" out of both kinds of translations referred to above—literal and homiletic. First the translator gives the meaning of the verse—not, however, in a verbatim translation, but in the accepted drill-fashion that had been passed on from generation to generation and to which teachers have remained faithful from the Middle Ages to the present day. For example, the first two words of *Shir Ha-Shirim* (The Song of Songs) are interpreted in the well-known way: "A song above all songs; while other songs are holy, this song is holy of holies. This was sung by a prophet who was the son of a prophet, a king who was the son of a king, a sage who was the son of a sage. This was sung by King Solomon to the King, the Holy One Blessed Be He, who is here called Shelomoh, for the peace of the world is His."

Only after this does the true "explanation" *(derush)* begin; it

7. Probably some shopkeeper well known to Sulkes.
8. We quote according to Staerk-Leitzmann's transcription, *op. cit.*, 287, 288.

consists of all kinds of quotations and tales from the Midrash that the common people formerly used to hear in the houses of study from the mouth of the *maggid* and expositor. Now that the printed book had become an available article and even reached as far as the "little stores" that supplied the needs of the "common man and of women," Isaac Sulkes presented this preacher's midrashic material in book form to the people. The "sermonic material" was transformed into "reading material."

The way of Isaac Sulkes was also followed by another translator, Leib bar Moses Melir, who published at the same press in Prossnitz in 1589 his paraphrase of the Scroll of Esther, *Di Lange Megile.*[9]

We mentioned above the medieval Scroll of Esther poems in the repertoire of the Jewish *Spielmann* which used to be declaimed even in the synagogue. The rich midrashic material that was woven around the Biblical story of Mordecai and Esther was also extensively utilized by the *maggidim* and expositors. The printing press, however, gradually began to displace the sober, epic *Spielmann.* For instance, people no longer had to depend on the *Spielmann* to declaim the *Shmuel-Bukh* epic; the printing press spread it abroad in thousands of copies, and whoever wished to do so purchased a copy and became familiar with it not through hearing but through reading. It was no longer necessary to wait for the *maggid* and the *firzoger* to familiarize the common people with the rich material of the Scroll of Esther found in the *Targum Sheni* and the Midrashim; Leib bar Moses Melir reworked all the material in book form and created his *Lange Megile*, which deserves an honored place in the history of Old-Yiddish literature and style.

A cultural-historical interest also pertains to the preface by the printer Isaac Prossnitz to *Di Lange Megile*. The German Jewish scholars of the nineteenth century, such as Güdemann, Grünbaum, Perles, Steinschneider, and other, always speak of Old-Yiddish literature as of a special "women's literature." This, however, is in fact incorrect. The following detail is worth nothing. We have collected the texts of some seventy title-pages of Old-Yiddish editions, and among them are only nine that address themselves exclusively to "pious women, young women, and maidens." The others—about seventy—

9. "The *Megillah* in the holy tongue and afterwards the German thereto, very beautifully translated and with the standard biblical commentaries and all the *midrashim* and explanations and novellae and beautiful stories and long admonitions that were made in it."

write, however, "not for women and maidens," but also for "both young men and householders," "for men and women, boys and girls." Some address themselves to the "dear brothers," to "common people, men and women," to "ordinary precentors *(ḥazzanim)* and teachers *(melamedim),*" to "dear people, men and women, boys and girls." Others again are addressed simply to *ben adam* (mortal man), to "either the scholar or the ordinary man, householders or women," or to "every Jew . . . whoever he is . . . whether man or woman, whoever can read."

The truth, however, is this. Even if the Old-Yiddish books were not composed especially for women, the authors and publishers realized quite well the enormous revolution which the popular literature had called forth in the life of the Jewish woman. Until the printing press created the possibility of the rise of folk-literature, the Jewish woman was entirely isolated from the national culture, for the language in which the national cultural treasures were assembled was alien and incomprehensible to her. Such a unique phenomenon in Jewish life, for instance, as Glückel of Hameln, with her harmonious world-view and outlook on life, was absolutely impossible in German or French Jewry of the earlier, medieval centuries. The story of Rashi's daughter, who supposedly would write responsa for her father when the latter was ill, proved to be a common old wives' tale. The responsa were written not by Rashi's daughter but by her son, the renowned scholar and Tosafist Rabbi Samuel ben Meir. Indeed for the medieval women the well-known lines of J.L. Gordon were most apt:

Jewish woman, who knows your life?
In darkness have you come, in darkness do you go.

The folk literature which blossomed in the sixteenth century, however, broadened the world-view of the Jewish woman very significantly. The great number of books imported from abroad gave her a familiarity with the outside world, portrayed in romantic and frequently also fantastic colors. Soon men with popular sentiment and feeling appeared, who set themselves the task of making the national cultural treasures available for the masses with the aid of the popular book. These persons greatly aided the publishers who, with their practical sense, promptly realized that the popular book might, in suitable hands, become a highly saleable item of merchandise. Thereupon the great revolution in the life of the Jewish woman took place. The woman, the mother of the coming generation, became a cultural factor in the life of the people. For her, the mistress of the house, the sources of the Jewish tradition, the Jewish religious-cultural and historical past, were opened to a significant degree. This was such a singular and uncommon phenomenon that those who took part in the folk-literature had to underscore it most sharply. For this reason, indeed, Isaac ben Aaron Prossnitz, in the preface to *Megillat Ester* pours out his anger on "the fools who prattle and think the world was created only for their sakes, and in whose eyes there is nothing else." He concludes that "everything that God Blessed Be He has created in the world, so that His Torah and *mitzvot* might be kept, whether great or small, women or men, poor or rich—with God all are alike." "The way of the world," Prossnitz further emphasizes,

is that women especially are considered nothing at all and are regarded as good for nothing, and whether young or old, they are done much injustice and violence, and it is contrary to God's will that one should mock and play with His creation. When the Holy One Blessed Be He wished to give the sacred Torah, He left the great, high mountains and showed Himself on the small, lowly hill. And the first words of God with the people of Israel were spoken to the women and the small folk, as you will find in the Pentateuch.[10]

Isaac Prossnitz also deems it necessary to stress that the work which he here issues "is not another ordinary book and was not written in Judeo-German only to pass the time. No, it is not such; we have a different case here." To be sure, many "amusing" stories were interwoven in *Di Lange Megile*. The whole work bears a clearly narrative character, and Staerk and Leitzmann rightly emphasize that "this book is a treasure of the most varied folkloristic motifs."[11] The author's intention, however, is certainly not merely to entertain but also to give ethical instruction, to educate morally, to disseminate knowledge of the religious-ethical foundations of Jewish culture among the broadest strata of the people. Our author is garrulous in places, but this, in the eyes of his readership, was by no means a defect. The material is extremely colorful and the style intimately

10. Isaac ben Aaron refers to the verse: "Thus shalt thou say to the house of Jacob and tell the house of Israel." The Midrash interprets this: "The 'house of Jacob'—these are the women and children; the 'house of Israel'—these are the men. God therefore commanded that the women be told first, and only then the men."
11. *Op. cit.*, 291.

popular. The author artfully braids the Biblical text together with a rich treasure of legends and maxims, generously drawn from the Aggadah and Midrash. Already in the first chapter the splendid description of King Solomon's throne, taken from the *Targum Sheni*, is interwoven with the dramatic and emotive scene in which the Jewish people, after the destruction of the Temple, is driven into exile by the powerful foe. With bated breath the common woman or the "ordinary householder" read one line after another:

And the prophet Elijah went with them until they came before the graves of the patriarchs. Here he cried, fell on their graves, and said, "Compassionate men, Abraham, Isaac, and Jacob, rise up and see how your children are being led!" And he left them and ran quickly to the graves of Sarah, Rebecca, Rachel, and Leah, crying, "Arise, and see how your children are being conducted into exile naked and barefoot and heavily laden!" So he fell on all the graves, those of Moses and Aaron and Samuel. "See how your little lambs are being led, those whom you grazed with sorrow! See how the vicious wolves tear them apart and mercilessly lead them naked and bare over all the mountains, heavily laden, without shoes, through all kinds of stones!" And when he spoke these words he quickly ran away from the graves, so that the pious ancestors might not embarrass him and say: "Are you not ashamed that you in your times have let such things happen, and come to give us the report thereof?" And they went, all of them, naked and barefoot, burdened with chains, kings and princes and slaves . . .[12]

The author endeavors at every step to give moral instruction to his reader, to strengthen in him the ethical-religious consciousness that every man's life is ruled by a higher moral power which evaluates men's deeds. Everything is weighed in the balances of justice, and recompensed according to the will of the True Judge. These moral maxims are illustrated by the author with intimate, genuinely popular stories. To familiarize the reader with the unique style of these didactic narratives, we present here one of them that is also reprinted in Grünbaum's well-known *Chresthomathie*.[13]

As a commentary to Mordecai's admonishing words sent to Queen Esther, "Think not that thou shalt escape in the king's house, more than all the Jews" (Esther 4:13), the author tells the following story that happened with Moses:

12. We quote according to Grünbaum, *op. cit.*, 210–211.
13. *Ibid.*, 215–218.

The custom of Moses our teacher was that he would frequently go into the fields to places where no people were, and there study by himself or experience the spirit of prophecy coming over him. For this reason he wandered to such places. Once he was under a tree that was not far from a well, resting and thinking about his study. Here Moses saw a man who came to the well and drank. The man's money-bag fell down, but he did not notice it and went his way. Thereupon another, a very poor man, came to drink and rested for a while at the well. It did not take long before he found the bag, whereupon he was very happy and went his way. A little while later a third man came along, and this simpleton rested there and drank well and was in his element. In the meantime the first man looked for his moneybag and, not finding it, thought: I certainly lost it at the well where I bent down to drink. He ran back very swiftly and there found the tired simpleton resting at the well, and he began to ask him what he was doing there. Then the simpleton said: I am tired, and I have been resting here for a while and have been sitting here for a bit and drinking, and now I will go my way. The other then said: Since you have been resting for a while, you found my moneybag which I lost here; no one else could have been here except you, for it is only a short time since I lost it. The foolish man said: My dear friend, in truth I do not have your bag, and make no libelous charges against me. If it is only a little while, you did not lose it here; therefore, go and seek elsewhere, and follow my advice. Perhaps you lost no purse at all, so go your way. You have picked the wrong man in me.—And they quarreled heatedly and came to blows. Here Moses our master ran up and wished to separate them, but he did not reach them before the man who had lost the bag killed the other and ran away. And Moses our master was very grieved for the simpleton whose fate had been so unjust, and he marvelled greatly that our Lord God should allow such a thing to happen. He ordains all things, Blessed Be He. And Moses said: Dear Lord God, here I have seen three things, all of which are unjust. You have brought it about that one man should lose his moneybag, and then that another should take the bag, carry it away, and no one say a word to him. Then you brought it about that the third man was unjustly killed. All this is still not enough. The wretch who lost the moneybag has, in addition, thereby become a murderer and will never have atonement. So, dear Lord God, I would wish very much to know how these things happened.—Here God Blessed Be He spoke: You reproach me unjustly, and so have many persons thought about many remarkable things that have taken place in the world. But man does not realize that they happen properly and justly. You must know, dear Moses, that the person who here lost his moneybag is himself a pious man but his father robbed it from the hand of the father of the man who found it; hence, I ordained that the second man should here find his legacy at the well. As for the third man who had to lose his head over this and apparently was not guilty, you must know that he once killed the first man's brother, but no one knew of it till this day. Since there was no witness here, the slain man's blood was not avenged. So I brought it about that the slain man's brother had to lose his money at the well, that the murderer should come here, and that the first man should suspect him and kill him and thus take vengeance for his brother. He killed him justly here. So I ordain all things, and no man can know My attributes and qualities. Therefore there is often wonder in the world why at times the wicked prosper and it goes ill with the righteous.[14]

Di Lange Megile is a harbinger of a new style in Old-Yiddish literature—the calm, flowing, midrashic style which weaves the text of the Bible together with the colorful and popular material of legend into a unique, artistic tapestry. This preaching, prose style gradually displaced the emotive, poetic style of the medieval *Spielmann.* It achieved ever greater dominance as a result of the printing press, whose invention enormously democratized the book and broke through for it a way to the broad strata of the people.

Shortly after the *Di Lange Megile* came off the press, there appeared a book which is the classic representative of this new style and which had the privilege of becoming the most beloved book among the people and to be crowned with the significant title "the women's Torah." This is the *Tze'enah U-Re'enah* of Jacob ben Isaac Ashkenazi of Yanov.

We noted earlier that the editor of the Cremona edition of the Pentateuch, Jehudah Leib Bresch, attempted to weave into the literal translation legends and sayings from the Midrash, and that at the side of the page he also introduced fragments of Rashi's commentary in Yiddish translation. Bresch's edition, which was later (1583) reprinted without changes, served as the model for the *Taytsh-Khumesh* which Rabbi Isaac ben Samson, the son-in-law of the Maharal of Prague, issued in 1610.[15] In the middle of each page is given the literal translation

14. The same story is presented in another, shorter version in *Simḥat Ha-Nefesh.* Later this story was transformed into a Hasidic legend in which Moses and God are exchanged for the Maggid of Mezhirech and the Baal Shem Tov. The Baal Shem Tov wished here to give his pupil a picturesque commentary to the well-known passage in the *Zohar,* "And these are the ordinances—they are the mysteries of transmigration." See also the article in *YIVO-Bleter,* Vol. III, 333–335.

15. Many bibliographers even indicate that the first edition of the *Taytsh-Khumesh* appeared already in 1608, but not a single copy of this edition has been preserved. We have used the copy that is in the Asiatic Museum in Leningrad. In this copy the title-page is missing, but at the end the date 1610 is noted. It is very possible, however, that this edition began to be printed in 1608 and this date was therefore noted on the title-page, but that it was completed only in 1610, and that the two editions noted by the bibliographers (1608 and 1610) are one and the same.

of the Biblical text, and at both sides in a different type-face are the commentaries in Yiddish of various Midrashim (on the right) and of Rashi (on the left).

The *Taytsh-Khumesh* had no great success. It was soon displaced by the "women's Torah," Jacob of Yanov's *Tze'enah U-Re'enah*, in which the Biblical text is forged together in a singular fashion with the various Midrashim and commentaries. We have very few biographical details about the author of this extremely popular book on which whole generations were nurtured. We do not know in which Yanov the author of *Tze'enah U-Re'enah* lived, for in Poland there were several towns that bore this name.[16] Also unknown is the year of his birth, and on the year of his death, too, the biographers do not agree. Eleazar Schulmann notes that Jacob ben Isaac Ashkenazi died in Prague in 1628.[17] According to Wolf,[18] he died in 1625, and according to Staerk-Leitzmann,[19] around 1620. Great confusion also surrounds the dates when the works with which Jacob Ashkenazi acquired such great renown appeared: *Tze'enah U-Re'enah* and *Sefer Ha-Maggid* (a paraphrase of the Prophets and Holy Writings). Benjacob and Schulmann[20] indicate that the first edition of *Sefer Ha-Maggid* appeared in Prague in 1576; according to Staerk and Leitzmann, however, the work was first published in Lublin in 1623.[21] The oldest edition of *Tze'enah U-Re'enah* that has been preserved is from 1622, but on the title-page of this edition (which appeared in Basel) it is noted that it is already the fourth edition and that the earlier ones appeared in Lublin and Cracow. However, it is virtually indubitable that the conjecture of Schulmann and Staerk-Leitzmann to the effect that the first edition was published at the threshold of the seventeenth century (around 1600) is correct.[22]

What Jacob Ashkenazi of Yanov had in mind with his *Tze'enah U-Re'enah* is to be seen quite clearly from the title-pages of his other two works. On the title-page of *Sefer Ha-Maggid* the author declares in Hebrew: "So that all the people of the land,

16. See *Russian-Jewish Encyclopedia*, XVI, 403–404.
17. *Op. cit.*, 36.
18. *Hebräische Bibliographie*, III, 469.
19. *Op. cit.*, 296.
20. The bibliographer S. Wiener also agreed with them.
21. *Op. cit.*, 308. This, however, contradicts their assertion that the author died in 1620.
22. See Schulman, *op. cit.*, 36; Staerk-Leitzmann, *op. cit.*, 296; Jacob of Yanov's Hebrew work *Shoresh Yaakov* (on laws treated in the *Shulḥan Aruch*) appeared in Cracow in 1585.

both small and great, might themselves know and understand how to read all of the twenty-four books [of the Bible], since previously only one from a city and two from a family had a name and a memorial [i.e., a book] out of which to exposit, and now the earth is filled with knowledge and there is no need to exposit." Indeed, he at once explains the same thought in Yiddish as well: "Hence the whole twenty-four books were translated completely, so that a person will not have to seek an expositor or interpreter who will tell him the twenty-four . . . and can study them himself. Hence, the book was called *Sefer Ha-Maggid*, to say that one does not need a *maggid* or expositor who will tell him the twenty-four."[23]

The same thought is repeated by Jacob ben Isaac in his *Melitz Yosher*: "For the people hear sermons in the synagogues and do not understand what the sermon is. They speak too rapidly in the synagogue, but in this book one can read slowly, so that he himself will understand."[24]

This desire that the popular book take the place of the preacher, that the written and printed word fulfill the task of the pulpit and the sermon, is an extremely interesting point in the history of Jewish culture and underscores most clearly the cultural-historical significance of Jacob Ashkenazi's *Tze'enah U-Re'enah*. The ancient custom introduced as early as the age of Ezra the Scribe—to translate and publicly explain to the people in its vernacular the weekly lections from the Torah— became in time extremely popular. From this "explanation" of the Torah, whole sermons filled with moral instruction and teaching about proper conduct were gradually born. Such sermons in the vernacular of the masses of the people, the Aramaic dialect, would be given on the Sabbath and festivals in the synagogues and houses of study by the people's teachers and guides. The renowned heads of the Sanhedrin Shemaiah and Avtalyon already bore the name *darshanim* (preachers) because they would preach to the people, provide them with moral instruction, comfort them in their distress, and strengthen their trust in God's speedy salvation. Such sermons would always begin with a verse from the *sidrah* or weekly lection from the Pentateuch. But the preacher by no means intended to explain the literal meaning of the verse in question. This was only a matter of accepted fashion. The verse was the introduction, the framework in which the preacher would spin

23. We quote according to the Prague edition 1657.
24. We quote according to Schulmann, *op. cit.*, 37.

and weave his ingenious tapestry of tender instruction, earnest words of reproof, and beautiful legends and proverbs. These oral sermons, the living word addressed to the people, was transformed in time into a national literature—the aggadic part of the Talmud and the ancient Midrashim.

These Midrashim, in which the cleverness and skill of the keen expositor and preacher is associated with the tender, naive simplicity of popular stories and legends, have in fact no specific author. The people, the community, laid building stones for them, and out of these the individual preacher constructed a building. Intimately beautiful legends from which the people wove laurel wreaths for their beloved heroes were explained by the scholarly preacher in his own fashion, wrapped in a mantle of ethical instruction, and adorned with verses from the Bible. The Midrashim that were written down served in later generations as handbooks and as an inexhaustible source for expositors who no longer addressed the people in the language of the Midrashim, the Aramaic-Hebrew dialect, but in the new vernaculars that the Jews employed. But now a new era began. The book penetrated among the masses of the people. A popular literature was produced in its *lingua franca*, Yiddish, which the majority of the Jewish people already spoke at that time. And the rabbi of the Polish town of Yanov, Jacob ben Isaac, created his *Tze'enah U-Re'enah*, which is the integral continuation of the ancient Midrash literature. Despite the difference in language, the new folk-Midrash in its classical exemplar, *Tze'enah U-Re'enah*, is permeated with the same rhythm and harmonious integrity as the ancient Midrashim. Different in their word order, etymological structure, and derivation, the two Jewish dialects, the ancient Aramaic and the medieval Judeo-German, were brought closely together, forged anew, and refined in the creative spirit of the people. Thus they form two rings in the "golden chain" of the ancient, wandering people.[25]

We noted earlier that the Old-Yiddish literature is not, as some German-Jewish scholars wished to demonstrate, a special "women's literature" but a genuine "folk-literature" which addresses itself to the broad strata of the people. On the other hand, there is very clearly discernible in the style and character of this literature the tender and womanly, the typically feminine, in which feeling and the emotive mood obtain dominance

---

25. We have spoken at length of this in our work, *"Der Kamf Far Yidish in Der Alt-Yidisher Literatur."* See also above, end of Chapter II.

over the logically intellectual and aridly abstract. And this amiable, intimate "feminine style" finds its clearest expression in Jacob Ashkenazi's *Tze'enah U-Re'enah*. Not without reason did this work become the most beloved book among Jewish women. The tender tone, the unique rhythm which breathes the harmonious integrity of the deeply believing soul, endowed the book with a special grace. Hence, it is not suprising that *Tze'enah U-Re'enah* became the "women's Torah," the guide of the Jewish mother and wife, her spiritual and intellectual mentor. For many generations *Tze'enah U-Re'enah* was not missing from any Jewish home.[26] From it the Jewish mother would read to the children every Sabbath about the historic events of ancient times, about the Patriarchs, mighty heroes, great sages, and righteous men who, in Jacob Ashkenazi's retelling, wore such a pleasantly domestic garment and were so comprehensible and easy to know.

The modern reader must take into consideration that the *Tze'enah U-Re'enah* text used to be printed without any changes (beyond the spelling), as long as Judeo-German books were printed with a special type-face called *tkhine-ksov* or *wayberish-Daytsh*.[27] Since the 1860's, however, the Jewish printers became so "contemporary" and "secular" that they not only began to print Yiddish books with the same type as Hebrew but also lost respect for the "women's Torah" and changed the text of *Tze'enah U-Re'enah* according to their taste. They threw out entire passages, altered the style, and inserted new quotations from various sources. To give the reader some notion of the text of Jacob of Yanov's work, we present here several fragments of the older editions.

I

(From *Parashah Noah* [Genesis 11:28]):

And Haran died before his father Terah. . . . Terah the father of Abraham was a seller of idols, and Abraham was once standing there, and when anyone came and wished to purchase an idol, he asked: How old are you? The person answered: Fifty or sixty years. Abraham then said: You are now sixty years of age, and you wish to bow down to one who is only a day old? Then the man would be ashamed and go away in embarrassment. Once a woman came and

26. Until 1732, thirty-four editions of *Tze'enah U-Re'enah* appeared. Since 1711 *Tze'enah U-Re'enah* has been printed with the *Targum Sheni* and *Targum Shir Ha-Shirim*; since 1722, with the *Targumim* to all five scrolls in the Bible.

27. Jewish girls were specially taught this "women's" alphabet.

brought a dish of wheat flour and said to Abraham: Take the wheat flour as a sacrifice for the idols. Abraham then took the dish of wheat flour and placed it before the idols. Then Abraham took a large stick and broke all the idols, leaving only one large idol standing and in the hand of this one he placed the large stick. When Terah returned, he said to Abraham: Who did this? Abraham said: A woman brought wheat flour for sacrifice, whereupon the idols began to quarrel with each other. Each one wished to eat first. Then the largest idol took a stick and broke all of them. Terah said: But do these things have any sense, or have they any vitality in themselves? Whereupon Abraham said: If they have no sense, why should we serve them? Then Terah his father took him and gave him into the hands of Nimrod. Nimrod said to Abraham: If you bow down to the fire, it will be well with you, but if you refuse, I will have you thrown into the fire. Then Abraham was thrown into the fire, but God saved him and he came out whole and unburned from the fire.

II

(From *Parashah Va-Yehi* for the verse "And when I was coming from Padan, Rachel died in the land of Canaan on the way"):

Jacob said to Joseph: No doubt you would wish to ask me why I trouble you so and beg that you carry me to the land of Canaan for burial and not leave me in the land of Egypt, seeing that I buried your mother Rachel in the field on the way where she died, and did not carry her to the cave to lie among the other patriarchs; even though she died quite close to the town of Bethlehem, I did not carry her there. You are certainly angry with me, but know that the Holy One Blessed Be He ordered me to bury her on the way, so that when the children of Israel will flee from Jerusalem and go into exile after their defeat by Nebuzaraddan, they will come the same way, and Rachel from her grave will pray for the Israelites and the Holy One Blessed Be He will accept her prayer."

III

(On *Parashah Yitro,* for the verse "And Jethro the priest of Midian heard"):

Because God commanded that He be revered and served, He ordained that one day in the week we should rest, to remember that God created the world and did many wonders for us in Egypt. You shall keep the Sabbath holy. You shall not think about money, but do holy things only on the Sabbath. God forgives the sins of one who properly keeps the Sabbath. There is a story about the wicked Turnus Rufus who once met Rabbi Akiba on the Sabbath. He said to him: Why is this day better than other days? Rabbi Akiba replied: Why are you more important to me than other people? He answered: God made me important. Rabbi Akiba thereupon said: God, who is our

Lord, also made this day precious. Then Turnus Rufus said: If God did, indeed, wish to have this day be more precious to me than other days, why does He Himself work on the Sabbath? He lets the rain fall and leads the clouds from afar on the Sabbath. Rabbi Akiba replied: You are familiar with the Torah of Israel. When two householders live in one court they must place an *eruv* between each other if they wish to carry any object, but when one householder has one court—even if it be three miles long—he may carry without any *eruv*. So also God to whom the whole world belongs. He alone may carry throughout the world, for no creature has any share in it. Therefore God may allow it to rain and also bring clouds to bear water throughout the whole world on the Sabbath. Rabbi Akiba said even more: The Israelites did not gather manna on the Sabbath; it did not fall on the Sabbath. And the river Sambatyon also, though it runs throughout the week, rests on the Sabbath.

IV

(From *Parashah Ki Tissa* for the verse: "But my Sabbaths you shall keep"):

This verse teaches us that even though the Holy One Blessed Be He commanded work on the sanctuary *(mishkan)*, nevertheless you shall keep the Sabbath and do no work, not even on the sanctuary. And our sages say: Therefore the Torah wrote, "*But* my Sabbaths you shall keep," to indicate that at times you may, indeed, profane the Sabbath, namely, when it is a question of saving lives. Know that the Sabbath was the first precept commanded to Israel, even before the Torah was commanded, for the Sabbath is equal in weight to the entire Torah. Our sages said Jerusalem was destroyed only because they did not properly keep the Sabbath and the Torah.

Tze'enah U-Re'enah, however, was not only the "women's Torah," the guide and educator of the Jewish woman. Its style dominated the elementary school as well. The generation that was growing up also became familiar with the text of the Pentateuch in the traditional midrashic fashion which achieved its classic form in Jacob of Yanov's masterpiece. This, however, called forth a negative attitude toward *Tze'enah U-Re'enah* in certain circles. From the cultural-historical point of view it is important to stress that the battle which a number of rabbis and scholars, such as the Maharal of Prague, Ephraim of Luntshitz, and others carried on against the abnormal method of study of that era,[28] also found a certain echo in Old-Yiddish literature. It is sufficient to mention the glossary-like Yiddish translation of the Pentateuch with the Five Scrolls

28. See our work, Vol. VI, pp. 87ff.

that was so popular in former times,[29] Moses ben Issachar Halevi Sertel's *Be'er Mosheh*, which appeared at the threshold of the seventeenth century.[30] In the long introduction the author deplores the fact that the text of the Pentateuch is taught in the elementary schools without any system or order. The parents in no way understand that one must first teach the children grammar and the literal meaning of the Biblical text. They wish only that their children should display their mental acuity in the *Gemara*, and it does not trouble them at all that the children do not properly know the simple translation of the weekly readings from the Pentateuch.

However, Moses Sertel's words had very little effect. About seventy years later, when the well-known bibliographer Shabbetai Bass reprinted *Be'er Mosheh* (1669), he also considered it necessary to indicate in the preface that the order of study is still in the same deplorable condition: "There are many students who know the *Gemara* well but are not familiar with grammar, and especially some of the teachers translate to the young whatever comes to their tongues."

Several years later we see the same Shabbetai Bass participating as editor in a great literary undertaking which had as its purpose to give the people an opportunity to become familiar with the text of the Bible in a faithful, verbatim translation. Even before the end of the sixteenth century (in 1590), the well-known printer Isaac Prossnitz reported in the preface to his edition of the Scroll of Esther that he intended soon, "God willing, to publish all the twenty-four [books of the Bible] in Yiddish translation." However, nothing came of this plan. And only in the 1670's did two printers of Amsterdam simultaneously publish two translations of the whole Bible. These were Uri (Phoebus) ben Aaron Ha-Levi[31] and Joseph Athias.[32] Like Ephraim of Luntshitz and Sheftel Horowitz, so Uri Phoebus

29. The extent to which Sertel's glossary was accepted by the people is attested by the ordinances, at the end of the sixteenth century, of the society "Talmud Torah" of Cracow, in which it is noted: "It is forbidden for any teacher to teach the Pentateuch with any commentary other than precisely the commentary *Be'er Mosheh* which is in our language that we speak here" (Güdemann, *Quellenschriften*, 233).

30. Since the Cracow society "Talmud Torah" already mentions *Be'er Mosheh* at the end of the sixteenth century, it must be conjectured that the Prague edition of 1604 that has come down to us was not the first.

31. The translator of Phoebus' edition was Yekutiel Blitz. The translation appeared in 1676–79.

32. The translator of Athias' edition was Joseph Witzenhausen, the publisher of the Arthur-romance (see above, p. 55). The largest part of this translation was edited by Shabbetai Bass. The edition appeared in 1679.

points out that all the people of the Sephardic communities, old and young, are quite familiar with the Pentateuch, the Prophets, and the Holy Writings, because they study the Bible according to its literal meaning and grammar. In order that the youth now growing up in the Ashkenazic communities might also be able to become familiar with the text of the Bible in the same way, he is issuing a complete new translation "in Yiddish, fully according to the literal meaning of the verse, and not by way of Midrashim or homilies—only the verse according to its literal meaning." The translator himself, Yekutiel Blitz, also complains that up until now the youth have not been provided with a Bible in Yiddish translated according to the literal meaning. All the glossary-like translations simply render each word by itself mechanically, not in a connected, stylistically constructed sentence, and utterly refuse to take account of "the nature of *Leshon Ashkenaz*," the spirit of the language into which the text is being translated. Blitz therefore intended to provide not a handbook for teachers but a reading book for adults, so that the reader might have before him an exact and scientifically accurate translation of the text of the Bible. Hence, he very indignantly attacks *Tze'enah U-Re'enah* which is "nothing but Midrashim and strange legends, asks many questions regarding the subject matter of the *parashah*, explains them according to the commentators and preachers, and does not give a thousandth part of the literal meaning of the verse."

The other publisher Joseph Athias also strongly criticizes *Tze'enah U-Re'enah* in which are "mostly *Gemarot* and Midrashim, all according to the method of homiletic interpretation, but not the chief thing of the Torah—so that one rarely understands how the verses in the literal meaning follow one another." Athias incidentally also deplores in general the order in which the children are instructed in the elementary schools. The teacher teaches the pupil only "one *parashah* or something more," and then begins to teach him *Gemara* "and stresses subtleties and *ḥillukim* (refined distinctions) but the chief element, the well of living waters, the written Torah, is left alone." The translator himself, Joseph Witzenhausen, complains of the fact that, because we expound the text of the Bible only according to the method of homiletic interpretation, the Christians laugh at us and assert "that we falsify the Torah."

Both translations appeared merely with the Yiddish text, without the original Hebrew. Both of them also, as we observed, set themselves the task of giving a literal translation, accurately and faithfully rendering the Biblical text, but "according to the nature of *Leshon Ashkenaz*," i.e., translating not mechanically, as do the glossaries, but taking account of the spirit of the language into which the translation is being made. But it is difficult to determine what the translators really understood by *Leshon Ashkenaz*—whether German or Yiddish. Staerk and Leitzmann, for instance, reproach Blitz and Witzenhausen in their well-known work[33] for the fact that they frequently "form non-German constructions." It is clear that neither Blitz nor Witzenhausen intended to provide a pure German translation of the Bible. They translated neither in the customary vernacular of the Jewish populace of that time, nor in the literary language, little colored with dialect, in which the morality books, travel descriptions, and memoirs of that age were composed, but in an artificial "translation" language which already had its ancient tradition. To make clear the marked distinction between this "translation" language and the customary language in which the Jew of that time thought and wrote, we present here two parallel passages of Blitz's and Witzenhausen's translations and prefaces, respectively:

.1 פון בליצס חומש־איבערזעצונג: אונ׳ ער הוב אן זיין ביא שפיל אונ׳ שפראך: עש רידט בלעם דער זון בעור: עש זאָגט דער מאן דעם דיא אויגן גיעפנט זיין, עש זאגט דער דא הערט גאטליכע ריד, דער דען אלמעכטיגן שיין זיכט (זיעט), די אויגן ווערדן גיעפינט אלש ער נידערפאלט! ווי פיין זיין דייני היטן יעקב, אונ׳ דייני וואוינונג ישראל. גלייך וואו זיך די בעכי אויז שפרייטן, ווי דא גערטן אין דען וואשרן.

פון בליצס פארערעדע: „איז דאש ניט אים צו בקלאגן אונ׳ צו בוויינן, דאש אונזרי גלערנטי ביז אלשהער אונש ניט פערזאָרגט האבן מיט איין עשרים וארבע אין לשון אשכנז אייגנטליך אויש גיליגט דען צחצחות פשט ווארט פער ווארט מלה״ק לל״א. חי נפשי, הרבה פעמים עצמו מספור האב איך גיהערט, דאש זי שפרעכן: וואָרום קאָן מן אויש ספרי גוים אייֽ הבנה האבן, אונ׳ אויש אונזרי ספרים קאָן מן קיין באשלוס פון רידן גיפונדן, אונ׳ דיא רייד אן זיך זעלבשט זיין קינדיש... אלי טוייטש ספרים זיינן אין איר שרייבונג פערמישט מיט אגדות זרות אונ׳ מדרשים, אונ׳ דיא מלמדים האבן עש ווייטר אין דען פורם איבר ליברט (איבערליווערט, איבערגעגעבן) אירי תלמידים".

.11 פון וויצנהויזנס חומש־איבערזעצונג: „ער היב זיין ביישפיל אויף אונ׳ שפראך: ער שפריכט בלעם דער זון פון בעור, אונ׳ ער שפריכט דער מאן דעם דאש אויג גיעפנט איז. ער שפריכט דער דא הערט גאטש ריד, דער דא זוכט דען שיין פון דעם אלמעכטיקן גאט, דער דא פעלט, אונ׳ דיא אויגן ווערדן אים גיעפינט. ווי גאר גוט זיין דיינן גיצעלט יעקב, ווי דייני וואוינונגען ישראל, גלייך אז וויא בעך (טייכן) ברייטן זיא זיך אויש, גלייך אן די גערטן ביי די דעם באך".

33. *Die Jüdisch-deutschen Bibelübersetzungen*, 1923, p. 162.

פון וויצנהויזנס פֿאררעדע, ווו ער פֿאלעמיזירט מיט זײַן קאָנקורענט, יקותיאל
בליץ: „כל הפוסל במומו פוסל, דאש האט גיטאן ה״ר כוסיל, ער האָט פֿאלשי הסכמות
גיבראַכט צו טראגן און׳ האט מיר וועלן דען חרם אויף דען האלז יאגן, און׳ מיך
פֿאר איין מוסר אויש גישאַלטן, און׳ האט ביגערט דש מיך קהל יצ״ו אין חרם האלטן
זאלטן; און׳ קהל יצ״ו און׳ דאש ב״ד מיט אייטל שקרים בירייכט; הערט אבר צו
וועש זא וייטר געשיכט: ער האט זיך זייער בירופֿין אויף זייני הסכמות, און׳ האָט
עורר גיוועזן אויף די גרוישי שווערי חרמות. . .

The attempt to displace *Tze'enah U-Re'enah* and other
homiletical translations was unsuccessful. The homiletical
style of *Tze'enah U-Re'enah* was more congenial to the contemporary reading public. For the old-fashioned system of education which even such an authority as the Maharal of Prague
could not destroy, the traditional style, was far more suitable
than Blitz's and Witzenhausen's new accomplishments. *Tze'e-
nah U-Re'enah* won the battle and displaced both new translations. Witzenhausen's translation did at least have the privilege
of being reprinted (in 1687),[34] but Blitz's did not. *Tze'enah U-
Re'enah* was triumphantly disseminated in scores of editions
throughout all the dispersions of Israel and ruled boundlessly
for generations over the minds and hearts of Jewish women.

34. Witzenhausen's translation was also reprinted in the well-known *Biblia Pentapla*
(Wandsbeck, 1711) together with the Catholic, Reformed, Lutheran, and Dutch
Bible translations.

CHAPTER SIX

Morality Books

Morality books in Yiddish—*Ein schön Frauen Buchlein (Seder Nashim)*—The Yiddish translation of *Sefer Ha-Yirah* (1546 and 1583) and the rhymed paraphrase *Hayyei Olam (Das Buch des ewigen Lebens)*—The Hebrew *Sefer Middot* and its Yiddish translation—*Roizn-Gortn (Sefer Ha-Gan)* and Abraham Ashkenazi's *Sam Hayyim*—The ethnographic interest of Ashkenazi's *Divrei Musar*—Moses Altschuler's *Brantshpigl* —Altschuler on the Jewish woman—Isaac ben Eliakum and his *Lev Tov*—The style of *Lev Tov*—Isaac ben Eliakum on prayers in Yiddish and on the education of children—To an impasse—Solomon Zalman ben Eliezer Ufenhausen and his *Yidisher Teryak*—The significance of the work.

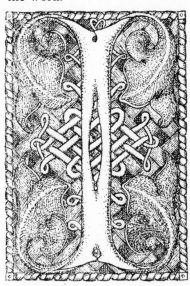 N *Tze'enah U-Re'enah*, as well as in *Di Lange Megile*, one basic tendency and goal is strongly discernible—to give ethical instruction to the people, to provide moral education, to disseminate the religious-ethical foundations of Judaism among the broadest strata. However, from the quotations that have been given, the reader may have realized that in these works another characteristic motif is quite noticeable, and that is the narrative element. It is not merely the moral but precisely the "entertaining" story itself, the belletristic part, that interests the ordinary reader. These works in fact combined two literary genres which at just that time, the close of the sixteenth century, constituted the two most powerful streams in Yiddish literature: morality books and story books. These two streams, however, did not flow quite apart and separate from each other; very frequently they mingled, and from this union, as we shall see later, were not

infrequently forged androgynous works of which it is quite difficult to determine to what genre they belong—whether we have before us a morality book or a belletristic work which is intended merely "to pass the time."

In the first chapter we noted the role of the so-called "patronesses" and *generins* in the medieval ghetto. As women of means, these ladies used to order from special copyists accounts of "the commandments incumbent on women" as well as other custumals that treat the religious laws of Jewish family life, interwoven with moral instruction and didactic maxims.

A handwritten copy of a *Seder Nashim* dated 1504 has been preserved in the library of Cambridge University.[1] Less than fifty years later (in 1552) a rhymed *Seder Nashim* (it is also called *Ein schön Frauen Buchlein*) appeared. This book was printed in Venice and edited, as the publisher Cornelius Adelkind indicates at the end of the work, "by a pious rabbi and a precious wife of a rabbi." The work was extremely popular, and in 1577 it appeared in an enlarged form in Poland (Cracow) in an edition by Benjamin ben Abraham Slonim and later in Basel in 1602.[2] In a tender, gentle tone the "little book for women" teaches the Jewish wife and mother how she ought to conduct herself in her family life and religious-social life. In the Basel edition the work begins as follows:

My dear daughter, see and mark well what I here teach you. If you follow me, you will live in propriety and honor and Almighty God will grant you happiness and welfare, and you will see joy in your children, and your days will increase, and your precious children will be as numerous as the stars in heaven, and all the wishes of your heart will be granted by God Praised Be His Name, and everyone will seek your blessed seed and desire it. Therefore, my dear daughter, I will teach you to follow the right way, and if you obey me, it will be well with your body and soul.[3]

Mitzvot Nashim was designated solely for women. But several years earlier (in 1546) there appeared in Yiddish a morality book

1. On this manuscript, see M. Weinreich, *Bilder*, pp. 149–50.
2. In the Venice edition this work has 123 chapters; in the later editions, 139. For a discussion of the various editions of the *Frauen Buchlein*, see Steinschneider, *Hebräische Bibliographie*, XIX, 82–83. The first book about "women's duties" in Yiddish was printed at the press of the brothers Helif in Cracow in 1535 (see I. Rivkind, *Bibliotek-Bukh*, Montreal, 1934, p. 49). At present this may be considered the oldest of the books printed only in Yiddish that have been preserved.
3. We quote according to Grünbaum, *op. cit.*, 269; see also Schulmann, *op. cit.*, 74–75.

which is chiefly addressed to men. This is the translation of Rabbi Jonah Gerondi's Hebrew *Sefer Ha-Yirah*.[4]

On the title-page it is noted:

This book was made by the very pious *ḥasid* Rabbi Jonah ben Gerondi, peace be upon him, and he called it *Sefer Ha-Yirah* (The Book of Reverence), inasmuch as he wrote in it nothing other than fear of heaven and, in a brief formulation, how every person ought to conduct himself in his whole life, whether in secular affairs or in religious matters, so that in this world he will be pleasing in the eyes of God and in the eyes of men, and that at the end he will be privileged to enjoy the life of the world-to-come. May God Blessed Be His Name grant this to each of us. Amen, so may it be His will.[5]

The translation is generally quite faithful. In places the translator gives not only the literal meaning of the text but also a short commentary—however, in rather clumsy, cumbersome language. We present here several parallel extracts from the original Hebrew and from the Yiddish translation.

A. *Original Text* (On being hospitable to guests and travelers):

And even if one have a hundred menservants or maidservants, he himself should take the trouble and wait on them. Was anyone as great as Abraham our father, who himself served the angels? ... And if they spend the night with him, he should give them the best of his beds, for great is the rest of the tired man when he lies down in comfort, and one who provides a good bed gives him greater pleasure than one who provides food and drink ... And in the morning he should accompany him and sustain him with bread, and remember that a wheel turns in the world; today one is rich, tomorrow destitute and ashamed ...

Yiddish Translation:

And even if he has a thousand menservants and maidservants, he should trouble himself and stand before them [the travelers or guests]

4. See our *History*, Vol. II, p. 113.
5. First printed in Zurich in 1545, reprinted in Freiburg-im-Breisgau in 1583. For extracts of this now extremely rare translation, see N. Shtif in *Filologishe Shriftn*, II, 164–165, and Weinreich, *ibid.*, 513–515. Shtif attempts to show (*Filologishe Shriftn*, II, 135–168) that the translation is by the publisher of the Constance edition of the Pentateuch in Yiddish, Michael Adam. His arguments, however, are not sufficiently persuasive. It is very difficult to believe that an apostate and missionary should have set himself the task of spreading among the Jewish masses such an extremely pious morality book as *Sefer Ha-Yirah*.

to serve them. For who is more revered to us than Abraham our father, peace be upon him, and he himself served the angels. . . . And he gives him [the traveler] more pleasure by placing him in a good bed than by giving him to eat and drink well . . . And there is a wheel that turns in the world: today luck strikes one, and tomorrow another.

B. *Original Text* (On deception)

You shall not deceive your comrade or a gentile, and you shall not refuse him excessively. And you shall not tell him something that you know never occurred. And you shall not say to him, I did this for you, when you did not do it for him. The principle of the matter is that every kind of deception is forbidden.

Yiddish Translation:

You shall not commit deception toward any man, not even a gentile. This means that one should not say something with one's mouth and think something else in his heart. And you shall not rebel against your comrades over much. And you shall not say to him, This and this thing I did for your sake, when you did not do it for his sake. But when he himself is mistaken and thinks that you did something for his sake, you need not say to him: I did not do it for your sake. For he himself is mistaken in this matter and you have not deceived him. This is the principle: In every way and manner it is forbidden to deceive any man.

C. *Original Text* (On exaggerated piety)

Be not righteous over much. If you see a naked woman about to drown in a river, do not say: I will run away and not look at her. But you shall rescue her and close your eyes as much as you can, and this will suffice. If you hear a man saying that he is going to smite his comrade, do not say: I will not reveal it to him and thereby be a tale-bearer. On the contrary, you shall not stand idly by the blood of your neighbor, but you shall tell him as much as you can, not using the language of tale-bearing.

Yiddish Translation:

You shall not be righteous over much. If you see a naked woman who is about to drown in the river, you shall not say: I will run away and I will not help her, for I do not wish to look on her while she is naked, and the like. If you hear from any man that he intends to smite his fellow, you shall not say to him(?):I will be silent and will not be a tale-bearer. For it is written: "You shall not stand idly by the blood of your neighbor." And you shall tell him according to all your ability, and not with the intention of bearing tales, and thus you will have protected yourself from sin.

In the same year (1583) that the second edition of this not very successful translation appeared, an anonymous author published in Freiburg a rhymed paraphrase of Jonah Gerondi's *Sefer Ha-Yirah* under the title *Das Buch des ewigen Lebens* (also *Ḥayyei Olam*).[6] This small work has a definite literary value. It is not simply a translation but a poetic reworking. The text is abbreviated in places, and the passages that have been worked over are presented in concise, pithy, popular language.

Ḥayyei Olam begins as follows:

> Good and blessed is the man who is willing to bear
> The yoke of the Torah in his youthful days.
> That his teacher struck him,
> He should not complain.
> Bethink yourself properly,
> And be the servant of God.

In the same tone he addresses the younger generation, the boys in the elementary school:

> Listen to me, dear, dear boys.
> You shall love the Creator,
> And keep His commandment always;
> So will you be quit of all sin.

To give the reader some notion of how the anonymous poet employed the Hebrew text, we present here several parallel extracts.

A. Hebrew *Sefer Ha-Yirah:*

A man should not rise from his bed naked, but properly dressed, as Rabbi Jose boasted: Never did the fringes of my gown see the rafters of my house . . . And from the time one rises to walk on the ground, he should bend his posture and bow his head, for the *Shechinah* is above his head, and therefore, it is proper to cover the head and not be bareheaded.

6. "The book of eternal life which, to those who read it and diligently keep what is contained in it and apply it in practice, brings grace in this world with God and among men; later it effects eternal life, to which the gracious God may help us all." This now very rare work is reprinted in extracts in Latin transcription in Grünbaum's *Chrestomathie*, pp. 251–265, and by Brüll in *Jahrbuch für jüdische Geschichte*, 1877, 100–115. See also N. Shtif in *Filologishe Shriftn*, II, 167–168.

Yiddish *Ḥayyei Olam:*

And be chaste and not loose.
The rafters should not see you naked.
As Rabbi Jose boasted: All my days I was swift;
The rafters did not see the hem of my shirt . . .
Walk somewhat bowed and not completely upright,
And remember that the Creator knows well what will be
  hereafter.
You shall think and do only what is right,
And not walk four cubits when your head is bare.

B. Hebrew *Sefer Ha-Yirah:*

Afterwards he shall go about his business, since study
of Torah is good combined with a worldly occupation, for a
man cannot serve the Creator if he does not take pains to
seek his sustenance. So David said: "Happy art thou when
thou eatest the fruit of thy hands, and it shall be well with
thee." And let his business affairs be in faithfulness, and let
him remove himself from falsehood and from the society
of evil men and the seat of scorners. And if he must abide
with them, let him take care lest they mock and jest at him,
and let him appear as one who esteems himself. Let him not
enter into their words, and let him not answer them except
briefly and impatiently, and let him rise immediately if he
can.

Yiddish *Ḥayyei Olam:*

And with God and honorably
Shall you earn your living.
Remember that you can avoid hunger;
Do not be ashamed even to trim another's beard.
And if you would have a good spirit,
Strive not after great wealth.
It is written: Forget not God;
Eat bread from the work of your own hands;
Let no lie come forth from your mouth;
And do not keep company with the idlers,
Even if it be necessary for your honor;
You shall not listen to them long.
Pretend you have forgotten something at home,
So that they do not charge you with conceit.

C. Hebrew *Sefer Ha-Yirah*

And if travelers come to one's house, he shall welcome them cheerfully and immediately set something to eat before them, for many a time a poor man comes who has not eaten and is ashamed to ask. And he shall give them of his bread and of his water; and everything shall be done cheerfully. Even if his heart be troubled and worried, he shall change his demeanor before them and comfort them with his words to refresh them.

Yiddish *Ḥayyei Olam:*

If a traveler comes into your house,
You shall receive him cheerfully.
He is ashamed to eat,
Therefore you shall not forget.
With a cheerful countenance you shall provide him food
    and drink.
You shall not complain to him about your cares and needs.
Make his spirit light,
Share with him your goods,
Speak kind words to him,
From your own hand let him not lack.

D. Hebrew *Sefer Ha-Yirah:*

Separate not yourself from the community, for if one isolates himself, he will not obtain reward with them. And the two angels who accompany a man place their hands upon his head and say: So-and-so, who separates himself from the community, will not see the consolation of the community. If the community appoints you as a *parnass* over it, be not arrogant toward the people and do not place upon them a fear that is not for the sake of heaven, but bear their burden, for great is the reward of the *parnassim* of the generation.

Yiddish *Ḥayyei Olam:*

You shall not clothe yourself in any kind of conceit
And not separate yourself from your community.
Whoever does separate from his community,
Even though things go well with him, it will still be to his
    misfortune.
And when this man departs from the world
Two angels accompany him.
They will interrogate him,
And placing their hands on his head,

Will say: You have separated yourself from your
   community;
Its joy will be vast and your's small.
It will have great favor and joy,
But you will not see it.
If a community appoints you *parnass*, you shall be modest;
You shall not take any conceit upon yourself,
You shall fear the Creator,
And you shall bear the community's burden willingly.

The passage of *Sefer Ha-Yirah* about going through the
weekly reading from the Pentateuch in the vernacular that was
quoted above is rendered in *Hayyei Olam* in the following way:

Now I would point out to you:
Every week you shall read the *sidrah* with lesser people.
Twice in Hebrew and once in Targum.
This is seemly for you.
Be prepared to read it once in German,
And with the accents, i.e., the clothing of the Torah.

Like *Sefer Ha-Yirah* and *Sefer Hayyei Olam*, so also the oldest
and most fundamental morality book that appeared in Yiddish
in the sixteenth century, the *Zitn-Bukh (Sefer Middot)* was translated from Hebrew.

Many scholars have taken an interest in the old *Zitn-Bukh*.
To be sure, it has not been determined whether this is the *first*
morality book in Yiddish which had the distinction of being
printed.[7] In any case, it is the oldest Yiddish morality book that
has come down to us. The origin of the book, however, has not
been cleared up to the present day. Not only has the author
remained unknown, but there is even a dispute about the language in which it was first written. Since the *Zitn-Bukh (Sefer
Middot)* was first published in Yiddish (Isny, 1542) and only
later appeared in Hebrew in 1581[8] under the title *Orehot Tzad-*

7. In any case, in the view of the bibliographer S. Wiener, a book of customs in
    Yiddish was already printed in 1537.
8. A year later, in 1582, there also appeared the second edition of the Yiddish *Zitn-Bukh*
    from the well-known press of the publisher of Cracow, Isaac Prosstitz. On the
    title-page is written: "*Sefer Ha-Middot*: this book writes what good qualities there
    are for men and how one should cleave to them, since through good qualities a man
    can fulfill the Torah and good deeds that are pleasing in the sight of God Blessed
    Be He forever and also in the sight of men. Printed in the major city of the holy
    community of Cracow in 1582 through Isaac the son of the pious Aaron, may his
    memory be for a blessing, of Prosstitz."

dikim, even such expert bibliographers as Steinschneider (*Cat. Libr. Bodleiana,* 521–522), Zedner (*Catalogue of Hebrew Books in the Library of the British Museum,* 623) and Benjacob (*Otzar Ha-Sefarim,* 51) at first believed that the Yiddish text is the original and *Oreḥot Tzaddikim* merely a translation. Subsequently, however, Steinschneider realized that he had been mistaken and conjectured that this morality book was first written in Hebrew (*Serapeum,* 1869, 135). Perles (*Beiträge,* 175–177) and Güdemann (in his *Geschichte des Erziehungswesens,* III, Ch. 6) also later came to the same conclusion. Eleazar Schulmann, however, categorically rejects this view in his *Sefat Yehudit-Ashkenazit* and asserts very definitely that the Hebrew *Oreḥot Tzaddikim* is merely a translation of the *Zitn-Bukh.*[9]

There is no doubt that it is not Schulmann who is right but Steinschneider and Perles, and that *Sefer Middot* was composed in Hebrew even before Gutenberg invented the printing press. That the morality book in Hebrew also bore the name *Sefer Middot,* not *Oreḥot Tzaddikim,* is to be seen from the Hebrew preface, where it is so referred to. It is, incidentally, virtually indubitable that the preface to the Hebrew edition was written not by the author but by the publisher. In the first edition (Prague) the preface is printed under the simple title *Hakdamah* (Introduction) and only in the later editions does it appear as *Hakdamat Ha-Meḥabber* (Introduction of the Author). It is possible that *Sefer Middot* had already been published in Hebrew even before the Prague edition of 1581. Testimony to this is provided by the following statement on the title-page of the Prague edition: "And because it is not found among us, for it has not been printed *in our days,* the idea came to our mind to become involved in it and to print it in order to benefit the many, so that they might read and study. . . ." To be sure, this is no more than a conjecture, for it is also possible that the Hebrew term for "in our days" is introduced here simply because it fits the rhyme. However, there is no doubt whatever that *manuscripts* of the Hebrew text already existed considerably before the Yiddish edition of 1542. In the library in Leningrad of the Society for the Promotion of Enlightenment and Culture Among Jews there was in Harkavy's collection of manuscripts an old copy of the Hebrew *Sefer Middot* written on parchment.[10] Unfortunately the manuscript is defective; sev-

9. *Op. cit.,* 86–88.
10. We have described this manuscript in our article in *Filologishe Shriftn,* III. On the Hebrew manuscript of Hamburg, which was completed in 1504, see M. Erik, *Geshikhte,* 273–274.

eral pages at the beginning are missing, and also a few pages at the end. It is written in the beautiful Rashi script of a skilled scribe, but on many pages letters have disappeared through age, and the text here can be read only through the incisions or markings in the parchment. The manuscript bears a special stamp which is also borne, as we previously noted,[11] by numerous old Hebrew parchment manuscripts of the Middle Ages: many pages have been cut off at the bottom deep "into the flesh" i.e., almost to the text. In our manuscript, which consists of eighty pages quarto, all of twenty pages have been cut. In eighteen of them entire strips have been cut off, and in two only half.

There is no doubt whatever that this manuscript was written *at the latest* in the second half of the fifteenth century, some seventy years and perhaps all of a hundred years before the first Yiddish edition of the morality book. When we compared the text of the manuscript in the Harkavy collection with the first Hebrew edition of 1581, we became convinced that the publisher employed a *later* copy, which was quite erroneous in comparison with our parchment manuscript. This is not the place to dwell on the matter, but simply as an example we give two passages from the same page. In Chapter 27 in our manuscript it is written: "Because the Talmud is very deep, for it is mixed up with the Aramaic language *(le-fi sheba-talmud amuk me'od, she-hu me'urav be-lashon arami).* In the first printed edition the sentence is corrupted and reads *be-lashon aravi*(?) (in the Arabic language). In our manuscript it is related: "And afterwards Rabbi Moses Maimon arose and included the entire Oral Torah in one book in very simple language, and following him arose Rabbi Moses of Coucy who composed a book that he extracted from that book of Maimonides." In the first Hebrew printed edition the entire clause about Maimonides is missing, and it begins immediately with "And following him arose Rabbi Moses of Coucy..."

As Perles in his day quite rightly noted, one can see from the Yiddish text itself that he has to do with a translation, not an original work. At the end of the Yiddish *Zitn-Bukh* comes a special supplement which begins with the following lines: "Honor to God the Almighty alone. To all women and maidens we extend our warm greetings, and, above all, to the honorable and modest Madame Murada, lady doctor of the liberal art of medicine, resident in Ginzburg. Kind lady! After I under-

11. Above, p. 13.

stood that you desire and long for the *Sefer Middot*, I ventured with the aid of Almighty God and published it."[12]

Thus we see that the "lady doctor of the liberal art of medicine," Madame Murada, already knew of the *Sefer Middot* but apparently could not read it because it was written in Hebrew. For this reason her friend and admirer decided to translate the work into the vernacular that she knew. Several other passages show even more clearly that we have here merely a translation. For example, at the end of the twenty-fifth chapter we read the following remark: "The little that stands here I found in another book which speaks of the evil inclination; so I wrote this down here and it does not belong to the *Sefer Middot*."[13] A similar remark is to be found also in a later chapter *(Shaar Ha-Teshuvah)*: "The little that is written here does not belong to the *Sefer Middot*; it was taken from another book and written down here."[14]

Who the author of the Hebrew *Oreḥot Tzaddikim* was has remained just as unknown as the name of its translator into Yiddish. Moritz Güdemann, indeed, attempts to show[15] that this work was produced by the well-known author of *Sefer Ha-Nitzaḥon*, Yom Tov Lippmann Mühlhausen. This conjecture is taken as an assured fact by Ignacy Schipper[16] and Max Erik.[17] We believe, however, that Güdemann's conjecture is ungrounded. It is difficult to believe that the *Sefer Middot* could have been composed by such an ardent Kabbalist as Yom Tov Lippmann.[18] One thing, however, is certain: the anonymous author of the *Sefer Middot*, who most probably lived in the fifteenth century,[19] was a man of broad knowledge and of clear

12. We have not seen the first edition of 1542, but the last two pages of *Sefer Middot* are reprinted in Isaac ben Eliakum's *Lev Tov*, Amsterdam edition (1670). See also M. Weinreich, *Shtaplen*, 108–109.

13. We quote according to Solomon Zalman London's edition (Amsterdam, 1735, 75) which is very close to the text of the first edition of Isny. The quotation agrees word for word with the text that Perles quotes from the first edition (*Beiträge*, 175). On the other hand the later edition (Horodno, 1795) of *Sefer Middot* is very much abbreviated and changed. This edition was also reprinted, with further abbreviations, in 1835.

14. *Ibid.*, 92b.

15. *Geschichte des Erziehungswesen*, III, 223–226.

16. *Di Kultur-Geshikhte*, 75–77.

17. *Op. cit.*, 279–280.

18. See our *History*, Vol. III, pp. 148–150.

19. In the twenty-seventh chapter ("Sha'ar Ha-Torah") the author mentions the final expulsion of the Jews from France (in 1395). It is possible that he himself was a descendant of the exiles from France.

mind who considered the world about him with sober eyes. His morality book is absolutely free of mystical elements, as well as of the rigorously ascetic spirit with which most of the morality books of that time are permeated. The author, to be sure, notes that "because the exile is so long" Jews must "separate themselves from the vanities of the world."[20] But he also admonishes that man must not look contemptuously on "this world" and must strive to find the beautiful in the ugly and disgusting. "A sage was walking with another man in the marketplace and they found a carcass lying on the way that stank exceedingly. Then the man who was walking with the sage said: 'Pfui! How vilely this carcass stinks!' Thereupon the sage said: 'See how the carcass has charming white teeth!' Thus, *Oreḥot Tzaddikim* declares, "he gave him to understand that one must always say the best of all things,[21] even of a carcass and —how much the more so—of a person."[22] While the author admonishes against drunkenness, he nevertheless deems it necessary to note that "it is good to drink wine in proper measure." Wine raises the mood of a person, "so that he should grow strong from it, and can study Torah and pray properly with concentration." And even "when two friends drink wine together, they like each other much better than before."[23] "The *Shechinah* rests only amidst joy," declares *Oreḥot Tzaddikim*. On the prophets also the *Shechinah* rested not otherwise than "through the power of joy."[24] Interesting, too, is the way the author of *Oreḥot Tzaddikim* endeavors to explain to the reader that man is unable to grasp the essence of the world-to-come and its pleasures:

Therefore you must understand and know that just as little as the bird that flies in the air can know the joy of the fish that swims in the water, the fish cannot know the joy of the bird, for the nature of the two is not the same. The bird suffocates in water, and the fish dies on the dry land. Thus also since we are, in this world, mixed up with bodily pleasures, we cannot attain knowledge of the pleasures that

20. *Oreḥot Tzaddikim*, Amsterdam edition, 1735, fol. 75b: "Now that, by reason of our many sins, the exile has continued too long, Israel ought to separate from the vanities of the world."
21. In the Hebrew text: "Why should you tell its disgrace? Tell the praise, for one should always tell the praise of the world."
22. "Sha'ar Leshon Ha-Ra," fol. 73b.
23. *Ibid.*, 29b.
24. *Ibid.*, fol. 35b.

the soul will enjoy in the world-to-come. For the pleasures of this world are lost and transient things, while the pleasures of the soul in the world-to-come are continuous and without cease, and the enjoyments of this world have no similiarity to the enjoyments of the world-to-come.[25]

Especially interesting is the twenty-seventh chapter, "Shaar Ha-Torah." We have spoken at length in the previous volume of the battle that some rabbis, such as the Maharal of Prague, Ephraim of Luntshitz, and others, carried on against the abnormal mode of education of that age, and how these rabbis attacked with special sharpness the *pilpul* which was then prevalent in the *yeshivot*. But considerably before Rabbi Loew of Prague, and even before Jacob Pollak's *seder ha-ḥillukim* (order of subtle distinctions)[26] was introduced into the Polish *yeshivot*, the author of the *Sefer Middot* declared war against the method of learning of his time. He deplores the fact that in his generation "everyone wishes first to sharpen his mind in *Tosafot, ḥiddushim*, and artificial accomplishments, without properly knowing the text of the Talmud . . . They occupy themselves with wild tricks, confuse their minds and waste their time with foolishness, and forget piety and fear of God." "Many of the students," the author further notes, "themselves now concede that their order of learning is absolutely worthless. They themselves realize that all these foolish tricks lead to their learning nothing, and through all these tortuous ingenuities of theirs they do not know any Torah, or the Prophets and Holy Writings. Nor do they know any *aggadot* or Midrashim or any other wisdom."

These sharp attacks on the contemporary mode of learning, however, are entirely missing in the Yiddish edition (Isny, 1542). The translator into Yiddish apparently considered it inappropriate to acquaint the "common" people who read the Judeo-German morality books with such "heretical" ideas.

Sefer Middot and *Sefer Ha-Yirah*, the latter of which appeared in Zurich, are both translated from Hebrew originals. The first morality book which apparently was originally written in Yiddish and only then translated into Hebrew is the little book *Roizn-Gortn (Sefer Ha-Gan)* which is divided into seven chapters, one for each day of the week. *Roizn-Gortn* was composed

25. *Ibid.*, fol. 33b.
26. See our *History*, Vol. VI, pp. 25ff.

in the fifteenth century by Isaac ben Eliezer of Worms but first appeared in print in Cracow in 1571,[27] and the abovementioned Moses Sertel translated the work into Hebrew and published it in 1597.

The first Yiddish morality book which appeared in print while its author was still alive is Abraham Ashkenazi's *Sam Ḥayyim* (Prague, 1590).[28] This little book was composed by Ashkenazi, an apothecary of Ludomir (Volhynia), in both Hebrew and Yiddish. On the title-page the reader is informed:

This book is called *Sam Ḥayyim*,
It came from a distant land,
But was made by a blessed hand.
Its author was Rabbi Abraham Ashkenazi the apothecary;
He sends it to the people as a gift,
For it shows how every man should guard himself from sin and shame,
And how man should be properly familiar with God's service.
Therefore do not let it out of your hand.
Through it you will come into the Holy Land."[29]

As the oldest morality book deriving from the Polish territories, *Sam Ḥayyim*, and its author as well, deserve extended discussion.

Abraham Ashkenazi is not a rabbi or preacher but a simple pharmacist. He himself attests that he "did not study *Tosafot* and *halachot*" and "is not very deep in learning." He does not introduce any quotations from the sacred books nor does he display any erudition. He is interested only in real, practical questions of life. His eye is directed chiefly to the earth, not to the heavens. Characteristic in this respect is his introduction:

27. Steinschneider gave an incorrect date (1579). On this, see *ZHB*, III, 62. *Roizn-Gortn* appeared under the following title: "This little book is called *Rose Garden*: just as it [i.e., a real rose garden] makes people very cheerful and strengthens man's heart, so also the heart of one who reads this little book will be strengthened and he will not fear, and his soul will be free of all wicked sins."

28. This edition is extremely rare. On the second edition, which a plagiarist published in 1772 under his own name, see our article in *Filologishe Shriftn*, III, 177–180.

29. On the title-page is written in Hebrew: "The Book of Life; to those who find it, it gives life and salvation double-fold. The commandment of the Lord is pure, enlightening the eyes. Let the man who desires life come here to buy the elixir of life which Rabbi Abraham Ashkenazi the apothecary of the holy community of Vladimir from the land of Volhynia has made (Prague, 5384)."

Sam Ḥayyim

The order of holy communities shall be conducted
So that with their deeds they may adorn themselves before
   God.
So the Holy One Blessed Be He will stand by them,
So that neither sin nor shame will come upon them.
Now I will present the matter properly,
How the leaders shall do right and pay no special attention
   to anyone,
Then I will distribute the little book
To all Jews, God's servants ever,
So that I Abraham and whoever brings it into print
   shall have the reward of it.
I beg all people and fall at their feet
All who read the little book,
Be it many persons or one creature only,
That he may not mock me or be angry with me,[30]
That I did not study *Tosafot* or *halachot*.
I am like the slave of the town of Hozai,
Who was sick when he had no work.
But you must not ask: What does he say more than other
   rabbis?
Believe me that I have written it only for sons and
   daughters.
Our Torah writes that a man should always study,
Even if people be angry with him.
Now I am like a chick still in the eggshell,
And beg all men everywhere
That I may find grace among all creatures
With my calling like a crier;
For I do not desire to say anything from my own mind,
But will present everything from many books,
So that you shall not consider me
As if I were the greatest fool.
I wish to explain everything with reason,
Not only as if it were pure air.
So would I root out all evil ways,
And will begin without delay with the leaders;
Then the order of the rabbis, the guardians of the city;
Then how one should raise sons and daughters.
After that we shall speak of community finances,

30. In our copy this passage is somewhat damaged, and we are not certain that we have
   read the word rightly. If we have, it must be *murren,* "to be angry" or "to be
   dissatisfied."

How they should administer the community's funds,
And manage to make the rich men give,
So that thereby they may practice charity properly;
Or when something is needed for the community's interest,
How they shall be compelled to contribute.

As a man of the people, Ashkenazi turns first of all to the "guardians of the city"—the rabbis, leaders, and *parnassim*—and demands of them not to wrong the common man and to lighten his tax burden. "One who wishes to be a *parnass* over the people must have compassion for them at all times . . . and for one who wishes to conduct an office of leadership with arrogance, all the doors in Hell are open . . . They shall not engage in flattery, and they shall also not always be exploiting their power. They shall not long for bribes; God will repay them elsewhere." Many times the author reminds the *parnassim* that "also when they demand taxes and collect them and know well that the poor have not wherewith to live, they should temporarily lend to them, for because of this do they stand at the peak—that they might be gracious to widows and orphans. So shall they be worthy of being crowned." Because the chief say in communal matters at that time was still exercised not by the *parnassim* and rich men but by the rabbis, our author reminds the leaders of the community that "they should not be timid before the rabbis."

The moral instruction of this apothecary undoubtedly also has an ethnographic interest. It presents us with characteristic features of the contemporary way of life. From the rabbis and heads of the Talmudic academies the author demands that "at least they should admonish the young men; otherwise, they will make carnival (celebrate Purim) the whole term." He also warns the students in the Talmudic academies: "Now I will be silent about the rabbis; they must endure a great deal. And I would say of the young men that they should not always be after the girls." He instructs the shopkeepers to carry on their business without deception and not have false weights, and to the town doctor "who goes about with remedies" he proposes that, instead of mocking others and busying himself with empty words, he would do better to look into a morality book such as *Sefer Middot* and *Menorat Ha-Maor*. One who is not very familiar with the Hebrew language, Ashkenazi emphasizes, should read Judeo-German books: "When one . . . does not properly understand the holy language, he can then read it in well-printed German . . . for the press has been given permission to print equally in all languages."[31] The Hebrew text stresses even more sharply that whoever is ignorant of Hebrew should read in Judeo-German or in any other language.

Sam Ḥayyim, as we have noted, is a little book. Several years later, however, there appeared in Yiddish a true *Kol-Bo*, an extensive anthology of ethics and moral instruction. This was Moses Henoch Yerushalmi Altschuler's thick volume *Brantshpigl*.[32]

The author addresses his readers as follows:

> Come here, good people,
> And purchase my instruction and teaching.
> Buy the lovely new mirror;
> Every one should run to it.

In the first chapter, where he explains the reasons why he wrote his morality book in German, he also indicates that "the book was made in German for women and for men who are like women in not having much knowledge," and that when "the Sabbath comes and they read it, they can comprehend, since our books are in Hebrew and at times write *pilpul* from the *Gemara*, so that they can not understand." Nevertheless, M. Erik and M. Grünbaum are, in a certain sense, justified when they declare *Brantshpigl* a special "women's book." We noted previously that those who took part in the creation and dissemination of the folk-literature were overwhelmed at the enormous revolution which the printing press called forth in the life of the Jewish woman. The woman, the mother of the coming generation, became a national cultural factor in the life of the people. We quoted earlier a rather long statement from the well-known publisher and translator Isaac ben Aaron Prossnitz which points to the great cultural role of "the women." Almost in the same terms as Isaac Prossnitz, the author of *Brantshpigl* endeavors in the first introductory chapter[33] to show that the woman is the "wheaten flour," the

---

31. We quote according to the second edition of 1727.

32. The oldest edition of *Brantshpigl* which has come down to us is the Basel edition of 1602. M. Erik, who wrote a special article on *Brantshpigl* (*Tsaytshrift*, I, 173–180), has, however, demonstrated that before this edition, there was an earlier one which appeared in the 1590's.

33. In the first edition *Brantshpigl* was divided into sixty-eight chapters. In the later editions certain additions were made, and it now consisted of seventy-four chapters.

"cream of the crop," and he bases himself on the same *aggadah* mentioned by Prossnitz. Moses Henoch declares:

"Thus shalt thou say to the house of Jacob and tell the children of Israel." (Exodus 19:3). Here the sages in the *Mechilta* explain that the house of Jacob means the women and children, while the house of Israel is the men. So that there it was the women who were first addressed, and later the men. It is said in the Midrash that they asked the rabbis wherewith the women deserved that Moses had to speak God's word to them before the men. They answered: because they accustom the children to study Torah from their childhood on and lead them to the teacher and devote their attention to the children, and speak God's word to them.

Because the woman is the "cream of the crop" and an important cultural factor in the life of the people, she also has numerous obligations. In many chapters of *Brantshpigl* the duties of the Jewish woman are specially treated: "This chapter explains how the modest woman should conduct herself in the home." "This chapter explains how a woman should behave with her servants in the house." "This chapter explains who is a good wife and who is a bad wife." "This chapter explains how a woman is wise to exhort her husband to the good." When a man comes home depressed and tired from worrying about earning a living, the modest woman should console him and speak tender words to him: "Dear husband, be not so grieved; God Blessed Be He is compassionate. Dear husband, we will trust in His holy name and accept everything for good."

Another chapter (Chapter 11) explains "that it sometimes happens that a righteous man has a bad wife and a wicked man a pious one." To give the reader some notion of the character and style of this morality book that was so popular in former times we present this chapter virtually *in toto*:

People marvel that a pious, decent man has a bad wife. In the Talmudic tractate *Ta'anit* it is written: Rabbi Jose the Galilean was a precious man and had a bad wife; if he asked her to cook peas she cooked groats; if he asked her to cook groats she cooked peas; she did everything to provoke him because he did not follow her in doing evil. It also sometimes happens that a wicked man has a pious, gracious wife. It is written in the Book of Samuel that a certain man named Nabal had as his wife Abigail, who was modest and gracious in all her deeds. King David blessed her and said, "Blessed be your discretion, and blessed be you." This is to be understood: Blessed are your words and blessed are you. It was a source of great wonder to our sages and prophets that things go ill for a just man and well for a wicked man. They wrote many explanations in our *Gemara*. Nevertheless, the conclusion remains among them that the Holy One wishes to test the righteous man with a bad wife to see whether she will not turn him to evil, and the wicked man with a good wife to see whether perhaps she will not turn him to good. . . . The wicked man is always reproved and instructed by his pious wife; perhaps he may thereby be made to turn and repent. The sages give the following example: A king has two servants. One is diligent in his service, and when he commits a slight offense against his master, the king shouts at him and reproves him. The other always does what displeases the king, but the king leaves him alone and does nothing to him. The king observes that his servants marvel at the fact that he reproves this one and says nothing to the other. So he says: Come here, I will explain this to you. With the good servant I am pleased and gladly have him near me. When he commits any little offense, I show him that he ought not to do this, so that he can remain with me. As far as the bad servant is concerned, I do not gladly see him by me, and in the next war that comes I will dispatch him with an order that they place him in the front rank so that he perishes. Then will his bad conduct be recompensed. Of this King Solomon says in Proverbs: "Him whom God loveth He reproveth." And of the wicked, King David says in Psalms: "Yet a little while and the wicked will be no more; though you look well at his place, he will not be there" (Psalms 37:10). That is to say, he ought to be in Paradise but is not there and never comes beneath the glory of the Holy One Blessed Be He and must perish. But the righteous man who stands here comes to other righteous men and receives the great reward and sees the love of the Holy One Blessed Be He who calls him "My servant." So God called our ancestors "My servants."

Brantshpigl, the first original morality book of large compass in Yiddish, at once became extremely popular and went through three editions while its author was still living.[34] It was chiefly disseminated, however, among the Jews of Germany. In the Polish communities *Brantshpigl* was soon displaced by its strong competitor, Isaac ben Eliakum's *Lev Tov*, which was first published in Prague in 1620. Testimony to the great popularity of the morality book written by Isaac ben Eliakum of Posen is provided by the fact that the renowned Rabbi Sheftel Horowitz[35] declares in his testament to his daughters that they should frequently read the Yiddish translation of the Pentateuch and *Lev Tov*. The rabbi of Prosstitz, Rabbi Yeḥiel

34. Moses Altschuler died after 1610, when the third edition appeared.
35. See our work, Vol. VI, p. 115.

Michal Epstein, of whom we shall have occasion to speak later, also declares in his *Derech Ha-Yashar:* "*Lev Tov* is a mighty book. It was made by a great sage who was a great scholar."

The title-page of *Lev Tov* is typical. We noted earlier the literary and ethnographic interest of the title-pages of the Old-Yiddish editions. In illustration, we present here in full the unique title-page of this popular morality book:

All you men and women,
And all who are fashioned by the Creator,
Who wish to build this world and the other for themselves,
Come, all of you, and look at this splendid book.
I believe no one will be sorry
Who reads it through completely.
One will find in it all of Judaism,
In its length and in its breadth,
Quite understandable and well explained,
Extending over twenty chapters.
Whoever reads through it
Will be happy with all his heart,
And have great and gentle joys.
Among all scholars it will call the tune.
But above all other things,
I would let you know
That knowing and reading is not the chief thing.
What is most important is observing and doing.
Whatever kind of person one may be,
It [this book] holds him in its power.
All the rules of conduct for man
From his birth, till he grows old,
And all behavior in any form.
Do not tarry, buy it quickly,
While you still find it cheap.
It also has good paper and ink;
Even a half-blind man can see it.
Buy it for yourself and for your wife and children,
For he who does not pay well for the book is a sinner.
Through it you will merit the world-to-come—
You and all your daughters and sons
That you will have throughout all generations.
Great honor and wealth will nevermore run away from you
And you will depart in good old age, Amen.

The author of *Lev Tov*, the deeply pious scholar of Posen, is not at all unjustified when he boasts that whoever reads his book "will find in it all of Judaism," all of "the rules of conduct for man" from birth to old age. Whereas *Brantshpigl* addresses itself chiefly to "the women," *Lev Tov* speaks to both sexes. Its favorite forms of address are: "Dear people" and "Householders and women." Indeed, it speaks first to the householders, and only then to the women. *Brantshpigl* teaches the women how they ought to behave toward their husbands; *Lev Tov* teaches householders how they should appreciate and honor their wives, for the woman is the mistress of the house and the educator of the children. When the author of *Lev Tov* speaks, for instance, of *hilchot derech-eretz* (the laws of proper conduct, Chapter 5), he notes that "proper conduct is divided into five parts: one part speaks of how a scholar ought to conduct himself; another part speaks of the conduct expected of old people; the third part discusses how householders and young men and youths should behave properly." Only at the end comes: "the fourth part speaks how women and maidens should conduct themselves properly."

Proper conduct and fear of God. And since fear of God is closely bound up with all the commandments and precepts that are written in the Torah, and the sages of the Talmud explained them so ingeniously, *Lev Tov* lists all the *mitzvot* which encompass man's family and social life, describes them at length, gives an estimate of their great importance, and weaves this together with extensive moral instruction and words of reproof. These long moralistic discussions make a painful impression on the modern reader, but in the God-saturated and melancholy ghetto of the seventeenth and eighteenth centuries the ascetic and God-fearing *Lev Tov* was highly congenial. Its reproving, admonishing style made a strong impression, and the common man would read the pages of this "mighty book" with a sense of humility and a trembling heart. Even now, however, *Lev Tov* has a significant interest for the historian of culture, because in it are preserved many singular details of the Jewish cultural life of that age.

As far as the structure of the work is concerned, *Lev Tov* is greatly indebted to the Hebrew *Sefer Ha-Musar* of Jehudah Challatz (Challas)[36] even in the order and number of its chap-

---

36. Zunz (*Zur Geschichte und Literatur*, 253) and several other bibliographers give this name in an erroneous form: Velez and Welez. The work was brought by a

ters. Indeed, Isaac ben Eliakum makes no secret of this and indicates quite frequently how extensively he employed Challatz' morality book. For instance, at the beginning of the fifth chapter he declares: "Now I will write the laws of proper conduct as they are well set forth in *Sefer Ha-Musar.*"

Nevertheless, *Lev Tov* is strongly distinguished from its Hebrew prototype by the fact that it is a truly *popular* book in all of its style and character. Almost half of *Sefer Ha-Musar* is taken up by the fourth chapter which discusses the great importance and value of prayer.[37] The chapter is filled with quotations from the *Zohar,* with fearful "combinations of letters" and the profound mysteries that are concealed in each individual prayer. The author of *Lev Tov* approaches this theme quite differently. For him it is most important to show that "prayer without inner concentration *(kavvanah)* is like a body without a soul." Hence, he declares it genuine blasphemy when common householders who are not very familiar with Hebrew pray from the *Maḥzor* with its difficult hymns and poems. "The mouth speaks, and the lips babble, and the heart knows nothing of it." The pious Isaac ben Eliakum of Posen comes to the conclusion: "Therefore every man should understand his prayer well, and he should know what he says and what he desires from the Holy One Blessed Be He; and whoever does not understand the holy language, let him say his prayer in the language that he does understand well, whatever it may be, German or Welsh (Italian), be it little or much, for a short prayer that he understands is better; and when he prays a little with inner concentration, it is a thousand times better than when one prays much and does not understand or has no concentration."[38]

The author of *Lev Tov* considers it necessary to repeat: "If he is a poor man so that he cannot afford to hire a teacher, let him read in German a German Pentateuch or German Psalms or other godly books in German."[39] The pious author, however, deems it necessary in this connection to warn the people: "But the German books that do not speak of the Torah or of *mitzvot* are words of scoffers. It is a sin to read them. These books are nothing but confusions."

---

relative of the author, Moses Challatz, "from distant lands" and first published in Constantinople in 1537.

37. We quote according to the first Constantinople edition of 1537.

38. *Lev Tov,* pp. 7–8. We quote according to the Frankfurt edition of 1681.

39. The author of *Lev Tov* in this connection recommends especially *Sefer Middot, Sefer Ha-Musar,* and *Brantshpigl.*

Like *Brantshpigl, Lev Tov* underscores the importance of the woman. In this connection it also refers to the abovementioned Midrash with its commentary on the verse, "Thus shalt thou say to the house of Jacob . . ." The author especially endeavors to inscribe in the consciousness of his readers that the woman ought to be *equal* to the man in the family. In a kindly, gentle, tone the mother teaches her daughter in *Lev Tov* how to value and honor her husband and serve him. "My dear daughter, stand before your husband and serve him. If you serve him and are a maid to him, he will in turn serve you and will be your slave; but if you hold yourself proud and precious and wish to dominate him, know that he will wish to be your lord by force, contrary to your wishes, and you will be low in his eyes as the worst of maidens."[40]

To raise a hand against one's own wife is, for the author of *Lev Tov*, the most grievous sin. "It is the most assured principle," Rabbi Isaac ben Eliakum warns,

that no son of Israel may strike his wife. This no Jew may do. It is not Jewish, but a great and grievous sin. It is far more grievous than to strike another Jew . . . Even one who does not strike but lifts his hand to strike is a wicked man and unfit to serve as a witness, like any other wicked man, and may not be called up to the reading of the Torah. . . . Also when he signs a letter, the letter is void as long as he has not repented properly.[41]

Quite different is the attitude of *Lev Tov* in regard to the raising and education of children. The most sacred duty is to raise children from infancy on to Torah, fear of God, and good deeds; and this must be done in strict fashion. Children must be afraid of their parents. "One who wishes to draw his children to Torah and good deeds should not display his love for his child . . . and everyone is obliged to raise his children so that they shall be afraid of their father and their mother."[42] Only in this way, *Lev Tov* asserts, can the rising generation be led in the right way, to be pious and just toward God and men. Not man as an individual personality is of chief significance for our ultra-pious author; he is firmly persuaded that far more important and precious are the *mitzvot*, God's precepts of morality and ethics, which man is obliged to fulfill in the most rigorous

40. *Ibid.*, Chapter 9, pp. 44. These maxims are also to be found in *Sefer Ha-Musar*, Chapter 6.
41. *Ibid.*, p. 45.
42. *Ibid.*, p. 43.

way and which he may not transgress in the slightest fashion. And woe to him who becomes "rebellious" and departs from the commandments of the Torah. On such a person one must have no mercy; he must be punished in the cruelest fashion. The author, who finds such tender and soft words when speaking about domestic tranquility, about the peaceable living together of man and wife, becomes barbarically cruel when he speaks about one who violates the seventh commandment and has sexual intercourse with a Christian woman. This passage is so characteristic that we present it here verbatim:

For the sin of lying with a gentile woman is more grievous than adultery with a Jewess, and anyone who finds a man lying with a gentile woman may freely kill him. Indeed, it is a great *mitzvah* to slay him immediately, and it is like bringing him as a sacrifice, as Pineḥas did. There is no need to give him any warning. Also, there is no need to obtain permission from any rabbi or from any judge or from any leader of the community, but whoever finds him . . . should kill him at once. One who slays him without judgment and without legal proceedings does a great *mitzvah*.[43]

When, in this connection, the passage of Maimonides' *Guide for the Perplexed*[44] about the "rebellious fools" is recalled, it becomes clear how a one-sided and arid rigorism brings men of quite contrary tendencies and world views to the same impasse.

Almost simultaneously with *Lev Tov* there was published another work which represents a unique phenomenon in Old-Yiddish literature. This is the *Yidisher Teryak*[45] by Solomon Zalman Tzevi Hirsch Ufenhausen.[46]

---

43. *Ibid.*, Chapter 6, p. 45.
44. Our *History*, Vol. I, p. 147.
45. The word *teryak* means a universal remedy against snake poison and various other debilities and sicknesses. We quote here the complete title-page of Ufenhausen's work: "*Yidisher Teryak:* This is a remedy and curing book, wherewith all ordinary Jews and Jewesses may justify themselves with truth against the Christians and reply to them with proofs from the Torah, the Prophets, the Mishnah, and the Talmud and the other codes, as well as with arguments from the sages, as well as becoming familiar there with the arguments of the sages and books of the Christians, i.e., that of the apostate, the devil Friederich Frenz of Ettingen, who, in his printed book *Der jüdischer Schlangen-Balg* falsely accused the Jews. Adorned with fine concordances and references. Also at the end, notations for the whole book in which it is indicated where everything is to be found. In honor of all men and women, in good High German, so that everyone may understand it, and the like of it for usefulness has never been printed. By Zalman Tzevi of Ufenhausen, composed in seven chapters and completed in press. Here in the holy community of Hanau with the permission of the praiseworthy government, may its majesty increase. Rosh Ḥodesh Adar Sheni 5375 (1615)." (We quote according to the second edition of 1680).
46. His work first appeared in Hanau in 1615. A second edition was provided in 1680–81

Yidisher Teryak

Polemics on religious questions, in which Hebrew literature is so rich, are rather rare in Yiddish literature. The *Yidisher Teryak* is, in fact, the only religious polemic work in Old-Yiddish, and even this work, as we shall see further, carries more of a social than a purely religious character. For the slight information that we have about the author of this interesting book, we are indebted to the author himself. From passing remarks in the *Teryak* it may be conjectured that Solomon Zalman Ufenhausen was born around 1550–1560. We also learn that "for many years" the author was driven away from his home by "evil Jews," and that he was an itinerant who traveled long and wandered over many cities and lands. These sojournings significantly broadened his world-view and level of culture. He was quite familiar with the German language, studied Luther's translation of the Bible assiduously, and was familiar with the works of Flavius Josephus (see *Yiddisher Teryak*, Chapter One, Section 13; *ibid.*, Chapter Three, Sections 7, 14, 15), Buxtorf the Elder,[47] and the apostate Antonius Margarita of Regensburg.[48] He also knew how Pico della Mirandola and Johannes von Reuchlin regarded the Kabbalah[49] and that the grammarian Elijah Baḥur familiarized Christian scholars with the Hebrew language and "held school at Rome and Venice."[50] He also displays great knowledge of Talmudic literature, and that he wrote elegant Hebrew is attested by the poem written in the well known *azharot*[51]-meter on the front page of the *Teryak*:

מומר — קם — מטוב ריקם — תפש הקם — מקרוב בא — וחדשים

יאפילו המאורות — זלזל התורות — מסיני נאמרות — כלפידים ורעשים.

הדפיס ספרים — עתק דוברים — כי נקלל השרים — ודתיהם מבישים. . .

On the basis of the author's remarks one may conjecture that he was a ritual slaughterer[52] and a circumciser.[53] But these professions, it appears, brought him a very scanty

---

by a Christian scholar named Wilfer, who published a Latin translation of Ufenhausen's work with many notes and comments. *Teryak* was reprinted for a third time in 1737 by Zussman ben Isaac Roedelsheim who further Yiddishized the language of the work somewhat, and in places changed purely German words into more Yiddish terms.

47. *Ibid.*, Chapter One, Section 20.
48. *Ibid.*, Chapter Two, Section 30.
49. *Ibid.*, Chapter One, Section 11.
50. *Ibid.*, Chapter Six, Section 2.
51. See our *History*, Vol. I, end of Chapter Two.
52. *Teryak*, Chapter Four, Section 12.
53. *Ibid.*, Section 23.

livelihood, and his wife and six children were not always well fed.

In the introduction the author tells at length for what reasons and under what circumstances he composed his work. A certain apostate, Samuel Friedrich Brenz of Ettingen, published in 1614 a rabid tract against the Jews and their religion entitled *Jüdischer abgestreifter Schlangen-Balg.*[54] Solomon Zalman Ufenhausen knew this apostate well and presents some biographical details about him. Brenz was a terrible usurer,[55] and if one added together all the horses on which he loaned money one could, Ufenhausen asserts, "put in the field" a regiment of riders. This, in fact, "brought him to baptism," for the Jews hated him for his ugly deeds and "pushed him away with both hands."[56] Brenz was a frightful ignoramus and in general a petty, good-for-nothing creature. His diatribe is written without any system or order.[57] Nevertheless, Ufenhausen relates, Brenz' talentless work had an effect on the rabble, and he therefore considered it necessary to declare publicly that *Schlangen-Balg* is filled with falsehoods and libels. When Brenz learned of this, he came riding in great wrath to Solomon Zalman Ufenhausen's dwelling, insulted him, and once again assured all and sundry that everything written in his work is nothing but truth and righteousness. Ufenhausen could not bear such a desecration of God's name. He told the author of *Schlangen-Balg* to his face that he was a shameless liar, and vowed to write a special book against all of Brenz's libels and falsehoods. Ufenhausen fulfilled his word, and in the following year his response, written in German, was already finished. In the same year he published his work in an abbreviated form in Yiddish under the title *Der Yidisher Teryak.*[58] Like *Schlangen-*

54. For the tract's complete title, which is enormously long, see Grünbaum, *op. cit.,* 560–561.
55. *Teryak,* Chapter Three, Section 11.
56. *Ibid.,* Chapter Six, Section 17.
57. Some notion of the wild confusion that prevails in Brenz's *Schlangen-Balg* may be given by the content-notation for the first chapter: "In the first chapter is a treatment of the blasphemies of the Jews, of magic with the Ineffable Name, and garlic eating on Christmas eve."
58. The author frequently mentions in *Teryak* the German work which he composed especially for Christian readers *(Ibid.,* Chapter One, Sections 2, 9, 13; Chapter Two, Section 27; Chapter Three, Section 11; Chapter Two, Section 4). It is very doubtful, however, whether the German text of Ufenhausen's polemic work appeared in print. In any case none of the bibliographers ever saw such a work with his own eyes. For a discussion of this, see N. Prylucki, in *YIVO-Bleter,* 1931, I, 423. *Der Yidisher Teryak* was translated into Hebrew, but the translation remained in manuscript.

Balg, the response to it is also divided into seven chapters. The author explains: "I present all his wickednesses word for word as he spoke them, and respond to all of them, great and small. But this ignorant apostate has written his work without any order, and all the subjects are mixed up . . . He jumbles everything together, and so I must also follow his lack of order."

From the scholarly point of view it is worthwhile to note the keenness and genuine historical sense with which the author endeavors to demonstrate[59] that the Jesus who is mentioned in a few passages of the Talmud has no relation whatever to the founder of the Christian religion, since the Jesus of the Talmud lived more than a hundred years before the age of Herod. It is not, however, in theological and scholarly matters that the chief interest of the *Yidisher Teryak* lies but in its polemical tone and in its secular, social character.

In accordance with the taste of that era, Solomon Ufenhausen is not chary of insults and epithets directed to his opponent, the ignorant author of *Schlangen-Balg*. Brenz's name Samuel is transformed in *Teryak* into Samael. He is also crowned with epithets such as the following: ignoramus, gross hooligan, disreputable bird, crude ass, crude tramp, water carrier, rogue, thief, wicked creature, etc. "In grammar," Ufenhausen asserts, "the author of *Schlangen-Balg* is as quick as an elephant." The apostate charges the Jews with kneading a *golem* out of clay and vivifying it through incantations and magic names. His opponent denies this. To be sure, he says, in the days of the sages of the Talmud such things did indeed occur, and perhaps such things occur at present in Palestine; but, he concludes sarcastically, "Our *golems* in *this* land we do not have from clay, but they are born from their mother's womb . . . and their father may have been a *baal shem*."[60] The apostate Brenz denounces the Jews for praying in the *Shemoneh Esreh:* "And for apostates let there be no hope." To this his adversary cold-bloodedly replies:

It is well known that one in a hundred lets himself be baptized for the sake of religion, except if he has himself committed some foul deed or intends to do it. As is daily experienced, apostates or converts abound in the lands of Germany like citrons *(etrogim)* in Muscovy. One lets himself be baptized because he wishes to eat pork; another is eager to be free of taxes; a third lusts after a Christian woman or hates his wife. One does it to provoke his family, and for many similar

59. *Teryak*, Chapter One, Section 7.
60. *Ibid.*, Chapter One, Section 13.

reasons they have themselves baptized. And when later the Christians grow tired of their baptismal children and are no longer willing to trust them, these make books or lampoons about us, as if to show thereby that they are good Christians. And if they are believed, they will make enmity for us among the Christians, in order to persecute us and drive us out.[61]

In the *Teryak* are many interesting details about the contemporary way of life. The author tells us about the role Jewish doctors played in such centers as Rome, Venice, Prague, and Constantinople. He notes that Christian midwives were often employed by Jewish mothers, and likewise that Jewish midwives were used in Christian homes. From the *Teryak* we learn that the Jewish populace in those days mainly utilized Christian barbers "in all places in the German and Welsh [Italian] lands." Especially interesting is the author's response to the charge that Jews live from usury:

You ask why. I tell you why. See, there is nothing in the world better than plowing fields. A farmer sows a measure of corn and reaps thirty fold from it. He has his bread assured, his cow, calves, butter, milk, fat, flour, meat, chickens, geese, and everything he needs. We Jews, however, have no land or strand, and must hope and wait for someone to give us something to buy. Concerning this the sages of the Talmud say that such a life cannot be called life . . . Lending money at interest was permitted us, but it produces for us great enmity, contempt, and much misery among the Christians. I would far rather that agriculture and all kinds of artisanries were allowed us and that we might leave compound interest alone. It makes expulsions and all kinds of misfortunes for us. Also we frequently forfeit both principal and interest. One ends up losing the money. In this respect the farmer or peasant is much better off and more secure, for no one can carry his field away . . . The fact that we were permitted to lend money at interest is like a piece of fat tied on a hook through which we are caught . . . And on this Scripture says, "And your life shall hang in doubt before you" (Deuteronomy 28:66). Lending money on interest is a curse and a chastisement, according to the Torah. It makes for us jealousy, hatred, contention, and anger. I would not expatiate; enough has been said about this for the person of understanding.[62]

In this writer of the beginning of the seventeenth century are already heard the same complaints that two hundred years later occupied such a prominent place among the battlers for

61. *Ibid.*, Chapter Four, Section 14.
62. *Ibid.*, Chapter Three, Section 11.

Haskalah. Solomon Ufenhausen realizes how abnormal and corrupt the economic foundations of the Jewish quarter are. He even concludes that in the external, Christian world not only is the economic situation more normal than in the ghetto, but the same is true of the spiritual realm. "The Christians," we read in the *Teryak*, "especially in these times . . . study diligently, and learning is highly esteemed among them. But among us, by reason of our sins, the opposite is the case. The Torah is put aside in a corner and counts very little. Always money, money! Money!—the whole world cries. . . . The rich man could study but does not wish to; the poor man would gladly study and cannot. Enough has been said about this for one who understands."[63]

Here we encounter the most interesting aspect of Ufenhausen's polemical work. The author of the *Teryak* is a skillful and temperamental polemicist. Nevertheless, it must be conceded that he does not always succeed in refuting his opponent's arguments and accusations. And at such times he endeavors to extricate himself through sophistical subtleties and explanations. We have frequently noted how, given the firm wall of venomous hatred and cold contempt with which the Christian world surrounded the ghetto, in the *Jewish* world also tendencies of isolation, the principle "It is a people that dwelleth alone," were strengthened. To hostility and calumny from the outside, the Jews responded from within with the same feelings. Hence the apostate Brenz charges his erstwhile brethren with having an attitude of hatred and contempt for the Christian world and the Christian religion. He mentions the verses that are said in the *Alenu* prayer by heart and that are concluded by spitting.[64] The apostate charges: Ask the smallest Jewish child,[65] and he will promptly tell you that the Christian church is called "an abomination." Of a deceased Christian it is said, "He has kicked off."[66] Holy water is called "unclean water."[67] Christ is called the hanged one, and the bastard born of uncleanness,[68] etc. The author of the *Teryak* here finds himself in the unfavorable situation of a battler whose hands are tied. He is, after all, unable to treat the question openly and comprehensively, and so he must resort to

63. *Ibid.*, Chapter Four, Section 7.
64. *Ibid.*, Chapter Five, Section 4.
65. *Ibid.*, Chapter Three, Section 17.
66. *Ibid.*, Chapter Four, Section 2.
67. *Ibid.*, Chapter Two, Section 25.
68. *Ibid.*, Chapter One, Section 3.

subtleties and evasions. Sometimes he gets off with silence. To Brenz's suggestion that the Jews in Poland and Bohemia kill informers or those who wish to convert, the *Teryak* replies: "I have never heard of this."[69] The ignorant Brenz had heard about the crude tract *Toledot Yeshu* which was spread abroad among Jews in many manuscripts,[70] but he did not know its proper name. Hence he called it *Maaseh Tola.* Consequently, the author of the *Teryak* pretends not to know anything about it, and declares: "I never in my life saw such a book." Brenz's charge that Jews call a church an abomination *(to'evah)* is refuted by the *Teryak* with the quibble that the apostate is mistaken; they do not say *to'evah* but *tevah* (ark). This derives from the phrase "one who goes down before the ark to pray." In a similar way he interprets the words *peger* (carcass), *mayyim teme'im* (unclean water), etc.

Max Grünbaum[71] and, after him, Max Erik[72] note that "a Yiddish edition of the *Teryak* was really not at all necessary," since "the Jewish readers by no means required that they be familiarized with all the slanders, stupidities and falsehoods of Brenz's *Schlangen-Balg.*" But that is not what the author intended with his *Yiddisher Teryak,* and he himself points this out at the end of the last chapter: "For the *benefit of the Jews* and at their desire, I also let it be printed in German in Hebrew letters, so that if cases arise, one should know how to answer Christians effectively, and also from it understand and realize what a great sin it is to defraud a Christian either in word or in deed." The much traveled Ufenhausen, who had a certain amount of education and had many Christian acquaintances in various lands, realized well how narrow and backward the world-view of the Jewish ghetto was. Not for polemic, apologetic goals but for purposes of enlightment did he publish his work in Yiddish. Ufenhausen utilized the apostate's charges to make clear to his readers that one ought to behave in the same way to all persons and be tolerant of the conceptions and views of those who believe differently from oneself. Brenz reproaches the Jews for not giving any alms to a Christian, for answering him with false words, and saying "*Lot* help you and burst" *(Lot helf dir un platz)* instead of "God help you in this

69. *Ibid.,* Chapter Three, Section 16.
70. In the Harkavy manuscript collection in the library in Leningrad of the Society for the Promotion of Enlightenment Among Jews, we found more than ten fragments of various Hebrew and Aramaic manuscripts of *Toledot Yeshu.*
71. *Op. cit.,* p. 561.
72. *Op. cit.,* p. 270.

place" *(Gott helf dir oyfn platz)*. Ufenhausen denies this and asserts that it is utter falsehood. But he also considers it an opportune time to instruct his reader that "all our books" stress "that we are obliged to give alms to Christians as much as to Jews . . . Everyone is obliged to feed and nourish people from the nations of the world as well as Jews." In this context he lets fly a barb: "Why should I write much that alms ought to be given to gentiles. Unfortunately, they do not give much to Jews, not even to a friend! Save us, O God of our salvation. Have mercy on the miserable poor. Give to the rich a heart of flesh, and take away the heart of stone."[73] Elsewhere Ufenhausen writes: "One must greet everyone, whether Jew or gentile, with sincerity and frankness, as the sages of the Talmud say in *Pirkei Avot*: 'Greet every man with peace.' This means: You must be diligent to greet all man and welcome them. Hence it says, *kol adam* (all men), so that there shall be no distinction between Jew and gentile, but all men equally."[74]

Similar thoughts are repeated by the author many times. Naturally, he understood quite well that such demands ought also to be addressed to the Christian world. But for this, in that age of discrimination and prejudice, the author of the *Yidisher Teryak* had neither the requisite courage nor the possibility.

73. *Teryak*, Chapter Four, Section 9.
74. *Ibid.*, Chapter Four, Section 4.

CHAPTER SEVEN

Folk-Tales;
THE *MAASEH-BUKH*

Story literature—From folk-tales to folk-literature—Rabbenu Nissim's *Ḥibbur Yafeh*—Handwritten collections of stories—The "wonderful story" of Meir the Ḥazzan—*Maaseh Beriah Ve-Zimrah*—The influence of the European romance and folk-literature—The *Maaseh-Bukh* and its significance—A tale of Regensburg—The fantastic tale about Rabbi Ḥaninah—The story about the Jewish pope—Yozpa Shammash's *Maaseh Nissim*—Marvelous and realistic tales—*Sefer Immanuel.*

T THE beginning of the previous chapter we noted that such paraphrastic versions of the Bible as *Tze'enah U-Re'enah* and *Di Lange Megile* combined two different literary genres which just at that time, at the end of the sixteenth century, formed the two major streams in Yiddish literature: morality books and story books. The narrative element, however, already made itself quite noticeable in the special morality books as well. Already in *Roizn-Gortn* and, to a greater degree in *Brantshpigl* and *Lev Tov*, ethical instruction is very frequently ornamented with tales and parables. This was by no means a new achievement; it was the continuation of the ancient, firmly established fashion. We noted in the first volume of our *History* how ingeniously the Jews of Europe in the Middle Ages took over the unique literary genre which was so admired in the lands of India and among the Arabs— the work that entertains, amuses, and at the same time also instructs and provides moral counsel, all with the aid of light ancedotes and lovely little tales. We also alluded there[1] to the fact, known to every cultural historian, of the importance of the mediating role of the Jews in the realm of European folk- lore. Themselves an Oriental people, familiar with the Arabic and Greek sources which had absorbed numerous Oriental and Indian legends, parables, and tales, the Jews were the connect- ing link and mediator between the eastern and western worlds in the Middle Ages.

The Jews, however, were not content with the role of the mediator through whom the European West became familiar with many Oriental motifs, with the treasures of the Indian and Persian-Greek tales and legends. The Jewish community produced its own legends and stories and spun tales about its beloved heroes with the golden threads of the most wonderful legends, interwoven with the loveliest hopes of speedy re- demption. It also modified and adapted to its taste and concep- tions the folkloristic material it had obtained as a legacy from previous generations. All this, however, remained mainly an "oral Torah," transmitted merely from mouth to mouth. Only by accident were some elements of this folkloristic material preserved, and this not in the vernacular but in Hebrew trans- lation and in the religious-ethical literature of that time, for instance, in the well known morality book *Sefer Ḥasidim*, in the historical chronicle *Sefer Yuḥasin*, and in the medieval Midra- shim, such as *Tanna De-Be Eliahu, Midrash Aseret Ha-Dibberot*,[2] and many others.

There have also been preserved in Hebrew manuscripts sev- eral stories, for example, the lovely tale of King Solomon and the ant,[3] the story of the two faithful friends *(Maaseh Bi-Shenei Anashim)*,[4] and the story about the Jewish pope.[5] Special collec- tions of tales and legends have also been preserved, for in- stance, *Meshalim Shel Shelomoh Ha-Melech*,[6] deriving from the

1. Vol. I, pp. 185ff. See also our article "Vegn Di Mekorim Fun Maaseh-Bukh" (*Literarishe Bleter*, 1927, No. 131).
2. In this Midrash there is a whole collection of seventeen tales.
3. First published in *Bet Ha-Midrash*, V, 22–26.
4. Published by Menaḥem de Lonzano at the end of *Maarich*.
5. *Bet Ha-Midrash*, V, 148–152; *Ibid.*, VI, 137–139.
6. *Bet Ha-Midrash*, IV, 145–152.

Middle Ages, and the collection composed in Arabic by Solomon Ibn Gabirol's older contemporary, the renowned Rabbenu Nissim of Kairouan.[7] To console his son-in-law Dunash who lost a beloved son, Rabbenu Nissim wrote for him (around 1030) a special collection of stories. This collection was soon reworked into Hebrew in two versions,[8] one under the title *Ḥibbur Yafeh Meha-Yeshuah* (first issued in Ferrara, 1557) and the second *Ma'asiyyot Sheba-Talmud* (first published in Constantinople, 1519). Much more interesting for medieval folklore is another collection of stories and legends that Israel Lévi first published in modern times.[9] Neither the name of the anthologist nor the time when the anthology was written down have been established, but it is indubitable that this anthology derives from the German provinces. Besides many stories taken from the Talmud and the Midrashim, it also contains narratives of the later era in which the influence of west European folklore is strongly discernible. The anthologist apparently was not an expert Hebrew stylist, and in his language many Germanisms or, more correctly, Yiddishisms[10] are noticeable. In this lies the strongest proof that the collector heard these stories from the mouth of the people in their *lingua franca* and translated them into Hebrew for his anthology.

Books of tales in the vernacular were first produced after the revolution which the printing press called forth in the cultural life of the people in Germany. We noted earlier that it was the printing press that first managed to separate the poem from the melody, to erect a wall between literary creativity and music, between the word and the song. Medieval knightly poetry in its essence was *oral*.[11] The knight generally could not write or read, and songs and poems were not read by him and his household but *listened to* as the jongleur and *Spielmann* declaimed them. The urban citizen class—the merchant, the shopkeeper, even the artisan—had to be able to read, write, and

---

7. Fragments of the Arabic original were published in modern times by Harkavy in the *Steinschneider-Festschrift*, 9–27.
8. In modern times Rabbenu Nissim's collection also appeared in Yiddish—the first edition in 1815, and the second in Warsaw (1837), under the following title-page: "*Sippurei Maasiyyot* of Rabbenu Nissim bar Jacob which he wrote for his son-in-law Dunash in order to comfort his sorrowing heart, as is stated in the introduction."
9. *REJ*, XXXIII, XXXIV.
10. In it one encounters, for instance, expressions such as the following: *yoda'at at li-lemod* (REJ, 32, 238); *zeh ha-shaar yesh me-roshah* (ibid., 245); *ehyeh shalit u-moshel me-otah ir* (ibid., 74); *lo hayah la-ani shum davar mi-mah li-k'not ḥittim* (ibid., 35, 68); *ve-tihyeh yoresh mi-kol asher li* (ibid., 79); etc.
11. See above, Chapter I, p. 27.

figure in connection with their livelihood, and this in the language of daily life. Not through listening but through reading did the urban citizen satisfy his cultural requirements, and when the printing press enormously democratized the book, there suddenly appeared in great quantity narrative reading material in the form of chapbooks or popular books in which the masses of stories, legends, anecdotes, and jests with which the imagination of the people adorned certain heroes and personalities with special affection was assembled. The same phenomenon was replicated in the Jewish quarter. The rich narrative material which previously lived in the mouth of the people was written down in the sixteenth century and spread among the broad strata of the population through the printing press.

We noted previously,[12] and will therefore not dwell on it here, that many of the German popular books which had just appeared were soon reprinted virtually without change in Hebrew letters for the Jewish reading public. Such editions can have only a cultural-historical, not a literary interest, for they do not in fact belong to the history of Jewish literature and style.

The oldest stories in Yiddish that have been preserved derive from the beginning of the sixteenth century. The scholars of literature Max Weinreich[13] and Max Erik[14] have described a Cambridge manuscript in which three Yiddish stories are written down. Each story derives from a different city—one from Danzig, one from Mainz, and one from Worms. The first tells of a Jewish woman, a beautiful seamstress in Danzig, who was separated from her husband. The latter went away to a distant country. The woman arrived in the same country disguised in men's clothing. The king's daughter became sick with love for her, and a match was arranged between the two. In the meantime the lovely seamstress found her husband, and the latter came to the bride on the wedding night instead of her. In the morning the seamstress fled with her husband on a galley, laden with the king's treasure, and they lived happily ever afterward.

The second story tells of two brothers of two different mothers who set out into the world to test which one of them would marry the most beautiful maiden in Mainz. One brother swindles, robs, and blinds the other. Nevertheless, the latter

12. See above, p. 50.
13. *Bilder*, 1928, 143–144.
14. *Geshikhte*, 343–344.

miraculously recovers his sight, grows rich, and returns as the lord of Mainz. No one knows that he is a Jew. On the day of the wedding he expels his murderous brother-in-law and marries the beautiful bride.

The most interesting of the three is the last story about a son of the rabbi of Worms. Once on *Lag Be-Omar* some boys were playing hide-and-seek. The rabbi's son, who was taking part in the game, looked for his comrade in a hollowed-out tree, saw a hand stretched out from the hidden recesses, thought it was his comrade, and in jest recited the marriage blessing with a ring over the hand. The owner of the hand, however, was a female demon who was hidden in the tree and took the ring. Later, on the young man's bridal night, she came and killed his wife. His second wife also perished in the same way. Only his third bride, a poor girl, pleaded with the female demon and was spared her life on the condition that her husband spend one hour each day with the demon. Once the wife found her husband with the demon at the stipulated hour sunk in deep sleep. The wife, a modest woman, tenderly laid the demon's long hair on the bench. The demon jumped up with great anger but was moved by the woman's courtesy. She surrendered the ring and disappeared.

This last story was extremely popular in the Jewish quarter. We encounter it later in the collection *Maaseh Nissim*, where the demon is transformed into the Queen of Sheba. The melancholy author of *Kav Ha-Yashar*, Tzevi Hirsh Koidonover, also introduced it into his morality book as a true story that took place in Posen.[15]

It is easy to see that all these stories do not carry a prominently Jewish coloration. The motifs were very probably taken from the external environment and reworked in Jewish fashion. Such stories have a very definite purpose: to amuse and entertain. But a quite different character pertains to the "wonderful story" about Rabbi Meir the *ḥazzan*, or precentor.[16]

---

15. See our *History*, Vol. VI, pp. 161ff.

16. Preserved in a manuscript deriving from no later than the beginning of the sixteenth century. The oldest printed edition that has been preserved is from 1694. It is beyond doubt, however, that there was a still older edition. Testimony to this is provided by the rabbi of Prague Rabbi Elijah bar Benjamin Shapira, who lived in the first half of the eighteenth century, in his *Eliahu Rabbah* (see L. Landshuth, *Ammudei Ha-Avodah*, 165). Both texts together, along with a critical-historical introduction, were reprinted by I. Rivkind in *Filologishe Shriftn*, III. However, it is difficult to agree with Rivkind, who endeavors to find a historical kernel in this legend.

This "wonderful story" is based on an historical date: "It was in the year that is written 5121 [1361]." So the story begins. The hero of the narrative is also a historical personality—the renowned Rabbi Meir ben Isaac Nehorai, the author of the popular Targum-poem *Akdamut*. However, he lived three hundred years earlier, in the generation before Rashi, and died in 1096. Rabbi Meir acquired great renown with his liturgical hymns and *seliḥot*.[17] He also wrote commentaries that are quoted by Rashi himself with great respect,[18] and composed a custumal which is frequently mentioned by the Maharil and many other eminent rabbis.[19] His numerous liturgical hymns and *seliḥot*, and also the manner and style in which he, as precentor, used to recite before the people his own prayers as well as those of others, made him extremely popular in the communities of Mainz and Worms, where he spent most of his life. Around his name a whole garland of legends was woven by the popular imagination, and in this way he became to later generations the hero of the wonderful "tale" about the wicked monk, the oppressor of Israel and sorcerer, and the little red Jew from the other side of the river Sambatyon.[20]

The plot of the story is as follows. In the time of King Martin de Lance "magic and sorcery increased in the world." Some of these magicians "made themselves monks with long cassocks." These monk-magicians "built castles and cloisters and lived in them." "Here they ruled the world at that time, and it could not be known who they were; they were able to bring to themselves all the most beautiful women and maidens that they knew." The greatest magician among them was a "black monk," a rabid enemy of the Jews. He would place every Jew whom he encountered under a spell with a simple touch of the hand, and the Jew would fall down and die as soon as he came home. In this way the black monk destroyed over thirty thousand Jews through magic. The leaders of the Jewish community dispatched a delegation to the emperor, begging him to protect them from their enemy. The emperor summoned the

---

17. On Rabbi Meir ben Isaac's work, see *Zunz, Literaturgeschichte*, 146–151, 248–250; *Synagogale Poesie*, 187–188; Landshuth, *Ammudei Ha-Avodah*, 162–167.
18. A. Geiger, *Nit'ei Ne'emanim*, 8.
19. Landshuth, *op. cit.*, 162, and A. Epstein in *Kaufmann-Gedenkbuch*, 291.
20. The "wonderful tale" about the emissary of the "little red Jews" who rescues the Jewish community from a terrible sorcerer-monk is also to be found, even though in another version, in the medieval Hebrew legends. See the legend "Ha-Tzayyad Veha-Of" in *Haggadot Ketu'ot* that Louis Ginzberg published in *Ha-Goren*, IX (Berlin, 1923).

black monk and, after long arguments, the latter declared that he would give the Jews a year's time in the course of which they must put forward a Jew who shall be more skillful than he in the realm of trickery and magic. If the Jews fulfill this condition, he promises them that he will do them no more harm; if not, he will kill them all, even if he himself dies in the process. The Jews had no alternative but to agree. First of all they betook themselves to their tried weapon; they decreed fasting, penitence, prayer, and charity. Afterwards letters were dispatched throughout the dispersions of Israel and inquiries were made about a miracle worker who might, with the aid of divine names, be able to overcome the fearful magician. But such a miracleworker did not appear. It happened, however, that a certain scholar of that time "fell asleep over his study" and in his dream he saw that the required person would not be found "either in this land or in Palestine, but you must travel beyond the river Sambatyon." There dwell the exiled Ten Tribes "who are masters of names and will come to your aid, so that the persecution will come to an end. They are called *benei moshi'im*, as the Scriptural verse says: 'And saviors (*moshi'im*) shall go up to Mount Zion' (Obadiah 21). This means the red Jews will come and help us in Zion." Thereupon the Jews sent for counselors to decide who should be dispatched to the *benei moshi'im*. "All agreed on Rabbi Meir, who was a great scholar and a pious man and always served the community for good. And they provided him with sufficient victuals and three pious rabbis who traveled with him."

After long trials the party arrived at the river Sambatyon precisely eight days before the end of the year that the black monk had stipulated. However, it was Tuesday, and they therefore had to wait until the Sabbath, when the Sambatyon rests and does not cast up stones. On the Sabbath Rabbi Meir told his companions to remain there, for "why should we all desecrate the Sabbath?" He alone sat down in the ship and set out over the Sambatyon to the little red Jews, the Ten lost Tribes of Israel. Upon his arrival, they immediately incarcerated him, because he "had desecrated the Sabbath." But he showed them the letter that the community sent with him, and thus they learned of the decree. They promptly released Rabbi Meir from prison and cast lots to determine who of them should desecrate the Sabbath and set out on a ship to help a community of Jews in distress. The lot fell on a little red Jew with a limp named Dan. The little red Jew explained to Rabbi Meir that he must remain with them, so that he should not desecrate the Sabbath a second time—and this deliberately. So Rabbi Meir remained forever among the red Jews on the other side of the Sambatyon. The little red Jew with the limp immediately sat down on the ship, sailed over the Sambatyon, and on the other side found the three rabbis. With the help of incantations the limping Dan managed, through foreshortening of the way, to arrive with his companions at Worms in the course of two days precisely at the end of the stipulated time. When the community saw the lame little man from the other side of the river Sambatyon they were beside themselves with terror; they could not believe that such a weak creature would be able to overcome the fearful magician, the black monk. At this point comes the most dramatic part of the tale. In the presence of the emperor and of an enormously large crowd ("the Jews stood around on the square, and the other peoples above") the contest between the monk and the little red Jew took place. The monk was aided in the contest by all kinds of demons and evil spirits, but the little red Jew, with the aid of divine names, nullified all his tricks and magic. The monk perished, the community was saved, and the joy of the people was boundless. The day of salvation was the day before Shavuot. The little red Jew told the community of Worms that on the Sabbath on which he set out on the boat, Rabbi Meir accompanied him and on the way sang for him a song which he had just composed and requested him to recite this song, which begins with the words *Akdamut Millin*, before the community. He also informed them that Rabbi Meir wished that the community each Shavuot at its prayers should "for the sake of his name, sing this song," because it is signed with his name: Rabbi Meir bar Rabbi Yitzḥak Gadol Ba-Torah Uve-Maasim Tovim Amen Ḥazak Ve-Amatz (Rabbi Meir the son of Rabbi Isaac, great in Torah and good deeds, Amen; be strong and of good courage). The story ends with two weddings. The little red Jew remained in the community of Worms, for he could not return to his home out of fear of desecrating the Sabbath, and he married Rabbi Meir's daughter. Rabbi Meir remained among the little red Jews and took Dan's grownup daughter as his wife.

This *wunderbare geschichtnis* is a typical medieval folktale, of the kind that used to be transmitted by the hundreds from mouth to mouth. And when, as a result of the printing press, the popular book was produced, this story was written down and brought into print. A very different character is borne by another story, more accurately, a novella, which has also been preserved in manuscript from the sixteenth century. This is *Maaseh Beriah Ve-Zimrah*, a story of a love that is stronger than death and to which God Himself gives His blessing.

A valuable contribution was made by Max Erik who first critically explored both versions of this remarkably beautiful novella and reprinted the older text that has been preserved.[21] This text is in a Munich manuscript (No. 100) written, along with several other items, by Isaac Reutlingen in 1580. There is no doubt, however, that Reutlingen merely copied from an older, probably printed edition. That Reutlingen is not the author of the novella is to be seen from the beginning of the narrative, where a complete confusion of names occurs. There "one called Hyrcanus" is mentioned. From the later text, how-ever, it is difficult to know who this Hyrcanus was and what relationship he has in general to the whole narrative. Only from the Venetian edition (1597) does one learn that Hyrcanus was Zimrah's grandfather. It is also indicated in Reutlingen's manuscript that Zimrah was the son of Tovat, but immediately afterward it is related that the king spoke "to his two sons Tovat and Zimrah." It is clear that Isaac Reutlingen copied from an older text of which the first page was defective, with blanks in some places. Later on, in the middle of the story, after the heroine of the novella enters Paradise, unexpectedly comes the following remark with stresses on each word: "Whoever does not believe this is also a Jew." It is clear that this skeptical remark belongs to the copyist Isaac Reutlingen, not the author. At the end, following the close of the narrative, there is again a statement of the copyist which begins with the words: "Now dear people, you have read in the *little book.*" Evidentally the copyist had before him a printed chapbook.

The story of the novella is as follows. The young Zimrah ben Tovat is greatly loved by the king of the Jews in Jerusalem and occupies a very honored position at his court. Zimrah and his father are once invited, along with the king, to a banquet at the house of the high priest Feigin.[22] There Zimrah sees Feigin's daughter Beriah "whose beauty is not to be described, and so I must refrain from doing so." The young couple fall deeply in love and pledge their troth to each other. Zimrah tells his father of his great love for the high priest's daughter, and so Tovat sends four officials to the high priest to request his con-

---

21. See M. Erik in *Landau-Bukh*, 153–162. Also Erik, *Vegn Alt-Yidishn Roman*, 147–172, and *Geshikhte*, 347–353.

22. In the Venetian edition the high priest has a Biblical name—Athaliah.

sent to the match. As in the romance *Paris un Viene*, here also the motive of family-pedigree appears as an obstacle. The high priest is an extremely arrogant and conceited man and tells the officials that he is not favorably disposed toward the match with Zimrah ben Tovat. The king, who greatly loves Zimrah, intervenes. Twice he summons the high priest and proposes Zimrah as a groom for Beriah. The arrogant high priest, however, is obdurate. "Dear king," he declares, "do you advise me to enter into a marriage with someone of lower class than my own? All the Jews will mock me." He would rather drown his daughter than marry her to a social inferior. In the meantime, the lovers see each other quite frequently in the high priest's house when all go to pray in the synagogue, and they "kiss each other a thousand times."

"After these things," the pope of Rome, who was a very wicked man, decreed that Jewish women may not go to the ritual bath and that Jews are forbidden to circumcise their children. In addition, the wicked pope would not allow any Jewish intercessors to come to him, and the gatekeepers were ordered to kill any Jew who would cross his threshold. Here the high priest finds a suitable occasion to be rid of Zimrah. He proposes to Zimrah that he go as an intercessor to the pope, and if he prevails upon the pontiff to nullify the grievous decree, he will have his daughter Beriah as a reward. The high priest is certain that the young man will not emerge from his mission alive. Zimrah, however, does not pass as a very clever man for nothing. He manages to gain access to the pope and to persuade him that the greatest evil from his decree will result not for the Jews but for the Christians. The pope marvels at Zimrah's wisdom, promptly annuls the decree, and presents him with many gifts. Zimrah returns home in great triumph. The stubborn high priest, however, breaks his word and refuses to give Zimrah his daughter. The meeting of the lovers is poignant. Weeping, they embrace each other, "and he kisses her, and she kisses him; it was such a kissing that if she was not beautiful before, she became beautiful now." Shortly after this, Beriah dies of grief.

Here suddenly the plot of the romantic novella, which until now had been realistic, assumes fantastic colors. After Beriah's death, a mysterious horse leads the grieving Zimrah to the other world. With the aid of prayer he goes through the *sher messer* or sharp knife, wanders through a house filled with corpses, and finally sees "his lovely, dear Beriah" sitting under the steps. This is a kind of punishment for the fact that she kissed him so many times. "Dear Zimrah," she says to her beloved, "I committed no sin on earth other than permitting you to kiss me." She warns him that he must not touch her, else he will have to die on the third day thereafter. Their love, however, is stronger than death. "I shall kiss you, and so I will die and remain with you here." He kisses Beriah and prays that she may no longer have to remain in torture. At once she passes over into Paradise. At parting Beriah declares to Zimrah: "Go home again and tell your father and my father: whether my father likes it or not, you will have me. He would not give me to you when I was alive; so he must endure your having me in the next world without his receiving silver and gold." Hereupon Elijah the prophet appears. He takes Zimrah by the hand, comforts him by saying "You have committed no sin," and leads him out of the yonder world. On the third day Zimrah dies. The angels Michael and Gabriel bear the dead Zimrah away to Paradise, "for he had never committed any sin." In Paradise his marriage with "his most beloved Beriah" is celebrated with great pomp. "The Holy One Blessed Be He recited the benediction, and the angels were the wedding jesters. Moses and Aaron led the bride and groom under the canopy. Afterwards they ate and drank and danced, and King Solomon recited the Seven Benedictions. It was a costly wedding such as has never been in any community."

Several scholars have rightly noted that in this novella the influence of the European romance and chapbook literature is strongly discernible. Testimony to this is provided even by the odd name of the high priest in the older version. Feigin certainly appears to be the corrupted Romance name Voeign. Many details of the second, fantastic part of the narrative—the mysterious horse, the sharp knife, etc.—undoubtedly derive from the German circle of romances and legends. The motif of the beloved finding his loved one at the gates of Hell and freeing her therefrom reminds one of the famous Greek legend of the inspired artist Orpheus.

The central motif, the dramatic, dynamic nerve of the whole novella—namely, the mighty love that triumphs over even the thirst for life and annihilates the wildest stubbornness, along with pride in family distinction—is certainly taken from the foreign milieu of chivalry. The material borrowed from alien sources, however, obtains a Jewish vestment and is interwoven with national Jewish motifs drawn from the rich treasure of Jewish folktales. For example, the motif about the pope with his oppressive decrees against the Jews is repeated in Jewish folk legend in different versions. From the variegated material the anonymous Jewish author managed to create a genuine work of art. He understood how to carry through his major motif that was not altogether acceptable in the medieval environment—celebration of the love that is stronger than death—artistically and modestly. Beriah, indeed, dies after kissing Zimrah, but she herself declares beforehand that she knows she will soon have to die "out of suffering," grief over the fact that her father separates her from Zimrah. With a pious mien the author admonishes: "Therefore let no one kiss anyone." But he himself weakens this admonition with the addition: "When one goes away from another." Beriah finds herself in the "hollow of the sling" because she permitted Zimrah to kiss her, but Elijah the prophet himself assures Zimrah: "You have not committed any sin." Zimrah binds himself to Beriah through kissing her, and the angels Michael and Gabriel at once bring him to Paradise "to his most beloved Beriah" precisely because "he had not committed any sin."

The love poem concludes harmoniously with the description of the extraordinary wedding such as "has never been in any community." The most characteristic thing here is that this wedding description, which bears such a typically Jewish national vesture, was borrowed from the outside and is undoubtedly under the influence of the closing scene of the novella that was extremely popular in the Middle Ages, "Cupid and Psyche," preserved in the *Golden Ass* of Apuleius.[23] There the hostile power which separates the lovers is the jealousy of Psyche's sister and Cupid's mother, Venus. However, love triumphs. Psyche is taken up to heaven, and a joyous wedding is celebrated. The god Vulcan was the waiter. The Oreads pelted everyone with red roses and other flowers. The Graces sprayed all the guests with spices and incense. Apollo sang with the harp in his hand. The lovely Venus danced to the beat of sweet music. All accompanied each other. The Muses played on flutes, and the Pans and Satyrs on drums and other instruments. So with great pomp Psyche was given to Cupid.[24]

Precisely this interweaving of foreign motifs with Jewish national motifs, the artistic reworking of alien material into a Jewish fashion, is quite frequently encountered in the most

23. He lived in the second century of the Christian era. His famous work is called in Latin *Metamophoseon Libri XI (De asino aureo)*.
24. See our article in *YIVO-Bleter*, Vol. III, 332–33.

important treasure of Jewish folktales and novellas that has been preserved in Old-Yiddish literature—the *Maaseh-Bukh*.

The oldest printed edition of the *Maaseh-Bukh* that has come down to us, and this only in three copies, appeared in Basel in 1602. The publisher was the book-peddler Jacob ben Abraham of Mezhirech who published several books at Basel in the period 1598–1603. On the title-page we read:

A beautiful storybook. Come here, dear men and women, and examine this lovely storybook which, since the world has existed, has never appeared in print. With three hundred and some stories, all of which are made out of the *Gemara*, and also tales out of the *Midrash Rabbah* and Bahya, and none of the stories of Rabbi Jehudah the Pious will you miss. Also tales out of *Sefer Hasidim* and *Sefer Musar* and the *Yalkut*, as you will see in the back in my listing. Therefore, dear women, before you had the German books; now you will also have the German *Gemara*. So you will also have the entire Torah.

No less typical is the prayer printed on the other side of the title-page:

Glory to God alone, Blessed Be His Name, who helped me realize the desire which I long ago undertook to serve pious women. I have now composed many books, but all of them are nothing in comparison with this one. For from it will read rabbis and rabbis' wives and every man. Even if one knows much *Gemara*, he will bring out of it midrashim and stories and legends, so that the whole world will be astonished at him and every man will say: "I believe he knows the whole Torah on one foot. As he has such great erudition in the Gemara, I believe he knows the whole Torah. Who has seen his like?" To every situation he gives a law to be carried out in practice applicable to the case. At times one will encounter a tale that will make him abandon his bad thoughts and bad deeds. For many a parable and tale teaches persons much good; it keeps many a man with God and with honor. Therefore, dear men and women, read frequently from it; so you will be edified by it and not read from the book of cows [*Ku-Bukh*]. And by *Dietrich von Bern* and *Meister Hildebrant* you shall also not let yourselves be entertained, for they are truly nothing but dirt. They give you neither warmth nor heat. Also they are not godly. You well require that God forgive you. Our sacred books write that it is a sin as big as a house to read from them on the holy Sabbath day. If you wish to spend your time reading, I will write a lovely storybook. Therefore, dear women, buy it quickly before it goes away into foreign lands—to Bohemia, White Russia, and Poland. So they will eagerly fetch them to still other lands. Therefore buy them. Later you will say: Why did I not buy any when it was in the land? Now I would gladly pay, when I cannot even get one. Therefore, let it not be too expensive for you at one thaler. So God will keep you from all things evil and terrible. Amen. Selah.

The magisterial Steinschneider noted in 1866[25] that the Basel edition of 1602 is not the *editio princeps* of the *Maaseh-Bukh*, despite the fact that on the title-page from which we have quoted above it is noted that "never since the world has existed, has it been brought into print;" for immediately afterwards we read on the same title-page: "three hundred and some stories, all of which are made from the *Gemara*," whereas the Basel edition contains a total of only 257 stories. Apparently the publisher of the Basel edition, Jacob ben Abraham, abbreviated the first edition and did not print all the tales, but left the title-page unchanged and only at the end noted the names of the publisher and printer.[26] Many years later Steinschneider conjectured that the *Maaseh-Bukh* was first printed no earlier than 1550.[27] This is not quite correct. In the form of the Basel edition, the *Maaseh-Bukh* was produced no earlier than the 1580's, for Max Grünbaum[28] and, after him, Max Erik[29] have shown that the last editor of the Basel *Maaseh-Bukh* undoubtedly utilized Jacob ben Isaac Luzzatto's work *Kaftor Va-Ferah*[30] which appeared in Basel in 1580.[31]

The report of the well known bibliographer Benjacob that the author of the *Maaseh-Bukh* is Asher Anshel Lezer Hazzan of Poland who spent most of his life in Germany is absolutely unfounded. The origin of the *Maaseh-Bukh* has, for the time being, not yet been cleared up. It is obvious, however, that one cannot here raise the question of an author, but only of an editor.

We noted previously that there were preserved from the Middle Ages special collections of stories and legends in He-

25. *Serapeum*, 1866, 11–12.
26. "At the command of Jacob bar Abraham, may the memory of the righteous be for blessing, of the holy community of Mezhirech in Lithuania, here in Basel in the year 1602, by Master Konrad Waldkirch."
27. *JQR*, 1904, 761.
28. *Jüdisch-deutsche Chrestomathie*, 449–453.
29. *Literarishe Bleter*, 1927, No. 22, 412; *Geshikhte*, 360–361.
30. See our *History*, Vol. IV, p. 123.
31. Jacob Meitlis, in his monograph *Das Ma'asebuch*, published in 1933 in German, rejects Steinschneider's conjecture that the Basel edition of 1602 is an abbreviated reprint of an earlier edition. Meitlis attempts to show (pp. 29, 31, 46, 122) that the Basel edition of the *Maaseh-Bukh* is indeed the *editio princeps*.

brew. Also in such works as *Sefer Ḥasidim, Sefer Sha'ashuim,* etc.,
folktales are collected in very considerable number, and many
of these are to be found in the *Maaseh-Bukh* as well. Moreover,
Yiddish manuscripts of the sixteenth century in which a certain number of folk stories that we also encounter in the *Maaseh-Bukh* are contained, e.g., the previously mentioned Munich
manuscript No. 100, in which Isaac Reutlingen wrote down
twenty-two stories of which only two are missing from the
Maaseh-Bukh, have come down to us.

Certainly the editor of this collection had before him
finished building material. All these stories collected by him
were taken from printed and written sources, as well as from
some transmitted orally. But he was "the right man in the right
place," a truly masterful editor. The material he assembled was
highly variegated. He drew most of his stories from the Talmudic and Midrashic literature, but he also derived much from
medieval European folklore, as well as from the special Jewish
folklore. From Gedaliah Ibn Yaḥya's *Shalshelet Ha-Kabbalah,*
which was published around the same time as the *Maaseh-Bukh,*
we see the rich cycle of legends with which the popular imagination adorned its beloved heroes, great Jews such as Abraham
Ibn Ezra, Jehudah Halevi, Rashi, Naḥmanides, Jehudah Ḥasid,
Eleazar of Worms, and others. These legends, which passed
from mouth to mouth and from generation to generation, are
also well represented in the *Maaseh-Bukh,* and this varied and
colorful material is harmoniously put together and transmitted
in a unitary, simple, popular style. Everything breathes the
same atmosphere. The knights and heroes of the tales borrowed from the outside world are transformed into pious and
righteous men. The great exploits are performed not by the
mighty hand armed with sword and spear, but by the divine
"name" and the heartfelt prayer. And all this is placed in a
framework of pious moral lessons, showing how well it is with
one who follows the right way and performs God's precepts
and good deeds. Certainly not all the reworkings belong to the
editor himself, but he was endowed in rich measure with the
popular sensitivity for choosing from the different versions the
most tender and substantial.

It is for this reason that the tales collected in the *Maaseh-Bukh*
have such great interest. If one compares any of these stories
with the old Jewish sources that treat the same material, the
well of folk-creativity is disclosed; one sees clearly how in the
identical milieu, the same motive, the same story, is gradually
changed and grows through the addition of new details, while

other details are removed. For example, the well-known story of *Yosef Mokir Shabbat* (Joseph who respected the Sabbath), which is given briefly and aridly in the Talmudic tractate *Shabbat* and in the old Hebrew sources *Hibbur Yafeh* and *Sippur Ha-Maasiyyot*, is retold in the *Maaseh-Bukh* in far more vivid and popular colors.[32] In many other stories the theme becomes more complex, and it happens not infrequently that a legend from the Talmud or other sources is here interwoven as a side episode. So, for instance, in the story of the testament which the pious man left to his three sons, a legend from the Talmud (*Sanhedrin*, 104) and a story from Rabbenu Nissim's collection (*Hibbur Yafeh*, 38, according to the Amsterdam edition, 1746) are utilized as extraneous details. Legends from the Talmud and Midrashim are also frequently forged with foreign, Oriental legends, e.g., the Indian story of the peasant who had pity on the half-frozen serpent is interwoven in the *Maaseh-Bukh* with the motifs of *Mishlei Shelomoh Ha-Melech*, and the peasant and serpent come for judgment to the sagacious King Solomon. Some of the stories are also extremely interesting by virtue of the fact that in them is reflected very clearly the stifling atmosphere of terror in the Jewish ghetto of the Middle Ages. Typical in this respect is the following story which belongs to the *Maasim Rabbi Yuda*, i.e., the cycle of legends that recount the praises of Rabbi Jehudah Hasid (Judah the Pious).

A story that happened in Regensburg. There were two bricklayers who worked at the house of a Jew in the Jewish street, and as they worked there they saw in the Jew's room much silver and gold. Thereupon they conspired to ascend together into the room while the Jews were in the synagogue and take everything away. And so they did, entering the room and taking many objects of silver and gold. Here one of the bricklayers bethought himself: "What need have I of my comrade? I will arrange it all myself." And he went and struck his comrade, who was crawling out of a hole, with a hammer on the head, so that he fell down into the room dead. He took the silver and gold from the dead man and ran away with it. Now all the Jews were in the synagogue, and when they came out, the owner of the house found a corpse lying in his room. They were greatly frightened, as they well should have been. They wished to remove the body in secret, for they were afraid of an attack, God forbid, as indeed almost happened. The people in the gentile quarter learned that the

32. It is worthwhile to compare this tale as it is related in the *Maaseh-Bukh* with the version in *Midrash Aseret Ha-Dibberot*.

Jew had killed a gentile, and many of them came running into the Jewish streets and were about to start a riot. Then came Rabbi Jehudah Ḥasid and ran swiftly to the burgomaster and said: "Sir, what will you do here? Will you, because of one dead man, destroy so many people, seeing that you know well that we have not done it? For the two men worked there, and I will prove to you that one killed the other." The burgomaster said to him: "If you will prove it to me, no harm will befall any of you." And he bade the gentiles[33] remain quiet for a time in the streets. Then Rabbi Jehudah Ḥasid spoke: "Let the gates of the city be closed, so that the murderer shall not be able to run away." This was immediately done. Then Jehudah Ḥasid wrote an amulet with holy names and placed it in the hand of the slain man. The slain man thereupon arose and looked about for the murderer. He saw him hiding behind another man. He ran up to him and said: "You murderer! You destroyed my life, and you did it so that you might have what was stolen all to yourself, and you went and struck me on the head with a hammer so that I fell down again into the room."[34] Thereupon they took the murderer and put him in prison and he was immediately condemned to death and executed. Then the pious Rabbi Jehudah said to the burgomaster: "See now, if I had not restrained you, you would have shed much innocent blood." The burgomaster replied: "Quite true. Therefore, dear master, forgive me. It will not happen again. If some such thing occurs in the future, I will first establish the facts of the situation." Now the dead man had many rich friends, who begged the pious rabbi to let him live, in payment for which they would give him a great deal of money. But this was not his intention, for he said that he was not permitted to do it. So he took the amulet away from the slain man, who again fell down like a corpse. And the burgomaster did Rabbi Jehudah much good thereafter.

One of the loveliest stories in the *Maaseh-Bukh* is the remarkable folktale about the righteous Rabbi Ḥaninah. It is difficult to say how this novella appeared in the Jewish quarter. In the old sources there is no mention of it. We encounter it only in the Hebrew manuscript collection that Israel Lévi published[35] (here the righteous man is called Joḥanan), but in another version. Many details in this version are recounted quite differently than in the *Maaseh-Bukh*, and several other details are

33. In some editions the word is Samaritans *(Kutim)*.
34. This motif of reviving a slain person through incantations before a court and having that person reveal the true murderer to the judges was very popular in antiquity among the Oriental peoples. It is already utilized by Apuleius in his *Golden Ass*.
35. In *REJ*, XXXIII, 239–254.

lacking completely. Apparently both sources drew the novella directly from the mouth of the people. The story is an extremely complicated one, full of fantastic events.

In Palestine[36] there lived a well-to-do Jew who had an only son named Ḥaninah. Before his death the father gave instructions in his testament to Ḥaninah directing the latter to study Torah day and night and support the poor generously. Then the father told the son that as soon as he arose from the seven days of mourning, he should go into the marketplace and buy whatever is first offered him. Ḥaninah fulfilled everything that his father directed him to do. As soon as he had completed the seven days of mourning, he went to the marketplace. Someone there put before him a silver vessel at a price of eighty gulden, and he bought it. He brought the vessel home, placed it on the table, and opened it. Inside it he found another vessel, and there he discovered a living frog. He nurtured the frog, providing it with food and drink. The frog grew daily, and the vessel became too narrow for it. Ḥaninah then made a chest for it, and when this also became too small for the frog, he built a small room for it. The frog continued to eat until it had consumed everything Rabbi Ḥaninah owned. Ḥaninah and his wife then said to the frog: "Dear friend, we can no longer feed you."[37] The frog replied that he should have no anxiety on this account. And in gratitude for Ḥaninah's receiving it so well and affectionately, the frog taught him all seventy languages and also familiarized him with the language of birds and beasts. The frog took leave of Ḥaninah and his wife, who accompanied it to the forest. There, at the frog's command, the birds and beasts brought an enormous number of precious stones and all kinds of roots and herbs. The frog bestowed all the diamonds and precious stones upon Rabbi Ḥaninah and taught him how to use all the herbs. Before taking leave of Ḥaninah, the frog explained to him that Lilith was its mother, that she gave birth to it from Adam the first man, and that it had the power to appear in all kinds of forms.

The report of Rabbi Ḥaninah's wealth and great wisdom spread throughout the land. The king also learned of him and invited him to his court, where he became a beloved royal counsellor. The king had not married and lived without a family. The elders of Israel therefore came to him and declared

36. In the Hebrew manuscript collection the land is not identified.
37. In the version of the Hebrew manuscript this detail is presented with many fine points that are lacking in the *Maaseh-Bukh*.

that it would be most desirable that there be a queen at his side, so that the people could hope for an heir to the throne, for a king is, after all, no more than flesh and blood and does not live forever. The elders had still another reason, but they were silent about it: the king was an extremely wicked man, and they hoped that perhaps if he took a wife, the queen would change him for the better and he would become good and pious. The king replied that they should return eight days later and he would then give them his answer. When the elders of Israel appeared at the appointed time, a bird suddenly came flying with a long hair in its beak and let the hair fall on the king's shoulder. The king looked at the hair. It was a woman's hair of extraordinary length and magnificent yellow-gold color. The king announced that he would take no other woman as his wife but the one to whom the hair belonged. He ordered the elders of Israel to bring this woman to his palace as soon as possible, else he would kill them all. The elders then decided that Rabbi Ḥaninah, who was very wise and knew all seventy languages, should assume the mission of finding the owner of the gold-colored hair.[38] Rabbi Ḥaninah parted with his wife and children, took with him twelve gulden and three loaves of bread, and set out on his way. His disciples accompanied him to the outskirts of the city, and from there he went on alone. The way was very difficult. He became tired and leaned against a tree to rest a bit. Then he heard a raven crying from the tree, complaining that it had not eaten for three days. Rabbi Ḥaninah understood the language of the birds. His compassion was aroused toward the raven, and he gave it a piece of bread. The second day he heard a dog baying mournfully. Rabbi Ḥaninah, understanding the language of all beasts, heard the dog complaining that it had gone hungry for six days now, and so he also gave the dog a piece of bread. On the third day Rabbi Ḥaninah found a fisherman at the river who was exerting strenuous efforts to draw out a large fish in his net. Rabbi Ḥaninah helped him in his work, then bought from him the fish that had been caught, and returned it to the water.[39]

At the other side of the river Rabbi Ḥaninah saw a large city with a magnificent palace in the middle of it. In this palace lived the owner of the golden hair, a remarkably beautiful

38. In the Hebrew version are several details that are missing in the *Maaseh-Bukh.*
39. According to the Hebrew version, the fish itself begs Rabbi Ḥaninah to throw it back into the water, and assures him that it will later repay him in gratitude for this.

princess. As soon as the princess saw Rabbi Ḥaninah from the window of her palace, she realized that he was a very wise man and summoned him for an interview. Rabbi Ḥaninah told her of the king's decree and that if she would not consent to become the king's wife, all the elders of Israel would—God forbid —lose their lives. The princess confirmed that the golden hair was, indeed, taken from her head; while she had recently been shampooing her hair in the garden, a bird came flying and plucked the hair from her head. She told Rabbi Ḥaninah that she would agree to his proposal if he would fulfill two conditions. For the time being she disclosed only the first: he must bring her two little jars of water, one with the water of Paradise, and the other with the water of Hell. Rabbi Ḥaninah left the palace extremely vexed and prayed before the Holy One that he might be able to fulfill the princess' demand so that the Jews would be saved from death. A raven came flying to him and said: "Dear rabbi, do you not recognize me? I am the bird you fed in the forest with your bread." And the raven told him that she would fetch the two kinds of water that were requested, and that he should simply tie the little jars to her wings. The jars were placed on her wings, and she soon brought them back to Rabbi Ḥaninah filled with water of Paradise and water of Hell.

The princess was satisfied and then put before him the second condition. She had once traveled over the sea, and from her finger a golden ring with a very expensive gem fell into the water. He must now bring this ring to her. Rabbi Ḥaninah was beside himself with grief, but the Holy One Blessed Be He helped him. When he came to the shore of the sea, the fish on which he had had pity at once appeared and assured him that it would obtain the ring. The fish swam to Leviathan and related the whole story. Leviathan issued a command adjuring all the fish, under pain of excommunication, that the ring must be surrendered. So a fish came and handed Leviathan the ring. It was immediately given to the fish that wished to express its gratitude to Rabbi Ḥaninah, and this fish spewed the ring out on the seashore. Just then, however, a wild boar came running and swallowed the ring. At this juncture the dog that Ḥaninah had saved from hunger with his bread ran up and offered its aid. The dog pursued the boar, tore it apart, and obtained from its viscera the ring which Rabbi Ḥaninah then brought to the princess.

The princess kept her word and went with Rabbi Ḥaninah to the king. She pleased the king greatly, and soon a marriage

was celebrated. Rabbi Ḥaninah became even more highly regarded by the king and queen. This aroused great jealousy
among many of the courtiers. Some of these "lay in wait for
him" in a hidden place and killed him. As soon as the queen
heard of this, she went to the place where the slain Rabbi
Ḥaninah lay and poured out the water of Paradise on him.
Rabbi Ḥaninah at once revived. The king witnessed this with
great wonderment. It pleased him greatly and he conceived a
desire to test the marvelous power of the water on himself. He
asked the queen to kill him and then revive him with the water.
The queen warned him, explaining that she could revive with
water only one who is completely righteous, but the wicked
king did not believe this and ordered one of his servants to kill
him.[40] The queen then poured out upon the dead body the
water of Hell, and the body was immediately burned to ashes.
The queen said: "You see, if the king had been pious, he would
have been revived. I see, however, that he was a very wicked
man." The counsellors of the king realized that Rabbi Ḥaninah
was not only a great sage but also a truly righteous man, and
so they decided to appoint him king over Israel. And since his
wife had died not long before, they gave him the queen as his
wife, and he ruled over Israel for many years.[41]

No less interesting but of a very different, realistic character
is the story of the Jewish pope. In the twelfth century, in the
period 1130–1138, the occupant of the papal throne in Rome was
Anacletus II, who was descended from Jews. In addition, he
was a friend of the Jews, and his enemies therefore called him
the "Jewish pope" (*Judaeus Pontifex*). This created such a sensa-
tion in the Jewish quarter that a legend was produced about a
Jewish child who had been kidnapped from his parents when
he was quite small and converted to Christianity. The child
had brilliant capacities and in time rose to greatness, attaining
the position of bishop, and was later elected to the papacy.
Finally he became a penitent reversioner to Judaism and died
a pious Jew. This story was extremely popular among both the
Ashkenazic Jews and among the Sephardim, and it is found in
different versions in Hebrew sources.[42] According to the Ashkenazic version, the Jewish pope came from Mainz; according

---

40. According to the Hebrew version, the king, relying on the aid of the miraculous
water, entered into a difficult war with a powerful enemy and perished in the war.
41. The story appeared in modern times (in 1917 in Petrograd) as a children's edition
under the title "The Story of the Pious Rabbi Ḥanania, Faithfully Transmitted by
Baal-Dimyon" (N. Shtif).
42. See Güdemann, *op. cit.*, II, 58–62; *Bet Ha-Midrash*, V, 148–152; *ibid.*, VI, 137–139.

to the Sephardic, from Barcelona, and his father was the renowned rabbi Solomon ben Adret.[43] The story is also contained in the *Maaseh-Bukh*, and indeed the version in this work
is the most interesting and substantial. In it is felt most clearly
the living breath of the popular narrative style. Hence, we
present the story here *in toto:*

It happened with Rabbi Simeon the Great[44] who lived in Mainz on
the Rhine. Now this Rabbi Simeon had three large mirrors hanging
in his house. In them he saw everything that had happened and that
would happen in the future. He also had at the head of his couch a
spring which issued from his grave in the cemetery. This Rabbi
Simeon was a great man and had a son named Elḥanan who was still
a small boy. Now it happened once that the gentile woman who lit
the fires on the Sabbath wished to heat the room one Sabbath, as was
customary. The woman took the child in her arms and went away
with him. The maidservant who was in the house did not take anything amiss, for she thought the gentile woman would bring the child
back, and everyone was still in the synagogue. The gentile woman
took the child and went away with him and had him baptized. She
believed she had brought a sacrifice, for in olden times gentiles
thought highly of converting Jews. When Rabbi Simeon the Great
returned from the synagogue the maid was not home, for she had run
after the gentile woman but did not find her. So Rabbi Simeon found
neither his maid nor his son at home. Suddenly the maid came running and shrieking. Rabbi Simeon asked the maid why she was crying so, and she said: "Dear rabbi, for our many sins the gentile
woman who lights the fires on the Sabbath took the child away, but
I do not know where she went with him." So they searched for the
child everywhere but could not find him. The child had disappeared
completely. The father and mother were greatly grieved about their
beloved child, as one can readily imagine. Rabbi Simeon fasted day
and night, but the Holy One Blessed Be He concealed from him the
place where the child had gone.

Now the child finally came into the hands of the priests, and they
brought him up so that he, who had the heart and mind of Rabbi
Simeon, became a great Christian convert. The young man went
from one university to another until he came to Rome and very
diligently studied all kinds of languages. He became a cardinal in
Rome, and his renown spread so far that people could not say enough
about him . . . and he was highly respected and very handsome.
Finally, it came about that the pope died, and the young man, because
of his intellectual keenness and mastery of all kinds of languages, was
made pope.

43. See Steinschnieder, *Letterbode*, VII, 170–176.
44. A well-known liturgical poet who lived in Mainz in the tenth century.

Now the man knew well that he had been a Jew and was the son of Rabbi Simeon the Great of Mainz. But things went so well with him that he remained among the gentiles, as one can well believe, considering how highly respected he was. He once thought to himself: I will bring my father here to Rome from Mainz. Thereupon he wrote a letter to Mainz to the bishop of the city, for he had now become pope and all the bishops were under his authority, ordering him to forbid the Jews to keep the Sabbath and to circumcise their children, and also to proscribe women's visits to the ritual bath. The pope thought that now his father would be sent to him, in order to bring about a revocation of these commands.

And so it happened. As soon as the letter from the pope came to the bishop, the latter informed the Jews of the decree. The Jews wished to intercede strongly with the bishop not to put the decree into effect, but the bishop showed them the letter from the pope and told them that he could not help them at all. If they wished to intercede, they must themselves go to Rome to the pope.

Who was more miserable than these poor Jews? They performed penitential exercises, prayed, and gave charity. Then they decided to dispatch Rabbi Simeon the Great with two rabbis to Rome, so that he might intercede with the pope, and perhaps the Holy One Blessed Be He would perform a miracle for them. In the meantime, they circumcised all the children in secret, for they arranged this with the bishop, but in great secrecy.

So Rabbi Simeon and his colleagues arose and traveled to Rome to the pope. When they arrived, they informed the Jews of Rome of their arrival and told them of their situation. When these heard of it they marvelled greatly, for they said that in the memory of man there had been no pope better to the Jews. He could not live without Jews and always had Jews secretly with him, and he also played chess[45] with them. Also they had heard nothing of the decree and said that they could not believe that it had come from the pope himself and that it must have been the bishop who had done it. Then Rabbi Simeon the Great showed them the pope's letter signed and sealed, and the Jews had to believe what they had been told. They began to say that this must be some punishment that the Jews in Germany deserved. And the Jews of Rome also engaged in penitence, prayer and charity, and the *parnassim* of Rome went to the cardinal whom they knew well and wished to make intercessions through him. The cardinal said that the letter was written by the pope's own hand to the bishop of Mainz, and therefore he could not do much. Nevertheless he promised to do his best, and told them to submit a petition. He would see to it that this came into the pope's hands, and he would do the best he could. So the Jews submitted a petition and gave it to the pope.

45. This game was very popular among Jews in the Middle Ages. On it, see Stein-schneider, *Schach bei den Juden*, 1873.

As soon as the pope read the petition, he remembered well how the situation had come about and ordered the Jews to appear in person before him. Rabbi Simeon the Great came to the chief cardinal, who showed the Jews in to the pope and introduced them as the Jews of Mainz who wished to see him and speak with him. The pope then ordered that the oldest among them should come to him. Now Rabbi Simeon the Great was the oldest among them. He was like an angel of the Lord of hosts, and as soon as he entered he fell on his knees. The pope was sitting in the room with a cardinal playing chess. As soon as he saw Rabbi Simeon, he was greatly frightened and bade him rise and sit until he finished the game, for he immediately recognized his father, although the father did not know him. When they had finished their game, the pope asked Rabbi Simeon what he wished. Rabbi Simeon told him with weeping and wailing, and was about to fall down again before him. The pope, however, would not suffer this and said: I have now heard your petition, but many strange letters came to me from Mainz, so that we had to issue our prohibitions. The pope then began to discuss the Talmud with Rabbi Simeon in pilpulistic fashion in such a way that he almost overcame him in the dialectical discussion. The rabbi marvelled that such a mind and heart should be found among gentiles. They remained together almost half a day and the pope said: My dear scholar, I see that you are highly educated, otherwise the Jews would not have sent you as their emissary. Now I have Jews visiting me every day who play chess with me. If you play with me once, you will not lose anything thereby.

Now Rabbi Simeon was a chess master whose like could not be found in the whole world. Nevertheless, the pope checkmated him. Rabbi Simeon marvelled greatly, and they began again to speak of religion. Finally, after the rabbi had complained long and urged his petition on him, the pope bade all the cardinals to depart from him. Then he fell on the rabbi's neck with tearful eyes and said: Dear old father, do you not know me? The father answered: How shall I know your royal grace? The pope said: Dear old father, did you not once lose a son? When the rabbi heard this he was greatly frightened and said: Yes. The pope then said: I am your son Elḥanan who was lost to you through the gentile woman. To say now what the sin is through which this happened or how it is—that I cannot know. I think God wished it so. I issued the decree expecting that you yourself would come to me, and so it has happened. For I wished to revert to Judaism, and therefore I will nullify the decree.

And he gave him good letters for the bishop of Mainz to the effect that the decree should be annulled. Then the son asked him: Dear father, can you give me some advice as to how I may have atonement? Rabbi Simeon replied: My dear son, do not worry. You are a forced convert, for you were still a child when you were taken away from me. Then the pope said: My dear father, since I have been so long among gentiles and I knew that I was born a Jew, and the good days —as you see—came to me so that I did not return to my religion, can I still have atonement?

Some say that Rabbi Simeon the Great noted something from the chess game that indicated he was of the seed of Jews. Then the son again said to the father: Go home in the name of the God of Israel, and bring the letters to your bishop and say nothing more of me. I will soon be with you in Mainz, but I wish to leave behind me as a memorial something that will be of benefit to the Jews.

So Rabbi Simeon returned to the Jews and showed them the letter to the effect that the decree, with the help of God, is annulled. They were very happy. So Rabbi Simeon with his colleagues went home and brought the letter to the bishop saying that the decree is, with the help of God, revoked. All rejoiced. And Rabbi Simeon told his wife what had happened to him and how their son was the pope. When she heard this she wept bitterly, but the rabbi said to her: Do not grieve. We shall soon see our son with us again.

And the pope wrote a book against the [Christian] religion, locked it in a vault, and wrote on it: Whoever becomes pope must read this. It would take too long to say what is in this book. Not long afterward the pope rose, took a great deal of money, and traveled to Mainz, where he again became a respected Jew. At Rome they did not know where he had gone. And Rabbi Simeon the Great commemorated the story in a hymn for the second day of Rosh Ha-Shanah into which his name and his son's are woven in acrostic form. Therefore you must not think that these are secular, fabricated stories, but it really happened as is written here. Some say that Rabbi Simeon the Great recognized his son in playing chess, for he had taught him a certain move when he was still very small, and the pope made this move when playing with his father; so he realized that it was his son. May the Holy One Blessed Be He forgive us our sins through the merit of Rabbi Simeon. Amen. Selah.

The *Maaseh-Bukh* is not only an anthology that was very popular and widespread;[46] it is also a great literary event, one of the major milestones in Old-Yiddish literature. With its publication, the narrative prose-style obtained a definitive victory over the poetic verse-style of the chivalrous romances and hero-epics. As in the earlier period the "melody of the *Shmuel-Bukh*" had become the pattern for versification, so the *Maaseh-Bukh* style became the model for all the later narrative litera-

46. In 1612 a German professor, H. Helwig, translated the *Maaseh-Bukh* into High German. A new German translation of the *Maaseh-Bukh* was published by Bertha Pappenheim under the title *Allerlei Geschichten* (Frankfurt, 1929).

ture.[47] Following the pattern of the *Maaseh-Bukh*, a whole series of larger and smaller collections of stories and legends were produced. The most interesting and important of these is *Maaseh-Nissim* by the author of *Minhagim De-Kehillah Kedoshah Virmisa*,[48] Jeptha Yozpa ben Naftali, the sexton and trustee of the ancient community of Worms.

Born in Fürth, Yozpa came as a young man of nineteen to Worms and spent his whole life there. The old melancholy city with its medieval mysteries and marvelous tales attracted his childish, artlessly dreaming soul with their poetic magic, and he felt himself called to note down for future generations all the stories and mystical legends that lurked in the shadows of the walls of Worms, in the narrow, crooked alleys of the Jewish ghetto. So was produced Yozpa Shammash's collection of tales and legends, *Maaseh Nissim*. The author wrote the anthology in Hebrew. The bibliographer Benjacob asserts[49] that the Hebrew text was published while the author was still alive, in Frankfurt-am-Oder (1662). However, it is extremely doubtful whether such an edition really existed, for not a single copy has been preserved. Apparently Benjacob was mistaken. Only eighteen years after Yozpa's death did his son Eliezer translate *Maaseh Nissim* into Yiddish and publish it in Amsterdam (1696).[50]

Since all the twenty-five stories published in *Maaseh Nissim* bear a local character and are bound up with the history and environment of Worms, it is quite understandable that this collection has a different thematic character than the *Maaseh-Bukh*. In Yozpa Shammash's collection stories from the Talmud and Midrashim, for instance, are missing. All the stories in *Maaseh Nissim* derive from the Middle Ages, and a considerable part of them were, indeed, produced in the narrow streets of Worms. Here appear most prominently two motifs that are highly characteristic of medieval Jewish life in Germany: (1) terror and dread before the hostile environment, before the slanders and persecutions that could break out at any time and bring enormous destruction, and (2) on the other side, ignorant superstitions, unshakeable belief in magic and incantations, in transmigrations and all kinds of demons. These two dominant

---

47. To what extent the *Maaseh-Bukh* influenced the *Tze'enah U-Re'enah* style ought to be especially investigated.
48. See our *History*, Vol. VI, Book One, Chapter Four.
49. *Otzar Ha-Sefarim*, 356.
50. We have employed the edition of 1776.

motives constitute the basic tone of all of the "marvelous" stories that the pious sexton of Worms wrote down for future generations.

Sedately and calmly *Maaseh Nissim* relates how the Jews were driven out of Worms. It tells of the massacres they had to suffer in the time of the Crusades, the terrors of the blood libel, the wild attacks of the students. The *Schüler-Gelauf* (student riot) was apparently a very ordinary, almost everyday phenomenon. The adolescent students of the middle schools were usually content with mocking the Jews who walked in the streets, spattering them with mud and dirt. On the other hand, the students of the seminaries and universities would show their strength by attacking the Jewish quarters, destroying their houses, and murderously beating the inhabitants. The Jews of Worms were so used to these "heroic deeds" of the students that when *Maaseh-Nissim* tells of the tragic destruction of the family of Rabbi Eleazar the author of *Rokeah*,[51] the Crusaders who killed Eleazar's wife and three children are transformed into students.

All the persecutions and massacres are frequently embellished with marvelous, fantastic details. So, for instance, it is recounted how in a time of dreadful persecutions (during the Crusades, or in the years of the Black Death), when the Christian populace attacked and destroyed the Jewish community of Worms, the Christians put a goose under a spell; this goose would point out every house in which Jews had hidden themselves, and thus almost all the Jews perished (Story No. 10). Several other stories also tell of the troubles that came through magic and enchantments. Story No. 4 tells of an idle rake who seduced a pious Jewish girl through magic. This rake had sewn into the girl's overcoat a magical love root, and as soon as the unfortunate girl put on the coat she lost her will and did everything her seducer ordered. She broke into her father's gold chest, brought the money to the rake, and surrendered herself to him. However, immediately upon taking her coat off, her love for the rake, who was a Christian, disappeared. Finally she understood that some magical power was in her clothing and so she ran away from her paramour naked in a chemise and told everything that had happened to her. She repented and was married off to a poor but pious young man.

Another story (No. 22) tells of a student who was a sorcerer and a beautiful only daughter "at the spring well of Worms."

51. See our *History*, Vol. II, pp. 70-74.

The story following it (No. 23) tells the sad tale of a bride and groom who were found after their bridal night in the cellar packed in a barrel. This, the author explains, happened through magic, or was perhaps a trick of the students. No. 21 tells of the "Queen of Sheba in the house with the sign of the sun." The Queen of Sheba herself appeared to a householder of Worms and, through magic, persuaded him to live with her, in exchange for which she bestowed great wealth on him. Some time later the Jew's wife learned the secret that her husband was living with a witch. The Queen of Sheba disappeared and, along with her, all the wealth.[52]

Of a completely different character is the amiable popular story about the *shlimazl* or ne'er-do-well (No. 20). "There lived a householder at the house with the sign of the crown." Things went very badly with this Jew; whatever he did turned out poorly. So he decided to leave the town, thinking that "one who changes his place changes his luck." He took counsel on this matter with the rabbi, who also advised him to move to another town. So he took his wife and children with his paltry household effects, placed them on a wagon, and locked the door of the little house in which he had lived. Just as he was about to sit down in the wagon, he heard a loud knocking from the little house at the door that had just been locked. The frightened householder asked who was knocking there and immediately received the reply: "Shlim Mazl (bad luck) is still following. I must go with you where you settle." All were frightened and astonished. "If so," the householder thought, "if bad luck wishes to accompany me, I would much rather remain here in the community." He sold his house for half its value, settled in another one in the neighborhood, and his luck changed. "So it went well with him again."

To give the reader a clear notion of the style and manner of *Maaseh Nissim*, as well as the milieu in which these wonder tales were produced, we present here *in toto* the marvelous story of the two *baalei shemot* or "masters of the name" of Worms:

A story of Rabbi Moses Reuben and Rabbi Lezer, masters of the name. One lived in Worms at the house where the shield of the black bears hangs. He was a precious man, a rabbi. His name was Rabbi Lezer of the family Ulma. He was the father of the *parnass* Rabbi Jacob, who was called by his surname Rabbi Jacob Weinstein. It once

52. For variants of the legend, see above, p. 177, and also our *History*, Vol. VI, pp. 161–63.

happened that Rabbi Lezer invited some young men to the third meal of the Sabbath to make a banquet on Saturday night. The young men became very merry and begged Rabbi Lezer to produce some marvel through the invocation of divine names, for he was a great master of the name. He said: I must have a can that is quite new and which has no cover but is just as the can-maker poured it out and has not yet been used. The young men fetched such a can. Rabbi Lezer then brought it about through names that the can became very large. Then he adjured Joab ben Zeruiah, who was King David's general. Joab had to come out of the can. First came an armored helmet. Then the head to the shoulders, then the body all encased in armor, and in the figure's hand a great iron bar. Then came the knees and the feet. So gradually, little by little, the figure came out in the room where the young men were. The room became extremely large and very high, for Joab was an enormously tall man. The young men became greatly frightened, for when he walked about the room, whenever he made a step, the whole house shook. The young men wished that they had not desired to see any trick, and they bade Rabbi Lezer to make Joab disappear again. Rabbi Lezer again brought it about through names that he went into the can little by little. Now when Joab had come in up to his arms, he would not go further. Rabbi Lezer himself was afraid and thought that Joab might—God forbid—do them some harm. Rabbi Lezer sent quickly for Rabbi Moses Reuben who was also a *baal shem*. He lived behind the synagogue in the house where the mirror hangs. Rabbi Moses Reuben said: It serves him right. Why does he attempt to perform a trick and cannot do it properly? Run swiftly and say to him: I will come at once and when I open the door of the room and am about to enter, he [Joab] will be frightened of me and will instantaneously run into the can, and the room will again become small as it was before. Now Rabbi Moses Reuben went to the house. When he opened the door of the room, Joab ran back into the can and everything came back properly, as it had been before. Thereupon the young men rejoiced greatly that no harm had come about.

In the *Maaseh-Bukh* the favorite hero is Rabbi Jehudah Ḥasid of Regensburg. In *Maaseh Nissim* this place is taken, for reasons of local patriotism, by the disciple of Rabbi Jehudah, Rabbi Eleazar author of the *Rokeaḥ*, who was a resident of Worms. *Maaseh Nissim* recounts his great praises and tells how Rabbi Eleazar flew on the eve of Passover on a cloud to Spain to Naḥmanides for the sake of performing a good deed; the lord of the city had arrested him in a street wherein Jews were strictly forbidden to walk and condemned him to burning. Rabbi Eleazar pronounced a "name" and, instead of him, the lord of the city, who was a very wicked man, was burned on the pyre. Rabbi Eleazar remained a rather long time with Naḥmanides and acquainted him with the mystical secrets hidden in the Torah.[53]

Among the marvelous stories collected in *Maaseh Nissim* a special place is occupied by a realistic tale of a gentile who wished to sell his child to the Jews for *matzot* on Passover. This story has a very definite ethnographic interest, and it is worth familiarizing the reader with its content: A gentile comes to a Jewish householder in Worms and says "he has a child of five or six years whom he would like to sell to the Jews, for he had heard that the Jews must have the blood of gentiles; he knows for certain that much blood can be obtained from the child." The Jew berates the gentile. He calls him "rogue and thief" for saying such things about the Jews. The next day, however, the gentile returns and says to the Jew: "Yesterday you turned me down and spoke harsh words to me in addition, but I know very well that it is true. You have no reason to be afraid of me. You may readily believe everything I say. You must not worry; I will not tell anyone. I would be risking my life if it were to be learned that I sold my child in this way and let him be killed for the sake of money." No matter how much the Jew argued, the gentile would not be dissuaded and "allowed the Jew no rest." The Jew then went to the *parnassim* to ask for advice. The *parnassim* immediately went to the city magistracy and told the whole story to the councilmen *(Ratmänner)*. "The councilmen gathered and discussed what they should do here." It was concluded that two *Ratherren* should disguise themselves in the clothing of *parnassim*, take along two servants dressed in the clothing of Jewish beadles, and go see "what lies behind the gentile." The two disguised councilmen sat down with the *parnassim* in the Jewish community council chamber, while their two servants stood dressed in the garments of beadles behind the door. They sent the Jew to go tell the gentile that he should bring his child to the council chamber if he really wishes to sell him. "The Jew performed his mission," and the gentile soon came with the child before the *parnassim* and the two disguised councilmen. He thought naturally that the councilmen were also *parnassim*. The councilmen adjured the gentile to keep silent for the sake of God, and tell no one about his dealings with the Jews. The gentile replied: "How should I say

53. This legend was already written down only one generation after the author of *Rokeaḥ*, while Naḥmanides was still alive, by the Kabbalist Rabbi Isaac ben Jacob (see *Madda'ei Ha-Yahudut*, II, 1927, p. 254).

anything? After all I would be in greater jeopardy than you Jews, for I wish to sell my own child to have him killed and have his blood drained." After the councilmen had reached an agreement with the gentile on the price that he wished for his child, they said to him: "We do not kill any person. Take a rope and bind your child hand and foot and slaughter him. He must be slaughtered, otherwise there is no deal." The gentile consented to this. They fetched a clean vessel "to let the blood be caught in it and had the slaughtering knife for cattle brought to them." At the moment the gentile took the slaughtering knife in hand and was prepared to slaughter his own child "the two councilmen called their two servants; these cast off their black cloaks and wide bonnets and put on their red cloaks with their hats and forcibly seized the gentile." "And the Jews had great honor for making this known. The councilmen placed the child in an orphanage, but the gentile was punished with death by torture. So let it be for all the wicked, but may it be well for all Israel and all good people, and may the Holy One Blessed Be He not let us experience any more suffering. Amen."

Such realistic stories were quite frequently printed in special editions in the form of chapbooks for the people. Many such stories were imported from the outside but presented to the Jewish reader in proper Jewish dress. So a certain number of novellas from Boccaccio's *Decameron* also penetrated into the Jewish quarter, after the erotic element had been covered with a heavy cloak of modesty. But competing very successfully with this realistic narrative material were the fantastic stories and wondrous legends with which the popular imagination adorned its beloved national heroes. As we noted at the beginning of this chapter, at first these legends lived only in the mouth of the people, wandering from generation to generation. Now they penetrated into the folk literature. They were printed in special collections, e.g., *Kevod Hachamim*, where it is noted on the title-page that "in this book are wondrous tales of Maimonides and Rashi, Ibn Ezra and Nahmanides, and in it is written the honor which Israelites had at those times even among the nations, while among them were heads of Talmudic academies."

Also printed in separate chapbooks were some marvelous tales of a great *tzaddik* or an astounding miracle worker, and in this connection it happened not infrequently that a historical personality obtained quite fantastic forms and was transported into a completely different era and legendary environment. Typical in this respect is the little book of stories *Sefer Immanuel* with the following title-page: "Dear people, pay attention to this story, for I translated it from Hebrew into German so that men may know how the Holy One Blessed Be He gladly accepts the repentence of people and shames no one. When a man repents with his whole heart, God heals all his wounds and pains. What happened to Immanuel you will read in the story. Therefore, dear people, run and buy the little book. In the merit of this, the redeemer will come unto Zion. Amen."

Sefer Immanuel tells of Rabbi Ishmael the High Priest who "learned all the mysteries of the Torah from an angel, and through the invocation of divine names went to heaven." This high priest "had a son named Daniel, and in his old age had another son who was called Immanuel. Shortly after the mother became pregnant with the child, the father Rabbi Ishmael died, and when the mother gave birth to him, she also died. So he was an orphan. His brother Daniel brought him up for good, but Immanuel did not wish to obey him and committed foolish deeds . . . Finally he became twelve years old, and did not know any of the prayers or any of the Pentateuch."

Following this, it is related how Immanuel's father once came to him in a dream and reproved him for not studying Torah. After all, man was created to study Torah and do *mitzvot*. Immanuel agreed to repent, and the father assured him that his repentence would be accepted by God and that he would be a great scholar. The following morning Immanuel arose "like a completely different creature" and requested his brother to give him a penance. Immanuel was washed like a corpse, dressed in shrouds, and laid in a coffin. When they wanted to pour a spoonful of molten lead into his mouth a miracle occurred; the molten lead was transformed into honey. This was a sign that the penance which he had done with inner intention and with his whole heart was accepted by God (a distant echo of the *Tannhäuser* motif). Immanuel became a great scholar and a very pious man. Once he prayed mightily and entreated God that he might have the privilege, while still alive, of seeing his portion in the world to come, as well as his brother's portion. A heavenly voice thereupon was heard: "If you fast forty days and every day perform forty-nine immersions, you will have your wish." So he did, and on the fortieth day, when he was on the field and praying, he fell on his face and slept. "Then God sent him Daniel Ish Ḥamudot and the latter said to Immanuel: Rise and open your eyes; you will

merit seeing more than the people who were before you."
Thereupon is told in great detail how Daniel Ish Ḥamudot, the
godly man, led Immanuel through all the departments of Hell
and then showed him the lower and upper Paradise. As soon
as one begins to read the description of what and whom Immanuel saw in hell, one immediately recognizes the source
from which this derives. It is a paraphrase of Immanuel of
Rome's *Ha-Tofet Veha-Eden.*[54] This is he, the clever wit, the
merry poet of love and passion, the "Heine of the Middle
Ages"—transformed into a son of the High Priest and a penitent. The talented Hebrew work of the poet, an echo of Dante's
Divine Comedy, is utilized as building material for a typical
Yiddish storybook with a sharply stressed pious moral lesson.

54. A verbatim Yiddish translation of Immanuel of Rome's poem appeared in Prague
around 1660–62 (see M. Erik, *Geshikhte,* 333).

CHAPTER EIGHT

Simḥat Ha-Nefesh;
THE BATTLE FOR YIDDISH

Morality books in the form of storybooks—Elḥanan Kirchhan and his *Simḥat Ha-Nefesh*—Kirchhan and his unique style—Kirchhan as storyteller—*Kav Ha-Yashar* and *Simḥat Ha-Nefesh*—Abraham ben Yeḥiel Michal and his *Berech Avraham*—The laws of the *Shulḥan Aruch* in Yiddish—The protest of the rabbis—The battle for Yiddish—The rabbi of Prosstitz Yeḥiel Michal Epstein as Yiddishist—The rabbis as opponents of popular books—A conflict of interests—The author of *Esrim Ve-Arba* on the question of language—Beyleh Perl and her husband's composition *Be'er Sheva*—Moses Frankfurter as battler for Yiddish—Aaron ben Samuel of Hergershausen and his *Liblikhe Tfile*—The significance of Aaron ben Samuel's work—The anger of the rabbis—Aaron ben Samuel's prayerbook under the ban.

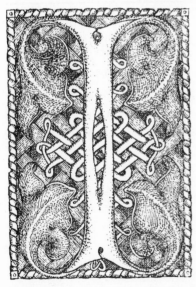

N THE previous chapter we observed that the pious moral lesson that was woven into the majority of storybooks erased, to a certain extent, the boundary between what were, from the sixteenth century on, the two most powerful streams in Yiddish literature: storybooks and morality books. Indeed, quite frequently the scholar of literature does not find it easy to decide to which genre he ought to assign a certain work, whether to the category of morality books or to narrative literature. We shall here dwell on one such work that is most typical and interesting—*Simḥat Ha-Nefesh*, written by Elḥanan Henlah bar Benjamin Wolf Kirchhan and extremely popular in its day.

Born in the little Hessian town of Kirchhan (near Marburg)

Simhat Ha-Nefesh

in the 1650's,[1] Elhanan Kirchhan in his youth wandered over
various countries. He lived in Holland and Poland,[2] and in the
latter of these countries married the daughter of the author of
Kav Ha-Yashar, Tzevi Hirsh Koidonover. He spent some time
in Koidanov,[3] then returned to his native town and remained
there his entire life. Kirchhan wrote a large commentary to the
Torah, and he himself bears witness that it was "a beautiful
composition."[4] However, it was not with this work that he
acquired renown, but with his tender *Simhat Ha-Nefesh*, published in 1707.

His father-in-law's morality book *Kav Ha-Yashar* appeared
only a year earlier. *Simhat Ha-Nefesh* not infrequently quotes
Tzevi Hirsh Koidonover's work, but the distance between
these two morality books is literally astounding. The author of
Kav Ha-Yashar wishes to cast dread on the reader; he drives him
on the way of repentance and reverence for God with the lash
of terror. But the goodhearted Elhanan Kirchhan thinks above
all of *simhat ha-nefesh*, "joy of the soul." He declares immediately at the beginning of his book that he will bring

many pure arguments to show men that they should not worry
. . . Then will his joy be very great. . . . Therefore I have given this
book the title *Simhat Ha-Nefesh* . . . He who reads the remedy here will
find that his care and worry depart from him . . . He will find great
consolations and pure arguments to show mortal man that he should
not grieve over anything. For everything that comes to man is from
God, and is for his good.

The humble author of *Simhat Ha-Nefesh* deems it necessary
immediately to call to the attention of the reader: "Do not
think that I have discovered something new, but only everything that stands in our beloved Torah." And in another passage he notes:

Do not think that I reprove somewhat and write moral instruction
and laws out of my head. I am much too unimportant for this. I am

1. He died after 1731.
2. Kirchan himself relates in his *Simhat Ha-Nefesh*: "I lived in the territories of
Poland."
3. The author of *Simhat Ha-Nefesh* relates: "When my mother, peace be upon her, the
modest woman Ehleh, died, I saw in the holy community of Koidanov in a dream
how she was carried out on a bed, and my father, may his days be long, wept and
mourned." There the author also relates, incidentally, that a son of his named
Moses died.
4. See *Simhat Ha-Nefesh*, Part Two, p. 22.

an ordinary man. My writing is a form of labor, and there is little
wisdom in it, but only all the ethical instruction and laws contained
in our holy Torah. Who will be so wicked and not keep the Torah?
... Therefore I beg people not to take it amiss; I write this book not
out of my head—everything in it is in our Torah—but somewhat to
remind people in another form, so that man should bethink himself
and speak the truth.

The modest Elḥanan Kirchhan is perhaps right when he
writes that he invents nothing and devises nothing "out of his
head." But it is certainly not true when he asserts that he
"discovered nothing," and that his writing is simply a "labor."
In every page of *Simḥat Ha-Nefesh*, in his manner of relating
things, Kirchhan's ardent, loving heart and his unique style
and mode of writing are discernible. Indeed, therein lies the
secret of the remarkable grace with which this book is permeated, and of the fact that it so strongly attracted the grateful
hearts of the common people.

A contemporary of the author of *Kav Ha-Yashar*, as well as
the author of *Shevet Musar*, Elḥanan Kirchhan firmly believes
in demons and evil spirits, and he knows of all sorts of deeds
that are wrought through magic. He also knows for certain
that "the male demons have hair on their heads and the female
demons have no hair on their heads." He tells of a woman with
whom "a demon united" and mentions the story of the gold-
smith of Posen which *Kav Ha-Yashar* relates.[5] Kirchhan asserts
that he "knew a child of three years in the holy community of
Szochozcov who recited great mysteries of the Torah and did
not himself know what he was saying." He is an ardent disciple
of Rabbi Isaac Luria and relates many marvelous things about
him. He admonishes the reader: "God has great sorrow when
man sins, for man is created in the image of God. When one
sins he makes a great defect; conversely, when he does a good
deed he gives power to the [supernal] worlds and brings great
abundance on the world. Just as when one touches a long chain
and the end of it shakes, the chain moves above." "Therefore,"
the author of *Simḥat Ha-Nefesh* concludes, "do not let yourself
be misled or seduced by the evil inclination."

Elḥanan Kirchhan knows the terrible punishment that
awaits a man as soon as he allows himself to be led astray by
the evil inclination. "There is much to write about this," he
notes. Much, indeed, is written in minutest detail on this sub-

5. See our *History*, Vol. VI, pp. 161–63.

ject in *Kav Ha-Yashar* and *Shevet Musar.* The kindhearted Kirchhan, however, endeavors to speak as little as possible of it. He does not wish to cast dread on his readers. Not with indignation and fear does he desire to lead men on the right way, but with soft and tender words of moral instruction, with lovely stories and parables that quicken the heart. "The story of a king"—with this *Simḥat Ha-Nefesh* begins. And immediately after the story comes a parable with a moral lesson in artless, amiable, genuinely popular fashion. If some trouble comes upon a man, let him not think that he alone lives in pain and grief. "There is no one in the world," Kirchhan notes, "who has not experienced troubles." And at once *Simḥat Ha-Nefesh* introduces the story, so popular in medieval Hebrew literature, of the testament that Alexander of Macedon left for his mother. Thereupon follows the author's moral: "The world is like a ladder. One goes up, another goes down. One dies, another is born. One gains much, another loses much. One has a peaceful life, another roams about the world. One is revered and honored, another is regarded as worthless. But rich or poor, it is all the same with God."

Man is blind. If some trouble comes upon him, he is beside himself with grief and does not know ànd understand that everything is for good and occurs only for his benefit. On this theme immediately follows a story of Rabbi Akiba, who always used to say that everything God sends is for good.

Once he [Rabbi Akiba] was traveling and wished to spend the night in a certain town. Upon being refused lodging, he said: This also is for the good, and spent the night in a forest where he had with him an ass, a rooster, and a candle. Along came a lion and ate up the donkey. Afterwards came a cat and ate up the rooster, then a wind extinguished the candle. Thereupon Rabbi Akiba said: "This also is for the good." That same night soldiers came and pillaged the town, taking its residents captive. Rabbi Akiba praised God for having performed a miracle and being for the good in everything. "If I had been in the town, I also would have been captured, and if the donkey or rooster had made a sound and the candle had burned, the robbers would have seen and heard where I am. So God saved me."

At the end comes the moral: "Therefore, mortal men, set your sorrow and your worries aside, and accept everything that God sends with good grace."

One story follows another in *Simḥat Ha-Nefesh.* The tale is told of a prominent man in Babylonia who was marrying off his son and arranged a great banquet for the Talmudic scholars. He bade the groom go up to the attic and fetch some good wine. The son went up to the attic, was bitten by a serpent, and died. When some time had elapsed, the father went to see where the son was and found him lying dead. However, he remained silent until the scholars had eaten and drunk and made merry. When it came time for reciting grace, he said to them: "Do not think that you should recite the Seven Benedictions. Do not think that you have come to lead my son under the bridal canopy, but rather to carry him out for burial."

Typical is the fashion in which the author of *Simḥat Ha-Nefesh* retells the familiar story from the Midrash about Rabbi Meir's two children who fell into a well on the Sabbath and were drowned. Rabbi Meir's wife, the pious Beruriah, did not wish to spoil the Sabbath, and so when Rabbi Meir came home from the synagogue she did not tell him of the tragedy. They sat down to eat and drink, and only after eating did Beruriah address to her husband the following query: "My husband, someone left me two golden *gulden* to keep. Now he comes and desires to have them back. Shall I return them to him or not?" Rabbi Meir replied: "Of course, you must cheerfully give back what is his!" Thereupon Beruriah said to her husband: "Your two children fell into the well and are dead; God has taken back His pledge." With this the story in the Midrash ends, but the kindhearted Kirchhan does not wish to grieve his pious readers. He wishes them to have "joy of the soul," and so he concludes the story on a happy note:

So they [Rabbi Meir and his wife] waited until the Sabbath ended, and they honored the Sabbath and did not mourn. Therefore God performed a miracle for them: when they were about to remove the bodies of the children at the end of the Sabbath, the children revived, because their parents had so cheerfully accepted what God had ordained. Now it may be seen what a great thing it is to accept everything from God with joy.

The author of *Simḥat Ha-Nefesh* is indeed, no innovator. All his stories and parables are, in fact, not contrived "out of his head"; they are taken from older sources. But Elḥanan Kirchhan possessed a rare skill of retelling stories in his own fashion. Every anciently known tale obtains in him a completely new vestment and shimmers with unique colors. For the reader to gain a notion of Kirchhan's singular style, it is worth dwelling on the well-known story, widespread among all peoples, about the custom instituted on a remote island whose inhabitants would choose a new king each year from abroad.[6] This artless, popular tale is already encountered in Baḥya Ibn Pakuda's *Ḥovot Ha-Levavot*.[7] But the author of *Simḥat Ha-Nefesh* veiled it in a new garment, and in his work it obtains a quite different style.

A parable. There was a certain land in which the people did not take as their king a man who was respected, but their custom was that, when they needed a king, they sent forth riders who traveled until they found a beggar who went about tattered and torn and did not have a penny of his own. Then they would give this beggar a sleeping potion, and in his sleep kidnap him, and ride with him to their land. There they washed him and anointed him with good, fragrant oil and spices, brought him into the city, and laid him in a bed, as is proper for a king. There he slept; this went on for three days and he knew nothing of what was happening to him. In the meantime they placed his watchmen at all the gates and doors, and all the princes and officials of the realm stood on watch to wait on him when he would wake up. So also did his manservants and maidservants. Now when he had waked up, all the princes of the realm and his manservants and maidservants came to him, bowed low before him, and asked him what he desired. When he looked about him, he marveled greatly and thought to himself: "What is this? How do I come into this bed? Am I a king? I was only a beggar and went about the world begging!" It was a great marvel to him. And so he decided: "It is not otherwise; I am a king and remain a king. That I was a beggar was a dream. I dreamed that I was a beggar but I remain a king."

Now every three years it was the custom in this country that they took another king. Giving the incumbent a sleeping potion once more and dressing him again in his beggar's clothing, they carried him back to the place from which they had taken him, left him lying there, and rode away. Now when he woke up he was astonished and said: "Where have I been? I was a king, and today I am a beggar." So he thinks: "It is not otherwise. I was a beggar, I am still a beggar, and that I was a king was a dream. So I dreamed."

Once they took for their king a beggar who was a very wise man. This man understood that he had become a proper king, and that he had been a beggar. This was the truth and no dream. He understood well and saw how all waited on him as on a king and that he possessed the keys of all the treasuries. So he remained silent for a whole year. After the year he took one of his servants aside in a chamber and confided the whole matter to him and said: "You must swear that you will tell me the truth. The thing is this: I am a king now, and I was

6. This theme was utilized in a unique way by the well-known German poet Gerhart Hauptmann in his play *Schluck und Jau*.
7. See our *History*, Vol. I, pp. 116–119.

a beggar before. If you should try to make me think that my having been a beggar was a dream—that cannot be, for when I was a beggar I fell into a ditch and was hurt; the bruises healed, but the marks of the wounds still remain on my body. Obviously it was not a dream. So tell me truthfully how things stand with me and what will happen to me. If you tell me the truth, I will make you a great lord and give you much money beyond calculation; if you do not tell me the truth, I will kill you. Therefore speak the truth." Now the servant saw that it could not be otherwise, and so he told him the truth of what had happened to him, and what the order of the country is: that when three years had elapsed, they would again give him a sleeping potion and return him to the place whence he had been taken. And he added: "And by this you may know that I am right: my lord the king has the key of all the treasures, but to one room alone he has no key; this is the room in which they stored your beggar's clothes until the time comes when they put them on you again." Now the king was frightened, but he was silent and paid strict attention to the servant's words and learned that the truth was such. So the king charged some officers with libels and killed them and made the servant who had confided the matter to him his viceroy. And during that time he emptied out all the treasuries and purchased large estates elsewhere and assembled great treasures. And he bought many slaves and arranged for his servants to wait with carriages on such and such day on the field at the place where he previously lay. And the residents of the country knew nothing of all this.

Now when the three years were up, they again gave him a sleeping potion and put his beggar's clothes on him and returned him to the place whence they had taken him. Now when he awoke, his servants stood there with wagons as he had ordered them, and they brought him to his country, where he became a great lord. And when they went home for their treasures they found great ruins, for the king had taken everything out.

After the story comes the moral:

So also is man. When he is created, he does not take to heart the fact that his soul came from the other world, and that he was a beggar. He was born naked, but he sees that he is a king over all the creatures and has all the pleasures of the world before him. And so he thinks: "I came thus from the other world. This was a dream. I am a king and will remain a king. And he follows all his lusts to enjoy the world in pleasure and does not think of Torah and *mitzvot*. Then his time is up. He is a king no more. He is given a sleeping potion—that is, death. And he is laid on the place whence he came. He came from the earth and is again placed in the earth. Then he thinks that his having been a king in the world was a dream. But he remains a beggar. He must go wandering. He is hurled in the "hollow of the sling" from one end of the world to the other, and in addition comes to Hell. But he who is wise reflects: "It is no dream. I was created from the earth and was born naked. That is the truth. In proof thereof I have an additional sign—the soul and the body as I was in the womb." And he takes his faithful servant, i.e., the good inclination, and he tells him the truth and says to him in proof thereof: "All the keys of all the treasures have been given to you save one—that is the soul, your garment which you previously had." And he thinks: "I will also remain a king; I will make treasures for myself." And he fulfills the Torah and *mitzvot* and does great charity. Thereby he purchases for himself the world-to-come. Now, when he dies, his servants come and bring him to his land, that is to say, the angels bear him to Paradise and he merits the world-to-come. Thus King David said: "When the Lord turned again the captivity of Zion, we were like those who dream." This means, when God redeems us and brings us again to Palestine we shall say: "That we were in exile was like a dream."

Quite according to the model of *Simḥat Ha-Nefesh*[8] did Abraham ben Yeḥiel Michal, the son of the author of the well known morality books *Derech Ha-Yashar Le-Olam Ha-Ba* and *Derech Yesharah* write his *Berech Avraham* (published at Wilmersdorf in 1731). Here also the moral instruction is heavily laden with belletristic material. Every chapter (the work consists of thirty-one chapters) is filled with countless tales and parables. But these stories, and in general all the materials, are thrown together without any order. Furthermore, the author is a very clumsy storyteller and his stories drag on colorlessly and tediously. So that the reader may have some notion of this book, we present here the content of several of its chapters:[9]

Chapter 25: In this chapter is explained what pious people there were in former times. May God grant that we may benefit through their merit.

Chapter 26: In this chapter is explained what novelties (*ḥiddushim*) of the angel of death occurred in former times. May God save us from him.

Chapter 29: In this chapter is explained how everyone should take care that the evil inclination not overpower him, and how he may assuredly come into Paradise.

Chapter 30: In this chapter are explained the new things of Jerusalem.

---

8. The second part of *Simḥat Ha-Nefesh*, which appeared some twenty years after the first, is written in a very different fashion, and we shall first speak of it only in later chapters.

9. We quote according to the Shklov edition of 1799.

Chapter 32: In this chapter is explained how our sages spoke with dukes and officials. It is to be marvelled at, for they were great sages.

Chapter 33: In this chapter is explained how everyone should take heed before all things that are magic. May God save all Israel therefrom.

Our sages write: The destroying spirits are more numerous in the world than people. And they stand in large numbers at mortal man's side, for they wish to harm him. And wherever holiness is greatest, they are most numerous. At times there is a sermon in the synagogue and there is a great press among the people; all this comes from the demons. If the clothing of the rabbis is torn—this is from the demons. They rub against it because the holiness in it is from the Torah. Often one's knees pain him and are very tired; all this is from the demons. If man could see them, then no one—God forbid—could remain alive, for a thousand demons stand at a man's left side and ten thousand at his right side. Therefore our sages declared a remedy to man: when he recites the *Shema* with concentration on his bed every night, they must depart from him. Everyone must be admonished not to pass over a sewer pipe from which refuse water is poured . . .

To add authority, the author introduces a long story about two men who went with a barrel of wine and sat down to rest at a sewer pipe. A demon sat there and "burst the barrel into two pieces."

Chapter 34: In this chapter are explained how the novel deeds (*ḥiddushim*) of dead people were, at which everyone marvels.

Chapter 36: In this chapter are explained all the new things that our sages saw when they traveled on ships.

Chapter 35: In this chapter are explained what days are not good as well as the days that are good for bloodletting, that all Israel may have a remedy.

Chapter 39: In this chapter is explained the story of how the prophet Elijah went walking in Hell with someone and showed him marvelous things.

Berech Avraham was not in a position to compete with *Simḥat Ha-Nefesh*. To the end of the eighteenth century it was reprinted only once (in Fürth, 1739), while *Simḥat Ha-Nefesh* in the course of the eighteenth century went through a large number of editions and became one of the most beloved books among Jews. The renowned Jonathan Eybeschütz considered it necessary to note (in his *Yaarot Devash*) that all women and maidens should read *Simḥat Ha-Nefesh* every day. The remarkable popularity of Kirchhan's work at that time is also stressed by Berthold Auerbach in his novel *Der Dichter und der Kaufmann* and Aron Bernstein in his *Voegele der Maggid.* Nevertheless, one edition of this popular folkbook aroused great indignation among the rabbis, and there is even a legend that it was burned.

Highly characteristic are the motives that called forth such wrath among the rabbis against Kirchhan's pious morality book. The author of *Simḥat Ha-Nefesh* does not tire of emphasizing that "an ignorant man cannot be pious, for he does not study and is dumb in the Torah." On the other hand, he is forever reminding the common reader that "now no one can have the excuse that he does not know what is a prohibition or violation [of the law], for there are so many morality books and law books printed in 'German' that everyone can himself study from them."[10] Elsewhere[11] he even lists by title the "German" morality books in which one can find "great Torah and laws": *Kav Ha-Yashar, Sefer Derech Ha-Yashar, Tefillah Derech Yesharah, Maaseh Adonai, Abbir Yaakov, Oreḥot Tzaddikim, Lev Tov, Brantsh-pigl,* and "other books besides." The author of *Simḥat Ha-Nefesh* therefore does not weary of reminding the reader to "buy 'German' books." "Do not begrudge any money, so that you may rightly learn all the laws regarding how you ought to conduct yourself."

To increase the usefulness of his own morality book, Kirchhan added, at the conclusion of *Simḥat Ha-Nefesh,* a special section containing laws for the religious year. This section, which occupies approximately half the entire book, begins with the words "Laws concerning how a man should conduct himself in the morning." The order and description of these laws in *Simḥat Ha-Nefesh* is taken directly from the *Shulḥan Aruch.* This section had no special heading. A later publisher in Vilna,[12] however, considered it necessary, in order to strengthen the authority of this section, to inform the reader that he has here an abbreviated *Shulḥan Aruch* in the vernacular. Hence the publisher added at the end of the first section, "Conclusion of the book *Simḥat Ha-Nefesh,*" and, preceding the second section, printed in large letters *Shulḥan Aruch Oraḥ Ḥayyim Ve-Yoreh Deah U-Minhagim Shel Kol Ha-Shanah.* But the pub-

10. *Ibid.,* 31a (we quote according to the Shklov edition of 1796).
11. *Ibid.,* 20b.
12. The date of this edition is unfortunately unknown. We have seen a copy of this extremely rare edition, but unfortunately the title-page was torn out. In any case, it was before 1796, the year in which the Shklov edition of *Simḥat Ha-Nefesh* appeared.

lisher fell into a bad trap with this move. The rabbis were greatly displeased by it. How can one do this—give the *Shul-ḥan Aruch*, even if only in extracts, into the hands of the rabble? Every ignoramus will think that he is already competent in the laws of what is permitted and forbidden in matters of food and may himself decide legal questions. Hence the whole edition was proscribed.[13]

From the standpoint of the history of culture it is worth noting that it was not only the Polish rabbis who were opposed to putting a collection of laws in the vernacular into the hands of the common people. They had fellow battlers in Italy who agreed with them in this matter. In 1565 an Italian scholar Ye-ḥiel Ha-Kohen of Anoscrivi put together, in Italian, a handbook for women called *Hochmat Nashim* in seven parts wherein the most important laws and moral instruction are presented. In the preface the author deems it necessary to note that many are angry with him for undertaking to explain the commandments of the Torah in the profane language of the people. He endeavors to show that this, according to all views, is quite proper, and refers to the men of the Talmud, the author of the *Zohar*, and Maimonides, all of whom explained the laws of the Torah not only in Hebrew but, indeed, in the vernacular.[14]

13. It is beyond doubt that it is precisely of this edition that Eleazar Schulmann tells in his *Sefat Yehudit Ashkenazit*, 74: "According to a story that I heard in my youth, generations ago they publicly placed on the pyre in Vilna the translation of the *Shulḥan Aruch* into the vernacular, because the masses, and especially the women, began to make legal decisions for themselves." It is interesting that in 1796 there appeared in Shklov a new edition of *Simḥat Ha-Nefesh*, but without the section dealing with laws. On the title-page it is noted: "Published in Shklov under the rule of the great and pious lord Major-General Cavalier Semon Gavrilovitch Zo-ritz, may his glory be exalted." The Shklov and the Vilna editions were noted down neither by Steinschneider nor by Benjacob, and also not by J. Shatzky in the introduction to his edition of the second part of *Simḥat Ha-Nefesh* (1926). For interesting details about many abbreviations and alterations in the later Russian editions of *Simḥat Ha-Nefesh* made by the Czarist censors, see N. Prylucki in *YIVO-Bleter*, pp. 222–227.

14. "And I also heard the wicked talk of many saying: Who permitted you to translate the commandments of the Torah from the holy language to profane language? For if our rabbis, may their memory be for blessing, permitted the Oral Torah to be written down because of the principle 'It is time to work for the Lord,' they did not permit it except in the holy tongue. I answer them that everything is included in one permission, for thus did many of the great scholars, like Maimonides, may his memory be for a blessing, who composed many books, his commentary on the *Mishnah* and his *Sefer Ha-Mitzvot* (in the Arabic language). And he was preceded in this by the men of the Talmud, which is written entirely in the Babylonian language that was the profane and vernacular tongue for them. And greater than this, the book of the *Zohar*, which is the tradition of the Kabbalah, was not written

This defense, however, was apparently of no avail, and Yeḥiel Ha-Kohen's handbook did not appear in print.

This indignation on the part of a certain segment of the rabbis towards religious-ethical works in the colloquial language is not at all an extraordinary phenomenon. We noted in previous chapters how hostile the learned circles were to the "foolish books" of secular content—all the knightly romances and hero epics imported from the outside world. The religious leaders of the people, however, were not in a position to drive out from the Jewish quarter, with their bans and prohibitions, the secular folk-literature produced according to foreign models. Some of the rabbis understood this quite well. The more farsighted among them soon realized that these books that were so loved by the people could be destroyed not through prohibitions but rather by giving the masses, the reading public newly created as a result of the printing press, another type of reading material more suited to the Jewish tradition and the Jewish world of ideas. An attempt was made to displace the "foolish books" through "godly books." We noted earlier how the pious and God-fearing Isaac ben Eliakum, who declared that "the German books that do not speak of the Torah or of *mitzvot* are words of scoffers, and it is a sin to read from them, for these books are nothing but confusions," immediately stresses in this connection that "whoever is poor, so that he cannot hire a teacher, should read in German a German Pentateuch or a German book of Psalms, or some other godly German books." He himself composed such a "godly German book," *Lev Tov*, of which he asserts in the preface that whoever "reads it through finds all of Jewishness in it." Proceeding from the principle that "prayer without inner concentration is like a body without a soul," he complains strongly of the fact that the common people recite prayers and liturgical hymns in a language they do not understand. He considers this literally blasphemy: "The mouth speaks, the lips babble, and the heart knows nothing thereof" (see above, Chapter Six, p. 162).[15]

Thus, those in whom the feeling for the people was aroused and who were concerned for the spiritual and intellectual requirements of the common folk, gradually became convinced

---

in the holy language. If so, then I did not turn aside from the way of the kings, that is to say, the kings—our rabbis." *Hochmat Nashim* remained in manuscript; we quote according to Steinschneider in *MGWJ*, 1903, 179.

15. We encounter these complaints later many times in various works, mainly in introductions to translations of the prayers.

battlers for Yiddish and Yiddish literature. Extremely interesting in this respect is another author of the seventeenth century, Yeḥiel Michal Epstein, rabbi in Prosstitz and father of the author of *Berech Avraham*. He lived at a time when the Jewish ghetto was veiled in melancholy and the mystical ascetic world-view of Isaac Luria ruled over it boundlessly. Yeḥiel Michal was also an ardent mystic[16] and dreamed of speedy redemption. More than anything else, however, he endeavored to show "that a common man can arrive at the highest level to which the scholars attain." In his morality book *Derech Ha-Yashar Le-Olam Ha-Ba*,[17] when speaking of the "conduct of him who is not a scholar," he especially stresses that "when any individual does according to his capacity, that suffices; God does not require more." "So also," Rabbi Yeḥiel Michal concludes,

in the case of study; everyone is obliged to study according to his understanding. When someone who does not understand Hebrew and studies every day, in a German book, the laws regarding how a man should conduct himself, or in other books that have been made, such as *Lev Tov*,[18] the *Taytsh-Khumesh*, *Orehot Tzaddikim* in German, *Sefer Ha-Yirah*—such study is accepted by God as much as when the scholar studies his Hebrew books according to his understanding.

Especially interesting is the thirty-first chapter of this work. "In this chapter," the pious author declares,

is stated that it is far better for one who does not understand Hebrew that he recite his prayers in the language that he does understand. There are many women who, when they are told that it is better that they say their prayers in "German" which they understand, rejoin: "It has been told us that the angels understand no other language than Hebrew." In truth, however, they are mistaken, for those who told them this have not studied many books . . . When one does not understand Hebrew and recites his prayer in the language that he does understand with his whole heart, with a broken heart, such a

16. An ardent follower of Isaiah Horowitz, he issued in 1683 a *Kitzur Shelah*.
17. Published in 1703. We quote according to the Vilna edition of 1874. In this work also the ascetic spirit of Horowitz's *Shenei Luḥot Ha-Berit* is strongly felt. In strong colors the author portrays the torments that await the wicked in hell and the great joys that await the righteous in heaven.
18. The author of *Derech Ha-Yashar* was a strong admirer of *Lev Tov*. "The book *Lev Tov*," we read in the twenty-sixth chapter, "is a mighty book. It was made by a great sage who was a great scholar."

prayer is far more acceptable to God, because it comes from the heart, than a prayer that one recites in Hebrew that he does not understand. Because God proves all hearts, no angel is required therefor, for God Himself accepts such a prayer. In Psalm 102 it is written: "A prayer of the poor, when he fainteth and poureth out his complaint before the Lord." "Poor" means one who is poor in knowledge, that is, poor in understanding. He does not understand Hebrew and recites his prayer in a language that he understands and does it for God, who creates no angel for this purpose but Himself accepts it. So also several books write: One word that a man understands has more effect than hundreds of words that are not understood . . . Therefore, my good friends, see that our ancestors translated all our prayers or Psalms or other petitions and everything into German. The whole order of prayers was made into German; also the Psalms and the *seliḥot* and *yotzerot* of all the festivals and some of the *Maḥzorim* have been printed [in German], as well as *maamadot* and all *teḥinnot* and *bakkashot*. Even in the case of the [regular] prayers, the German was printed alongside them for many years. And as for the statement to the effect that the angels do not understand German, our ancestors took a great deal of trouble to translate everything so that persons who do not understand the holy language should say everything in German. For what one understands goes to the heart. This is certainly done with complete concentration and inner intention. So their prayer is definitely accepted.

Under the conditions in which the Jewish quarter lived in that era when the ascetic-religious world view ruled without restraint over the life and cultural requirements of the people, the battle for Yiddish necessarily had to bear a strictly religious character. The need for books in Yiddish is mainly urged from the purely religious point of view: "One who cannot study [in Hebrew], and women also, should read German books so that they may know and understand how to serve God." And on the Sabbath they should "rest from all work and also from words that one ought not to say, but speak only words of Torah; and they should study, each according to his capacity." The publisher of *Shevet Yehudah* in Yiddish, Eliakum Shatz, stresses that he is issuing this historical work "because the people on the Sabbath and festival days stand about in the marketplaces and the streets and discuss with one another matters that are not good, all kinds of scoffing and gossip and falsehoods; so it is better that they should read such books, wherein one can see the miracles and wonders that were done for our fathers in ancient days." Highly typical in this respect is the chapter "Sabbath Morning" in the book *Minhagim* that Simeon Hanau of Frankfurt published:[19]

After table Jews should study, and one who cannot study should read godly books in German, for the Sabbath complains before the Holy One Blessed Be He that all things have their partner and the Sabbath has no partner. To which the Holy One Blessed Be He replies: Let Israel be your partner, that is, let them study the Torah on you when they are idle. The Torah also complains and says: When Israel comes to Palestine, this one will go into his field, this one to his garden, but who will study me? To which the Holy One Blessed Be He replies: On the Sabbath they are at leisure; let them study you then.

Nevertheless, many of the rabbis were very displeased not only with the secular literature in Yiddish, the knightly romances and fairy tales, against which, as we previously noted, such Yiddishists as Cornelius Adelkind, Eliakum ben Isaac of Posen (author of *Lev Tov*), and the like battled, but also with the religious, didactic book in Judeo-German, with the popular book in general. We have observed[20] how an author of the sixteenth century, the man of the people Isaac Sulkes, complains in the preface to his translation of the Song of Songs that the scholars look with contempt and distrust on religious books that are written in Judeo-German and that aim to teach the common people morality and piety. We noted there how Sulkes endeavors to calm the scholars, "the great masters who are full of Torah and sit whole days and nights over their books," telling them to have no fear that he and others like him wish to trespass on their domain. He attempts to show that, alongside the "rich shops" satisfying the requirements of the "noble people," must exist "small shops . . . that can also give to the common man for his money."

This, however, was of no avail. The demands and requirements of the common people, of the artisan and handworker, very frequently came into conflict with the conceptions and interests of the scholars. Thus, there had to be a collision. The previously mentioned Joseph bar Yakar,[21] with his popular views and ironic attitude toward the *yotzerot* and liturgical hymns, could not be especially pleasing to the rabbis and scholars. We noticed, however, that even such a God-fearing and pietistic writer as the author of *Lev Tov* had the courage to

19. We quote according to the 1733 edition, 26b.
20. See above, Chapter V.
21. See above, Chapter IV.

declare that, when the ordinary person recites in the synagogue pieces of liturgical poetry with their difficult language
that are incomprehensible to him, he is a "blasphemer and
denier." And Yeḥiel Michal Epstein argues in his *Derech Ha-
Yashar:* "But let the women not say any *maamadot* and *korbanot*
. . . The less one says that he does not understand the better
it is." Joseph bar Yakar at least still acknowledged that "the
holy language is the wheaten flour, the cream of the crop," but
among the authors in Judeo-German there were also those who
went much further and declared that in general it is all the
same whether one reads in Hebrew or in the vernacular. The
author of the Yiddish *Esrim Ve-Arba,* Ḥayyim ben Nathan of
Prague (1674), declares: "No man needs to be ashamed to read
these books, because it is no shame for him to read German, for
in former times our sages translated the *Gemara* and the *Mishnah* so that they could be understood; for when one knows
nothing—then this is a shame . . . an eternal shame. *It is equally
valid if one studies in the holy language or in German,* for in learning a *halachah, he also uses German."* Therefore, the important
thing is understanding well."[22] "There is no difference," main-
tains the unfortunate Beylah bat Jacob Perl, who buried all of
her seven children, "with what one benefits the many—
whether the holy tongue or German (Yiddish)." This she argued to her husband Issachar Ber Eybeschütz, the scholarly
rabbi, requesting him to write, "as a memorial for their seven
children who died," a book of consolation and moral instruction in Yiddish, "that he may describe the expectation of his consolation, and perhaps some other person who will read this book
will also find his consolation." But the rabbi refused to occupy
himself with a book in common Yiddish. He preferred to finish
scholarly Hebrew works, a commentary to the Torah and novellae to the Talmud ("But he would not do it, because he had to
complete his book"). The miserable mother begged "from day to
day" until finally, "through my much talking, he said: Since I
have found that such a scholar as Maimonides wrote his books
in France (?) so that everyone might understand . . . So he sat
down and made the book." Nevertheless, the scholarly Issachar
Ber refused to publish a common Yiddish book, and his composition (it was called *Be'er Sheva*) remained in manuscript.[23]

22. We quote according to Schulmann, *Ha-Shiloaḥ,* VIII, 135.
23. A complete copy of *Be'er Sheva* was in the hands of Eleazar Schulmann (see his
work, 104–105).

The folk literature, however, spread ever more widely. And while the publisher of the *Maaseh-Bukh* writes, "You presently have all the German books; now you also have the German *Gemara*, and so you will have the entire Torah," several generations later the author of *Emunat Yisrael*, Gedaliah Teikus, declares proudly, "In truth all the things which he [the schoolboy] hears from the teacher, he can better read in German [i.e., Yiddish] books, for today, in our times, literally the whole Torah and all the laws are in German" (we quote according to the Vilna edition, 1816).

In fact, however, many were strongly displeased with this. The scholars could not derive much joy from the fact that the "German books" explained things better than they,[24] and it also did not please all the rabbis that "literally the whole Torah and all the laws" were easily accessible for the common people. Furthermore, the preachers could find little to delight them in the statement of the author of *Tze'enah U-Re'enah* in the preface to his *Ha-Maggid:* "They completely translated the twenty-four [books of the Bible] so that a person would not have to seek a preacher or expositor who should tell him the twenty-four . . . but he can study himself. Hence they called the book *Sefer Ha-Maggid*, that is to say, *one needs no maggid* (expositor or preacher) who should tell him the twenty-four." All this makes quite comprehensible the indignation of the rabbis when the publisher of Vilna issued the second section of *Simḥat Ha-Nefesh* under the heading *Shulḥan Aruch*.

However, the *Shulḥan Aruch* was not the only book that the rabbis found it unsuitable for women and ignorant persons to be able to use. They concluded in general that it is forbidden to disclose to the common people the profound mysteries hidden in the Midrashim and other sacred books. They also concluded that such morality books as *Ḥovot Ha-Levavot*[25] and *Menorat Ha-Maor* are too holy and profound to be translated into *Leshon Ashkenaz*. Only when one takes all this into consid-

24. The author of *Masach Ha-Petaḥ*, Feivish of Metz, also considered it necessary to note that he gives in his textbook "many convenient instructions for common people, men and women, on how they can themselves teach their children grammar, without a teacher."

25. First published in Yiddish translation only in 1716 under the following title-page: "The book is called *Ḥovot Ha-Levavot.* It is unique in the world. It was made and well thought out by the great and pious scholar, Rabbenu Baḥya of former times, so that men and women and all people should turn to it. It is organized into ten gates and portals, so that young and old may understand it.

eration does the polemic of the *dayyan* of Amsterdam Moses Frankfurter (1672–1762)[26] become comprehensible. In 1722 he published *Menorat Ha-Maor* with his Yiddish translation. In the introduction[27] Moses Frankfurter considers it necessary to attack the "scholars" who believe "that it is not rightly done to write such books in *Leshon Ashkenaz* and to disclose to everyone the things that are written in the Midrashim and *Gemarot*. Therefore I have shown that the contrary is the case. It is a commandment to make books in all languages . . . One who cannot study in Hebrew should study in his own language."

Moses Frankfurter writes further:

An even greater thing do I wish to show you, that all our books that are most difficult to learn were very little made in the Hebrew language but in the language that the common man spoke. First, the *Talmud Yerushalmi* was made in the language that men, women and children spoke in Palestine, and not in Hebrew. Also in our *Gemara* that is called the *Talmud Bavli* there is much that is not Hebrew. In the Midrash also there is much that is not in Hebrew but in the language that the common man spoke in the countries where the book was made. The *Targum Jonathan* and *Yerushalmi* in which there are many mysteries was made in a common language so that everyone should be able to understand. The *Zohar* is a very holy and fearful book which consists only of mysteries of the Torah, and it was made not in the holy tongue but in the language they spoke in Babylonia. And so it is with many other books.

A contemporary of Moses Frankfurter's went much further than the *dayyan* of Amsterdam in his battle for Yiddish as a literary language. This was a "common man," a resident of a small town in south Germany, Aaron ben Samuel of Hergershausen. Orphaned at a very early age, he wandered about among strangers from childhood on and used to be given his meals at different homes each day. His youth passed without light and joy. "Only distress and poverty and troubles and the contempt of enemies forced me to call on God for help, for my parents left me and I had no friend in the whole world, so I placed all my hope in God." Samuel "sought consolation" in the Torah and in the holy books, but he knew very little Hebrew. He found what his solitary soul longed for so greatly in

26. The historian Menaḥem Mann writes in his *She'erit Yisrael* of Moses Frankfurter: "The renowned judge our master our teacher, Moses Frankfurter, who was also rabbi of the holy society *Gemilut Ḥasadim.*"
27. About this introduction we wrote many years ago in our article "Di Ershte Yidishisten" (*Moment*, 1911, No. 26).

the "precious" books in Yiddish, in the folk literature. In this literature he discovered the loyal friend and guide that he sought; it became his comfort and support throughout his life. In tender, moving prayers he expresses his praise and gratitude to the Creator for the vast grace He has shown him. But he was not content with this. He also wanted to benefit others, to open the eyes and illuminate the hearts of those like him. May they, he explains, enjoy much happiness through him. May men, women, and children who are even lower than he perceive, through persons such as he, the good and right way that leads to the source of living waters, which he himself drew from the books in Yiddish. Samuel proceeded to write a unique prayer-book entitled *Liblikhe Tfile Oder Greftige Artznay Far Guf Un Neshome* (Furth, 1709).[28]

I know, the author declares beforehand, that some proud scholars will laugh at my simple words, but Ben Sira has said: Better less learning but with fear of God than much wisdom mixed with hypocrisy. Even though arrogant persons with false hearts laugh at me and will not understand my sincere wish, I hope that all upright, good hearts will recognize in my work the good will of my heart.

The author does not exaggerate when he declares on the title-page that his is a work "that has not appeared in such German [Yiddish] print since the world has existed." This is sufficiently attested by the lengthy introduction that the author placed before his *Liblikhe Tfile.*[29] Aaron ben Samuel, this common man of the people (*Lantz-Man* as he himself expresses it) had the courage to issue forth decisively against the whole system of educating children that was prevalent at that time among Jews, and he stresses that he wrote this "quite long introduction in German" so that the ordinary man might be able to see and understand the great mistakes that are made among us. After all, we *Lantz-Layt* understand very little of the Hebrew books.

28. The title-page of Aaron ben Samuel's *Liblikhe Tfile* reads as follows: "Dear brethren, buy this dear prayerbook or mighty remedy for the body and the soul that has never been printed in such a translation since the world has been in existence. And let your wife and children read in it diligently, so they will properly refresh body and soul, for this light will shine into their hearts. As soon as the children read it over, they will immediately understand its prayers. Thereby they will enjoy this world and the world to come. Amen, so may it be God's will."

29. In the nineteenth century (1846) a German rabbi published this introduction in Isidor Bush's *Jahrbuch für Israeliten*, but unfortunately in very Germanized form. It would certainly be worthwhile to reprint it.

Simḥat Ha-Nefesh

In the *Sefer Ḥochmot* (Book of Wisdom), Aaron ben Samuel notes, it is written that if it be desired that a wise generation grow up, care must be taken that the children are brought up well and familiarized with moral instruction and proper conduct in clear, comprehensible language. All this must take place in the mother tongue, otherwise the child will not understand. Further, the author invokes *Oreḥot Tzaddikim*, where it is written that "the child's heart is like a new book on which one wishes to write; now the book comes into the hand of a fool who writes all kinds of silliness in it until it is spoiled." If the child falls into the hands of a foolish teacher, the latter instructs him in his silly fashion and fills the child's heart with nothing but foolishness, for, Aaron ben Samuel insists, a child from five to twelve years is like a new, still unwritten book, and what is inscribed in the child's heart in the course of these years remains throughout his whole life. If one writes on it wise things, clearly and comprehensibly, so that the child may grasp and understand, then he can become a wise person. But if one teaches during these years of infancy in such fashion that the child is unable to grasp what he is taught, his mind and heart remain stopped up all his years. "Therefore, the child should be taught in the mother tongue," the author repeats. If one teaches in another language, he plows with the child for six or seven years successively, and the child's heart remains stopped up, and he knows "neither of reverence nor of love." Unfortunately, Aaron ben Samuel emphasizes,

among us the custom is that a child from his earliest years must learn Hebrew, which his young mind does not understand at all, and the teacher cannot teach otherwise than he also has been taught. Thus no one can have pure reverence, as Elishah ben Abuyah said, for in his youth he did not understand it; and when he comes to years that he understands how to read German [Yiddish] his mind is stupefied and he cannot obtain from the German any proper attitude, for he reads it over superficially and takes the Hebrew much less to heart. From this come all frivolous, heedless ways, and the basic cause of all our evil is that the children in their youth do not have their learning brought to their hearts.

For this reason, indeed, Aaron ben Samuel explains further,

to help us out of this bad situation, I ventured and undertook to print as well as I could in the German mother tongue the foremost prayers and meditations *(kavvanot)*, together with some chapters of the Psalms, that such prayers may rise to Almighty God and also penetrate man's heart, so that he may improve himself in many deeds and no longer be so evil and bring great peace . . . And also the children will learn to read and speak in fine language without mistakes.

In point of fact Aaron ben Samuel did not produce a simple translation of the customary *siddur* or prayerbook. He translated only a certain number of established prayers and certain chapters of the Psalms; mainly he presented quite new prayers that he himself had composed—prayers for children, a prayer when one "goes to the synagogue," "a lovely supplication *(te-hinnah)* for a man of the country *(Lantz-Man)* who is not a scholar," "a beautiful prayer to ask that man and wife live together affectionately," and many others. And he printed his *Liblikhe Tfile*, not as all the Yiddish books were ordinarily printed, in the special *Wayber-Ksov*, but in square Hebrew letters with vowel points, as all the *siddurim* and *mahzorim* were published.

Aaron ben Samuel believed that his work "would bring great peace," but he was mistaken. His prayerbook produced not peace but indignation and resentment. In his introduction, and generally in his entire undertaking, the rabbis saw nothing but heresy and profligacy, and they banned his work as soon as it came off the press. No one dared take the heretical prayerbook into his hands. Several generations later, in 1830, in the attic in the house of study of Aaron ben Samuel's native town, hundreds of copies of this confiscated prayerbook were found.

CHAPTER NINE

Historical and Travel Literature;
MEMOIRS AND *TEHINNOT*

Historical literature in Yiddish—The Yiddish translations of *Josippon, Tam Ve-Yashar, Shevet Yehudah*, the Apocrypha, and *Tzemah David* —The chronicles *Bashraybung fun Shabsay Tzvi* and *Gzeyres Vermayza* —Menahem Mann Amelander and his *She'erit Yisrael*—The significance of Amelander's chronicle—Travel accounts in Yiddish—The legendary and fantastic elements in these accounts—*Gelilot Eretz Yisrael* and *Maaseh Amsterdam*—Abraham Levi's *Rayze-Bashraybung*— Memoirs in folk literature—*Megillat Shemuel, Megillat Eivah, Megillat Gans*, and *Megillat Berens*—The memoirs of Glückel of Hameln and their significance—The woman in folk literature—The women's prayers *(tehinnot)*—The *tehinnah* style—*Tehinnot* written for women and *tehinnot* written *by* women—Sarah Bas-Tovim as legend—Sarah Bas-Tovim as an actual personality—Composers of *tehinnot*.

N THE previous chapters we noted how intimately associated the two major streams in Old-Yiddish literature—storybooks and morality books—were. In close affinity with the morality literature was the third branch of Old-Yiddish prose—historiography. Here also the narrative material, the description of historical events, was placed in a didactic framework, interwoven with moral lessons, with a pious commentary and conclusion. The story of the event must let us "hear something," so that we may learn a lesson from it. The sins and temptations of our ancestors must be an admonition for us not to embark on evil paths, and the good deeds and dedication of former generations must be for us a mirror and guide in our grievous exile.

The first building stone for historical writing in Old-Yiddish literature was laid down by the convert to Christianity Michael Adam, the well-known publisher of the Constance translation of the Pentateuch. In 1546 Michael Adam published in Zurich a Yiddish translation of the famed *Josippon*, following the later Hebrew version that Tam Ibn Yaḥya issued in Constantinople in 1510.[1] This Zurich edition is a truly splendid monument of the Yiddish book-printing art. With its richly illustrated woodcuts, it is in general the most beautiful printed work in Old-Yiddish literature. The book itself, which is most interesting and written with great talent, found enormous favor among ordinary Jewish readers, and was several times reprinted in various translations and reworkings.

No less popular was the Yiddish translation of *Sefer Ha-Yashar* which Jacob ben Mattathias published in 1670 under the title *Tam Ve-Yashar*. On the title-page the publisher declares: "Because in this book are related the deeds that God Blessed Be He did from the creation of the world till Joshua brought the people of Israel into Palestine, we have translated it from Hebrew into Judeo-German, so that all may know the miracles and wonders."

As early as 1591 there appeared in Cracow an anonymous translation of Solomon Ibn Verga's popular historical chronicle *Shevet Yehudah*.[2] On the title-page is the statement: "Well translated in brief, for reading by common householders, men and women. One will find in it wonderful stories that happened to our ancestors in exile, and how many times they sanctified God's name [i.e., were martyrs] . . . With it man will awaken his heart to the fear of God. May God further preserve His people and send the redeemer, the Messiah son of David speedily, in our days, Amen. So may it be His will." This work also enjoyed great success among the people and was reprinted a number of times.

Very popular was Ḥayyim ben Nathan with his excellent translation of the historical books of the Apocrypha (Judith, Susannah and the Elders, Tobit, etc.) which he issued in 1625 under the title *Sefer Ha-Maasim.* "These books," the translator explains,

I translated word for word from the priestly twenty-four [i.e., from the Christian edition of the Bible], and simply abbreviated them in several places. They are charming to read and bring much reverence

1. See our *History*, Vol. II, p. 143.
2. See our *History*, Vol. IV, pp. 65ff.

for God, for one sees how our ancestors suffered many troubles but nevertheless remained with God. Therefore God helped them again. I called it *Sefer Ha-Maasim* because it is not as highly esteemed as the twenty-four [canonical books of the Hebrew Bible]. Nevertheless, they are charming, godly books.

On the other hand, the translation of David Gans' *Tzemaḥ David* which Solomon Zalman Hanau published in Frankfurt-am-Main in 1698 had very meager success. Gans' chronicle[3] is written in an overly arid, protocol-like tone, and it was unable to attract the common reader. Better fortune was enjoyed by Nathan Hannover's *Yeven Metzulah.*[4] Two years after this sad chronicle came off the press in the original Hebrew, there appeared (in 1655) a rhymed translation in Yiddish,[5] and some decades later it also appeared in a new translation.

Historical literature in Yiddish, however, does not consist of translations only. Old-Yiddish also has some original descriptions of important historical events. So, for instance, the most reliable description of the Shabbetai Tzevi movement was given us by a contemporary resident of Amsterdam, Yehudah Leib ben Ozer in his *Bashraybung Fun Shabsay Tzvi.* The author declares in his preface:

Since all my days I inquired and asked everywhere possible to me of respected and truthful men who knew anything at all of Shabbetai Tzevi, and since I spoke with many people who were personally with him and ate and drank with him and had good knowledge of his affairs, with the help of God it will be portrayed below and everything described in detail as far as my knowledge goes. You will hear fearful things that happened in those days when the whole world was literally deluded, and both Jews and Gentiles all believed that this Shabbetai Tzevi was the redeemer and actually moved worlds. And it was not only that Jews, "believers sons of believers," had faith in him, but his dread also fell upon the Christians and the princes of Edom were astonished and considered it real. When at that time any post came to Amsterdam, there was such a crowding that one person nearly crushed the other in order to hear the latest news of Shabbetai Tzevi. And so it was in all of Europe, aside from the tumult that he

3. See our *History*, Vol. VI, pp. 47ff.
4. *Ibid.*, pp. 122ff.
5. "The terrible persecutions that took place in the year 1648 and later in White Russia, Lithuania, and Poland; and because of our many sins, many thousands of souls of rabbis and scholars, men and women, young men and maidens, perished through horrible deaths—may the Lord avenge their blood. And it was made into German in rhymed verses out of the holy tongue by Moses ben Abraham Amsterdam (1655)."

aroused in Turkey, Egypt, and Palestine. So I have made from this a description as a memorial, that posterity may take an example from it.

Many sad events and bloody persecutions were written down as a memorial for future generations in the Yiddish vernacular. Around 1609 there appeared in Cracow the *Wiener Gezeyre* in which is described how, at the time of the Hussite War (1420) an entire community sacrificed their lives for the sanctification of God's name.[6] However, as early as 1582 (therefore, before the Cracow edition) one Yeḥiel ben Yedidiah of Orovchik translated this report from Yiddish into Hebrew.[7] One of the tragic episodes of the Thirty Years War, the siege of Worms in 1636, was described at length by a resident of Worms of that time in his *Tzores (Gzeyres) Vermayze* (published in *Kovetz Al Yad*, 1898). The disturbances of 1696 in Amsterdam also obtained their Yiddish historian who portrays them in his *Ayn Bashraybung Fun Der Rebeliray Tsu Amsterdam*. The blood libels, too, found their echo in Yiddish historical literature. The blood libel at Metz of 1669 was described in all its details by an anonymous resident of that city. In the introduction the author declares that he wrote his description in Judeo-German so that "everyone, women and men, young men and maidens, might be able to read it and see how many miracles God performed and protected us from the enemies of Israel; let everyone, therefore, learn from this to serve God with fear and with his whole soul until the coming of the redeemer. Amen."[8]

Considering the blood libels that occurred so frequently in the first decades of the eighteenth century in various Polish provinces, a Jewish communal leader named Ḥayyim Alshech published a work entitled *Teshuat Yisrael* in which he presents in Yiddish translation three important apologetic documents that deal with the blood libel of 1706 in the Italian town of Viterbo. "This book *Teshuat Yisrael*," writes Alshech in the introduction, "I took pains to obtain in Rome, where it was printed with the permission of the pope—may his glory increase. But it was printed in Italian and in the Latin tongue which few persons in these provinces understand. So with

6. The persecution is described in a different fashion in *Gzeyre Mimdinas Estraykh* which is printed at the end of Akiva Baer ben Joseph's *Maasei Adonai* with the subtitle: "The persecution took place in the year that is counted 5180, on the tenth of Sivan, and on the ninth of Nissan 5181.

7. See Steinschneider, *Geschichtsliteratur der Juden*, 1905, p. 67.

8. First published in full by Dr. Meir Halevi in *Filologishe Shriftn*, III, 243–282.

enormous trouble and expense I translated it from these languages into Yiddish, and every man will be able to see the content when he reads all three books through."[9]

The most important work of all of Old-Yiddish historiographical literature is undoubtedly *She'erit Yisrael*, which Moses Frankfurter's pupil Menaḥem Mann ben Solomon Halevi Amelander (died 1767?) published in Amsterdam in 1743. Menaḥem Mann was a scholarly Jew and, because of his great learning in grammar, was known as *der medakdek*, "the grammarian." A faithful disciple of Moses Frankfurter, he considered it his duty to spread abroad books in the colloquial language. With his brother-in-law Eliezer Zussman Roedelsheim,[10] Mann in 1725 began to issue *Maggishei Minḥah*, a splendid edition of the Hebrew text of the Bible with Rashi's commentary, accompanied by a Yiddish translation. Since the partners were not in a position to finance such a comprehensive work (716 pages folio) with their own capital, they employed the subscriber system; subscribers would receive the work by separate printers' sheets and pay for each sheet individually.[11] In 1743 Mann issued a corrected edition of the *Josippon*-translation, and in the same year his original historical work *She'erit Yisrael* appeared. *She'erit Yisrael* is conceived as a continuation (Part Two) of *Josippon*, beginning from the period after the destruction of the Second Temple until modern times. "Dear people," it is stated on the title-page,

run swiftly and quickly buy this mighty work, for herein are related all the wondrous stories of the things God did for us Jews from the time Josippon stopped writing and we remained in exile. For we Jews were scattered to all the ends of the earth—east and west, north and south, as they are called. May God further preserve the remnant of Israel and send us our rightful redeemer. May this happen speedily. Thereto we shall say Amen.

Menaḥem Mann diligently collected the material required for his chronicle not only from Jewish sources but also from various European sources. Like the majority of historians of that day, he was not in a position critically to distinguish common legends from reliable historical facts. Nevertheless, his work contains much valuable information regarding the

9. For a discussion of this work see Dr. J. Shatzky's notice in *Pinkes*, Vol. I, 1928, p. 12.
10. Who later in 1737 reprinted *Der Yidisher Teryak* (see above, Chapter VI, pp. 164ff.)
11. See Naḥum Shtif's notice in *Yidishe Filologye*, 1924, 388–389.

history of the Jews in Germany and Poland. Unusually rich material is presented by *She'erit Yisrael* about the Jewish community in Holland, especially Amsterdam. To acquaint the reader with Menaḥem Mann's style and mode of writing, we present here two extracts from his *She'erit Yisrael*.[12]

Beginning of Chapter 15: The author of this book says: Because the purpose of this volume is to describe how it went with us Jews to the present day, I could not refrain from taking out the main things and the novel things (*ḥiddushim*) that are written in the book *Massa'ot Binyamin*. This work was written by one called Rabbi Benjamin Rofe ben Rabbi Jonah. He was from the city of Tudela that was in the land of Navarre. He described what he himself saw in the world, in whose three parts, called Europe, Asia, and Africa, he traveled. Whatever he saw he wrote down, and he notes in what places he found Jews, and how things went with them at that time, and from what tribe and descent they are, and who their rabbis and leaders at those times were, and under what kind of sovereignty they lived. And this man was truthful, a credible and reliable person, for when he had finished his journey he returned to the land of Castile. This was in the year that is reckoned 4933. Here he was tested in regard to his credibility, and it was found that he was a very wise and understanding man in the Torah and in all of the matters in which he was examined. It was found that he was a truthful man.

Beginning of Chapter 32: "It was in the days of King Vladislav (Ladislaus IV) who was king in Poland and was a very good and pious king, worthy to be counted among the righteous, for he always did much good for the Jews of Poland. In his times there arose a low people called the Cossacks, who were Greeks. They were peasants who revolted against King Vladislav and against his nobles. This was in the year 1648, and the persecution commenced in the month of Nissan. They began to kill many hundreds of the Jews. Then numerous high officials of the Poles, with many people, rose to fight against the Cossacks, and it happened that the Poles came close to their camp in the land of the wicked, which is called Ukraine. Here the Cossacks came against them to do battle.

She'erit Yisrael achieved great success. It was reprinted twice during the author's lifetime (Fürth, 1751 and 1757) and, after his death, in 1771 (Amsterdam). To the latter edition a supplementary chapter, presenting subsequent historical events up to 1770, was added. Shortly thereafter *She'erit Yisrael* was pub-

'12. We quote according to the edition of 1771.

lished in Hebrew translation, and in the nineteenth century
Menaḥem Mann's work also appeared in Dutch.

To the historiographical literature must also be reckoned
travel accounts, whose historical value is pointed out by the
author of *She'erit Yisrael*. The Jews, the "knowers of ways,"
would frequently embark on distant voyages. Special handbooks were even produced for travelers with various items of
practical information and explanations, e.g., the work *Derech
Eretz*, which the well-known Shabbetai Bass published in Yiddish (1680) for merchants and traveling agents. Hence it is not
surprising that travel accounts were preserved in rather considerable number among Jews. In Yiddish translation appeared not only the famous travel descriptions of Benjamin of
Tudela[13] and of Petaḥiah of Regensburg,[14] but also the fantastic report of the renowned adventurer of the ninth century
Eldad Ha-Dani, who claimed that he was descended from the
tribe of Dan and came from a country of East Africa where a
substantial part of the Ten Lost Tribes reside. All the legends
and fairy tales which this unique representative of the "little
red Jews" relates in his report were taken by the translator as
pure truth. The title-page of the Yiddish translation[15] announces:

The book of Eldad Ha-Dani, who was from the tribe of Dan and told
of the dwelling place of the tribes of the sons of Moses, as is explained
in this book. In it are told the great deeds of God Blessed Be He, and
the gracious things He did for Israel. Also in it are reported where
the Ten Tribes are and how they have a king over themselves. And
the righteous Eldad is from the tribe of Dan. He told everything, and
also how beyond the Sambatyon are the sons of Moses our teacher,
peace be upon him. All of them are very righteous men, and God
Blessed Be He always does great miracles and wonders for them.
Therefore we have translated it into Yiddish, so that everyone may
see the great miracles and wonders and gracious things that God
Blessed Be He does with Israel. May God send us the righteous
redeemer, so that we may witness all these things with our own eyes,
Amen.

13. See our *History*, Vol. II, pp. 78ff. The Yiddish version of Benjamin's work appeared
    in Amsterdam in 1691.
14. Petaḥiah of Regensburg made his journey around the world in the period 1170–1180.
    The Yiddish translation of his *Sibbuv Ha-Olam* appeared in Prague in 1600 under
    the title-page: "The encircling of Rabbenu Petaḥiah the pious of Regensburg."
15. The year and the place of printing are not given. From its appearance, the edition
    comes from the eighteenth century.

Stories about the Ten Lost Tribes and the sons of Moses on the other side of the Sambatyon were in general greatly loved among the people, and a whole series of chapbooks with accounts of them appeared. One of these, *Tela'ot Mosheh*, was published in 1712 by the convert to Judaism Moses ben Abraham Avinu.[16] No less popular were travel descriptions of Palestine and the neighboring lands. The authors of such accounts assert that they witnessed with their own eyes everything they relate. Nevertheless, their reports are filled to overflowing with the most fantastic and marvelous tales. Typical in this respect is the work *Gelilot Eretz Yisrael* which appeared in Lublin in 1635. This is the report of one Gershon ben Eliezer Edels of Prague about the journey he made through various lands of the East on the way to Palestine. In this report the most marvelous novelties in the world are related as actual things that the author supposedly saw with his own eyes. Beyond Damascus, for instance, our traveler witnessed fearfully large, multi-colored beasts with three eyes, and in another place he encountered enormous creatures with five feet and three eyes. Our author further asserts that he himself saw a man without a head whose mouth and eyes were on his breast, who ate only fish, and whose speech was a kind of Greek. The reader need not be surprised that our traveler also saw birds that spew fire, gazed at the Tower of Babel built by the Biblical "generation of the dispersion," and at the ford of Jabbok marvelled at the narrow passage where the patriarch Jacob wrestled with the angel. Gershon ben Eliezer even asserts that with his own eyes he saw still inscribed in stone the footprints of the mighty wrestlers. In Shushan he saw with enchantment the casket of Daniel Ish Ḥamudot hanging high over the river and shining like pure gold. Our traveler was also at the river Sambatyon and himself heard the noise and rushing of the fearful hale of stones that rages ceaselessly through the six days of the week. Not far from the brook Kidron he saw the pillar of salt into which Lot's wife was transformed. At midnight, our credulous traveler relates, one can observe the pillar of stone in its natural size. At dawn, however, it has shrunk to two cubits. Gershon ben Eliezer explains this "naturalistically." Sheep, as is well know, are great lovers of salt, and so they come in the dark hours of the night by the hundreds and lick the heap

16. See Zunz, *Gesammelte Schriften*, p. 193; Schulmann, *op. cit.*, 126.

of salt; in the course of the day, however, the column grows again to its former size.

The most characteristic thing in this connection is that the foremost rabbis of that age, e.g., the well-known "Baḥ," Joel Sirkes, gave their approbations to the fantastic reports of our Baron Munchhausen.[17] *Gelilot Eretz Yisrael,* however, found some disfavor among the Jesuits in Poland, and at their command the work was burned in Warsaw. But it was soon reprinted under a different title, *Derech Ha-Kodesh.*[18] It was also translated into Hebrew and several times reprinted.

There also appeared numerous travel accounts which, from the outset, were written with the definite purpose of entertaining the reader, providing him with some interesting material for his perusal. These are, in fact, plain storybooks in the form of travel descriptions. One such little book bears the name *Maaseh Amsterdam.*[19] On the title-page we read: "A story of Amsterdam. A travel account made by Rabbi Levi of Amsterdam describing how he and nine other Jews departed from Amsterdam on a ship. *Maaseh Amsterdam* tells how in the year 5442 a ship was fitted out from Amsterdam with much food and persons, as well as many weapons, so that men might travel on the sea to discover unknown islands. Hence, we Jews also decided to send along several Jews, to find out whether there are not places where there are Jews of whom we did not as yet know."

There also appeared in Yiddish, even though in rather small numbers, quite realistic travel accounts, without any legendary and fantastic embellishments. The most important among these is undoubtedly the *"Rayze-Bashraybung* (Travel Description) of Abraham Levi through Germany, Bohemia, Moravia, Hungary, Styria, Austria, Tyrol in Italy, Lombardy, the Marches of Antona, Romagna, Tuscany, and Bologna."

Abraham Levi was born in 1702 in the little town of Horn (in the German state of Lippe). As he relates in his report, when he was still a boy the "historical books" aroused in him an intense desire to travel through the world, so that already then he decided to set out as soon as he was grown up. "At the end of the seventeenth year of my life," he relates, "in the year 5479

17. Baron Munchhausen is the hero of collections of extraordinarily mendacious and exaggerated tales popular in European literature.
18. The title *Derech Ha-Kodesh* (Holy Way) is taken from the first line of the author's introduction: "Do not wonder at the act of a man poor in knowledge such as I, for he took his way, the *holy way,* to go up to the house of God."
19. The place and year of printing are not noted.

(1719) I began my journey. Through Germany to Bohemia, Hungary, Austria, Styria, to Tyrol in Italy, and finished . . . in the year 5484."[20]

From the Hebrew acrostic which the author placed before his *Rayze-Bashraybung* it is clear that Abraham Levi was a learned man and had a good command of the language of the Bible. However, he was absolutely free of the mystical world view which then dominated the Jewish ghetto. He was a man who looked with sober, open eyes on God's world, and in his chronicle he noted everything that interested him and attracted his attention factually, aridly, in protocol-like fashion, without lyricism and without the least effusiveness.[21] Youthful and eager for knowledge, he regarded everything attentively, and his report therefore yields a wealth of interesting and reliable detail regarding the contemporary life of the Jews. Abraham Levi gives us the number of residents of many Jewish communities that he visited. We find a precise portrait of the way of life in such important Jewish centers as Prague and Nikolsburg. He acquaints us with the wealthy tax farmers, bankers, and Court Jews of that time, such as Samson Wertheimer, Mendel Oppenheimer, and Abraham Ulma. He also describes the little village houses in Moravia, the care and feeding of silk worms in Italy, the grand military parades before the emperor's court in Vienna, and the marvelous panorama disclosed before the enchanted eyes of the traveler when he approaches the magnificent city of Venice by ship. One can only regret that this travel account remained for more than one hundred and sixty years in manuscript and was then published in such an inaccessible journal as the Amsterdam *Israelietische Letterbode.*[22] Hence, we present two sizeable extracts from Abraham Levi's travel account.

I

The Jewish Ghetto in Nikolsburg

The *Judengasse* is also one of the suburbs and has about six hundred houses. They have two large synagogues which are called the Old Synagogue and the New Synagogue. They are also, just as in Prague, very assiduous in study, so that one finds here, too, many Jewish

20. Abraham Levi died in great old age in the year 1785.
21. A characteristic feature: Abraham Levi deliberately avoids Hebrew words and expressions in his report; this makes his protocol-like style even more arid and monotonous.
22. Vol. X, 1884–1885.

students from abroad. The clothing of the Jews is here similar to that of Poland, with long coats called *rek-shubtz* and another one over them called *hilrok* . . . and a wide fur coat that they call *oyshoyb*. The women, however, call their clothing *mieder* and *funti*. They also wear cloaks with a four-edged piece of black velvet on their backs that is called *mantil*. On their heads they wear a veil like a funnel or a hunter's horn. The girls all go about with braided hair—rich or poor, all alike. The married men wear beards, long beards, and do not allow themselves to be sheared by any knife; they are pious people. They mourn their dead very keenly. When someone dies, the women as well as the men follow [the body] and raise a mournful cry that is heard throughout all the streets. The cemetery is also close to the Jewish street. They do not make a casket when one dies but lay him in the grave on the earth. However, they place on each side a board on which a cover may be laid. But when it is a *kohen* (priest) who dies they do make a casket.

As far as the Jews' ceremonials and customs are concerned, everything is to be praised. They take care on Fridays, as soon as the afternoon arrives, to close their shops and do no more business, but undress and go to bathe. They wash their bodies clean, put on their Sabbath clothes, and read through the prescribed lection from the Torah for the week once in Hebrew and twice in Aramaic. They themselves decorate the house with ornaments; they are the most painstaking servants. They do not ask this of their servants but do it themselves to honor the Sabbath. Each one has a baking oven in the kitchen, and every Friday they bake fresh bread. All must have three kinds of food—wine, fish, and meat. Even if they be among the poorest, they must have these three things and purchase them on Friday to honor the Sabbath. When the day grows late, a synagogue beadle comes dressed in his best clothing and calls out: In half of a quarter hour *Kabbalat Shabbat* (the service for the welcoming of the Sabbath) will be held. And so everyone goes to the synagogue. Here [i.e., in the synagogue] the practice is the same as that carried on in Prague, and described by us, with singing and music and a beautiful postlude which frequently goes on for quite a long time. Their singers are also renowned; not many of their like are to be found. The most outstanding is called Mordecai Ḥazzan.

II
The Jews in Vienna

They [the Jews] lead here [in Vienna] a peaceful life, except for one difficulty that they have—the so-called *Glöckelei* (bell-ringing). This is when the priests go to visit a sick person. Then they come with a little silver statue [of Jesus] and a bell in front of it. Before this all passersby fall down on their knees. When a Jew meets such a procession, the priests or the students they have along with them are fully authorized to force the Jew to his knees; if he refuses, they may slay him on the spot. When a Jew encounters such a sight, he must take care to cross the street or withdraw. I myself was in this danger two or three times. Once as I was going to Prince Eugene's Garden and came into the neighborhood, I saw a procession from a distance coming very quickly toward me. I wanted to withdraw, and so I went into a house. I ran into a maidservant, and she informed the owners that there was a Jew in the house. The people realized why I had come, and one of them wanted to conduct me out forcibly as the priests passed by. I gave the maid a coin, and so she let me out through a back door and I ran away. Another time I was standing in the marketplace to buy several things and I saw a student looking at me. Suddenly he asked me if I was a Jew. I replied affirmatively, and he said to me: Turn around and look. Then I saw a party of men carrying candles with many following them. I realized at once that these were the men with the bell, and so I ran away. The student who had recognized me ran after me crying all the time: Jew, take off your hat! I ran, with him pursuing me, until he seized my hat from behind me. I did not want to stop and was afraid of a wicked crowd following. I ran away into another street and bought another hat for my head.

Abraham Levi's *Rayze-Bashraybung* is, in manner and tone, quite close to another genre in the history of literature, namely, memoirs. This genre is rather poorly represented both in Hebrew and in Yiddish literature. Most of the memoirs that have been preserved in Old-Yiddish literature bear the title *megillah* (scroll). Such scrolls tell of tragic events which certain families or individual persons lived through. So, for example, there is a *Megillat Shemuel*. From the title-page we learn: "The Scroll of Samuel, the head of the community of Prague. In this are related the miracles and wonders which the Holy One Blessed Be He, in the greatness of His compassion and in the greatness of His lovingkindness, did for the leader and chieftain, the *parnass* and renowned intercessor Rabbi Samuel Tausk, head of the holy community of Prague and the whole community of Israel, in the year 5464, when he was saved from a calumnious libel. May the Holy One Blessed Be He further save all Israel and send our Messiah." In this scroll, written in 1720,[23] is related at length how the leader of the community of Prague was imprisoned through a slander in 1704 and the whole community was in grave jeopardy. A similar character is borne by the memoirs of the renowned Rabbi Yom-Tov Heller, *Megillat Eivah*, which was also originally written in Yiddish,[24] and by

---

23. First published in *Kovetz Al Yad*, 1899.
24. See our *History*, Vol. VI, pp. 100ff. Rabbi Yom-Tov Heller also considered it necessary to translate into Yiddish (1626) the well-known testament of Rabbi Asher

the scroll that tells of the ill fortune of the brothers Berens who were incarcerated at the beginning of the eighteenth century on the basis of a libel.[25] *Megillat Gans*, published by David Kaufmann in 1896, gives us a melancholy picture of Jewish life in Germany in the middle of the seventeenth century. A significant interest is also aroused by the *Megillat Rabbi Meir* (first published in *Kovetz Al Yad*, 1904) which originated in 1631. Its author, Meir ben Yeḥiel, relates how as a fifteen-year-old boy in 1608 he set out, along with eight other boys, from Ungarisch Brod to Cracow to study at the *yeshivah* there, and on the way all of them were taken captive by some "landowner."

The true pride and glory of Yiddish memoir literature, however, is represented by the *Memoirs (Zichronot;* in Yiddish, *Zikhroynes)* of the well-known Glückel of Hameln. We pointed out earlier how, as a result of the printing press and the development of popular literature associated with it, the woman became a significant cultural factor in Jewish family life. Books were especially produced for her, and efforts were made to point out her newly risen cultural worth. But women were not content with associating themselves with the national culture through the popular book; they also ventured to take part themselves, according to their powers, in its creation, in preserving and disseminating its collected treasures. Already in the middle of the sixteenth century the *firzogerin (ha-rabbanit ha-darshanit),*[26] the precentress for women Rebecca bat Meir Tiktiner, acquired a great reputation with her learning. She even aroused interest in the Christian learned world; the scholar Wagenseil speaks of her with enthusiasm in his work on the Talmudic tractate *Sotah* (printed in 1674), and in 1719 a German professor wrote a special Latin essay on her. Rebecca Tiktiner composed a morality book entitled *Meineket Rivkah* in which she presents numerous statements from the *Gemara* and Midrashim. The work was first published many years after her death, first in Prague (1609) and later in Cracow (1618). However, already in Wagenseil's time the book was extremely rare,

---

ben Yeḥiel (Rosh) entitled *Sefer Ha-Hanhagah* (see our *History*, Vol. III, p. 84) so that all, "small and great, should understand it." Rabbi Yom-Tov Heller also issued a booklet in Yiddish entitled *Berit Melaḥ* (on laws concerning the salting of meat) which was several times reprinted.

25. This *megillah* was in the hands of the historian Jost. He greatly deplored the fact that such an interesting document was written in a "corrupted jargon" and therefore "improved" it and published it in a Germanized re-working (in *Jahrbuch für Geschichte der Juden und des Judenthums*, II).

26. On *firzogerins*, see above, Chapter I, pp. 23ff.

and we have, unfortunately, not had the opportunity to become familiar with this work of the "first woman writer in Yiddish," as Wagenseil calls her.[27]

In 1586 Roizl Fishels published Moses Stendal's translation of the Psalms and, along with it, wrote a lengthy preface in verse:

Roizl bas Reb Fishel people call me.
This they do because they do not know my father, may his
    memory be for blessing.
Rabbi Joseph Levi is his name, of the tribe of the Levites,
Who are all servants of God Blessed Be He.
And his father was Rabbi Jehudah Levi the older, peace be
    upon him,
Who conducted a *yeshivah* for fifty years in the holy
    community of Ludomir.[28]

Elis bat Mordecai Michals of Slutzk made herself known with her translation of *Maavar Yabbok* (1704), and also a translation of the prayers. Another translation of the prayers was set in type by Gele,[29] the eleven-year-old daughter of the convert to Judaism Moses ben Abraham. The young typesetter set before the edition these artless lines:

Of this beautiful new prayerbook from beginning to end,
I set all the letters in type with my own hands.
I, Gele, the daughter of Moses the printer, and whose
    mother was Freide, the daughter of Rabbi Israel Katz,
    may his memory be for a blessing.
She bore me among ten children;
I am a maiden still somewhat under twelve years.
Be not surprised that I must work;
The tender and delicate daughter of Israel has been in exile
    for a long time.
One year passes and another comes
And we have not yet heard of any redemption.
We cry and beg of God each year
That our prayers may come before Him Blessed Be He,
For I must be silent.
I and my father's house may not speak much.[30]

27. On Rebecca Tiktiner's "Simḥat-Torah poem," see the next chapter.
28. See Schulmann, *op. cit.*, pp. 24–25.
29. Born in 1702.
30. A reference to the fact that her father was not born of Jews.

As will happen to all Israel,
So may it also happen to us,
For the Biblical verse says,
All people will rejoice
Who lamented over the destruction of Jerusalem,
And those who endured great sufferings in exile
Will have great joy at the redemption.

These simple, artless lines of the youthful typesetter lead us into the intimate spiritual world inhabited by the Jewish woman. In them is felt the breath of the unique atmosphere that was created around the feminine population of the ghetto as a result of the newly blossomed folk-literature, with its narrative-didactic style. In this respect the *Memoirs* of Glückel of Hameln are extraordinarily interesting.

Glückel was born in 1645 in Hamburg into the wealthy family of the *parnass* of the community, Leib Pinkerle. At the age of fourteen she married the wealthy jeweler Ḥayyim of Hameln and thereafter lived happily with him for thirty years. Then her husband died and left her with twelve orphaned children. The grieving widow became extremely melancholy, and in her sleepless nights filled with bitter despair she arrived, as she relates in her *Memoirs*, at the idea of describing for her children as a memorial the life of their father and, incidentally, acquainting them with the highly prestigious family from which they were descended and with the good deeds and piety of their ancestors. "My dear children," Glückel reports on the first pages of her *Memoirs*,

I began to write this with the help of God after the death of your pious father, for it was something of a relief and pleasure to me when melancholy thoughts came and grievous worries, for we were like sheep without a shepherd and we lost our faithful pastor. So I spent many nights sleeplessly and I was worried that I might—God forbid —come to melancholy thoughts. Hence, I frequently rose at night and passed the sleepless hours with this.[31]

From the outset Glückel undertook to present a portrait of very broad compass, to write up her recollections in seven

31. *Zichronot* (Memoirs), 1896, pp. 3-4, 20.

volumes. Her project was completely fulfilled. She began her life's work in 1691 as a middle-aged woman and finished it as an old lady of seventy-four in 1719.[32] Glückel's *Memoirs* undoubtedly have a significant historical-social value. They provide a wealth of extremely important information about the economic and social conditions of the Jews of that time, about their business relationships, and about the entire contemporary community in Germany and the neighboring lands. It is impossible to write the history of the communities of Hamburg, Altona, Hannover, Hildesheim, and Metz during the second half of the seventeenth century without employing Glückel's *Memoirs*.

These *Memoirs* are important, however, not merely as a historical monument but also as a significant literary phenomenon and a fascinating *document humain*. The wife of the merchant Ḥayyim of Hameln, the pious and God-fearing Glückel, was endowed not only with a phenomenal memory that absorbed like a sponge all the important events of her past life; she was also blessed with a poetic, deeply feeling soul and with the spark of a true artist. She is not content with telling us about the years of her past. She also provides a moral portrait of her environment, the way of life in her milieu. In this respect it is especially interesting to compare Abraham Levi's *Rayze-Bashraybung* with Glückel's *Memoirs*. In Levi's work there is a protocol-like, dry narration of personal experiences and social events, while in Glückel's there grows before the reader a colorful portrait of the old-fashioned Jewish life. In the center of this portrait clearly emerges, in its very extraordinary form, the remarkable Jewess who was endowed not only with a clear, practical understanding but also with an ardently loving heart and a poetic, richly imaginative soul.

Glückel did not possess any European education. She notes (p. 26) that as a child "she had to sit in the *ḥeder* (elementary school)." But it is very doubtful whether she was able to read the text of the Bible and the Hebrew morality books in the original. All her learning, which she displays in broad measure in her *Memoirs*, was drawn chiefly, if not exclusively, from the folk-literature. The Judeo-German "godly" books disclosed to her the treasures of the Jewish national culture, familiarized her with the ethical world view of Judaism and with the colorful tapestry of *aggadot* and legends. The singular world of ideas and concepts that dominates the Jewish ethical literature (*mu-*

---

32. Glückel died in 1724.

sar) became our memoirist's intimate world of feeling and experience. From it, too, she drew her unshakeable belief in God's infinite grace and mercy that are poured out over the world, despite all the sufferings and troubles that man must endure in life. She also endeavors to implant this faith in her sons and daughters. "Therefore," Glückel tells her children,

let every person who has the fear of God in himself accept punishment from God willingly and joyfully, for sufferings are a redemption for his body and his merits in the world-to-come that is eternal, and he is assured that his Creator will give him everything good if he relies on his Creator . . . Dear children, I may not expatiate on this, for otherwise I would enter too deeply into it and ten books would not suffice. Read in the German *Brantshpigl,* in *Lev Tov,* or—he who can do so—in the morality books. You will find everything there. Therefore, I beg you, my dear children, be patient. If the Holy One Blessed Be He sends you some punishment, accept everything patiently and do not cease to pray. Perhaps He will have mercy. And who knows what is good for us sinful men—whether it is good for us to live in this world in great wealth and comfort and spend all our time in this transient world in pleasure and enjoyment, or whether it is better for us that our Heavenly Father always keeps us under the rod of His correction in this sinful world, so that we may always have our eyes directed toward heaven and ever call upon our gracious Father with our whole heart and with our hot tears? So I am confident that the faithful, gracious God will have mercy and redeem us from the long, grievous exile. His compassion is great, His mercy vast. What He has promised us will certainly come. Let us only wait patiently.[33]

The influence of *musar,* or the traditional ethical literature, is also very strongly discernible in Glückel's writing. She constantly repeats: "My dear children, I do not intend to make and write for you a morality book."[34] The style of the ethical literature, however, powerfully dominates her whole world view, her entire way of thinking and feeling. Her *Memoirs* are not only filled with quotations from the Talmudic sages and traditional moral instruction; she also very eagerly utilizes parables, fables, tales, and all kinds of "morality book stories." Glückel even apologizes occasionally for this practice, and when introducing a tale "as one finds it in the account of Alexander of Macedon," she remarks immediately: "I do not write this story as the truth; it may be only a heathen fable. I placed it here in

33. *Ibid.,* pp. 13–14.
34. *Ibid.,* p. 4 and other places.

order to while away the time."[35] The rich narrative and folk-loristic part of the morality literature was dear to her poetic soul and became an organic, characteristic aspect of her style. The parables of the Talmudic sages, all of the "morality book stories" and "heathen fables," grew into Glückel's intimate world, became the air that she breathed and the essential material out of which she wove and with which she embellished her tapestry of recollections. And this is done with such artless simplicity and sweet sincerity that even the modern reader is unwillingly attracted by the magic of this singular, harmoniously integral and firmly believing world. Thus, the ordinary family recollections of an impoverished woman, depressed by great trouble, are raised to the level of an artistic work of broad scope and significance.[36]

However, it is not only the influence of the Yiddish morality books that is discernible in Glückel's style. In every page of her *Memoirs* is also felt the *woman*, the old-fashioned Jewish woman, with her humble, sorrowful mood, her intimate tenderness. Through this, her style obtains the specific coloration that is so characteristic of that very unique branch of Jewish religious literature whose heyday began in the seventeenth century and is known under the name *tehinnot* (in Yiddish, *tkhines*).

We noted previously[37] that as early as the Middle Ages, before the printing press was invented, Judeo-German translations of the prayers already existed. One of the oldest printed books in the folk language that has been preserved is Joseph bar Yakar's translation of the *Siddur* (1544). After bar Yakar's translation came another which was published in Mantua (1562), and then many others.[38] Numerous translations of the Festival Prayerbook and of collections of customs *(minhagim)* also appeared. *Sefer Hanhagot Hayyim Bo Yi'matze Hayyim* (The Book of the Conduct of Life in Which One Will Find Life) we read on the title-page of such a custumal translation:

This little book is well thought out. He who lives according to it will find eternal life, and in it are also many supplications *(tehinnot)* and petitions *(bakkashot)* wherewith one can live in God's service. I have

35. *Ibid.*, p. 21.
36. On Glückel's language, see A. Landau's work in *Mitteilungen der Gesellschaft für jüdische Volkskunde*.
37. Above, p. 23.
38. Yeḥiel Michal Epstein also published a translation of the prayers (*Derech Yesharah*, 1697).

translated it into German so that the whole world may understand. One will well perceive in it how a person should conduct himself in the synagogue. What is written in it cannot all be set forth here. But he who reads it will be well pleased by it. Therefore, dear people, let the small price of this little book not bother you, for, holding it, you will enjoy the world-to-come because of it (Wilmersdorf, 1724).[39]

"Wherewith one can live in God's service"—to this end Samson Frankfurter also printed in Yiddish (1703) the second part of his *Sefer Ha-Ḥayyim* (laws of mourners and instructions on the purification of a corpse): "All the rules of mourning, well explained in German, for men and women, boys and girls." In the introduction it is noted: "Hear, dear people, why I made this book in German. This is brought about by this time when the people of Israel are scattered in all places and do not everywhere have rabbis who may teach them and show them what everything signifies, and not everyone knows the right way to deal with the bodies of the dead."[40]

The "German form of speech" was also provided so that everyone should know "what is to be said at the graves of parents and friends. Also on the eve of Rosh Ha-Shanah and the eve of Yom Kippur, that one should pray for a good year, that the Holy One Blessed Be He forgive us our sins and grant us what we ask of him and prosper us in all our ways."[41] Even special handbooks containing religious instructions on how a man ought to conduct himself while traveling were published (*Siaḥ Ha-Sadeh*, Fürth, 1736).[42]

All these editions are permeated with a very definite tendency: to give the common reader the possibility of praying in his own language that he understands well, i.e., Yiddish. This

39. This custumal published by Samson Hanau in Hamburg in 1733 has the following title-page: "Much more beautiful than were the first—This, one will easily note in reading—About all the customs in Germany throughout the whole year—Also in Poland, Bohemia, and Moravia—And many laws set properly—Therewith everything you know to live in God's service—In addition, the book is well formed —And ornamented with all kinds of lovely new copper engravings."
40. We quote according to the Sulzbach edition of 1767.
41. We quote according to the Fürth edition of 1766.
42. There also appeared in Yiddish practical handbooks for travelling merchants. Such a handbook was published anonymously in 1680. In the same year the well-known Shabbetai Bass (see our *History*, Vol. VI, p. 152) published his above-mentioned handbook *Masechet Derech Eretz* with all necessary instructions for travelling businessmen.

tendency is most clearly expressed in the preface to the translation of the Festival Prayerbook published in Amsterdam in
1721:[43]

A prayer without inner concentration is like a body without a soul.
This means when one prays before the Holy One Blessed Be He and
does not do it with a diligent heart, the prayer is like a cripple of a
man who has no life or vitality. Now our sages, may their memory
be for blessing, said: Every Jew who wishes that his prayer be heard
at the Days of Awe should read it before Rosh Ha-Shanah and Yom
Kippur so that he may be fluent in it and understand what he is
saying. Let everyone take an example from the situation when one
has to speak before a king of flesh and blood regarding his person or
property. In such a case he sees to it that he has thought out well what
he should say, so that he does not stumble and understands what he
speaks. How much the more so before the King of kings, the Holy
One Blessed Be He. And if any man be affected in his body and
property and soul, the chief thing is that he should know what he
says. It so happens that the commentaries are also not for the common man, for they do not grasp all the words so well . . . And
especially the women, who do not understand any commentary or
what they are saying. Now our sages, may their memory be for
blessing, said: In regard to prayer, women are equally commanded
with men. Therefore we considered this and let the Festival Prayerbook be printed in German, well translated in the best fashion and
with interpretation and good explanations, that it may be useful and
good for each Jew, no matter who he be, as you will well see. This
is the rule: Be it man or woman, whoever can read, must concede that
such a Festival Prayerbook is as useful and good for his soul as gold
and silver, and when one reads in it diligently and prays with intention and inner concentration and understands what he says, the
prayer will certainly be heard. Then we shall merit the advent of the
Messiah, Amen.

In some editions, however, a different tendency is discernible. We observed previously[44] the contempt with which Joseph bar Yakar speaks of the liturgical hymns and other prayers that are written "in very difficult expressions," so that it is
hard to find possibly one in a thousand "who knows what they
mean." Aaron ben Samuel, the author of the *Liblikhe Tfile*,[45]
declared war against the canonized Hebrew Prayerbook, and
even the pious Rabbi Yeḥiel Michal Epstein declares in his

43. It is quite possible that this is a reprint of an earlier edition.
44. Above, pp. 97–98.
45. Above, Chapter VIII.

Derech Ha-Yashar Le-Olam Ha-Ba (end of Chapter 31): "But let the women not say any *maamadot* or *korbanot* . . . The less one says that he does not understand, the better it is." Thus, it is not surprising that, parallel to the canonized prayers, there were also created free Yiddish "supplications and petitions *(te ḥinnot u-vakkashot)* written in a very plain, popular style. Such printed *teḥinnot* are preserved from as early as the sixteenth century. The author of *Sama De-Ḥayyei* (or *Sam Ḥayyim*) Abraham Apteker, published in 1590 a collection of *teḥinnot*. A Yiddish *teḥinnah* is also printed at the end of *Maaseh Bet David Be-Yemei Paras*, which appeared in Basel in 1599.[46] To be sure, some of these *teḥinnot* were translated from Hebrew. In the headings of numerous old *teḥinnot* it is directly noted that they "are taken out of exalted books." One *teḥinnah*[47] begins with the following lines:

This lovely *teḥinnah* [was] translated into German from the
    holy tongue
Out of all the petitions in the world.
As you read it, your heart will rejoice.
Twenty-two prayers and petitions are listed in it;
Also twenty-two letters of the alphabet set forth according
    to an eight-fold acrosticon.
Every woman should always carry this *teḥinnah* with her.
It may be recited either on the cemetery or in the
    synagogue.

In the case of other *teḥinnot*, it is noted that they were composed by a pious and God-fearing man. For instance, in the "Teḥinnah Kodem Ha-Tefillah" we read the following report:

This holy *teḥinnah* was thought out anew;
It was made by a pious and good man.
Whoever always has the fear of God in view,
Whoever prays with intention and concentration and takes
    care,
Will be protected from evil happenings by day and by
    night.

In another *teḥinnah* ("Teḥinnah Shaarei Ratzon") it is noted: "This *teḥinnah* was brought from Jerusalem; so it is proper to

46. See N. Shtif in *Tsaytshrift*, II–III, 544.
47. Found in the collection *Teḥinnot U-Vakkashot*, No. 50 (year of printing not noted).

say it every day with weeping and lamentation."[48] The announcement that the *teḥinnah* was "brought from Jerusalem" is by no means accidental. We have already had occasion to note[49] that in the collection of prayers entitled *Shaarei Tziyyon* that Nathan Nata Hannover published, there are numerous prayers which undoubtedly had a certain influence on the *teḥinnah* literature. The "Lion's Cubs," the Kabbalists of Safed who were disciples of Rabbi Isaac Luria, and among whom prayer was the profoundest mystery, could not be content with the canonized *Siddur*. They also composed emotive hymns and tender prayers of their own in which they expressed their feelings, their ardent love for God. Many of these prayers are distinguished by their simple, popular style. Some of them were not only translated into Yiddish[50] but also served as a pattern for the *teḥinnah* literature with its unique manner and style.[51]

The number of the *teḥinnot* is enormous. For every day, for every incident and event in human life, there is a *teḥinnah* that "one should say." There are *teḥinnot* to be recited when going to the synagogue, and others to be said on departing from the synagogue. One *teḥinnah* is said before kindling the Sabbath and festival candles, another after kindling them. There is even a special "mighty prayer" which a husband is to recite in the course of the last two months of his wife's pregnancy. In addition, there are special *teḥinnot* for a widow, for a woman when her husband is traveling, when she goes to or comes from the ritual bath, when she is pregnant, when she is about to deliver a child, when she goes to the cemetery, and "when she becomes sick and lies in bed." There are also *teḥinnot* for a livelihood, for pious and good children, etc.

As we see, certain *teḥinnot* were designated especially for men. The overwhelming majority, however, were composed exclusively for the use of women. Hence, they are adapted to the feminine spirit, to the unique qualities and psyche of the woman. We have noted that some *teḥinnot* were translated

48. We quote according to the edition of Novy Dvor, 1813.
49. See our *History*, Vol. V, pp. 66, 80–81.
50. For instance, the prayers of Rabbi Isaac Luria which are printed in *Shaarei Tziyyon*, and others as well.
51. According to a notice in the American *Pinkes*, (1928, 171), Solomon Freehof in his study in English on the *teḥinnot* has shown that Hannover's *Shaarei Tziyyon* strongly influenced the *teḥinnot*—literature. Unfortunately we have not had the opportunity to read this work.

from Hebrew; on the other hand, of some it is noted that they were "made by a good and pious man." But, along with the *teḥinnot* that were produced *for* women there also appeared, in incomparably larger numbers, *teḥinnot* composed *by* women themselves. And it was the woman as composer of *teḥinnot* who created the classic *teḥinnah* style—the uniquely diffuse and wordy, intimately tender, humbly feminine style.

It is beyond doubt that the cradle of the *teḥinnah* stood at the *firzogerins* who used to read or sing prayers and supplications in the vernacular before the women in the synagogue.[52] The *firzogerins* were not content merely with translating the canonized prayers for their audience; they would also present these in paraphrase and reforge them in simpler, more popular forms. The author of these lines saw in the collection of the deceased bibliographer S. Wiener a page of an old, handwritten *teḥinnah* which Wiener conjectured was written no later than the beginning of the seventeenth century. On the page was the text of a *teḥinnah* which later came into the frequently reprinted collection *Teḥinnot U-Vakkashot* with the notation: "To be said every Thursday with great intention and concentration." This *teḥinnah* is undoubtedly a paraphrase of a Hebrew prayer, apparently reworked by a *firzogerin*. It begins as follows:[53]

May it be Your will, God of our ancestors, our Creator, Creator of the whole world from the beginning of the world with the word of Your holiness, with Your will and the will of those who fear You and the will of Your household Israel. You were alone, and no one else will be in eternity. One only and no one alongside you to rule this world and the other world. Here, I, Your maidservant, come, daughter of Your maidservant with great humility before Your holiness, that You may give me honorable sustenance . . . me and my husband and children and all who trust in You.

To gain some notion of how the female composers of *teḥinnot* would utilize and rework their Hebrew models, it is worthwhile to dwell on the "beautiful *teḥinnah* that one should pray every day for a livelihood." We quoted in the fifth volume of our *History*[54] in verbatim translation the prayer "Ana Ha-El

52. See above, pp. 23–24.
53. Unfortunately, we have a copy made by a strange hand, not the author's, and we are very doubtful whether the spelling is properly given.
54. p. 82.

Ha-Mechin Parnasah Le-Chol Beriah" from Nathan Hannover's *Shaarei Tziyyon.* Now we present, as a comparison, the
"beautiful *teḥinnah*":

Almighty God! You are a King of the whole world, and You are a
Helper above all helpers. So I beg You, great, merciful Father-King,
that You may have compassion over me and my husband, and that
You may protect us and guard us from everything evil, and that You
may show us the way to have a livelihood in honor, and that we may
not—God forbid—need to be sustained by any man and that we may
not be ashamed, but that we may be nourished always through Your
faithful and kind hand. And may You nourish us, just as You nourished the wife of Obadiah and her children through the hand of the
prophet Elisha—the pious, godly man. And may You lead my husband in the right way and send him good angels to accompany him
and be with him. Just as You sent angels with Jacob our father, peace
be upon him, so may You also send with my husband angels who may
protect him in all his ways and paths; wherever he takes a step, may
they protect him from everything evil, and may he come in health
and peace and nothing but happiness and rejoicing to his house, to
his wife and children. Let the merit of his little children who are still
pure of sins and transgressions be with him. I beg You, Master of the
whole world! If my husband has sinned before You and You have
ordained that he should—God forbid—be punished on the way, I
implore You, Almighty, Compassionate One, to tear up all the evil
decrees concerning him and not treat him with the attribute of strict
justice but only with the attribute of mercy. Do not examine his sins
when he goes in a place of danger. And may the merit of our ancestors Abraham, Isaac, and Jacob be with us, and may the merit of our
little children who are still pure of transgressions be with us always.

The considerably larger part of the feminine *teḥinnot* are
anonymous, but a few names of composers of *teḥinnot* have
been preserved in the memory of the people. The most popular
among them is Sarah Bas-Tovim. This name was so beloved
and well known in the Jewish world that it became something
of a legend, the living symbol of the woman's *teḥinnah* with its
lyric, tender style. S. Niger relates in his interesting work
Shtudies Tsu Der Geshikhte Fun Der Yidisher Literatur that when,
in a conversation with old Mezaḥ, he once asked who Sarah
Bas-Tovim was, Mezaḥ led him to the mirror, pointed to his
own hairy face, and said with a smile: "Here she is."[55] These
words of Joshua Mezaḥ require some explanation. Until the
second half of the nineteenth century, as long as religious

55. *Pinkes* of Vilna, 1913, p. 127.

books in Yiddish were still printed in the special *Wayber-Ksov*, the old-fashioned and God-fearing publishers regarded the women's *teḥinnot* with a certain respect and reprinted them without any changes of text. To be sure, the "young man, the typesetter" would frequently make troubles and, through terrible mistakes, greatly distort the text.[56] All this, however, was unwitting, without any previous intent. Quite different was the situation later, from the 1860's on. The publishers became "contemporary" and "this-worldly" and saw in the editions of *teḥinnot* primarily a current article of merchandise. If old merchandise was lacking, new stock had to be supplied immediately. Thus, they would order from *maskil*-writers "beautiful new *teḥinnot*" of Sarah Bas-Tovim; and those battlers for Haskalah—I. M. Dick, M. A. Shatzkes, and others—who regarded the old-fashioned "foolish and tasteless" women's *teḥinnot* with extreme contempt and disgust,[57] would, for a very small honorarium, copy the *teḥinnah* style, falsify and imitate the humble, tender, elegiac petitions of the Jewish woman to her faithful Protector, her merciful God, her compassionate Father in heaven. Joshua Mezaḥ also used to fabricate *teḥinnot* for a few *groschen* under the name of Sarah Bas-Tovim, and so he naively believed that this Sarah was someone who never existed, simply a legend the "foolish" women had devised, since in fact all the *teḥinnot* bearing her name were fabricated for small sums by himself and other imitators such as he. Old Mezaḥ, however, was mistaken. Sarah Bas-Tovim is an actual historical figure, and it is, in general, not difficult to discover her genealogy and to establish her literary legacy.

The surname Bas-Tovim is an indication that the composer of the *teḥinnot* was descended from distinguished ancestry. Indeed, she came from a quite prestigious family. Her father Mordecai was a great scholar. Her grandfather Isaac was rabbi in Satanov,[58] and her grandfather's father, also named Mor-

---

56. For instance in, Sarah Bas-Tovim's "Tekhine Fun Rosh-Ḥodesh Bentshen" there is a line, "Lord God of Hosts you probe all the chambers of all thoughts, of all hearts." In an edition from the beginning of the nineteenth century (the date is not given) this line obtained the following clumsy form: "Lord God of Hosts, *here I see* all chambers; You probe all the thoughts of all hearts." Further on in the same *teḥinnah* the expression "Master of the Universe, how my *heart* breaks" is transformed into "How my *head* breaks."

57. On Dick's attitude toward the womens' *teḥinnot* see Niger, *op. cit.*, p. 129.

58. In the sub-title of the *teḥinnah* "Shaar Ha-Yiḥud" we read: "This *teḥinnah* was made by the respected woman Sarah Bas-Tovim (the daughter of distinguished men): the scholar and rabbinist, distinguished in Torah, our renowned master and teacher Mordecai, the son of the rabbi, the great light, our master and our teacher Isaac

decai, was rabbi in Brest-Litovsk.[59] In Brest-Litovsk there lived
in the second half of the seventeenth century two rabbis named
Mordecai, Mordecai Zusskind (died in 1684) and Mordecai
Ginzburg (died in 1688). Very likely Sarah was a great-grand-
child of one of these, and she therefore lived in the first decades
of the eighteenth century. From her *tehinnot* we also learn that
her mother was named Leah.[60] In her personal life she was
unfortunate ("punished," as she herself expresses it). For some
time she was a wanderer. She was probably also a *zogerin*, a
precentress in the women's synagogues, and she poured out
her embittered and grieved heart in elegiac petitions, lyrically
tender *tehinnot*. Two collections of *tehinnot* by Sarah Bas-
Tovim have been preserved. The first is called *Sheker Ha-Cheyn*.
"The book *Sheker Ha-Cheyn* I translated into German," we read
on the title-page. "It is a remedy for the soul in this world and
in the other world, and you should not spare your money as
long as you can obtain this book. Thereby we shall merit the
world-to-come in the other world, and may the Messiah come
in our days speedily, Amen."

Following this comes the introduction by Sarah:

Dear women and girls. Read this *tehinnah*, and your heart will rejoice.
The prayers were taken out of[61] books. In the merit of this you will
be privileged to come to the Land of Israel. I have set before you a
beautiful new *tehinnah* that should be said Mondays and Thursdays
and on fast days and the Days of Awe. "Grace is deceitful and beauty
is vain" (*sheker ha-hen ve-hevel ha-yofi*). Beauty is nothing: only virtu-
ous deeds are good. "Every wise woman builds her house." The chief
thing is that the woman should conduct her household in such a way
that those in it can study Torah and that she may lead her children
in the right way to the service of God. I, a poor woman, was scattered
and undone. I could not sleep. My heart murmured in me, and so I
reminded myself whence I came, and whither I shall go, and how I

—may the memory of the righteous be for blessing—of the holy community of
Satanov."

59. In the sub-title of the collection of *tehinnot* entitled *Shloyshe Sheorim* it is noted:
"This *tehinnah* was made by the modest woman Sarah, the daughter of our master
Rabbi Mordecai, may the memory of the righteous be for blessing, the grandson
of Rabbi Mordecai who was president of the rabbinic court of the holy community
of Brisk, May the Lord establish it."

60. In the preface to *Shlyoshe Sheorim* it is noted: "May I not have to be a wanderer for
a long time in the merit of our mothers Sarah, Rachel and Leah; and may my dear
mother Leah also pray to God with me." (we quote according to an edition which
appeared around the beginning of the nineteenth century; the date is not indicated.)

61. Here a word is certainly missing.

shall be taken. And a great fear came upon me. And so I begged the living God Blessed Be He, weeping bitterly, that this *teḥinnah* may come forth from me.

I, Sarah Bas-Tovim, the distinguished and well-known woman, who has no strange thought but who made this *teḥinnah* for the sake of dear God Blessed Be He, that it may be a memorial after my death.[62] Whoever reads this *teḥinnah*, his prayer will certainly be accepted before God Blessed Be He. I. Sarah Bas-Tovim, the daughter of the scholar, the rabbi, distinguished in Torah and renowned, our teacher Rabbi Mordecai, the son of the rabbi, the great light, our teacher Rabbi Isaac, may his memory be for a blessing, of the holy community of Satanov, may God be over her. Amen.

Also in the preface to her other collection of *teḥinnot*, entitled *Shloyshe Sheorim* (Three Gates), Sarah Bas-Tovim explains why the collection bears this name. She also incidentally presents several autobiographical details:

I, Sarah Bas-Tovim, do this for the sake of dear God, Blessed Be He and Blessed Be His Name. I arrange for a second time another beautiful new *teḥinnah* in three gates. The first gate is based on the three commandments that were given to women: separation of dough, purification from menstrual uncleanness, and lighting of candles. Their name is *ḥallah, niddah,* and *hadlakat nerot.* The second gate is a *teḥinnah* to be prayed when the new moon is blessed, and the third gate is for the Days of Awe.

I take for my help the living God Blessed Be He, who lives forever and eternally and place this other beautiful new *teḥinnah* in German with great love, with great fear, and with trembling, with affright, with broken limbs, with great supplication, with great[63] ... May God have mercy on me and on all Israel, so that I may not have to be a wanderer long, through the merit of our mothers Sarah, Rebecca, Rachel, and Leah. And may my dear mother Leah also pray with me to God Blessed Be He, that my being a wanderer may be an atonement for all my sins. And may God forgive me for the fact that in my youth I talked in the synagogue when they were conducting the service and reading the dear Torah.

Lord of the whole world, I lay before You my petition, and as I begin to arrange my *teḥinnah* with all my intention and concentration and the depth of my heart, may You protect us from suffering and pain. I implore dear God Blessed Be He to have great mercy on all Israel and on my old age, that I may no longer have to be a wanderer[64] ... as He listened to the petitions of our patriarchs and matriarchs.

62. Apparently Sarah Bas-Tovim did not have any children.
63. A word is missing.
64. Here, apparently, several words are missing.

Remember when our father Abraham with his left hand took hold of Isaac's neck and in his right hand grasped the knife to slaughter his son Isaac. This he did for the love of You, and did not recoil from doing Your bidding where You sent him. So do You turn to have mercy upon us. And I beg heaven and earth and all the holy angels that they pray for me, that both my *tehinnot* may become a crown on His holy head, Amen.

The "third gate," which is "of the Days of Awe," contains Sarah Bas-Tovim's *tehinnah* for measuring candle wicks at the cemetery, a *tehinnah* of which the aged Mendele Mocher Seforim speaks with such enthusiasm in his *Shloyme Reb Khaims.*[65] *Shloyshe Sheorim* is concluded by Sarah Bas-Tovim with the following "moral lesson for women":

I, Sarah, entreat you young women not to converse in the dear synagogue, for it is a great sin. I remember that the *Tanna* Rabbi Eliezer bar Simeon encountered officials who led two asses laden with punishments. He asked the officers for whose sake this was. They said: This is for the sake of the people who converse in the synagogue from after "Baruch She-Amar" until after the "Shemoneh Esreh." Therefore I warn you, that you may not be punished—God forbid—as I was punished, with homelessness and wandering. Hence, you should take proof from me and confess your sins before God Blessed Be He. Also I entreat you to have mercy on widows and orphans and strangers and captives, and on aged people and sick people. For when you fast, your heart is bitter; so you should also believe that the heart of the poor man is bitter; he has not wherewith to refresh himself. Therefore I beg you to pay attention to this matter, and God Blessed Be He will grant you great prosperity. Also I implore you not to laugh and mock at other people, for God does not pardon this. You should take proof from me, that you may not—God forbid—be punished, as I was, with homelessness. And you should stand in the dear synagogue with fear and dread. I also arranged the other beautiful new *tehinnah* so that I might thereby have atonement for my great sins. Through our remembrance of our sins, may God Blessed Be He grant us life, Amen. Selah. The woman, Sarah Bas-Tovim, daughter of Rabbi Mordecai, may his memory be for blessing.

Sarah Bas-Tovim is the most popular but not the only composer of *tehinnot* whose name has been preserved. The names that have come down to us, however, are only prestigious names—all daughters of rabbis and wives of rabbis. Very popu-

65. Chapter V.

lar, for instance, in its day was a "Teḥinnah of the Matriarchs for Rosh Ḥodesh Elul" which was composed, as is indicated on the title-page, by "the woman, the rabbi's wife, Serel, daughter of the renowned rabbi, our teacher Rabbi Jacob Halevi Segal of Dubno, and wife of the rabbi, the great light, learned in wisdom, our teacher Rabbi Mordecai Katz Rapoport, president of the rabbinic court of the holy community of Olesnica."[66] We present several extracts from it to acquaint the modern reader with the typical *teḥinnah* style:

"Do with me according to Your great lovingkindness." Do with me lovingkindness and justice with great mercy, I entreat You; accept my petition . . . I pray that You may accept my bitter tears, as You accepted the tears of the angels who wept when our father Abraham brought his dear son Isaac to the binding. The tears of the angels fell on Abraham's knife and did not permit him to slay his son Isaac. So also may my tears fall before You and not allow me or my husband or my children and all my good friends to be taken away from the world . . .

"All gates are closed but the gate of tears are not closed." Therefore, merciful Father, accept my tears with which I entreat You. Place them in Your vessel. Wash away our sins with the tears, and remove Yourself from the attribute of strict justice to the attribute of mercy, Amen.

"Teḥinnah of the Matriarchs" is the title given to these prayers, for the authoress always turns to the matriarchs of the Jewish people—Sarah, Rebecca, Rachel, and Leah, asking them to be present with their merit and to protect their sinful, homeless children. In the *teḥinnah* for the sounding of the *shofar*, Serel bat Jacob addresses the following petition:

May there be present for us at the judgment the merit of the four matriarchs, and the merit of the three patriarchs, and the merit of Moses and Aaron . . . First we beg our mother Sarah that she may pray for us at the hour of judgment, that we may go out free from the judgment . . . Have mercy, our mother, on your children, and especially pray for our children that they be not separated from us. You know well that it is very bitter when a child is taken away from its mother, how it was with you, how grieved you were when they took your Isaac away from you. And today you have occasion to pray, for now they are blowing the *shofar* of a ram, so that God may remember the merit of Isaac who let himself be bound like a sheep

66. In Steinschneider the edition of 1783 (in Frankfurt-am-Oder) is noted. See also E. Schulmann, *op. cit.*, p. 69. We have employed the Vilna edition of 1852.

for the sacrifice. Therefore Satan becomes confused and cannot now accuse us. Therefore you now have occasion to pray for us, that the attribute of mercy may be aroused in our behalf. I also beg our mother Rebecca to pray for her children, and pray for our father and mother that they may not—God forbid—be separated from us. For you know well how strongly one longs after a father and mother, for when the servant Eliezer took you away from your father and mother to your husband Isaac, you wept greatly. So you know how bad it is without a father and mother. Therefore pray for our father and mother, that they may have a year of life, a good year, that I and my husband and children may have an ample livelihood. We also entreat our mother Rachel to pray for us to be inscribed and sealed for a good year and never to have any grief. We know well that you cannot endure the sorrow of your children. For when your dear son Joseph was taken away to Egypt, the Ishmaelites afflicted him greatly, and he fell on your grave and began to weep: Mother, have mercy on your child! How can you look at my sorrow? You loved me so much, and today I am in such dark straits, and you do not have compassion on me. So you could not listen to the affliction of your child, and you answered him: My dear child, I hear your weeping and your bitter cry. I will always have mercy and pray for you and listen to your sorrow. Therefore, have mercy upon our sorrow and anxiety and trembling before the judgment, and pray for us that a good year may be inscribed for us, so that we may never have any sorrow, Amen.

Another "Teḥinnah of the Matriarchs," also composed by a rabbi's daughter, is known. She herself bore the name of all four of the matriarchs, as is indicated in the subtitle of the *teḥinnah*: "This *teḥinnah* was arranged by the scholarly woman, Sarah Rebecca Rachel Leah, daughter of the rabbi, the renowned scholar, Rabbi Yokil Segal Horowitz, president of the rabbinic court of the holy community of Glogau, wife of the rabbi, the great light, the keen scholar, our teacher Rabbi Shabbetai—may his Creator keep him and preserve him—president of the rabbinic court of the holy community of Krasny." She also appeals to the matriarchs of the Jewish people, requesting them to protect their children, with their great merit, in the latter's deep distress.

Appealing to the holy matriarchs, to righteous women—this is the favorite motif of the women's *teḥinnot*. "Dear God," we read in a *teḥinnah* composed by the rabbi's wife Memael,[67]

67. "A *teḥinnah* on penitence, prayer and charity. This beautiful new *teḥinnah* was made by the woman Memael of rabbinic family, the daughter of the renowned and faithful Rabbi Tzevi Hirsch, the wife of the rabbi, the great and holy light, Rabbi

let me benefit from the merit of our pious Hannah. She went to the temple to pray before Eli the priest. She only moved her lips, and he said to her: Depart from hence, you drunken woman. Thereupon she answered: No, my lord, I am a woman with a grieved spirit. And You answered her. Therefore I implore You to answer me also. I beg You, dear God, do not punish me with any anger but treat me with the attribute of mercy, as our father Jacob, peace be upon him, prayed when his children might—God forbid—be guilty. Remember what troubles he endured before he raised them. All the more how much should I beg that I may not have any sorrow in my children? I know very well that I ask too much. I am not worthy to stand before You. But You desire that man pray to You. So You have compassion upon him. Here I entreat You, O God, not to cast me off in my old age.

Isaac, may the memory of the righteous be for blessing, president of the rabbinic court of the holy community of Belz." We quote according to the Vilna edition of 1855.

CHAPTER TEN

Parables and Maxims;
ELEGIES AND SOCIAL PORTRAITS

The later poetic literature—Collections of fables in Yiddish—The translations of *Mishlei Shualim* and *Meshal Ha-Kadmoni*—Abraham ben Mattathias' *Ku-Bukh* and Moses Wallich's *Sefer Meshalim*—The significance of the *Ku-Bukh*—Social motifs in the *Ku-Bukh*—*Tsukht-shpigl* and *Der Kleyner Brantshpigl*—Jacob Siegel's *Kehillat Yaakov*—Historical poems—Elḥanan Helin's *Megillat Vintz*—"Conflagration poems" and "stench poems"—The historical importance of lamentation poems in connection with oppressions and persecutions—Elegies on the massacres of 1648—The poem on Shabbetai Tzevi by Joseph Tausk—The social motif in this poem—Liturgical poems in Yiddish—Rebecca Tiktiner's "Poem for Simḥat Torah"—Sabbath songs—The second part of Elḥanan Kirchhan's *Simḥat Ha-Nefesh*—The desire to spread moral instruction and God's precepts with the aid of songs—The description of village Jews in *Simḥat Ha-Nefesh*—Anonymous religious poems—Social poems and mocking poems—*Di Bashraybung Fun Ashkenaz Un Polyak*—The polemic against *ḥazzanim* or cantors—Joel ben Eliezer's rhymed apology *Re'aḥ Niḥoaḥ*.

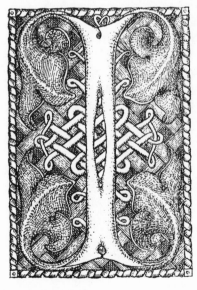

T HAS been indicated above[1] that at the threshold of the seventeenth century the prose narrative style obtained its definitive victory over the epic *Spielmann*-style in popular Yiddish literature. The *Shmuel-Bukh* epic and the *Artus-Hof* romance displaced the *Tze'enah U-Re'enah* and the *Maaseh-Bukh*. This, however, in no way means that rhymed poetic forms disappeared from the folk-literature; they merely lost their dominance and ceased to be the most significant factor in literary creation. Though their impor-

1. See above, p. 197.

tance was diminished, it did not disappear and was not lost. In the later era also numerous works were produced in rhymed verses and in stanzas constructed according to the principles of meter. However, these works are, in regard to style and content, of quite varied genres. In them the influence of three distinct sources is discernible. One group derives sustenance from the secular and religious poetic literature in Hebrew. In the second the influence of the German epic is felt; here the echo of the *Shmuel-Bukh* melody is heard. The third rises directly out of the popular poem and is intergrown with it. In the present chapter we shall attempt to familiarize the reader with these three groups.

In the first volume of our work we observed[2] how extremely popular among Jews was the literature of parables and fables. Hence, it is not surprising that the collections of fables which appeared in Hebrew were also disseminated in Judeo-German translations. As early as 1583 Jacob Koppelman published in Freiburg[3] his translation of *Mishlei Shualim* from which we have already presented several extracts.[4] In 1693 Gershon Wiener issued in Frankfurt-am-Main a Yiddish translation of Isaac Ibn Sahulah's *Meshal Ha-Kadmoni*. On the title-page is explained: "This speaks of many lovely parables that will be found in this book, when it is read through from beginning to end." The most popular of all, however, was the collection of fables by Abraham ben Mattathias which appeared in Verona in 1594[5] under the unique title *Ku-Bukh* (Cow-Book). The publisher of the *Maaseh-Bukh*, Jacob ben Abraham of Mezhirech, expresses the hope that his edition will so absorb the "dear men and women" that they will have no more desire "to read from the Book of Cows."[6] In fact, the *Ku-Bukh* was so thoroughly read through by the "dear men and women" that not a single copy of it has been preserved. And of all the bibliographers only the aged Shabbetai Bass in his *Siftei Yeshenim* noted Abraham ben Mattathias' book of fables as an eye-witness who had still had the opportunity to become personally acquainted with the work. It is virtually beyond doubt, however, that the *Ku-Bukh* was not lost but has come down to us under a different title.

2. *Ibid.*, pp. 185ff.
3. Reprinted in Frankfurt in 1767.
4. See Vol. I, pp. 203–205.
5. According to Benjacob and Schulmann, in 1555.
6. See above, p. 185.

In 1697 in Frankfurt-am-Main Moses ben Eliezer Wallich of Worms published a book of fables entitled *Sefer Meshalim* with many lovely woodcuts. That Wallich is merely the publisher and not the author is noted on the title-page. Also in the long rhymed introduction with the acrostic "I Moses ben Eliezer Wallich, may the memory of the righteous be for blessing, of the holy community of Worms," written in the meter of Jehudah Bresch's introduction to his well-known translation of the Pentateuch,[7] Wallich indicates: "It is usually called *Ku-Bukh*— Let one go and seek it—A year and a week—And wear out his shoes." Because the *Ku-Bukh* had become such a rarity, he, Moses Wallich, decided to reprint it on "pure and white paper —with the letters like a sapphire—with charming illustrations —like an apple into which one bites."[8] It is clear that *Sefer Meshalim* is merely a reprint of the old *Ku-Bukh*. Apparently Wallich reprinted the work with certain stylistic changes. A certain allusion to this is found on the title-page: "Now set again with diligence—devised in print in a new way."

Abraham ben Mattathias derived the parables of his *Ku-Bukh* chiefly from the two popular Hebrew books *Mishlei Shualim* and *Meshal Ha-Kadmoni*.[9] However, he did not translate these but reworked them anew in poetic fashion. It suffices, for instance, to compare the fables of the *Ku-Bukh* about the dog with the scrap of meat in its mouth, the town mouse and the field mouse, the sick lion in his old age, and the well-known story of the widow and the young watchman with the Hebrew versions in *Mishlei Shualim*,[10] or to observe the form obtained in the *Ku-Bukh* by the reworked humorous tales about the peasant and the writer and about the young woman and her lover taken from *Meshal Ha-Kadmoni*,[11] to become convinced that the author of the *Ku-Bukh* was, indeed, a talented fable poet with his own style and manner.

Not without reason did the pious publisher of the *Maaseh-Bukh* complain so strongly about the *Ku-Bukh* and include it among the "foolish books." Despite the moral lessons with

---

7. See above, p. 100.
8. *Sefer Meshalim* is now also extremely rare. Of this edition only three copies have been preserved—at Oxford, Hamburg, and Amsterdam. In 1925, however, the Soncino Society published in Berlin a splendid anastatic reprint of *Sefer Meshalim* and added a German translation by Dr. R. Beatus (1926).
9. Approximately two-thirds of the fables in the *Ku-Bukh* come from these two sources.
10. See our *History*, Vol. I, pp. 203–205.
11. *Ibid.*, pp. 200–203.

which Abraham ben Mattathias frequently concludes many of his fables, one feels in his work the breath of the Italian Renaissance (it is no accident that the *Ku-Bukh* was printed in Italy). Like the author of *Meshal Ha-Kadmoni*, the author of the *Ku-Bukh* makes no distinction between fables about beasts and stories about men. One is forcibly reminded of Immanuel of Rome's *Maḥbarot* and Boccaccio's *Decameron* when Abraham ben Mattathias relates smilingly how a young woman cuckolds her pious husband, and while the latter "goes to the synagogue with his whole heart and holds in his hand the festival candles" and there prays before God, his wife enjoys herself with her lover. The *Ku-Bukh* refuses to acknowledge any veil, any bashful allusions; what is not stated explicitly is revealed by the illustration of the amorous couple lying in bed. Immediately afterwards is portrayed the cuckolded husband, with two horns on his forehead, and over the illustration the inscription: "Here is the man with the great horns—His lament is endless and measureless."

With acid sarcasm the *Ku-Bukh* portrays a Jewish Tartuffe, an old usurer and cheat who commits all kinds of frauds, but with a hypocritically pious mien. This is his portrait:

> His figure was very terrifying
> And could make one surmise
> That even if he were very pious and very good,
> He still had a false character.
> He entered with cleverness and good sense.
> Every day he rose at dawn
> And prayed with great devotion,
> As if each day were Yom Kippur or Rosh Ha-Shanah,
> With much bending and bowing.
> And looking at the heavens above,
> With a loud, clear voice he called to God
> And at the prayer "Modim" bowed very low.
> He recited many hymns and Psalms;
> The whole day he went about in *tallit* and *tefillin*.

The merchant whom this Tartuffe defrauds with his pious tricks in the basest fashion is left waiting long, since the hypocrite must serve God:

> Therefore, dear friend, wait a little while;
> I may not speak now with any man.
> I must bless the *etrog* and *lulav*,

And also have to recite the *Viddui* (Confession) now
And lament my distress before God.
I also have to say "Al Ḥet."
Leave me for an hour, and then we shall talk.

The beasts and birds in the *Ku-Bukh* are much more talkative
than in Berechyah Ha-Nakdan's *Mishlei Shualim*. But the dialogue is highly vivacious; each personage speaks in his own
distinctive way. When the dog courts the cow whom he intends to kill[12] and promises her that he will "give her costly
presents, make a precious marriage contract with all things and
good provisions," the cow half-wittedly declares: "All the dogs
are very impudent; all day they do nothing but bark and yell."
The dog immediately responds:

But I am pious and honest,
And do nothing other than the right.
For I am of good stock,
My native piety guards me
For many long years.
I am descended from the pious and quiet canines
Who refused to bark in Egypt
On the night Israel left the land.
And therefore they received a good reward from God;
He bade that they be given all the ritually forbidden food
That they, too, might live in luxury,
As is proper according to the law.
Of canine stock, I claim my pedigree
From all the best and pious;
From these have I come here.
The dog named Schlager was my cousin
And the dog Muftil belongs to my family.

Not infrequently a sharply expressed social motif is detectable in the *Ku-Bukh*. In this respect the fable about the wolf
who is a judge and to whom the "wild deer" and the "quiet
sheep" come for litigation is typical. This fable develops in our
poet into a keen social satire. With biting sarcasm he relates
how the king, a lion, could not find a more suitable judge in
the whole land than the wolf. The latter does not have to be
begged long and swears "to judge the whole world justly."
Coming before him with a case are the deer, a usurer, and the

---

12. *Ku-Bukh*, 35–36.

poor sheep, the marrow of whose bones has already been sucked out by the usurer. The deer demands money from the sheep and calculates that the latter still owes him "twenty-two pounds." The sheep complains: "One man's statement is half a statement—Unless both are heard—So it is written in the Council House of Nuremberg." And she demonstrates through strong proofs that she has already paid her debt with enormous interest. The deer brings false testimony, and his witnesses "all stated that it was true." Naturally the wolf was "very much inclined towards the deer." He does not permit "the poor sheep to speak" and promptly issues the verdict: they are to "shear the sheep's wool and not give her a penny to spend for food; the wool is to be sold and the sheep to be let run about naked." At the end comes the poet's moral:

The example is well known to me,
A member of the council and judge of the land,
How some sit in the court,
And justice is for him quite round; he turns it about just as
    he wishes,
According to the demand for it.
This frequently must prevail.
Falsehood puts its foot
Thus in the world,
And has constructed its tent,
Firmly sunk its foundation.
Truth has closed her mouth,
For falsehood has triumphed throughout the world.
Justice has now fled completely;
Truth is hardly to be found anymore;
Lies make the people blind,
So that they do not wish to see the right.
How can justice take place in the world?
For violence prevails over justice.
This I, poor wight, lament.[13]

It also happens not infrequently with our poet that, under his pious moral lessons, is suddenly felt the joker, the scoffer with the sarcastic smile—for instance, in the epilogue to the fable about the town mouse and the field mouse. The moral is that a person ought to be content with little; it is better to eat a dry crust of bread than "the food of a king with grief and

13. *Ibid.*, 22a.

distress." Suddenly, however, the poet interrupts and smilingly addresses the reader:

This makes me well believe
That one would better take a young and charming wife
Than an old one who is a disgrace to her husband.[14]

Also very popular among Jews from ancient times, like fable poetry, was the other genre of didactic poetry—the parable, the moral lesson, the finely pointed gnomic maxim. Testimony to this is provided by the classic works of ancient Hebrew literature: the Book of Proverbs, Ben Sira, the "Chapters of the Fathers" *(Pirkei Avot)*, and the literally countless proverbs in Jewish folklore.

It is therefore quite understandable that, contemporaneously with the Yiddish translations and poetic reworkings of the Hebrew fable collections and of didactic books such as *Ben Ha-Melech Veha-Nazir*,[15] there also appeared Yiddish reworkings of rhymed maxims and moral lessons collected from ancient Hebrew literature. Most popular and best known was *Der Tsukhtshpigl*[16] of Seligmann Ulma (of the family Günsburger)[17] which first appeared in Hanau in 1610 and was later several times reprinted. From the title-page we learn that this is "a godly and worldly book taken from the words of the sages, whose like has never been printed. It was collected from all the six orders [of the Mishnah] and other books besides. All the proverbs were made with care, well translated, well considered, and arranged according to the alphabet. He who reads in it will rejoice." In the preface the author complains of the "women and girls" who spend "the holy days of Sabbath and festival" with vain things, "some in cursing and scolding, some in promenading, courting, or some in other empty things and other street talk." They let no one through, "whether he be foreign or native, woman or man, they bell him with mockery

---

14. *Ibid.*, 13b.
15. See above, pp. 35ff.
16. In several later editions (Prague 1678, Frankfurt-am-Main, 1680 and 1691, Offenbach, 1716) also under the Hebrew title *Sefer Mareh Musar: Der Tsukhtshpigl*, a godly and a worldly book."
17. A. A. Roback (*Filologishe Shriftn*, II, 390) notes that Seligmann Ulma was a rabbi. However we greatly doubt this. It is difficult to believe that a German rabbi of the end of the sixteenth century would have allowed himself to come forth publicly with such frivolous and witty verses as we not infrequently encounter in *Tsukhtshpigl*.

and other taunting words, with tongues that cut more sharply than swords." It is clear that the cheerful and witty author does not mean this seriously; it is only a matter of style.

As we know from the title-page, the author of *Der Tsukht-shpigl* assembled, according to the alphabet, proverbs and epigrams (over five hundred) from the Talmud and the Midrashim, as well as from other sources, and reset them into rhymes. Only in a few cases is the translation faithful and verbatim. Ulma proves himself a genuinely artful translator who knows the secret of reforging the foreign text into new, artistic forms. For example, the Talmudic epigram "He who immerses himself with the unclean creeping thing still in his hand, and love that does not come from the heart, and prayer without inner intention and concentration—Satan will find these things an indictment," is translated by Ulma as follows: "Penitential ablution without regret, love without fidelity, prayer without devotion—these three has Satan devised." The clever maxim given in the Talmudic tractate *Sanhedrin*, 7a: "When love was strong, we could have lain on the edge of a sword; now that our love has become weak, a bed of sixty [cubits] is not large enough for us," is rendered in *Der Tsukht-shpigl* in the following verses:

When love between my wife and me was great,
On the edge of a knife did I lie with her;
Now that love is no longer so strong,
A bed of sixty cubits width is too narrow for us.

The Hebrew maxim *Da'agah ve-rov shanim ya'asu levanim* is translated by Ulma as follows: "Worry and many years produce gray and white hairs." And the familiar dictum "More than the calf wishes to suck, the cow wishes to give suck" is reworked into the following verse:

The calf never has so much desire to suck
But that the mother far more eagerly extends her breast to it.

Ulma, however, very rarely gives a faithful translation. Mainly he paraphrases the text. It also happens quite frequently that the sense of the Hebrew or Aramaic proverb is substantially altered. The author of *Der Tsukhtshpigl* also quite often employs, in his commentary and paraphrase of the old epigrams from the Talmudic literature, proverbs taken from the later Jewish or German folk-literature, as well as directly from the mouth of the people. The Talmudic proverb "Either fellowship [with other people] or death" is explained by Ulma with the following German proverb: "One for a legacy, two for bed, three for the road, four for gaming, five for drinking." Some maxims grow in *Tsukhtshpigl* into entire didactic poems —for example, the frequently quoted admonishing verse:

Truth has died,
Piety has been corrupted,
Vice and shamefulness
Have obtained dominance . . .[18]

Seligmann Ulma pours out his wrath particularly on women. He uses cutting words found in the Talmudic literature in regard to women and makes out of them sharp, if not always finely pointed, epigrams. Ulma introduces with pleasure the well-known dictum "The understanding of women is light, but their garments are long, wide, and large" and translates it:

From the wisdom of women you will gain little.
They have long dresses and short sense.
Therefore bethink yourself well before following them.

The Talmudic statement "Haughtiness is not seemly for women" is paraphrased by Seligmann Ulma in the following verse:

High rank is ill suited to women;
It is fitting only for the man.
In women, power goes to their head,
And they quickly become arrogant.

The well-known Talmudic maxim "A woman of sixty is like a girl of six to run after the sound of music" serves Ulma as a motto for the following somewhat immodest lines:

An old woman of sixty,
Like a girl of six,
Lusts with all her heart

18. Quoted by Brüll in *Jahrbücher fur jüdische Geschichte und Literatur,* 1877, p. 118; M. Bassin, *Antologye,* Vol. I, p. 30; Z. Rejzen, *Leksikon,* 1914, p. 35; and by many others.

To sing and dance
And is eager for every joy
As the loveliest maiden.
I believe they desire to have husbands
As no virgin desires a young swain.
I marvel they never lose their taste for the love-game.
If you ask her heart
What she often desires,
It is—in summer—one who drives the flies away from her.
The rest I will not write . . .
I let it stand with the common proverb:
Old cows that give neither milk nor butter
Also like to lick salt.

It is beyond doubt that, in his acid epigrams against women, Ulma employs not only Talmudic but German popular literature as well. This is noticeable, for instance, in an epigram such as the following:

Great lords and beautiful women
Should be served well and trusted ill,
For their heart is like a bathhouse:
One goes in, another goes out.

It is possible that the author of *Der Tsukhtshpigl*, like the poet Jehudah ben Shabbetai[19] in his day, was made a misogynist by certain circumstances in his personal life. Ulma does not tire of hurling his pointed arrows at "bad women":

Would you restrain a woman's wickedness?—
Then suggest that you will take another wife.
For this, women cannot bear at all.
Every woman is jealous of her fellow-woman,
With such defense you accomplish more than with beating
   her,
For you beat ten devils in for each one you beat out.

Seligmann Ulma further complains:

A bad, quarrlesome wife
Is for her husband a leprosy in his body.
If you would have rest,

19. See our *History*, Vol. I, pp. 178ff.

Der Kleyn Brantshpigl

Send her to Satan.
Give her her marriage contract and divorce;
You will easily find another to go with you to bed.

Der Tsukhtshpigl also warns:

He who runs over the pavement,
Or jumps over a bridge,
Or takes a wife he does not know
Remains a fool to his end.

Also very popular was another "mirror" (*shpigl*). This, too, was a collection of proverbs and maxims. It was called *Der Kleyn Brantshpigl* and was first published (Venice, 1566) under the title *Mishlei Hachamim.* Most of the maxims (fifty out of seventy) are taken from Jehudah Alharizi's *Tahkemoni* (*Makama* 44), as the anthologist himself notes in his epilogue: "I Jehudah bar Israel Regenspurg, who is also called Leib Shevril of the holy community of Lumpenburg—Read in a Hebrew book— In which the sayings of fifty of these sages were found—And I translated twenty stanzas from Hebrew into German—I hope I will not be vilified for this—I brought it to seventy maxims—Corresponding to the seventy members of the Sanhedrin I conceived it."[20]

The construction of the work is quite simple. First comes an introductory stanza:

There was a king of Israel most precious and wise,
Who had with him seventy sages greatly deserving of
    praise.
Once he said to them: Let each one say something of use,
Wherewith his sagacity may be proved.

Following this, each sage comes forth with his maxim. It is characteristic that *Der Kleyn Brantshpigl* also speaks with great indignation of "bad" women. The sixty-ninth sage declares:

---

20. At the end the author notes:
    I hope to God to have many other books printed
    That I have made, that are very cheerful and very beautiful,
    Some that are all in Hebrew
    And unrhymed,
    And some are entirely in German, rhymed very well.
    And some in Hebrew and German, rhymed very well and without number.

A sage was asked why he cheated himself
With taking a small, skinny wife.
He replied that he could not order his life without a wife,
And so chose the least of what is so bad.

Immediately after him the "seventieth sage" appears with his maxim:

A sage wrote above the door of his house:
God grant that everything bad remain outside this door.
Another sage passed by;
This grieved and angered him.
So he wrote underneath: If you have so resolved,
When your wife goes out—by which door will she come
    home again?

Among the rhymed works in Yiddish that are based on a definite Hebrew text, a special place is occupied by the work entitled *Kehillat Yaakov* which the *hazzan* or cantor of the Franconian town of Roethelsec, Jacob bar Isaac Siegel, published in 1692.[21] The author himself indicates that, regrettably, he is very weak in "the language of the rabbis" and feels strong only in *Leshon Ashkenaz*, i.e., the Yiddish vernacular. In this language, the only one available to him, he decided to write a long Biblical poem "in the melody of the *Shmuel-Bukh.*" Whereas the poet of the *Shmuel-Bukh* utilized the old Midrashim and legends that were produced on the text of the Biblical Book of Samuel, our author based himself chiefly on the midrash of the later era—*Sefer Ha-Yashar.*[22] Naturally our naive author, the cantor of the little town, was quite certain that this "hero epic" is identical with the ancient *Sefer Ha-Yashar* which the Bible mentions so frequently.[23]

On the title-page it is announced that *Kehillat Yaakov* contains "much of a pleasant nature to read, and no foolishness but only a pious, godly thing, made in the melody of the *Shmuel-Bukh* and pleasantly rhymed, and also well thought out. The first part is mainly taken from *Sefer Ha-Yashar*, but at times some lovely proverbs are added to it. But in the other part *Sefer Ha-Yashar* comes to an end. Here I turned only to Midrashim and *Gemarot.*"

21. We have utilized the Wilhelmdorfer edition of 1718.
22. See our *History*, Vol. I, pp. 186ff.
23. See the preface to *Kehillat Yaakov*.

The author's statement that he made his work in the "melody of the *Shmuel-Bukh*" is not quite correct. The verses in *Kehillat Yaakov* are generally not constructed according to the meter of the *Shmuel-Bukh* stanzas. But one thing is certain: *Kehillat Yaakov*, like the *Shmuel-Bukh*, had its special melody according to which its verses were sung. The author was, after all, a cantor, and so he devised for his verses a melody and used not only to declaim his work but to sing it. This, indeed, is indicated in the preface: "He who rhymed and sang this book." The author relates that all who came to know his work in manuscript advised him to publish it as soon as possible. He hopes that his poem will so interest the people "that many a man will leave off dice-throwing and card-playing and will spend the same time in refreshing the heart in this lovely book."

The poetic value of *Kehillat Yaakov* is very slight. The work is overly drawn out, and in places the verses limp. Nevertheless, it must be conceded that the *ḥazzan* of Franconia was not entirely without talent and certain passages read with interest. To give the reader some notion of the style of *Kehillat Yaakov*, we present here a description of the rape of the Sabine women:[24]

The men of Kittim[25] considered how they could bring it about
That they might also obtain beautiful wives . . .
So they considered how they would attack the problem.
They bethought themselves that the time of cutting the grain would soon arrive . . .
Then we young fellows will all run to the city of Safina;
There we will take brides as beautiful as we can find.
The action began; they [the Sabine men] went out and left the city open.
When the young Romans came running here swiftly,
They were—poor things—glad, and yet greatly affrighted.
But each was clever enough to seize his merchandise.
The merchandise was delivered, and they began to run home with them;
They had not a penny in their purse and yet bought fine merchandise.
But they were pressed for time; they could not tarry,

24. The author bases himself on *Sefer Ha-Yashar.*
25. The Romans.

For if any had been caught, his pack would have been taken away.

But the good maidens definitely helped faithfully in this [i.e., their escape].

They ran as fast as they could, but they were also glad that it turned out so well.[26]

Unfortunately, the small amount of talent discernible in *Kehillat Yaakov* is drowned in a sea of watery rhymes. The work is further marred by the author's great defect—his tastelessness. Some legends in *Kehillat Yaakov* are presented in a form and with details such that any reader with a bit of literary taste simply cannot stand them.[27]

Jacob Siegel naively believed that the legends and stories that he utilized from *Sefer Ha-Yashar* in his *Kehillat Yaakov* reported reliable historical events. Old-Yiddish literature, however, is quite rich in poems, elegies, and songs based on actual historical facts. It is difficult to single out any significant event in Jewish life of recent centuries that did not immediately find a certain resonance in Yiddish poetry. The songs and poems connected with history were not only declaimed but, in the majority of cases, also sung to a special tune, and in many of them the melody with which they used to be chanted is even noted.[28]

One of the most important and popular historical poems is *Megillat Vintz*[29] (or *Vintz Hans Lid*) in which the attack that the Christian mob made in 1614 in Frankfurt-am-Main on the Jewish community under the leadership of the cakebaker Vincent Fettmilch is portrayed. The poem was composed in Hebrew

26. *Kehillat Yaakov*, 12.
27. For instance, the stanzas which describe how the daughters of Moab seduced the sons of Israel (*ibid.*, 85–86).
28. Several examples: (1) "A new lament about the expulsion from Tannhausen. This poem was made by an honorable young man, Seligman the son of Rabbi Itzik Shalit of Tannhausen in the land of Swabia in the year 1721 with the melody of Rabbi Simeon of Prague." (2) "A new lament that was made by a martyr whose name was Rabbi Ezekiel. He made it before his death with the melody 'They who dwell in houses of clay' on Thursday, Erev Rosh Ḥodesh Iyyar, in the year 1719." (3) "A new lament of the great fire in the holy community of Frankfurt, with the melody of Haman in the *Akhashveyrosh-Shpil*, 1711."
29. First printed in Frankfurt in 1616, reprinted in Amsterdam in 1648 and Frankfurt in 1696. Wagenseil reprinted the Yiddish text in his work mentioned above, and Schudt printed both the Hebrew and Yiddish texts. In modern times Max Weinreich reprinted the Yiddish text (in the collection *Onhoib*, 1922, and in *Shtaplen*) with a long introduction and many notes.

and Yiddish by Elḥanan bar Abraham Helin, a resident of Frankfurt.[30]

The *Vintz Hans Lid* used also to be sung to a special tune, as is indicated on the title-page: "The melody for it is composed like 'The Battle of Fabia.'" The Hebrew text is in places cumbersome; one senses that the author does not have a free and complete command of the Hebrew poetic art. The Yiddish text is incomparably stronger. Here the author feels far more at home and freer; here he can express his feeling and enthusiasm without hindrance, pour out his sentiments in powerful, genuinely poetic verses. The entire poem consists of 103 eight-line stanzas constructed according to the principles of contemporary German meter. In all the stanzas the rhymes follow a definite order (*ac, bd*). Every line consists of four beats (in a few cases, only of three), but the meter (in consonance with old German poetry) is not syllabic but tonic, i.e., only the number of beats is preserved in the line but not the regular exchange of accented and unaccented syllables. The number of accented syllables among, and also before, the accented ones can be quite different. So, for instance, in the following stanza:

מיטן אין גאָרטן אויף דער עֵרדן
זיין גיזעֵסן אין איינם ריִנגן
צעֵהן קינדבעטרן נוך אירם גֶעבערטן
מיין הֶעֵרץ מיר דארִיבֵר האָט וועֵלן צו שפרינגן.

In all four lines there are four accented syllables, but as far as unaccented ones are concerned, there are in the first —1,1,2; in the second—1,1,2,1; in the third—2,3,1; in the fourth —1,1,2,2,1.

Like the great poems of the *Spielmann* era, *Megillat Vintz* begins with a paean to the Creator and His great deeds:

> I would recount God's power,
> His wonders and great signs,
> His might and also His works,
> How He has never forsaken us,

---

30. Elhanan Helin composed another poem also in Hebrew and Yiddish entitled "Shir Ve-Zemer Na'eh Al Orech Ha-Galut," published in the year he died (1624).

In all our journeyings and in all lands;
I would testify to this.
I would make His name known
With truth, and will not lie.

The author then proceeds to the matter of his poem and portrays how the artisans and lower strata of the Christian populace attacked the Jewish quarter under their leader—the "new Haman" Vincent Fettmilch:

A great rogue, an evil beggar,
His like hardly ever existed.
He was a great burden for us—
Such a one they made their king.

The poet describes all the troubles that the Jews of Frankfurt had to suffer, and he concludes bitterly:

They ruled over us with full force;
We were always in great anxiety.
In the morning we wished it were night,
And at night that it were morning.

Of all of the sufferings and persecutions that the community had to endure, the poet emphasizes two which apparently made the strongest impression on him. The rioting mob, in plundering the Jewish houses, pitilessly threw out from their beds the new mothers along with their newborn babies and took away the beds:

The bandits cast them out of their beds
And dragged the beds away.
I would have wagered much against this,
Had I not seen it with my own eyes.

The other motif that made the most painful impression on the poet was the mockery and contempt with which the rabble burned the holy books and hurled them in the dust:

Also many mighty books that are precious
And rejoice a scholar—
They threw in the dirt
And scattered in the streets.

Vintz Hans Lid

The rioters made pyres of the costliest books and roasted meat
on them, and parchment books they sold to the bookbinders:

> For a joke to bind other books in them.
> No fear went to their hearts
> That thereby they sinned.

A bitter fate, too, befell the manuscripts:

> Also the best merchandise
> That has ever been seen by human eyes,
> Manuscripts, we lost;
> They carried all of them away.

After this comes a portrayal in powerful stanzas of how the
entire Jewish community left the city:

> We set out with great joy,
> But also with sorrow close by—
> Sorrow on parting from the community,
> And joy that our life was preserved.
> . . . .
> Many thousands placed themselves on the bridges—
> They wished to look on our misery,
> How hurriedly we set out on the field—
> Men and women and children.

After the poet reports the later episodes of the expulsion—
the sentence of death carried out on the ring-leaders of the
rising by the executioners, and the return of the expelled Jews
to their homes—he concludes his poem with these pious lines:

> All my words that I have spoken here,
> Everything that I have sung—
> No falsehood have I told you
> But testified to the truth with my tongue.
> Only turn away from all evil,
> And hold fast to the good with both hands;
> So God will redeem us from all troubles
> And send the Messiah son of David.

About a hundred years later the community of Frankfurt
lived through a new catastrophe. A great conflagration broke
out and destroyed the whole Jewish quarter (in 1711). A resident

of the community, David Zoigers, described the destruction in an elegy which used to be sung to the tune of the Haman-song in the *Akhasheyrosh-Shpil*.[31] Because fires occurred very frequently in the narrow, wooden streets of the ghetto, the number of conflagration poems that have been preserved is quite considerable.[32] No smaller is the number of the *Ippush-Lider* (literally, stench poems), elegies and laments on the terrible epidemics with their numerous4 a victims. The poetic value of these laments is quite small.[33] Nevertheless, they have a certain historical significance because they not infrequently report details that are of interest to the historian of culture. For example, in Moses Eisenstadt's elegy on the epidemic in Prague (1713),[34] when the terror the residents experienced is reported, there also breaks through the great indignation of the author against the wealthy men and leaders of the community who, in the time of trouble, fled from the city and left the poor without protection and help:

One saw them carrying coffers and chests all day.
How woeful it was for the poor people,
As they realized that the rich were all departing,
And we must remain here stuck in the affliction.
Many, many thousands were taken away.
Literally not a single rich man remained in the community;
Similarly, many scholars and other prominent people
All fled elsewhere.

Numerous elegies and laments that mourn the frequent persecutions of Jewish communities have also been preserved. So for instance *Gezerat Kehillah Kedoshah Pozna* in which the following lament is given:

31. The conflagration poem is reprinted in Schudt, *op. cit.*, p. 63–73.
32. The oldest of the conflagration poems that has been preserved is the above-mentioned poem of Elijah Baḥur ("Now I will sing to you a bit with my bad voice").
33. Among some of the composers of the "conflagration poems" who themselves suffered from the fires, the most important motive for creation was: "to obtain some gain after the fire." This, for instance, is noted quite openly by Abraham Moses Latz in the close of his "Conflagration Poem from Prague":
    This poem have I, Abraham Moses, made with broken heart.
    When I remember my house and property, how can I endure the pain?
    For I was burned by the great fire.
    Therefore, buy this poem from me, so that I may have something to gain.
34. "A new lament over the great, fearful epidemic that took place here in Prague and began on the 28th of Tammuz 1713."

It was such a persecution
That a father knew not what had happened to his child . . .
. . . They said: First we shall take your money,
Then you must leave this world.
Will your God come down from heaven?—
We will make you a shame and a mockery.[35]

There is also "A Beautiful Poem of Vienna with the Melody *'Akedat Yitzḥak'* on the Expulsion from Vienna of 1670" and "A Lament on the Destruction of Ungarisch Brod That Took Place in 1683."[36] The grandson of Yozpa Shammash (author of *Maaseh Nissim*), the young Zekli ben Liebermann Segal, mourns the destruction that the French wreaked on Worms in 1689 in "a new lament" in which every verse ends with a Hebrew line from the Bible.[37] The poem concludes with this moving stanza:

O God, Shepherd of Israel, Your sheep are very scattered!
O God, gather us together again, for we are very far from
   one another!
O God, let the day that you have assured me come—
"In My anger I smote you, and in My favor I have had
   mercy on you."

The frequent blood libels also found an echo in a whole series of "martyr poems," some of which were published in modern times by Max Weinreich with numerous pertinent explanations and comments.[38]

As in Hebrew literature,[39] so in Yiddish the terrible destruction of the communities of the Ukraine in 1648 found a strong resonance. Weinreich[40] also reprinted several of the most important laments dealing with the Chmielnitzki persecutions (two elegies and an *El Male Raḥamim*). Among these is also the long lament that Joseph ben Eliezer Lippmann Ashkenazi first composed in Hebrew, but "because numerous people cannot

35. Reprinted in *Letterbode*, XI, 166, and in Bassin's *Antologye*, pp. 84–85.
36. See our *History*, Vol. VI, p. 126, Note 16.
37. First printed in 1696 at the end of *Maaseh Nissim*; reprinted in several later editions of *Maaseh Nissim*. In modern times the poem was reprinted with an historical introduction by J. Shatzky in *Filologishe Shriftn*, III, pp. 43–56.
38. *Shturemvint*, 1927, pp. 165–220.
39. See our *History*, Vol. V, Chapter VI.
40. *Bilder Fun Der Yidisher Literatur-Geshikhte*, 192–218.

understand it and so it cannot go to their hearts," he was entreated by many to "print it in German."[41]

In these elegies, as in the *Vintz Hans Lid*, the desecration of the Torah perpetrated in the hurling of the Scrolls of the Law into the dust and the trampling of them by the mob with their feet is stressed with special pain. In the lament on "the persecutions of 1656" the author complains:

They spread holy Scrolls of the Law on the earth
And kill women and children on them . . .
They desecrate Scrolls of the Law
And of their parchment they make shoes.
O God, how can You look on at this?[42]

Joseph Ashkenazi also writes:

Now might each cry and tear his garments,
At what the wicked, the peasants in White Russia, have
    done here—
Eagerly torn the holy Scrolls of the Law . . .
Hacked up scrolls, made of them slippers for the feet.
O sacred Torah, how should this not anger you?
Men should place dust and ashes on their heads,
For the pain is not to be described on many pages . . .
Still I would ask the Torah a question:
Did the sacred letters really fly up again to heaven?
An answer can be given: It is no lie,
For those who studied it were killed by the sword and the
    bow.

As in the Hebrew elegies on the Chmielnitzki persecutions,[43] so in the Yiddish laments the longing for vengeance is strongly heard. In the *El Male Raḥamim* reprinted by Weinreich we read:

Such an evil decree has not been
Since the destruction of the Temple—what a great sin this
    must be.

41. This poem which was composed to the melody of "Addir Ayom Ve-Nora" was first printed in 1648 in Prague.
42. It is worth noting that in this lament the social motif is also heard:
    For what reason did the misfortune come?—
    Because the rich did not defend the poor.
43. See our *History*, Vol. VI, pp. 129ff.

O Master of the Universe, You know well the blood cries to
    You, You are the Creator,
And You are called a God great and fearful!
How can You restrain Yourself and be silent? . . .
Avenge Yourself with Your burning wrath,
For such is Your holy Name.
Let the earth not cover the blood, let it be cursed,
Until the Holy One will Himself look down from heaven
And avenge the blood of the righteous
At the hands of the vile enemies,
And let the souls of the righteous rest under Your Throne
    of Glory, O God of vengeance.

The elegy for the persecution of 1656 ends with the following
chord:

> Master of the Universe, revive the dead . . .
> For they lie buried in all corners.
> Wipe out Amalek . . .

Highly characteristic are the final verses of Joseph Ashkenazi's elegy. In previous volumes[44] we noted that the terrible
destruction of the communities in the Ukraine intensified messianic—mystical hopes. In Chmielnitzki's massacres men saw
the "pangs of the Messiah," the harbingers that very soon the
redeemer would appear. It was even calculated that *ḥevlei
mashiaḥ* is equivalent in *gematria* to the letters for the year
1648.[45] This hope-filled messianic motif resounds very clearly
in Joseph Ashkenazi's closing verses:

> Cease to weep, rise from the ground;
> Fear not—better times will soon be here.
> Elijah the prophet who rode on fiery horses comes
> To afflict the enemy.
> The Messiah will awaken his servants,
> Erase the name of Amalek and the enemy
>
> . . . .
>
> Consolations and good tidings shall we see;
> All we who hope and trust in God,

44. Vol. V, pp. 137ff. Vol. VI, pp. 156–57.
45. In the first stanza of Joseph Ashkenazi's lament we read: "In the year *ḥevlei
    mashiaḥ* (1648) the Cossacks persecuted us."

Men and women, will bring peace offerings to Jerusalem
To the Temple which God Himself will build.

We shall say Amen with mouth open wide
When our scattered brethren are brought as a present.
All sorrow and suffering will be forgotten;
There will be nothing more to put on save great joy.

When the messianic hope was incorporated in the mighty
Shabbetai Tzevi movement, it found a living resonance not
only in Hebrew but in Yiddish literature as well. Among the
hundreds of elegies and laments that mourn the burnings,
epidemics, expulsions, massacres, and all the other afflictions
which the Jewish communities had to endure, the "Beautiful
New Poem of the Messiah," which one Jacob Tausk of Prague
published in Amsterdam in Tammuz of 1666, when Shabbetai
Tzevi's star attained its zenith, is distinguished by its triumphant, joyous tones.

Jacob Tausk was a Polish Jew, an ordinary Jew; in his
conceptions and entire world-view he stands not a whit
above his milieu. Moreover, he had generally only a very
slight notion of poetry and the poetic art. However, as Max
Weinreich, who published the "Poem of the Messiah,"[46]
rightly points out, precisely the fact that our author does
not try to grasp stars from heaven gives a special interest to
his composition. For we see here a faithful reflection of the
spiritual condition of the masses of Jews at that time.[47]
From Jacob Tausk's poem the multitude itself speaks; it expresses its enthusiasm and joy that finally the great miracle
has occurred and the golden hope for which the homeless
nation has waited so many generations has at last disclosed
itself in all its splendor:

O Jews, dear brothers mine, rejoice once more,
For God has given him to us; we have our king.
He will help all the people,
We have long hoped and waited.
Amen and Amen and Amen.

46. *Tsaytshrift*, I, 158–173.
47. Weinreich, *Bilder*, 223.

Jacob Tausk's Messianic Poem

O Jews, dear brothers mine, we will all have great
happiness.
Soon we will travel to the Holy Land, dance and jump for
   joy.
Forgotten will be our sorrow;
There will be nothing but great joy.
Amen and Amen and Amen.

Israel, dear brothers mine, stay hidden no more!
We hear and see good tidings—now we need worry no
   longer.
God has sent us the time
To sit in pure joy.
Amen and Amen and Amen.

Typical is the picture Tausk gives of how Jews will live in
the land of the fathers after the Messiah has brought them
there:

Come here, dear brothers mine, we will mention no
   troubles,
The Turks will be our slaves, they will rinse our
   glasses.
We will wink to one another
And drink to the health of King Shabbetai Tzevi.
Amen and Amen and Amen.

We will do no work but only study Torah,
God will guard us all, we will have no fear.
Many will acknowledge that our God
Created heaven and earth.
Amen and Amen and Amen.

Joy and happiness resound from the masses.
The merit of our ancestors have we enjoyed.
Praise God with reverence
Because He has given us such a time.
Amen and Amen and Amen.

Stir, O poor, sick people! You are released from your pains
Praise God with great joy and all your heart . . .

Another theme in Jacob Tausk's messianic poem must be
stressed. This is the social motif. In the poem is related how the

Messiah's secretaries dispatched "emissaries in the land" who "write of the great joy":

That we should set forth and not remain here long.
He who has no money or property—
Let them help one another.

There, in the land of the fathers—the author asserts—Jews will be able to get along without money. But there were rich men who refused to rely on miracles; in their view, in Palestine also, and even in the times of the Messiah, money would remain a very respectable item and be extremely useful. Hence they had no desire to part with their wealth and to give funds to the poor for expenses. There were also those who openly stated that exile was not so bad for them, and hence they had no desire to move to the land of Israel. On these wealthy people the author pours out all his scorn:

The rich pursue nothing but pleasure and joy with their
     money
And pay no attention to the poor.
Amen and Amen and Amen.

Our prophets[48] wrote from their land to the rich,
Asking them to share with the poor, so that they also may
     come betimes.
If they refuse to listen to the poor,
They will use up their money en route with trouble,
Amen and Amen and Amen.

Some of the rich believe they will not have wherewith to
     live in the land of Israel
If they treat the poor well and give charity.
They will there be considered ever so much higher;
They should only bring beautiful *kiddush* cups,
Amen and Amen and Amen.

Honor will be done to the rich when they come to the land
     of Israel,
Those who were of use to the poor and took them along.
Some of the wealthy hold the redemption for naught—

48. Shabbetai Tzevi's associates—Nathan of Gaza and others.

They will die here miserably on the dung heap.
Amen and Amen and Amen.

Some of the historical poems, such as the abovementioned *El Male Raḥamim* or the elegy on the Gonta massacres of 1768 which begins "Our Father in heaven, how can You look on this?"[49] are written in the style of the Hebrew *seliḥot* and form a transitional stage to the purely religious poems which are also quite richly represented in Yiddish literature. We noted earlier that many persons were opposed to having the poor people, and especially women, break their teeth over the difficult and incomprehensible hymns in the Festival Prayerbook. Such a prayer that is said without any intention and concentration, these persons contended, has no value whatever. Thus, a Yiddish liturgical poesy, religious hymns and paeans in the common vernacular comprehensible to all, was produced. Such religious poems in Yiddish are preserved from as early as the sixteenth century, for instance, the "Simḥat Torah Poem" of the aforementioned Rebecca bat Meir Tiktin (Tiktiner).[50] We present here the first part of the poem according to a later reprint:[51]

Our God is one—You are my God,
Who created my soul and body—Hallelujah.

You created heaven and earth;
Therefore is your praise eternal—Hallelujah.

You were and will be eternally.
You created us all—Hallelujah.

All things are in Your power;
Therefore we praise You day and night—
   Hallelujah.

True and pure is Your command:
Therefore we thank You, O true God—Hallelujah.

49. Published in Litinski's *Korot Podolyah*, 53–55; reprinted in Bassin, *op. cit.*
50. Above, p. 241.
51. In a "Teḥinnah Imahot Gedolah" (year and place of printing not given).

Living and eternal, You are our consolation,
As You did promise us—Hallelujah.

You live eternally on Your heavenly throne;
For the pious You keep their reward—Hallelujah.

Omnipotent are You, our God, alone;
Your enemies must go to ruin—Hallelujah.

Beside You there is no other God;
Therefore heaven and earth abide—Hallelujah.

He will adorn us with His crown,
All who have accepted the Torah—Hallelujah.

Take as your help the heavenly host;
Everything will prove true—Hallelujah.

In Frankfurt-am-Main and in many other communities it was customary to welcome the Sabbath while it was still daylight (in order "to add from the profane to the holy"). To extend the Sabbath meal into the night or at least until sunset and thereby not speak any "vain words," a resident of Frankfurt, the author of the custumal *Yosif Ometz*,[52] composed in 1596 a rather long "New Song for Sabbath Eve" in which he celebrates the great importance of "the candles of Sabbath." Because this commandment is a special "women's commandment," the author, immediately after each Hebrew verse, also provided a translation in Judeo-German in rhymed lines. We present here several verses of this song:

I will sing today
In the presence of Sabbath candles
That shine toward me,
That one sees through the room.
On the Sabbath candles alone
Is light directed
To sing over the table against night.
For only when it is night
Do the lighted candles first shine.

---

52. See our *History*, Vol. VI, pp. 70ff.

The commandment of kindling lights
Was given to women alone,
For Eve extinguished with her sin
The light of every man.
Also they [the women] are usually at home,
But not so the man.
When he comes from the field towards night,
When it is about to become dark,
She must kindle the lights.

When she has said the benediction
Let her pray in the light of the candles
That her children may be privileged
To study well and be pious.
Such a benediction is priceless;
It goes to the portal of heaven.
The gate is not closed till night.
When it is about to become night,
The lighted candles shine.

The author of the chronicle *Tzok Ha-Ittim*[53] also composed in Aramaic a hymn for the Sabbath day *(Mizmor Shir Le-Yom Ha-Shabbat)*. From Aramaic it was soon (in 1654) reworked into Judeo-German by one Gimpel Segal and published in Amsterdam with the following introduction: "This hymn for the Sabbath day was made by our teacher Rabbi Meir of Szcebrzcyn, and the one who translated it into German is Gimpel Segal of Vienna. He desires to show no mental acuity in this so that he might be praised and lauded, but he made it comprehensible for common people and women and maidens, that they might also know how to spend the holy Sabbath and what is the significance of the extra souls. This hymn is set to the melody of *Akdamut*. And when you read it, it will rejoice your heart. Late every Friday it should be sung with a petition. So will we merit that the Messiah will soon lead us into the Land of Israel."

Another figure who acquired renown with his religious poems in Hebrew and Yiddish was the *ḥazzan* or precentor Jehudah Leib Zelechover. He published his poems in his old age[54]

---

53. See our *History*, Vol. VI, p. 127. Both texts of this Sabbath poem are reprinted in *Otzar Ha-Safrut*, III, Part Two, 147–161.
54. For biographical details on the author of *Shirei Yehudah*, see J. Shatzky's article "Yehude-Leib Zelechover Un Zayne *Shirei Yehudah*," *(YIVO-Bleter*, Vol. III, 138–147).

in Amsterdam (1697) under the title *Shirei Yehudah*. In the long rhymed introduction, which has a certain cultural-historical value, the author complains that at banquets and weddings the guests do not conduct themselves properly.[55] They speak only "profane words;" they are concerned with nothing but dancing and jumping, and the *hazzanim* sing at table songs "that should not be mentioned." For this reason he, the author, has composed especially for *hazzanim* and singers his hymns, that they "may not spare their voices in honor of God" at banquets after dinner. One hymn is composed "in honor of the unity of the Holy One Blessed Be He and His *Shechinah*," to be sung at all religious banquets "in order to arouse and maintain the memory of the destruction of the Temple." Another is written in honor of Hannukah.

Considerably more interesting in their broad scope are the Sabbath and festival poems written by the author of *Simhat Ha-Nefesh*. Twenty years after the appearance of the first part of *Simhat Ha-Nefesh*, Elhanan Kirchhan published the second part of his work (Fürth, 1727). This part is distinguished very sharply from the first in form. It is a collection of poems to be sung, and with every poem the notes of the melody are given. What purposes he intended with his work, and for what reasons he set his poems to popular tunes taken from musicians, are explained by Kirchhan in the introduction:

Having seen what great indecency occurs in communities,
And that they do not take to heart that all is vanity—
The books in German and the first part of my *Simhat Ha-Nefesh* being without effect among many—
For to bring them diligently to read ethical instruction and laws is an art;
Of what avail is it to make edifying books
If they are not read, and piety is set aside because of worldly things?
Considering such things with pain,
I have made these hymns.

55. "I have seen in many places what happens at banquets and weddings . . . At a wedding all run after eating to the dance, and thereby the religious 'precept of the banquet' is soon completely destroyed. Very few remain sitting at the table. They run around like fish in water, and when they return to the address there is a great tumult. No plea helps to make them quiet . . . They play with the maidens who sit by the bride and do things that are not of much use."

Many laws of every day and Sabbaths and festivals are
   portrayed in them
And set according to song and rhyme.
Also provided with musical notes, to make known,
Through the practice of a musician,
The right melody . . .

The work consists of fifteen poems or "hymns" *(zemirot)*,
as they are called by the author. Of these, three celebrate
the Sabbath. Others are devoted to the New Moon, Rosh
Ha-Shanah, and Yom Kippur. So, also, special hymns cele-
brating Sukkot and Simḥat Torah are given, and, following
them, hymns for Ḥannukah, Purim, Passover, and Shavuot.
After this comes a poem "for a wedding and circumcision
feast," a "bridal poem," and a "song for everyday" which
had already been printed in the first part of *Simḥat Ha-
Nefesh* under the title "A Beautiful Awakening Song." After
the "song for everyday" comes a poem without a title—a
rhymed description of Jewish life in the villages and rural
settlements. This poem is not merely of great interest for
Jewish cultural history; it is also the key to the entire work.
Through the frequent persecutions and strong competition
that Jews had to endure from the urban Christian populace,
they were increasingly pushed out of the cities and moved
into the villages.[56] This process was most clearly discernible
in the seventeenth century. At the end of that century a
very considerable, if not the largest, part of the German
Jews consisted of villagers who lived among the peasants,
keeping shops, taverns, and inns. The peasant environment
naturally exercised a powerful influence on the village Jew.
The well-known type of the crude, ignorant villager was
formed. Elḥanan Kirchhan, who was—according to Shatzky's
undoubtedly correct conjecture—an itinerant preacher, had
opportunity to become intimately familiar with the way of life
of the village Jews. He portrays this life in rather somber colors
in the above-mentioned poem:

56. Already in 1544 Michael Adam notes in the above-mentioned preface to his
Constance edition of the Pentateuch: "We see the communities, by reason of
our many sins, ever declining and destroyed through many expulsions, so that
where formerly there were ten communities, one now finds only one, because
of our many sins. And through such expulsions, the householders are compelled to dwell in the *villages.*"

In many villages women and virgins go about everywhere
    without a chaperone
And pay no attention to transgression, be it light or small,
Pronounce permissible what is forbidden . . .
There are also women who drink a great deal of liquor at a
    wedding or circumcision,
As much as is required for a ritual bath,
And carry on, at the same time, wanton talk and laughter
    with men and youths.
As they do, so also do their daughters.
In villages on the sacred New Year
They have ignorant precentors and youths who do not
    know a single prayer formula,
Do not understand one word;
And on Purim they read to the congregation with a
    benediction out of a paper *megillah.*
Some have made a mouthpiece out of horn
And place it in the *shofar,*
Sounding the ram's horn through the mouthpiece
Just as they do with the trumpets and forest horns with
    which they hunt hares.
Village people are mainly their own ritual slaughterers,
    none of whom understand a Hebrew letter.[57]
Rarely does one encounter here a man who has a good
    slaughtering knife . . .
I also found an ignoramus declaring proper to his comrade
    something that is ritually unfit,
And they also ate of it, giving it no further thought . . .
The conduct of weddings is not to be reported;
In any case, words of Torah are rarely heard . . .
When a scholar preaches, whether of things small or great,
It is like the work of Satan—
No word of holiness is allowed to come to them;
At once they fall asleep or drowse.
Many a time they play tricks and pranks,
And women and maidens let their voices be heard like
    whores,
And will not be shut up,
So that in the middle of the sermon they must stop.
And when the sermon is over,
The impudent songs come again.

57. Jehudah Zelechover also complains in the above-quoted preface that there are
    many young Jews who cannot read and write.

The Second Part of Simḥat Ha-Nefesh

They carouse and shout and sing,
They clap with hands and feet and jump on the table . . .

Further on the author portrays how the crude villagers
behave at weddings and how badly they fulfill the commandment of visiting the sick and the precepts regarding the sanc-
tity of the Sabbath:

Also many village people burden their youth and servants
With walking or pasturing their cattle on Sabbath and
    festivals.
Thus, much desecration of the Sabbath occurs; one ties his
    prayer-book in the horns of the ox.
They walk them beyond the permissible distance and
    sometimes go many such distances looking for the
    animals. . . .
If a villager has a tutor in his house,
He is regarded as having learned the whole Torah through,
And must give decisions on all the laws.
But the tutor and the householder who do such things are
    worse than heretics . . .
Tutors instruct for the sake of money,
Teach only Gemara and leave aside the Pentateuch and
    other books of the Bible.
At *bar mitzvah* they do not let the children study further;
So the child knows nothing, but remains a horserider.
Many women treat men like dogs.
Curses are always issuing from their mouths.
Even if nothing else is wrong, she is arrogant in her
    conceit.
And this is a principle: In a house where there is cursing
    and swearing, there is no blessing and good fortune in
    anything . . .
I report such things, so that people should know how to
    desist from them.
Unfortunately, there is much more to say,
But it is very grievous for me to have to tell such things.
My prayer, however, is always: Dear, merciful God, do
    not recompense according to their evil works!
A blind man who walks alone stumbles on the way;
But when he is led, he follows the right path.
So, because the people do not read earnestly, they err with
    many transgressions . . .

"The people" refuse not merely to read any books "earnestly;" they do not read books at all. They refuse even to listen to sermons and wish to hear only gay songs and tunes. Elḥanan Kirchhan not without reason complains very strongly of the "ignorant" *ḥazzanim* or cantors.[58] Among the singers who used to amuse the common people with merry songs and couplets, a rather significant role was played by the wandering *ḥazzanim* and their singing assistants who used to employ the time between the holy days in making tours through the smaller Jewish villages and presenting evenings of song and concerts.[59] The number of these itinerant *ḥazzanim* rose considerably after the massacres of 1648, when emigration from Poland into the German territories grew. Many prominent rabbis of the seventeenth and eighteenth centuries deplore the "desecration of God's name" perpetrated by the fact that the "emissaries of the congregation" are transformed into "comedians" and sing "impudent songs" to amuse the people. The author of *Etz Hayyim* is filled with indignation at the fact that the *ḥazzanim* sit together with "common jesters" and sing "whore songs" and utter "obscenities." These songs and melodies which the *ḥazzanim* sang not merely at circumcisions and banquets but even in the taverns were greatly loved by the common people in the village settlements.

The pious Elḥanan Kirchhan, as we observed, complained strenuously of this and decided to fight against the *ḥazzanim* with their own weaponry. Since the *ḥazzan* tears the common people away from the book and amuses them with songs and melodies, Kirchhan desires, through the aid of song, to spread moral instruction and God's commands. "He wishes," the cultural historian J. Shatsky correctly notes, "to penetrate the masses not with tales and fables for reading, but with songs. With and through singing, he would become one of their own among the masses of the people. Let the religious rules, the

58. The ignorance of most of the *ḥazzanim* is often deplored in the literature of that time. Typical in this respect is the following passage in the preface which Jacob Joseph ben Meir Sofer wrote to his textbook *Even Yisrael:* "I had compassion on the common people and their children and on the common *ḥazzanim*. Therefore I wrote in German the principles that are necessary for speaking and reading, so that each one can study by himself . . . Therefore, I hereby beg all *ḥazzanim* and teachers that they only have as much pity on themselves as I had on them; so they will rejoice."

59. For more about this, see I. Schipper, *Geshikhte Fun Yidisher Teater-Kunst,* I, 153–154, 170, 187, 188; J. Shatzky in *Filologishe Shriftn,* II, 225–226; in *Pinkes,* 1928, 177–181; and in the preface to *Simḥat Ha-Nefesh,* 1926, 43–45.

stories, and the parables be sung. Through singing, the people will become familiar with all the laws which it was desired that they keep and not simply know of."[60] The first part of *Simḥat Ha-Nefesh* was written by Kirchhan for urban Jewish readers; the second part, for rural residents, village Jews.

Kirchhan was not a poet and his poems have very slight literary value. Nevertheless, the second part of *Simḥat Ha-Nefesh* possesses not only the cultural-historical significance that we noted previously; it is also interesting for the history of the evolution of the meter and poetic forms of the Yiddish folksong. A man with a profound feeling for the people, Kirchhan frequently managed to render the supple rhythm of the common folksong. Typical, for instance, is the first stanza of his previously mentioned didactic poem:

> O man, O man, how you delude yourself!
> You fly, you run—what good will it bring you?
> Death waits unexpectedly behind your door.
> Your money and your houses and golden chains
> Cannot help you out of your distress,
> When the angel of death comes and would slay you.

Tender and sincere also are Kirchhan's stanzas in which national motifs resound:

> Remember how Israel is scattered in all places
> How can one take pleasure in joy and merriment . . .
> Merciful God, stretch forth Your mighty hand
> To gather in those who are scattered in all corners . . .

In another place the author laments:

> We are despised
> In the exile;
> Dear God, change it!
> Day and night
> We have nothing but tumults.
> Merciful God, send the Messiah!

Kirchhan's "bridal song" also ends with the same motif:

> Dear God, send us the Messiah soon
> To quicken our grieved hearts,

60. *Simḥat Ha-Nefesh*, 1926, 44.

For we are weak and feeble in exile.
Let us hear the sound of joy and the sound of happiness,
The sound of the groom and the sound of the bride,
In Jerusalem the holy city,
In Jerusalem the holy city.

Aside from the many Jewish religious poems and hymns (*zemirot*) that were produced by well-known authors, there have also been preserved liturgical poems in Yiddish the names of whose creators are unknown, as is also the time when they were written. It is worth mentioning the two well-known poems "Eḥad Mi Yodea" and "Ḥad Gadya" that are sung on the nights of the Passover *seder*, the first in Hebrew and the second in Aramaic. The singular style and rhythm of these songs bears a clearly stamped European popular character. Similar songs are to be found in considerable numbers in the medieval folklore of most of the peoples of Europe. A Latin poem that is very similar to our "Ḥad Gadya" has even been preserved from the Middle Ages (see Wagenseil, *op. cit.*, 97). It is highly probable that these two Passover songs existed in the vernacular of the Jewish masses before the Hebrew-Aramiac text appeared in the *Haggadah*.[61] We present here the opening stanzas of both poems in Yiddish:

I

אײנס װער װײסט?
אײנס װײס איך: אײניג איז אונזער גאָט
דער דאָ לעבט און דער דאָ שװעבט
אים הימל און אַך אױף דער ערד.
צװײ און דאָס איסט אבער מער, און דאָס זעלביג װײס איך:
צװײ טאָבען (טאָװלען) מאָזעס, אײניג איז אאַז״װ.

II

אײן ציקלײַן, אײן ציקלײַן, דאָס האָט געקױפֿט דאָס פֿעטערלײן
אום צװײ שילינג־פֿעניג. אײן ציקלײַן, אײן ציקלײַן.
דאָ קאָם דאָס קעצעלײן, און אַס דאָס ציקלײן
דאָס דאָ האָט געקױפֿט אאַז״װ.

---

61. It is worth noting that in the first printed Haggadot, e.g., in the Prague edition of 1526, these poems are still not present. On the other hand, in the Prague edition of 1590, the "Ḥad Gadya" song is already printed both in Aramaic and in Judeo-German.

Among the anonymous poems that have been preserved there are also a significant number in which it is not the religious but the social motif that resounds most sharply, despite the fact that they are not infrequently written in the fashion of religious supplications *(seliḥot)* and elegies *(ki-not).* Typical in this respect is the long mocking poem against the *parnassim*[62] in the well-known Wallich[63] collection. In this poem the poor complain:

We poor people must lament what occurs in the world,
What has happened here in the land of Bamberg,
How the *parnassim* commit very shameful things against the
    poor.

Further on it is related that "once a feast took place" and the *parnassim* let the poor stand behind the door. The food they gave them was half warm and half cold, and "so little that one could not be satisfied from it." The mocking poem concludes in quite pious fashion:

Now we will close the *seliḥah.*
May God let us enjoy the merit of the fathers.
So that we may proclaim [His salvation] on the cathedral
    square.
To this we would say Amen.

No less typical is the "New Lament with the Melody of *Ani Ha-Gever* on a Communal Servant of Frankfurt" which was first published in 1708.[64] In this poem the itinerant poor complain very strongly of the troubles they have to endure from the gatekeeper of Frankfurt, Jacob Fullwasser:

Listen, dear people
To what transpires in these times
When we try to go to Frankfurt.
O we poor people—
When we itinerant beggars march to Frankfurt,
They do not let us past the gates.

---

62. The poem occupies all of six pages in manuscript. Two of the *parnassim* are
    even mentioned by names, Hirsh Schwartz und Shmerle Shupfalk.
63. See above, pp. 88ff.
64. Reprinted in Bassin's *Antologye* and *Filologishe Shriftn,* II, 169–174.

They receive this dismal welcome when "Jacob Fullwasser with his staff" comes toward them. The situation is even more grievous in the winter time:

But in winter he behaves much worse with the poor;
He lets us stand, old and young, before the gate,
And allows no one before the officials (*gabbaim*) until our
    hands and feet are frozen.
And we cry loudly:
O dear God, how cold we are!
And the gentiles, because of our many sins, stand there
    looking on.
Out of great pity they bid the wicked
To let us go in and warm ourselves.

The poem is filled with bitter hatred for this strict gate-keeper:

How we suffer pain through this wicked man,
And we beg night and day
That thunder may quickly strike him.

To be sure, God is "slow to anger" and He allows this wicked man to "enjoy his merit in this world." The author of the poem, however, hopes that:

In the world to come they will break his bones.
The destroying angels will shatter his limbs
And hurl him in the hollow of the sling . . .

Even at the end, where the author refuses to disclose his name and declares jestingly

Would you know who made this little poem?
A man on two feet thought it out

it is immediately added: "And may Jacob Fullwasser break his neck, Amen and Amen."

Of significantly broader scope is the mocking poem *Di Bashraybung Fun Ashkenaz Un Polyak* which was composed and printed in the second half of the seventeenth century.[65]

65. Reprinted by M. Weinreich in *Filologishe Shriftn*, III, 540–551.

Di Bashraybung Fun Ashkenaz Un Polyak

After the enormous destruction which Polish Jewry lived through in the bloody years 1648–1649, Germany was flooded with Jewish refugees fleeing from the Polish territories. We noted in the previous volume that for generations Poland was renowned as the chief hostel of Torah. Young people used to go from the settlements in Germany to the Polish *yeshivot* to study Torah, and Polish scholars settled in Germany as teachers, rabbis, and other religious functionaries. German Jewry was regarded as unlettered in comparison with Polish Jewry. The great catastrophe changed many things in the mutual relationships of the two communities. The large numbers of physically and morally broken and greatly impoverished immigrants who suddenly flooded the German communities were regarded by the long-settled, indigenous Jews as an embarassing and heavy burden. In addition, one must take into consideration the great differences in the way of life of the two Jewish communities. The German Jews regarded the refugee "Polish beggars and vagabonds" with contempt and disgust and were always thinking of ways to get rid of them. The "Polyaks," for their part, looked with bitterness on the "Ashkenazim" who refused to recognize the commandment of welcoming strangers. This controversy between the old settlers and the undesired "aliens" is portrayed in very prominent fashion in *Di Bashraybung* in the form of an argument among the representatives of three Jewish settlements—Poland, Germany, and Prague.

The name of the author is not indicated, but it is beyond doubt that he was a Polish Jew.[66] Indeed, the "Polyak" is the first to come forth with his complaints against the German Jews. When he lists their failings—what misers they are, how badly they welcome strangers—he presents, incidentally, interesting genre-portraits of the mode of life in the Jewish communities of Germany. The German Jews of the seventeenth century for instance, were not very strict about beards, and the "Polyak," whom the "Ashkenaz" addresses with contempt, "You Polyaks with your wide beards," considers it necessary to note:

I would mention the matter of trimming the beard.
He trims it away like leaven [on the eve of Passover],
He leaves only a small goatee.

66. We have pointed to this in our work in *Yevreyskaya Starina*, XIII, 156.

With intense bitterness the Polyak declares:

One other thing I must tell you,
For I cannot bear it.
The Polyak may be a scholar of good family,
But the Ashkenaz will not intermarry with him, except if
  the girl be not especially blessed.
But when the Ashkenaz wishes to obtain a rabbi or cantor
He must, nevertheless, send to Poland.
You would be as the dumb and speechless in Torah,
If teachers did not frequently come to you in Germany
  from Poland.
We would not be eager to come and receive shame in
  Germany,
If the war had not come to our land . . .
You Ashkenazim also fled to Poland in the past
When war[67] struck you in Germany.
You were favored with money and in your persons,
And were given funds and the best wives.
Therefore take it not amiss that we come to you . . .

Like Elḥanan Kirchhan, the "Polyak" also portrays in dark
colors the low cultural level of the villagers in Germany:

Another thing lies on my stomach;
This I must relate and say:
How the villagers conduct their synagogue-going
Young and old . . .
When they come together on the Sabbath for services,
They begin to laugh,
Their mouth does not stand still.
One speaks of his filly, one of his horse—
Why should I say much?
Often they even come to blows in the synagogue.

Here the "Ashkenaz" enters with his complaints:

It is true that in Poland there are great Torah scholars,
But none of them is to be trusted in money or in
  merchandise.

....

67. The Thirty Years War.

We give you food and drink and money thereto;
Nevertheless, we Germans have no rest before you Polyaks.

The Polyaks—the "Ashkenaz" or German contends further
—are swindlers and thieves, and it happens not infrequently
that one welcomes a Pole as a respectable traveler, and the man
purloins items and clothes from the house. In addition, the
Poles are enormous trenchermen: "You think the oxen come
into the stable already roasted." They are also tremendously
arrogant. A Pole may not even know how to recite the *Kiddush*
or *Havdalah*; yet "he gives himself out as if he were the rabbi
of Cracow."

After this, the debate of the "Ashkenaz" with the man from
Prague commences. The Jews of Prague are also reproached
for being gluttons and frauds who even swindle their own
progeny:

To cheat their own children is no shame among them.
He promises his son-in-law three years of maintenance, in
   addition to a portion in the house.
Four weeks after the wedding: "Son-in-law, do you wish to
   eat?
Pawn your prayershawl and robe; your maintenance is at
   an end."

Along with polemic works, apologetic brochures in
rhyme have also been preserved, e.g., *Re'ah Nihoah*, which
the precentor or *hazzan* Joel ben Eliezer published in Fürth
in 1724.[68] We spoke previously of the battle carried on
against the precentors because they refused to content
themselves with the religious functions of "emissary of the
congregation" and also endeavored to amuse the people as
singers and entertainers. This battle, too, found its resonance in literature. At the beginning of the eighteenth century there appeared in Hebrew a sharply-worded, anonymous brochure entitled *Sheloshah Tzo'akim* against *hazzanim*,
who are charged in it with violating grave precepts of the
law. "They are gluttons and drunkards" and "void of all
precepts and good deeds." Against this brochure Joel issued
forth with two apologies, one in Hebrew and the other in
Yiddish "so that everyone may understand." This apologetic

68. Reprinted with a thorough introduction by J. Shatsky in *Pinkes*, 1928, 177–192.

brochure has a certain cultural-historical significance. In it we hear not only of the *ḥazzanim* and their conduct. We also have before us a portrait of a typical cantor of that time with all his gestures, inclinations, and naively petty notions.

CHAPTER ELEVEN

The Beginnings of Drama in Yiddish

The factors that hindered the normal development of dramatic art among Jews—The Azazel-cult and Yahweh-cult—Dialogue as ornament—The "Jewish scenes" and the medieval mystery plays—Entertainers and masquerades—Purim parodies—The influence of the secular humanist theater in Italy—The first Hebrew Purim comedy *Bediḥuta De-Kiddushin*—The influence of the German *Fastnacht*-plays and of the Biblical dramas—The *"Shpil Fun Tab Yeklayn"*—The Purim play of the "King's Young Men"—"English Comedies" and *Staatsaktionen*—Yiddish *Staatsaktionen* and their transformations.

HE ANONYMOUS *Bashraybung Fun Ashkenaz Un Polyak* is written in a dramatic form. After the dialogue between the "Polyak" and the "Ashkenaz" comes the debate between the latter of these and the man from Prague. Nevertheless, this work has no relationship whatever to dramatic art; the *Bashraybung* was produced to be read or declaimed, not acted. However, there have been preserved (*in toto* and in fragments) a certain number of anonymous works written in rhyme that are closely connected with the theatrical art and were created as "theater pieces," for the special purpose of being played on the stage.

Historians of literature and culture have long suggested that the ripest fruit of poetic creativity, dramatic art, was treated as a stepchild in Hebrew literature. Franz Delitzsch, for instance, notes that "dramatic poetry is that form to whose cultivation the Israelite spirit . . . was least favorable."[1] Steinschneider remarks also, as if it were a well-known matter, that "Semitic literature until modern times has nothing of the dramatic to exhibit."[2] Dr. Ignacy Schipper also concludes that the Jews in the Middle Ages, in comparison with the Romance and Germanic peoples, "were extremely backward in their dramatic creativity." These scholars, however, were content merely with noting the fact and did not consider it necessary to attempt to discover its causes.[3]

In Greece, the classic land of ancient theater and ancient tragedy, the theater—as we know—was closely connected with the religious cult. Its cradle stood at the altar where men would bring sacrifices to the god of vitality and fertility, Dionysus, in the form of a he-goat. People danced in a joyous circle around the altar and sang paeans in the form of dialogues between the first singer (coryphaeus) and the choir. The word "tragedy," in fact, derives from the Greek words *tragos* meaning he-goat, and *oide*, an ode or song of praise. In our work *"Tsu Der Geshikhte Fun Der Yidisher Folks-Dramatik"* (*Bikher-Velt*, 1929, I, III) we speak at length of the fact that these living seeds, these vital kernels of theatrical representation out of which the classical Greek theater blossomed, were also not lacking in the case of our ancestors, among the ancient Israelite tribes. Signs and memories of popular plays filled with theatrical moments are preserved in Judaism's oldest literary monuments. In our work we touched on the point that in ancient times the children of Israel also worshipped *se'irim*, i.e., gods whose emblem was the he-goat. And the "scapegoat," the *azazel* who was so closely associated with the ritual of Yom Kippur, is, in fact, a twin brother of Dionysus. It was in *his* honor that the Israelite maidens would dance on a certain day (the tenth of Tishri) in the vineyards and sing erotic songs, as the Greek maidens did

1. *Zur Geschichte der jüdischen Poesie*, 77.
2. *MGWJ*, 1903, 84.
3. As far as we know, only L. Philippson in his foreward to *Ezechiel und Philo* attempted to throw light on the reasons why the kernels of drama which had been sown in Jewish cultural life since ancient times could not ripen to maturity.

at the time of the Dionysian rites. Greek tragedy, however, derives not only from the religious cult of Dionysus but was itself considered, in the consciousness of the people, a religious act, a rite of worship. The popular myth, clarified and refined by the inspired creativity of the poet, obtained flesh and blood and was incorporated on the stage in real, substantive forms and there disclosed itself before the audience, the entire community, in living, palpitating word and image. Precisely for this reason, among the Jewish people, dramatic art could *not* be born from the *azazel* and he-goat cults, despite the fact that the Yom Kippur ceremony with the "scapegoat" is so rich in theatrical effects and that we already detect in it the most important nuclei of the later Greek tragedy which bloomed so magnificently.[4] Jewish religious-dramatic art could not be born because precisely in the Yom Kippur ceremony we see quite clearly the *decline* of the *azazel*-cult, of the pictorial folk-myth. The *azazel*-cult still lived in the psyche of the people, but the Yahweh cult had already triumphed over it. Not to the god Azazel but to the God Yahweh did the Israelites offer sacrifices on the golden altar, and the "scapegoat," the *azazel*-sacrifice, which becomes the symbol of the people's sinfulness and guilt, is dispatched outside the camp into the wilderness, to be hurled off a mountain peak. The God Yahweh, the God of the prophets, who, from being a local, national deity became the *universal* God who cannot suffer any other gods near Him, triumphed —this God who cannot and may not be conceived in any pictoral form whatsoever, the God who commands with utmost strictness: "You shall not make for yourself any likeness . . ."

The fact that the inconceivable and infinite God of the prophets displaced all other gods and myths in the popular consciousness excluded the possibility that the lyric dithyrambs, the prayers and praises of the God of Israel, the dialogue and choral singing of the Psalms which the Levites used to sing in the Temple to the accompaniment of musical instrumentation, should obtain more concrete forms associated with mime and gesture and be transformed into a pictorial, personified, dramatic-religious representation. The religious sentiment, the feeling of love and reverence for the universal God, the Creator God, who refuses to know of limited, human, corporeal forms could not express and disclose itself in theatrical, sculptured images and figures, but only in the *word*, in the trembling of the human soul.

4. See our work, *Bikher-Velt*, 1929, I, 40.

In this respect the Book of Job is highly instructive. Precisely this work that is so rich in theatrical elements and was created in dramatic forms shows most clearly that in the ethical-mono-theistic world-view established by the Hebrew prophets there was missing the most significant life-moment of Greek tragedy: the belief in blind fate, in the predetermined decree which man is unable to evade and in the face of which, the more stubbornly he struggles against his fate fixed beforehand by alien and merciless powers, the more inevitable and deeper becomes his downfall. And precisely because, in the Book of Job, God carries on a conversation with Satan and His voice is heard "out of the whirlwind," this work had to remain a book merely for reading and could not be represented in living dialogue on the stage. The whole world-view of the monotheis-tic Jew, with his firm belief in the unembraceable and hidden God "who has no form of body and no body," protested against the idea of making out of the Book of Job a "theater play," of transforming the narrative of the great struggle of man's soul, of the proud human personality yearning for justice, into a dramatic "presentation."

In the realm of dramatic art, virtually the same phenomenon that we observe in regard to another art that is also associated with embodiment in clear, three-dimensional forms—sculp-ture—was replicated. Given the strict prohibition "You shall not make for yourself any likeness," the Jewish artist did not have the possibility of creating in prominent forms not only human but even animal figures, out of fear that idols would be made of these. So he carved with his chisel in wood and stone, elaborated the most marvelous arabesques with a delicate brush, spun and wove ingenious ornaments of plants, animals, and birds, all together. Thus the *decorative* became the intimate and beloved realm in which Jewish art could disclose its own nature, its own unique style.

So it was also with dramatic art. Because the dramatic could not evolve normally into the "play" and "presentation," it developed in the word, in narrative form. The popular imagi-nation created an enormous mass of legends and tales which literally astonish one with their wealth of dramatic moments. It suffices to mention the cycle of legends associated with the "wisest of men," King Solomon, sitting on his magnificent throne, the throne so well known to everyone that is portrayed in the Midrash literature with no less masterfulness than Achilles' shield in Homer's poem. Or, to cite another example, the legends associated with the destruction of the Temple. The terrible event has taken place. God's sanctuary has been burned. The holy city and the entire land are destroyed. The finest children of Jerusalem are led away by the enemy in chains and sold as slaves. As soon as they hear the bitter tidings, the patriarchs rise from their graves. Abraham, Isaac, and Jacob come before the Throne of Glory to implore mercy. The holy shepherd Moses also comes and begs for his sheep over whom he watched forty years in the wilderness. The patriarchs silence the twenty-two letters of the Torah that appear to testify before the Throne of Glory that great is the sin of Israel which has violated the commandments of the holy Torah. But the wrath of God is not stilled, and the harsh decree is not tempered. Then the matriarch Rachel, the symbol of mother love and mother pain, comes. She pours out her great anguish before the Throne of Glory, and against her mother's tears God cannot stand fast. From the heavens the divine voice is heard: "Weep not, Rachel. I will bring back your children from exile."

The dialogue, the debate, is the favorite form of numerous Midrashic and Talmudic legends, which were, however, transmitted only from mouth to mouth. The dialogue is employed merely as an ornament, not as a dramatic "play." And the finest Hebrew poets of the Middle Ages, from Solomon Ibn Gabirol to Israel Najara, produced by the hundreds dialogue-poems, dialogues between the homeless lover, the congregation of Israel, and her Loved One who is angry with her but cannot forget her—the Master of the Universe.

Hence, it is not at all surprising that in Arabic Spain there bloomed so beautifully in Hebrew literature the poetic *makama*-form which the Hebrew poets adopted from their neighbors, the Arabs, among whom theater and dramatic art could also find no proper ground, and—indeed—for reasons similar to those that prevailed among the Jews.[5]

It was different, however, among the Jewish communities in *Christian* Europe. We know quite well that, as among the ancient Greeks, so among the Christian peoples of Europe in the Middle Ages, theatrical presentations were closely bound up with the religious cult. The cradle of theatrical art in Christian Europe stood in the church, and the priest with his cross was its father. The theatrical presentations (mystery plays, miracle plays) evolved from Catholic worship. The Christian populace at that time was still at a rather low level of culture and had not yet completely forgotten its previous idolatrous worship. Hence, the priests familiarized the people with the foundations of the faith and with the history of Jesus' life in a very unique way. They would not read or narrate the text of the gospel, but *represent* it in images and mass processions. Not through the word, through abstract concepts, did they teach the common, unlettered multitude the content of the Christian faith, but through clear, prominent symbols that could be seen by the eye and touched by the hand. The story of Jesus' birth, crucifixion, and resurrection used to be *represented* in the church in dramatic scenes that were an organic part of Catholic worship and gradually grew into quite lengthy liturgical dramas, in which not only the clergy but the common people as well would participate. The church became too narrow for the mysteries, and so they moved into the churchyard and later even outside the churchyard. But the life-nerve of these dramas remains, as before, the sharply stamped religious, worshipping factor. Among the characters of the cumbersome and often enormously long mystery plays[6] were not only saints, prophets, and apostles, but also "God the Father" Himself, His "Son," and the Holy Virgin Mother.

Dramatic works which bore such a typically Christian religious character were very little suited to interest the Jewish populace to the extent that the barrier, already standing for many generations, should suddenly be broken through, and Jews should obtain a strong desire to imitate the gentiles and plant in their own midst the alien growth —theatrical art. Moreover, one must bear in mind that it was precisely in Germany that the association of the mystery play with the churchyard lasted longest. Until well into the fifteenth century the mysteries were presented mainly during the week before Easter when Jews, the "enemies of Christ," had to lock themselves up in their ghettos so as not to be visible to Christians. In addition, it must be taken into consideration that the mysteries were not only purely of a Christian religious character but were also

6. The text of such dramas would reach 60,000 lines. In the presentation several hundred persons would take part, and the play would go on for many days successively.

strongly hostile to Jews. It is a historical fact that the German mystery plays, which reached their period of efflorescence only after the Crusades, are permeated with venomous hatred and bitter contempt for everything having any relationship to Judaism and Jewry. In the Easter and Christmas mystery plays there were not a few scenes in which, among the characters, Jews also figured; in these scenes the hatred and contempt felt for Jews would disclose themselves in their genuinely medieval crudeness. When hell was represented on the stage, the most prominent place there was occupied by the crater especially for *Judaei*. To show the ugliness and ridiculousness of "false" Judaism, the Christians used to present a special allegorical play called "The Church and the Synagogue."[7]

From the time that not only the clergy but the common people as well began to take part in the religious plays, there penetrated into the pious mystery, along with the popular language, which gradually displaced Latin, elements of the profane, everyday way of life. Together with the didactic-religious, there appeared also the comically witty, the vulgar and popular. Amidst the serious and pious scenes intrude comic little episodes, the so-called "farces," interludes with crudely witty, merry laughter. And the victim, the dart-board for all these jests and funny pieces, was —most of the time—the Jew. In Frankfurt, for instance, the comically caricatured Jewish masks which used to appear on the stage in certain scenes of the mysteries bore the family names of the most prominent members of the Jewish community. The scene where Judas Iscariot appears on the stage was utilized to amuse the audience, and the Jews were there represented as the vilest swindlers and wretches. The favorite "numbers" for making the audience happy were the scenes with Jewish dances and songs. On the stage in the Jewish "loge"[8] stood the figure of a calf filled with beer, and the "Jews" used to drink the beer not from the calf's mouth but through its other orifice (*Judaei bibunt ex culo vituli*). In another mystery play Jews lie stretched out on the ground sucking the udders of a pig. This "clever" display of medieval tavern wit and crude barbarity was even perpetuated for many generations on one of the town

7. See Weber, *Geistliche Schauspiele und kirkliche Kunst*, 1894.
8. The medieval theatre stage was divided into separate loges.

walls of Frankfurt, and the tasteless Johann Jakob Schudt decorated his thick anthology with this picture.[9]

All this, naturally, could do little to arouse in the Jewish populace the desire to overthrow the barrier which for centuries had separated Jewish culture from the art of the theater. The Old-German religious mystery plays were incapable of influencing the neighboring ghetto in such a way as to help a Jewish drama come into being. On the other hand, the influence of the Christian environment in regard to old customs, wedding and festival entertainments, dances, song, witticisms, and jests is very strongly discernible in the Jewish ghetto. Many of these customs and entertainments were even, in their time, closely connected with idolatry and the cult of demons. However, in the course of generations their religious character evaporated and the customs remained in the consciousness of the people only as a way of life. The Calendes and Caliades, for example, which are bound up with wearing the disguise of animals or with exchanging men's and women's clothing, were, in fact, associated in earlier generations with the religious cult and with erotic moments in idolatrous worship. It is from this that the prohibition in the Torah of "wearing the garments of a woman" derives. In time, however, the living symbol lost its religious content and was transformed into ordinary folklore, into accessories of popular amusement. The Christian environment did have a great influence[10] in this area on the pioneers of "entertainment" in the medieval ghettos —on all the Jewish jesters, "fools," and *badḥanim* with their dance, song, and play.

As early as the twelfth century the pious author of *Sefer Yere'im*, Rabbi Eliezer ben Samuel of Metz, deplores the fact that at weddings and other happy gatherings men and women disguise themselves in strange clothing.[11] Other rabbis complain of the "sinful jesters" who spout rhymes and speak obscenities.

In Italy, where the gay and colorful carnivals attained their most extraordinary brilliance and splendor in the Middle

9. See *Jüdische Merkwürdigkeiten*, II, 257.
10. Dr. Schipper collected interesting material on this influence in his *Yidishe Folks-Dramatik*, 26–100.
11. *Sefer Yere'im*, No. 96: "And to dress thus even by chance or in play is forbidden . . . And because I saw men temporarily wearing women's clothes and women temporarily wearing men's clothing at banquets for bride and groom and also at many [other] affairs, I have written thus."

Ages, the custom of wearing masks was also highly popular in the life-loving Jewish communities. The celebrated Italian rabbi of the fifteenth century Jehudah Minz relates that on the happy days of Purim, when "to increase joy" is recognized as a religious precept by the Talmud, everyone used to participate in the cheerful masquerades—young men and maidens, children and old people.[12] But even in the life-loving Italian ghettos there did not exist at that time any dramatic "Purim plays." The Italian Jews of the Middle Ages also kept apart from Melpomene's art.[13] Only gay parodies which used to be recited over foaming beakers of wine were widely utilized. Parodies in which the earnest style of the Bible and the Talmud were employed for merry and even frivolous slapstick and buffooneries were extremely popular among Jews already in the Middle Ages. As early as in the poem *Minhat Yehudah Sone Ha-Nashim* by Jehudah Shabbetai, the text of the *Ketuvah* or marriage document and the *Kiddush* is parodied. Another author of the twelfth century, Menahem ben Aaron, parodies the style of the *piyyut*, or liturgical hymn, in his gay *Maariv Le-Purim.* Kalonymos ben Kalonymos' well-known parody *Masechat Purim*[14] served as a model for hundreds of other parodies.[15]

Only in the first half of the sixteenth century was a bridge between the Jewish ghetto and the European theater produced and were the first foundation stones for Jewish theatrical and dramatic art laid. In our previously cited work on the Jewish theater in the Renaissance, we noted that only at the threshold of the sixteenth century, when a national theater with its *secular* repertoire was formed in Italy and the purely humanist drama triumphed over the Christian mystery plays, was a suitable environment created for Jews to become interested in the art of Melpomene. It is by no means accidental that the first information about a Jewish play in Europe comes from Italy in the year 1531. The Italian historian Marino Sanuto indicates

12. *Pesakim U-She'elot U-Teshuvot*, Venice, 1553, fols. 35–36: "On the matter of wearing masks which the young men and virgins and maidens, the old and the young, are accustomed to do on Purim . . . I wished to bring forth an argument to permit it . . . Great and pious men—may their memory be a blessing—among whom I grew up saw their sons and daughters, their grooms and brides, wearing masks."

13. For a discussion of this, see our work on the Jewish theater in Italy in the Renaissance (*Yevreyskaya Letopis*, IV).

14. See our *History*, Vol. II, p. 223.

15. See Steinschneider's "Purim und Parodie," *Letterbode*, VII, IX; *MGWJ*, 1902–03; I. Davidson's *Parody in Jewish Literature*, 1907.

in his notebook that on March 4, 1531 (Shushan Purim) he witnessed in the ghetto of Venice a splendid comedy *(una bellissima
commedia)*. Whether this comedy, which was undoubtedly
played in the vernacular (Italian), dealt with the theme of the
day, that is, the plot of the Scroll of Esther, is difficult to say.
In any case it was in Venice in the middle of the sixteenth
century that the talented translator of Petrarch into Spanish,
Solomon Usque, in collaboration with Eliezer Graziano, composed in Italian a Biblical drama *Esther*[16] which did not appear
in print and was apparently intended especially for the stage.
Usque's contemporary and acquaintance, the well-known director of the court theater of the dukes of Mantua, Jehudah ben
Isaac Sommo,[17] attempted to produce a Purim comedy in Hebrew. In his *Dialogues on the Art of the Theater (Dialoghi sull Arte
Representativa)* Sommo stresses how rich in dramatic elements
many of the old Jewish legends and tales are. He relates, incidentally, that he himself employed such a legend written in
Aramaic for his play "Corso della Vita." Another narrative of
the Midrash (*Tanḥuma*, "Parashah Lech Lecha") was utilized
by the same author for a cheerful Purim comedy *Bediḥuta De-
Kiddushin* which was preserved in manuscript and not long ago
became known to wider circles as a result of Jefim Schirmann's
interesting treatise.[18] In the preface it is explicitly noted that
the comedy was composed for the purpose of being presented
during the Purim festival ("to laugh with it on the days of
Purim and at the time of joy"). In the prologue the author
stresses that the peoples of the world consider it a defect and
one-sidedness that the Jews have not produced any dramatic or
theatrical works in their language. Hence, he undertook to
show them that in the realm of art and poetry the Hebrew
language is no less worthy than all other languages.[19]

Sommo's attempt to create a theater repertoire in Hebrew,
however, was unsuccessful. We know that precisely in the

---

16. This drama was later reworked by Leo de Modena (see our *History*, Vol. IV,
Chapter V).
17. For more about Jehudah Sommo, see our above-mentioned work in *Yevreyskaya
Letopis*, and also in our *History*, Vol. IV, pp. 97, 99.
18. *MGWJ*, 1931, 97–118. In the manuscripts that have been preserved the name of the
author is not mentioned. J. Schirmann however, presents quite convincing arguments to justify his conjecture that Jehudah Sommo is the author.
19. *Ibid.*, 115: "Behold, I have chosen this day to show all the peoples of the earth that
the Hebrew language is not inferior, for every work of art, to all the tongues of
the nations, but indeed the beauty of its greatness is far above them."

second half of the sixteenth century, the dramatic works that were produced in the vernacular finally pushed out from the Italian theater the classical repertoire, the Latin comedies of Plautus and Terence. For the Jewish theater also, which in Italy was born in the Renaissance era, a repertoire in the vernacular was produced. For the theater was a requirement not of the elect few but of the broad masses of the people.

The same thing occurred in Germany. We know quite well that, while a whole chain of cultural, social, and political factors called forth the broad religious movement of the Reformation, it ended with Germany's secession not only from the foreign Catholic Church of the pope but also from the *Latin* Church. We noted earlier[20] that the culturally matured urban bourgeoisie demanded that its intellectual and religious sustenance, the Bible, be made available to it in its mother tongue. The celebrated German translation of the Bible was not a brilliant invention of Martin Luther but a result of a long and significant cultural process. And, indeed, it was the same cultural process which brought it about that Luther's contemporary and ardent disciple, the renowned Hans Sachs, also came forth as the reformer of the German popular theater, the true founder of a *secular* theater.[21] The merry scenes filled with crude jests, the "farces" that were woven into the pious mystery plays, eventually separated from them and were transformed into independent entities. But thanks to Hans Sachs, the crude and debauched *Fastnacht* carnivals and plays were raised to the level of talented folk-comedies which not only cast off every religious vesture and moved from the churchyard into taverns and special theater buildings,[22] but were also not infrequently utilized as a weapon against the Catholic church. Not without reason did Luther declare the popular comedy an excellent pedagogical instrument for his reforming purposes.[23] In fact, Hans Sachs composed a whole series of anti-papal farces in which he mocks the Catholic clergy and discloses their moral degradation and profligacy.

Even for the pope's patron saint, the apostle Peter, into whose hands the keys of heaven were given, the *Meistersinger* of

---

20. See above, p. 46ff.
21. On Hans Sachs as reformer of the theater, see Eduard Devrient, *Geschichte der deutschen Schauspielkunst*, 1905, Vols. I–II, 57–64.
22. The first theater for German plays of secular content was built in 1550 in Hans Sachs' native city, Nuremberg.
23. See Devrient, *op. cit.*, 71.

Nuremberg has very little respect. In one of his *Fastnacht* plays[24] Hans Sachs represents the keeper of the heavenly gates as a gay chess player who spends his time quite convivially with chess partners in a tavern over full bottles of wine and beer, and in his intoxicated state forgets that at the gates of heaven the righteous stand and cannot enter because he has the keys with him.

As a result of the humanist movement and the Reformation, both of which powerfully stimulated interest in the Bible and at the same time greatly obscured the former brilliance of the Catholic-colored mystery plays,[25] Biblical dramas of a more or less secular character were produced in large numbers in the first half of the sixteenth century. Indeed, Hans Sachs, the great master of *Fastnacht* plays, also composed a certain number of secular dramas on Biblical themes—"Esther," "Judith," "King Solomon's Judgment," etc.

All this perforce made a powerful impression in the Jewish ghetto, whose residents generally listened with bated breath to the struggle that had erupted in the Christian world, and where, in the Reformation movement, were seen the "footsteps of the Messiah," and it was hoped that the rebellious monk Martin Luther would succeed in shattering the worst enemy of Judaism—the Catholic Church.[26] Under these circumstances a bridge between the Jewish ghetto and the European theater was finally formed, and the barrier which separated the Jewish populace from the temple of Melpomene was overthrown. In the ghetto also appeared theater pieces following the pattern of the *Fastnacht* plays and dramatic productions modeled after the Biblical dramas. And precisely in these dramatic creations could the extraordinarily rich dramatic kernels scattered in the Midrash literature finally be utilized in a theatrical form, even if quite primitively.

---

24. "Sanct Peter vergnügt sich mit seinem Freunden unten auf Erden": Ein Fastnachtspiel mit vier Personen (*Hans Sachs ausgewählte dramatische Werke*, II, 177–190).

25. Under the influence of the Reformation movement, the mysteries and miracle plays were proscribed at virtually the same time in several countries—in England in 1543, in France in 1548.

26. See Steinschneider, *Hebräische Bibliographie*, V, 45; Graetz, *Geschichte der Juden*, Vol. IX, Note no. 5. The Kabbalist Abraham ben Eliezer Halevi (see our *History*, Vol. V, pp. 20–21) announces with great enthusiasm: "A man named Martin Luther, he whose reputation is spread abroad in all lands, began in the year 5284 (1524) to battle against the religion of the uncircumcised . . . demonstrated publicly the falsity of their religion . . . and showed himself against the hanged one . . . and he brings them gradually closer to the religion of Moses . . . In fine, redemption for the poor inheritance will spring forth" (*Kiryat Sefer*, VII, 444–445).

It is beyond doubt that as early as the sixteenth century merry *Purim-shpiln* or Purim plays were produced in Yiddish following the pattern of the German *Fastnacht* plays and Biblical dramas, which were also apparently presented at Purim time. However, the texts of these dramatic works have not been preserved. Only about two Purim farces which used to be played in the sixteenth century do we have more or less precise information. An unknown author of the sixteenth century reports that in the dancehouses every Purim they used "to make a play about Tab Yeklayn, his wife Kendlayn, and his *tsvey zindlech fayn* (two little sons fine)."[27] The text of the play has not come down to us, but in the frequently cited Wallich collection there is a poem of thirty-one eight-line stanzas in which the content of this comical genre-piece is presented. The poem is called *Ayn Hipsher Khotonu:*

> Khotonu, We have sinned: let me speak and be relieved.
> I would tell you what happened here in the year 1598
> In the holy community.
> Ask nothing and let nothing puzzle you.
> Let it not puzzle you, for it is only a Purim meaning
> That they make a play about Tab Yeklayn
> With his wife Kendlayn
> And with his two little sons fine.

Then comes an account of the odd behavior of the couple, of their foolish deeds whereby they become a mockery and a derision.

In the same Wallich collection there is another *Purim-shpil.* This one is especially interesting by reason of the fact that in it we encounter certain characteristic elements which pertain to the major accessories of many later *Akhashveyrosh-shpiln:* the "clown" or "courier" who also plays, in a certain respect, the role of the director; the king and his retinue; and afterwards song and dance. The piece is played by a group of merry *yeshivah*-students who put on their play in wealthy homes and obtain for it food and drink in generous measure. The play is begun by the "clown" with his greeting to the people sitting at table:

> Fumei! Dear comrades!
> God give you a good Purim!

27. See Steinschneider, *MGWJ,* 1903, 170; idem., *Serapeum,* 1864, 102.

I come in with my bells
[To sing] about the king's young men.

The choir of youths requests the "dear, gentle people" not
to take it amiss and treat the "king's young men" well:

Give us, then, rich wine,
For we are well turned-out,
Short on sermons and long on delicacies.
Bring forth the best victuals
That you have in the house.
Give us wine without measure;
We will guzzle it all.
Let us praise and carouse
Whole days and whole nights.

Afterwards the clown asks the young men, in the name of
the king, to "hold a dance with the goats." As the young men
dance with the "goats," the king (Purim-king) appears, and the
clown introduces him:

Now our king comes crawling,
He has a belly like a pillow-case.[28]

In this *Purim-shpil* elements of the old Calendes and Caliades,
as well as of the later popular farces, are very much in evidence.
Unfortunately, however, no complete texts whatever of the
Yiddish dramatic works that were produced following the
models of the Biblical dramas of the humanist and Reformation era have come down to us. Only fragments from the seventeenth century have been preserved, and these not in their
original form. Nevertheless, from these fragments one can obtain a more or less clear notion of the singular new branch that
sprouted forth in the field of Jewish literature—Yiddish popular drama.

In this connection it must be borne in mind that in seventeenth century Germany the theater was under the strong
influence of the "English comedians." Itinerant troupes of
English actors and their repertoire enjoyed great success in
Germany as early as the beginning of the seventeenth century.
called "English plays" with the title *Komödie-und Tragödie-*

28. *Op. cit.*, 280–291.

Spiele. Under the influence of the English plays and their style, a very unique genre of dramatic works which eventually obtained the odd title *Haupt- und Staatsaktion* was produced. These were not comedy and not drama, but simple "action," theatrical performance. The characters of these "actions" had to be exclusively "heroes" of very lofty stature: kings, princes, chancellors, military leaders. Among these dramatic heroes with their emotive, exalted speech and deeds there suddenly had to appear "out of thin air" the "merry character"—the buffoon known as Hans Wurst or Pickelhering with his crude jests and roguish tricks. "The role of the merry character," writes the historian of the German theater Eduard Devrient,

is actually not a firmly established role but a vacuum, an empty space, which Hans Wurst filled, according to his taste, with a mixture of shrewdness, mockery, laughter, foolishness and obscenity . . . This was a theatrical trick, a kind of comic choir which grotesquely sharpened the comic and ridiculous aspect of the scenic action; it is the personified folk-wit which bursts with crude impudence into the midst of serious dramatic scenes to mock and deride the proud and prestigious, the exalted and emotive.[29]

The king and the clown, the hero and his caricature, tragic pathos and crude tavern wit, the rapid exchange of the tragic and comic—in this contrast of images, this pairing of two contrary elements on the scene, consisted the chief attractive power of the *Staatsaktionen.*

As in the Shakespearian theater, so in these *Aktionen* the rule of the classical theater about the "unity" of place and time was cast off. On the contrary, in the English *Aktionen* everything was extremely "scattered and dispersed." As in a kaleidoscope, one scene after another in which are extraordinarily mingled the elevated with the comic, the emotive and rhetorical with the crude and vulgar, appeared before the spectator. All this was accompanied by dancing, loud choral singing, colorful fireworks, trumpets and fifes. No less "kaleidoscopic" is the language of the *Aktionen.* The "heroes" speak an inflated, artificial language in which the echo of the pseudo-classical French tragedy and the mannered court literature of the seventeenth century is heard. The "princesses" and "chancellors" show off with Latin words and French expressions, and immediately thereafter Hans Wurst, the "merry character," with his abu-

29. Eduard Devrient, *Geschichte der deutschen Schauspielkunst,* 1901, Vols. I–II, 98–99.

sive language, his fishmarket dialect, and his wanton street witticisms, appears on the scene.[30]

The "English comedies" attained their greatest brilliance in Germany thanks to the "Magister" of Leipzig Johann Velthen (or Veltheim) who, at the beginning of the 1670's, organized, out of a group of students, his famous troupe *(die berühmte Bande)* with which he wandered for more than twenty-five years through various cities of Germany.[31]

Following the pattern of these *Staatsaktionen*, a whole series of plays in Yiddish, especially intended for presentation in the theater, were produced.[32]

The similarity is not only in the construction and style but even in the plot. The "English plays" very frequently utilized Biblical plots, e.g., the stories of Haman and Ahasuerus, the selling of Joseph, David and Goliath, Judith and Holophernes, and the like. The Yiddish repertoire also consisted of plays dealing with the same plots. However, one very important distinction must be noted here: the Christian reworkers of Biblical plots utilized only the Biblical text in their work. Quite different was the case in the production of the Yiddish *Aktionen*. The Jewish author drew extensively from the enormously rich Midrash material and utilized the legends and *aggadot*, abounding in dramatic elements, which the popular imagination had woven around its beloved heroes and defenders. Frequently the material is taken not directly from the Midrash but from a poetic reworking of the older Yiddish epic-literature.[33]

In exploring the history of the development and the metamorphoses of the Yiddish plays on Biblical plots, one must, however, also bear in mind the following factors. First of all, these pieces were played mainly in the course of the Jewish "carnival," i.e., the Purim season, when it is a commandment "to increase joy," when, since ancient times, comic and jesting tricks were played, when all kinds of parodies were recited,

---

30. For more about the German repertoire of the "English comedies," see K. Weiss, *Die Wiener Haupt- und Staatsaktionen*, Vienna, 1854, Eduard Devrient, *op. cit.*, 83–160. Al. Veselovski, *Starinni Tyeatr v Yevropa*.

31. For more about Velthen's troupe and its repertorie, see Eduard Devrient, *op. cit.*, 125–148.

32. The titles even remain the same: *Akta Ester mit Akhashverosh, Aktion von König David und Goliath.*

33. It is interesting for this reason to compare, for instance, the older fragments of the *Meluchat Sha'ul* (Reign of Saul) and Goliath plays that have been preserved with the corresponding passages in the *Shmuel-Bukh.*

and when—in later times—merry farces *(Purim-shpiln)* were presented. Much is also suggested by the fact that the Biblical plays used to be presented not only by actors or *yeshivah* students on specially arranged stages; they were also presented by primitive *Purim-shpiler* or "Purim players"—artisans' apprentices who used to go about to wealthy homes on Purim and there extemporaneously present the *Purim-shpil.* Above all, these had to curtail greatly. We know that an *Aktion* would generally last about four or five hours. Our *Purim-shpiler* did not have that much time. Furthermore, the play had to be as elementary as possible and the number of players as few as possible. It must also be borne in mind that most of the *Purim-shpiler* belonged to the humblest classes that had very little book learning. Naturally, they remade the roles in the plays according to their taste, strongly spiced with crude jests and obscenities. As a result of these factors, the text of the *Aktionen* was gradually changed. The distinction between the "merry person" and the sentimental, emotive heroes became ever smaller; gradually it disappeared altogether, and the role of the "merry person" was occasionally even merged with the "heroic" characters. It also happened not infrequently that the pathetic, emotive style of the play was completely displaced by the Purim parody-style, and the tragedy was transformed into a grotesque parody.

To make clearer to the reader this metamorphosis, which is highly interesting from the literary-historical point of view, we shall consider more closely the transformations sustained by the most popular of the Yiddish plays—the *Aktion Fun Ester Mit Akhashveyrosh* or *Akhashveyrosh-Shpil.*[34]

34. We have treated the transformations of the *Akhashveyrosh-Shpil* in a special work in *Zukunft*, 1926, I.

CHAPTER TWELVE

Akhashveyrosh- Plays
AND OTHER DRAMAS

The transformations of the *Akhashveyrosh-Shpil*—The influence of the Christian Bible dramas and *Aktionen* on the Yiddish *shpiln*—The original text of the *Akhashveyrosh-Shpil* and its solemn, emotive tone —The *Akhashveyrosh-Shpil* of 1708—*Akta Ester Mit Akhashveyrosh*— Fragments of old *Akhashveyrosh-Shpil* texts—Mordecai "the Jewish prince" and Mondrish the clown—The parodying style—*Mechirat Yosef* and its versions—*Akedat Yitzhak* and *Avraham Ve-Sarah Shpil*— The *Shmuel-Bukh* and *Melokhim-Bukh* texts in dramatic reworking— *Goliath-Shpil, Meluchat Sha'ul, Hochmat Shelomoh* and *Ashmedai-Shpil*— *Mosheh-Rabbenu-Shpil* and *Moyshe Mit Di Lukhes.*

HE *Ester-Drame* or *Akta Akhashveyrosh* was one of the most popular plays in medieval Europe in the period from the sixteenth to the eighteenth centuries.

Some scholars have even written special scientific works on it.[1]

In the above-mentioned collection *Englische Piesen*, which appeared in Germany in 1624, the *Komödie wegen der Königin Esther und dem stolzen Haman* is printed at the beginning.

When in 1682 the first attempt was made to build a theater

1. See above.

in Russia at the court of King Alexei Mikhailovich and the cultured German pastor Johann Gregory was commissioned for the task, the first "comedy" that was played for the pious Russian king was *Akta Akhashveyrosh (Artaksierskovo dieistvo)*.

The *Akhashveyrosh-Shpil* was even more favored among Jews, for it was closely bound up with the Jewish "carnival"—the happy Purim season, when it is a religious duty to be merry. How beloved this *Aktion* was among the masses of the people even in the earlier generations is to be seen from the characteristic fact that the abovementioned David Zoigers[2] who published in 1711 "A New Lament on the Great Fire in the Holy Community of Frankfurt," considers it necessary to note that his poem is written "in the melody of Haman in the *Akhashveyrosh-Shpil.*"

The text of the Yiddish *Akhashveyrosh-Shpil* was quite different from the Christian Esther dramas and comedies. The latter, as we have already indicated, were, above all, *Biblical* dramas, in which the text of the Biblical Scroll of Esther was dramatically reworked. In the Yiddish *Akhashveyrosh-Shpiln*, however, it was not merely the Biblical text that was utilized but chiefly the legendary material regarding the miracle of Purim which is woven into the various Midrashim, such as the Aramaic *Targum Sheni* and the medieval *Midrash Abba Guryon*, *Midrash Ester Rabbati*, *Midrash Megillat Ester*, etc.[3]

The oldest printed text of an *Akhashveyrosh-Shpil* that has been preserved is from 1708 and has come down to us only thanks to Johann Jakob Schudt who reprinted it in his well-known work *Jüdische Merkwürdigkeiten* (Part Three, 202–225).[4] Schudt himself relates that the copies of this *Akhashveyrosh-Shpil* published in 1708 were burned by order of the *parnassim;* the edition therefore quickly became a bibliographical rarity, but he managed to obtain a copy through great effort.[5] When one

2. See above, p. 278.
3. But the technical theatrical means, all of the necessary instruments, the music and interludes, were also used in the Jewish *Esther*-dramas in the same measure as on the Christian stages.
4. On the title-page the anonymous publisher announces: "A lovely new *Akhashveyrosh-Shpil*, devised with all the artistries; it will never be made so well again. With many lovely laments set up in rhyme. So we hope that he who buys it will not be sorry for having spent his money. Since God Blessed be He ordained for us to be merry on Purim, we have made for it this *Akhashveyrosh-Shpil*, charming, extensive and fine. So, you householders and young men and youths, come quickly running and buy this lovely *Akhashveyrosh-Shpil* from me. You will not be sorry for spending your money. When you read it you will again enjoy your money."
5. *Jüdische Merkwürdigkeiten*, Part Two, p. 316.

begins to read the text, it is immediately apparent that the anonymous author (apparently one of the *Purim-shpiler* or Purim-players) who "made this *Akhashveyrosh-Shpil* lovely and fine" was a wild ignoramus. Every Hebrew word comes out suffering great loss, so that in places it is difficult to recognize. For instance, *kushah* for *kushyah*, *mis tami* for *mistama*, *tanna* for *ta'anah*, *arich appayyim* for *ereh appayyim*, *leibris* for *la-brit*, *shehe'eheh yoneh* for *sheheheyanu*, etc. As regards content, two points are most interesting. First, the *Akhashveyrosh-Shpil* begins not with the story of Vashti but immediately with the story of Esther. Second, the role of the comical person (Pickelhering or Hans Wurst of all the *Haupt-* and *Staatsaktionen*) is represented by one of the chief characters in the play, Mordecai, and also in places by other characters—Haman, the writer, etc. This is not merely the echo of the parody-style in which so many gay Purim songs and jesting pieces were already produced in earlier generations. Here it must also be borne in mind that for the *Purim-shpiler* it was highly desirable that in their "plays" there be as few "roles" as possible. It is quite comprehensible that the role of the "merry person" had to be bestowed on Mordecai, the only Jew in the play, for he, after all, was the only one who could spout Jewish puns and witticisms, parody Hebrew prayers, and perform jesting tricks.[6] Because the taste of the *Purim-shpiler* and his colleagues who, in this instance, reworked the *Akhashveyrosh-Shpil* in their fashion was at a very low level, Mordecai's jests and buffooneries are so dirty and crude that it is quite understandable why the *parnassim* and leaders of the community persecuted the work so intensely and why Schudt, who notes that "the Jews themselves are ashamed of this Haman-comedy," reprinted only the Yiddish text without a German translation, "to avoid vexing innocent hearts."

It is clear that we have before us here not an independent work nor an *Aktion*-play nor a farce, but a crude, cynical reworking of an older text.[7] To obtain a more or less clear notion of the character of the serious Biblical plays in Yiddish that were produced according to the model of the German Biblical dramas, it would be necessary, first of all, to determine

6. A. Landau already noted this in *Mitteilungen*, 1904, 31.

7. We here consider the *Akhashveyrosh-Shpil* that was preserved thanks to Schudt only from its literary aspect. From the scenic, theatrical point of view, there are in this play several quite successful moments, e.g., the last scene with Haman's "resurrection," where he declares "I was in the other world and saw much money."

whether older Yiddish texts have been preserved that derive from the seventeenth century when the *Haupt-* and *Staatsaktionen* obtained their highest splendor in Germany. Regrettably, however, this is a very difficult task, because the oldest printed texts that have firmly established dates derive from the first half of the eighteenth century.

Best known of these editions is *Akta Ester Mit Akhashveyrosh*, which was printed in Prague in 1720 and was also, as is noted on the title-page, "played in a public theater with trumpets and other instruments this year by the delightful young men, the students of the *yeshivah* of our master, our teacher, and our rabbi, the renowned scholar Rabbi David Oppenheim, may his light shine."[8]

In its style, language, and structure, *Akta Ester* is a typical play of the *Haupt-* and *Staatsaktionen* repertoire, but with one important exception: the "merry person," the role of Hans Wurst, is played, as in Schudt's *Akhashveyrosh-Shpil*, by Mordecai himself, who declares that the king is his relation by marriage and that he is called "Printz Reb Mordekhay." But in the play itself there is an allusion to the fact that, at that time, the tradition was still quite fresh of having two separate roles in *Akta Ester Mit Akhashveyrosh*: the role of the "merry person," the improvised Pickelhering, and the role of the respected courtier, the counsellor "Printz Reb Mordekhay." On the last page of *Akta Ester* there are three woodcuts. On the upper two are pictures of Mordecai and Haman, the former in the rich clothing of a courtier, and the latter dressed in the warlike garb of a medieval knight. On the third woodcut are portrayed three clowns in their "fools' clothing." The "merry person," therefore, still has no relationship whatever to "Printz Reb Mordekhay."

In fact, two years before *Akta Ester*, there was published (1718) in Amsterdam an *Akhashveyrosh-Shpil* under the following title: "Akhashveyrosh-Shpil in a new Manner like an Opera, and which is Drawn from *Targum Sheni* and the *Midrash Yalkut* and Other Midrashim, and set in Such a Manner as It is Played by

8. *Akta Esther* was reprinted in 1763 and 1774. Large fragments are to be found in Weinreich's work in *Filologishe Shriftn*, II, 439–449. Not only was *Akta Esther* presented in "open public theaters" with "trumpets and other kinds of instruments," but also all the other *Akhashveyrosh-Shpiln*—even those which used to be presented by the primitive *Purim-shpiler* in wealthy homes (see, e.g., *Mitteilungen der Gesellschaft für jüdische Volkskunde*, 1928, 151, where there is an account of a *Purim-Shpil* in Berlin in the year 1703).

Proper Comedians."[9] In this *shpil* Mordecai is not a comic figure. He speaks in the same emotive, strongly Germanized style as the other "heroes." However, in the Amsterdam *Akhashveyrosh-Shpil* the "merry person" is lacking, and the *Aktion* style is thereby marred. Not without reason is it stressed that this *shpil* is "in a new manner like an opera."

Interesting indications about the transformations of the *Akhashveyrosh-Shpil* are given us, however, by certain texts that were preserved as a result of oral tradition. Steinschneider mentions in his *Purim und Parodie*[10] a Lemberg edition of the *Akhashveyrosh-Shpil* published in 1876. On the title-page is printed: "*Akhashveyrosh-Shpil* in *Ivre-Taytsh;* everyone may read, great and small, so that everyone may understand. Brought to the press by Rabbi Moses Tzevi Hirsch Zucker, may his light shine." This text was already printed thirteen years earlier in Czernowitz,[11] and we shall therefore designate it by the letter C. Dr. Schipper, in his history of the theater, has a good deal of confusion about this text. In the second volume of his work Schipper dismisses this version with a few lines and is content with the notation that this text is of the same character as the *Akhashveyrosh-Shpil* that was published in 1912 in the Vilna "*Lebn Un Visenshaft*" (Nos. 5–6, 189–197). This, however, is certainly not correct; these two versions are strongly distinguished both in language and in the construction of the scenes. It appears, however, that Dr. Schipper learned of text C only at second hand. He himself, in fact, confirms this conjecture. In his *Yidishe Folks-Dramatik* (p. 265),[12] Schipper indicates that after he published the second volume of his *Geshikhte Fun Yidisher Teater-Kunst Un Drama*, a new, hitherto unknown to him, "very important version of the *Akhashveyrosh-Shpil*" appeared. This version, which S. Bastomski issued in Vilna (1926), Schipper stresses, "*is the only known version of the Akhashveyrosh-Shpil in which large portions of the role of Mondrish are preserved*" (ibid., 267). Schipper, however, is greatly mistaken here. In Bastomski's *Akhashveyrosh-Shpil* there is not a single line that is not to be found in version C. However, the —according to Schipper—new, "very important version" is, in

9. Dr. Weinreich also presents some large extracts from this play in his work cited above.

10. *MGWJ*, 1903, 86.

11. We have not seen the Czernowitz edition. The quotations that A. Landau presents from it in his notice mentioned above agree completely with the Lemberg text.

12. Published in 1928.

comparison with version C, greatly abbreviated (so is the role of Mondrish) and the language in it is modernized. For this reason it happens quite frequently that the rhyme is lost.[13]

The text of version C is so greatly confused that at first it is literally impossible to obtain the plain meaning. The cues of various characters are very frequently mixed up, and when the first sentence is on one page, one must search for the next somewhere on another page in the mouth of another character. Nevertheless, when the text is carefully analyzed, it becomes clear that we have before us an extremely erroneous and distorted, but therefore undoubtedly very old *Akhashveyrosh-Shpil* text which derives, in all probability, from the seventeenth century and is certainly quite close to the text of the original *Akhashveyrosh-Aktion* which was produced following the pattern of the "English plays."

The list of characters in this *Akhashveyrosh-Shpil* is most interesting: Ahasuerus—the king; Vashti—the queen; Rotz—the courier; Bigthan—the chancellor; Mordecai—the Jewish duke; Esther—the queen; Haman—the prince of the Amalekites; Zeresh—his wife; Mondrish—the court fool. Thus we see that Mordecai and Mondrish are two quite different characters. One is a "duke" or "prince"; the other, the "court fool," the clown, Pickelhering. This becomes quite clear from the text itself in the course of the first half of the play. Here Mordecai, in fact, plays the role of a "duke," a lord of the king's court. When a quarrel between him and Haman occurs, Ahasuerus quiets them with the words: "Having such great power, I need *kingly people.* Therefore, dear people. do not kill each other." When the wrathful king proposes to condemn Queen Vashti to death, he takes counsel with both nobles, with the "prince of the Amalekites" Haman, and with the "Jewish duke" Mordecai. And Mordecai responds to the king in the tone of an authentic lord.

As we noted in our abovementioned work,[14] in the C text there is a mechanical intermingling of two different versions. One occupies the first twenty-two pages[15] and also those from page 39 to the end. The intervening sixteen pages derive from another version. The first version is certainly quite old, un-

13. Only in one important point does Bastomski's version differ from version C. In the former it is Mondrish who conducts the marriage ceremony (p. 27); in version C it is Mordecai.

14. See *Zukunft*, 1923, 1.

15. We quote according to the Lemberg edition of 1876 (the press of Hirsch Zucker).

doubtedly much older than the text which Schudt reprinted (this text we will henceforth designate as S), but, therefore, containing many mistakes, confusions, and interruptions. In this older text the chief characters speak, as in all the *Aktionen* of that time, in emotive, primitive, dramatic style. Their speeches (even Haman is no exception) are free of comical elements, especially of obscenity and common jesting. On the other hand, as in all the *Aktionen* of that time, the dramatic treatment is interrupted by special comical interludes (intermedias).[16] The "merry person," the unique Jewish Pickelhering—Mondrish, appears and performs all kinds of pranks, amusing the people with puns and crude slapstick. But suddenly (on page 23 of the Lemberg edition), as Mondrish spouts puns and parodies Hebrew prayers, he is transformed out of a clear blue sky into Mordecai. Mordecai and Mondrish are forged into one person, who performs foolish tricks and spouts obscenities. It is clear that here begins a quite different, later version—no longer of the drama *Akhashveyrosh-Shpil* but of the *Purim-Shpil*. Even in version S (which Schudt published in his *Merkwürdigkeiten*) are still detectable—to be sure, only in a few passages—remnants of the old, original text, in which Mordecai and the "merry person" were two different characters. On page 205 we read: "Mordecai says"; then comes the comment: "Mordecai goes out and comes in again and says." Mordecai thereupon tells the king that he "ran day and night" and found for him a maiden "whose first name is Esther." And suddenly, immediately after Mordecai's speech, comes the unexpected and quite senseless report: "Enter Mordecai." But the Mordecai who first enters here is a completely different person. This is Mondrish, the jester who amuses the people with his foolish pranks and spouts cynical, obscene talk.

The same thing happens again further on (pages 214–215) in the scene between Queen Esther, Hatach, and Mordecai, after Haman has obtained the king's permission to destroy the Jews. The whole scene follows the *Targum Sheni* faithfully; but, on page 215, after "Mordecai says" that he "would prefer to visit the graves of his fathers," again comes the quite unexpected remark: "Mordecai enters." Once more the Mordecai who enters here is not Mordecai the Jew, Esther's uncle, the advocate

16. These comical interludes also had no fixed text in the German *Aktionen*. The text used to be improvised by the "merry person"—Pickelhering. Hence, one often encounters in the text of the *Staatsaktionen* the remark: "Here Pickelhering acts" or "Intermezzo of Hans Wurst."

who wishes to save his people, but a jester, a clumsy Kuni-Leml who spouts crude witticisms and foolish notions. Thus the dramatic, emotive scene of the popular play is suddenly interrupted by the tasteless *Purim-shpiler*.

We know that, according to the *Targum Sheni* and other Midrashim,[17] after Hatach's mission, Esther and Mordecai both pray before God, and their prayers are tender and full of emotion. That his dramatic moment was properly utilized in the first text of the folk-play we learn from an older version which was preserved through oral tradition and which the ethnographer S. Weissenberg wrote down and published.[18] Linguistically this text is greatly modernized, but it is beyond doubt that the source of this *Purim-Shpil* was a quite old text, and some scenes in it are generally more faithful and more accurately rendered than in other versions that have been preserved. This is also the case in the scene that has just been mentioned. In this version, instead of Mordecai-Mondrish's foolish tricks that we encounter in version S, are given both prayers of Mordecai and Esther in a highly emotive style. The *language* of the prayers is already contemporary; in it is detectable the pithy dialect of Volhynia. But the *content* certainly derives from a very old text. Common *Purim-shpiler* who intended merely to amuse the people would not have been able to employ so ingeniously in Mordecai's prayer the beautiful legend of the *Targum Sheni*[19] which relates that on that certain night when "the king's sleep fled," the cries of Jewish children rose to the heavens, and that they seemed to the Creator like the cries of lambs and little goats.[20] The angels on high then trembled. Frightened, they rose and asked one another: "Has the time perhaps come for the world to be destroyed?" They all assembled before the Lord of the universe who asked them: "What is this voice of little goats that I hear?" The Attribute of Mercy answered as follows: "It is not the voice of little goats that You hear, but the cry of Jewish children whom the wicked Haman wishes to slaughter." In version W we read in Mordecai's prayer:

17. A special fragment "Prayer of Mordecai and Esther" is preserved in Aramaic and Hebrew.
18. *Mitteilungen*, 1904. Henceforth we shall designate this version by the letter W.
19. Chapter VI, 1. It is also to be found in later *midrashim*—in *Abba Guryon* and in *Midrash Megillat Ester*.
20. In *Midrash Megillat Ester*: "And the Holy One Blessed be He heard . . . and said: "What is the sound that I hear, like lambs and goats?" (*Agudat Agaddot*, 1881, 73).

When the children begin to cry from the cradles,
The angels will ask: What voice is this of little goats?
Then the Attribute of Mercy will answer: It is a voice of
  Jewish children;
The wicked Haman has risen against them and wishes to
  kill them like sheep and cattle.

We see the same thing also in the scene in which Haman
demands of "all the lords," as well as of Mordecai, that they
bow down before him. In the W text the conversation develops in a dramatically serious tone. In S, however, Mordecai performs idle, foolish pranks; he is not the courtier,
one of the "dukes" and counts," the Jewish intercessor, but
the foolish apprentice lad who wishes to amuse the people.

Hence, it is beyond doubt that in the old *Akhashveyrosh-*
Aktionen of the seventeenth century which used to be
played on the Jewish stage, the comical person was quite independent, not merged with Mordecai or any of the other
major characters. Also, this figure was certainly not directly
associated with the dramatic action; he appeared merely in
the interludes to amuse the people. It is also beyond doubt
that in the old *Akhashveyrosh-Shpiln*, Mordecai, in complete
agreement with the Biblical Scroll of Esther and the Midrashim, is (and this, in fact, is the case in the *Akhashveyrosh-*
Shpil of 1718 and in the older parts of versions C and W) the
pious Jew, the righteous man and advocate through whom
salvation comes for the Jewish people. The same thing is
true in regard to Queen Esther. There is no doubt whatever that in the older versions of the *Akhashveyrosh-Aktion*
Esther from her first appearance to her last is the royal
lady, the proud queen who speaks in the artlessly popular,
exaltedly emotive style.

This is the case not only with the two major figures but
also with the third major figure, more accurately, the central figure of the drama—Haman. It is very characteristic
that in the Jewish tradition Haman does, indeed, appear as
an extremely wicked man. He is the symbol of hatred and
vengeance. He is literally the *sitra ahara* (the demonic) itself,
but without the least comical feature, without a trace of
petty vanity. Even Ahasuerus' wrathful words, "Will he
force the queen?" are explained by an old Midrash to the
effect that Haman did not at all intend to offend the queen,
but the angel Gabriel came and pushed him on the bed

where Esther sat. The folk-imagination, insofar as it disclosed itself in the old, popular *Akhashveyrosh-Shpil*, went even further. We see this very prominently in text C, which, as we noted previously, is closest to the oldest text of the play.[21] Already in his first appearance, where he turns with a petition "to the great God," Haman declares that he has for many years now "looked in the books" and discovered there that the Jews must "be destroyed through his hands." His hatred toward the Jews is not a caprice; it is literally a matter of Providence, a sort of fate. It inheres in his blood; he obtained it as a legacy from his ancestors. He is, after all, "the prince of the Amalekites," a descendant of King Agag whom the prophet Samuel hewed into pieces. More than anything else, he fears "that people will laugh at him" and wishes to avoid this. And it is literally astonishing how, in the text of version C that has been preserved, the anonymous author endeavors to fulfill this wish of Haman "the enemy of the Jews." When Haman's downfall occurs, the author does not permit laughter at him; all his sympathies are on the side of the fallen wretch. And the spectators suddenly realize that the "prince of the Amalekites" is not merely the "enemy of the Jews," the grim villain, but a strong personality with deep feelings and, in addition, a kindly father of a family. Beautiful and moving are the lines in which Haman speaks of his father and mother, and full of gentle, tender sorrow is his final speech which ends with the following humbly pious chord:

> No man should hold himself high;
> At the end they hide him in a dark grave.

In what sharp contrast this closing scene stands with the foolish, crude end of the *Purim-Shpil* that Schudt reprinted. To the hanged Haman the author merely bids "a good farewell":

> Woe, woe, was he beautiful;
> He loved to eat pig's feet with horseradish
> Woe, woe, was he clever;
> The wine of idolaters he drank from a jar . . .[22]

21. It is worth noting that, even in Schudt's *Akhashveyrosh-Shpil*, the only few tender and poetic lines in the whole play are heard from Haman's mouth, when he bids farewell to his wife Zeresh.
22. Here follow two obscene lines which we omit.

Woe, woe, how he ate with beautiful knives.
In the homes of counts and princes he broke all locks . . .
The king said to the writer: Writer, give him a glass in his
    ears;
Perhaps he will be born again.

Indeed, Haman is "born again" and at once proclaims:

I was in the other world
And saw much money.

And when the writer asks: "You rogue, why did you not take
it?," Haman declares, "I was afraid I would lose my life."

Another characteristic feature in the original text of the
Akhashveyrosh-Shpil, insofar as it has been preserved in the older
versions that have come down to us, is worth noting. In the
first act Vashti is condemned to death at Haman's advice. She
thereupon implores Haman to spare her young life. When
Haman refuses, Vashti asks the chancellor to admit her to the
king to beg mercy from him, but she finds no favor with the
king either. In the last act these scenes are repeated, but now
with Haman himself. Through Vashti's successor, Haman falls
into disfavor with the king and is condemned to death. Now
Haman begs the chancellor to admit him to the king so that he
may plead for his life before Ahasuerus. This time again the
king is adamant, and the judgment is executed.

These transformations which the dramatic material of the
Akhashveyrosh-Shpil sustained, the later changes from the earnestly emotive tone of the older version of the popular play
into a vulgarly parodying tone, are not difficult to explain
when the following circumstances are taken into consideration. Aside from the serious *Aktionen*, as we previously noted,
the merry *Fastnacht* plays were extremely popular in the Jewish quarter. The comic element was also strongly represented
in the interludes of the *Aktionen*, the so-called intermedias.
Here were interwoven all kinds of parodies which for many
generations had been favored among Jews and served as entertainment material on the cheerful days of Purim.[23] This
parody style refused to content itself with the narrow bounda-
ries of the intermedias and ventured to lay its stamp on the
entire scenic repertoire, to tear away from the "heroes" their

23. See above.

emotive, solemn dress and transform them into comic masks and cheerful parodies. It was in this way that Mordecai "the Jewish duke" was transformed into a tramp, a beggar with a hump on his shoulders, and Queen Esther appears "in torn shoes," is "a picture of a girl."

> In spots green, in spots yellow . . .
> Enough to make you want to trample with the feet . . .
> Today she wears all her weekday clothes . . .
> Today all her festival clothes.
>
> If she wears the festival clothes, they are
> A disaster sewn with red thread,
> Straw trousers,
> Trimmed with wire . . .
> . . . .

Considerable literary historical interest is also presented by the metamorphoses that certain passages or lines of the *Akhash-veyrosh-Shpil* had to sustain in their long peregrinations from one version to another. We content ourselves with only two or three illustrations.

In Vashti's speech imploring Ahasuerus to spare her life we encounter in the older C version the following lines:

> Why should you not remember
> The time that you possessed my white body?

These modestly pure words obtain in the later W version a gross and crude form:

> Why should you forget all the time
> That you fondled my clear, snow-white sides?

Not always, however, does it happen that a line in its later wanderings is dipped in dirty clay and crude cynicism. Sometimes it is improved and raised to a higher level. The text occasionally falls into the hands of a talented *Purim-shpiler* with a poetic, popular feeling; in him awakens the artless child of

24. See the *Akhashveyrosh-Shpil* variant that is published in *Leben Un Visenshaft*, 1912, 5–6, p. 195. A much more vulgar "portrait" of Queen Esther is given us by another variant of the *Akhashveyrosh-Shpil* that P. Marek published in *Perezhytoye*, II, pp. 228–229.

the people, the intimate soul of the common multitude with its hidden, tender feelings and touching moods, which then disclose themselves in primitive and clumsy but, nonetheless, poetically beautiful forms. The line in question then is not made crude; it bursts forth in gracious and moving verses.

In the humble speech of Vashti that we quoted earlier from the older C version, the miserable queen begs:

Therefore, King, think that in your eyes I am like a young
  little bird;
Therefore, Father King, spare my young little life.

This motif expands in the later W version into a whole poem, a typical folksong, primitive and artless, yet modestly gentle:

Vashti:
Father King, kingly Father!
I will be with you
A little bird.
I will always sing for you and play for you;
Only spare me my young little life,
Very lovely and very fine.

The King:
No, this cannot be;
You must die.

Vashti:
Father King, kingly Father!
I will be to you a little dog.
I will yap for you and bark for you;
Only spare me my young little life,
Very lovely and very fine.

The King:
No, this cannot be;
You must die.

Vashti:
Father King, kingly father!
I will be to you a maidservant.
I will sweep for you and clean for you;

Only spare me my young little life,
Very lovely and very fine.

The King:
No, this cannot be;
You must die.

Even in the Vilna version,[25] where we have before us in fact
not a dramatic *Akhashveyrosh-Shpil* but a typical Purim parody,
Vashti also turns to Ahasuerus with the following movingly
solemn lines—the only lines of such a character in the whole
play:

So I go,
And so I stand,
And so I fall,
Before the Father King at the doors,
Before the Father King's eyes.
Forgive my sins,
As a father forgives his own child!

Some of the textual changes are interesting from a social
standpoint. In the *Targum Sheni*, for instance, in Haman's
denunciation of the Jews not a word is said about Jewish artisans. The denunciation speaks merely of Jewish beggars and
poor people "whose like is not to be found in the world," then
of Jewish lords and officials, Jewish merchants and traders ("in
wax and candles") who are great swindlers in business. Very
likely in the oldest *Akhashveyrosh-Aktionen* there was also no
mention whatever of artisans. The *Purim-shpiler*, however, who
were themselves mainly artisans and apprentices, perceived in
this a bit of impugnment of their honor. Thus, out of professional pride, they took care that Haman in his denunciation
not forget the Jewish artisans and also accuse them before
Ahasuerus. We see, in fact, that in the older C text Haman
already mentions the artisans, but in an offhand fashion, in the
following lines:

The Jewish artisans are terrible swindlers;
They are not to be endured.

25. Published in *Leben Un Visenshaft,* 1912.

On the other hand, in the later texts, for instance, in version W, the artisans are spoken of at considerable length (lines 486–509). There is a detailed account of the swindleries of the "makers of gold rings, cloakmakers, capmakers," etc. The same thing is repeated in the version that P. Marek published in a Russian anthology.[26]

Other Yiddish plays that are based on Biblical plots did not go through as many metamorphoses as the *Akhashveyrosh-Shpil*, because they were not associated with the miracle of Purim and with the special Purim parody-literature. Of the Biblical episodes which served as themes for Yiddish plays the most popular were the following.

1. *Mechirat Yosef or Yoysef-Shpil*. The magnificent Biblical narrative about Joseph and his brethren was already in the Middle Ages employed for all kinds of mystery, miracle, and morality plays. In the era of the Reformation also many poets dramatically reworked the "story of the beautiful Joseph and his brethren." In 1546 there appeared a Joseph drama composed by Mathias Reuter. A pupil of Hans Sachs, Adam Fischman, produced "A Large Comedy of the Pious Ancestor Jacob and of His Dear Son Joseph, Together With His Brethren, To be Acted in Four Hours." A Latin school comedy on the same subject appeared five times in German translation by 1612. Very well known at the end of the seventeenth century was the play of Christian Weise "The Excellent Chaste Joseph in Egypt."[27] Velthen and his "renowned troupe"[28] also presented in Dresden in 1678 at the royal court theater "The Comedy of the Patriarch Jacob."

It is beyond doubt that as early as the seventeenth century dramatic plays on the theme of the selling of Joseph were produced for the Yiddish stage. The structure and style of the *Mechirat Yosef* plays were under the powerful influence of the European repertoire, but the major source for the Yiddish reworkings of the Joseph plot was the well-known medieval Hebrew epic *Sefer Ha-Yashar*.[29] Of the printed texts of the plays

26. *Perezhytoye*, II, 231.
27. First performed on the stage in 1690.
28. See above, p. 330.
29. See our *History*, Vol. I, pp. 186–88. considerably later (in 1729) a *Yosef-Aktion* under the title *Milḥamah Ve-Shalom* was also produced in Hebrew on the basis of *Sefer Ha-Yashar* and other Midrashim. The author, Hayyim Abraham of Mogilev, himself indicates in the preface: "All the narrative in this composition is built on the words of our sages—may their memory be for blessing—in the Midrashim, and on

on the selling of Joseph that have come down to us, the oldest is the *Mechirat Yosef* preserved by Schudt which was presented on the stage in 1708 by the Yiddish theater director Bermann of Limburg, printed in 1712 and later reprinted in Schudt's *Jüdische Merkwürdigkeiten*. According to Schudt's report, the "completer" of the play was Bermann himself. In all likelihood, however, the "completer" merely reworked an older text. Following the pattern of the "English comedies," poems for singing were woven into the play, and in the intermedias appears the "merry person" who, in *Mechirat Yosef*, bears the name Pickelhering. However, the style and language are drier than in the "English plays." The director Bermann apparently was under the strong influence of the didactic-rationalist drama that was highly popular at that time. Hence he lets the "heroes" of *Mechirat Yosef* speak in an arid, wooden language that is filled with an enormous number of French and Latin words and expressions. To give the reader some notion of the singular style in which the characters of this play talk, it suffices to present the following speech addressed by Joseph's brother Asher to his brother Issachar:

ברודער ישׁשׂכר, האשטו אׇבשׁערפֿירט
וואשׁ אׇלהיר איז וואׇרדן אׁופֿ(ע) רירט?
ווען זיך שׁוין אׁונזׇר פֿאׇטׇר האׇט טרוׇציג געשׁטעלט
זׁא האׇט ער אׁבער דאׇך גׇרן גׁיוואׇלט
אׁלז דׇר טרוׁים אׇטׇעשׁטירט,
זׁונדׇרן ער האׇט אׁונז רעשׁפֿעקטירט
אׁין דׇם יעדרׇר פֿון אׁונדז בעשׇׁר טוׁט מאׇרידירן
אׁײן קיׁניגרײׁך צוׇ פֿירׇן.

Brother Issachar, have you observed
What has operated here?
Even if our father took an opposing position,
Nevertheless he wanted it,

the words of the great commentators; I also plucked a bit from the words of *Sefer Ha-Yashar*." The work was first published anonymously (on this, see the interesting statement of the author in the preface to his *Pat Lehem*, Shklov, 1803). The scribe of the community of Zolkiew, Eleazar Paver, in 1801 issued an abbreviated translation in Yiddish under the title *Gedulat Yosef* which was very popular and went through numerous editions (on this, see J. Shatzky's bibliographical study in *Arkhiv Far Der Geshikhte fun Yidishn Teater Un Drame*, I, 151–158, and N. Prylucki's notices in *YIVO-Bleter*, I, 408–414). *Gedulat Yosef* was later reworked by Eliakum Zunser in *Mechirat Yosef*. A Polish reworking *Milhamah Ve-Shalom* was presented successfully in Warsaw (see A. Berliner, preface to *Yesod Olam*, XVII).

As the dream attests;
But he respected us,
In that each of us would be a better marauder
To lead a kingdom.

The text of most of the versions that were preserved through oral tradition and were published only in modern times indicates a definite affinity of these versions with a general original text which is certainly older than the *Mechirat Yosef* that was presented on the stage in 1708 by Bermann of Limburg. This original text was undoubtedly more popular and vital than the aridly rationalist text which this Bermann "completed."

2. *Akedat Yitzḥak-Drama.* We noted above that the rich legendary material about the Biblical partriarchs and especially about the binding of Isaac which was woven into various Midrashim was reworked in Hebrew, as well as in Yiddish, in various liturgical hymns and epics. In the era of the Reformation when, among other Biblical dramas and comedies, there also appeared a whole series of dramas on the theme of the binding of Isaac,[30] attempts were also made in the Jewish ghetto to work up the Midrashic material for the newly created Yiddish theater. Dr. Ignacy Schipper in his history of the theater[31] attempted, on the basis of four fragmentary versions[32] that N. Prylucki published in his collections of Yiddish folklore (II, 64–83), to reconstruct the probable schema of the oldest text on the binding of Isaac. Unfortunately, however, Dr. Schipper did not know of an important version that was published in Vilna in 1875.[33] The language of this edition is a popular, modern one, but it is beyond doubt that the version

30. Hans Sachs also composed a play *Opferung Isaak* in 1553.
31. Vol. II, pp. 27–28. Schipper's conjecture that the Jewish reworker of the *Akedat Yitzḥak*-drama employed as a model the Polish mystery *Sacrificium Abrahamae* and his conjecture that the Yiddish play *Akedat Yitzḥak* has points of contact chiefly with this mystery are, however, false. We know, after all, that the Christian Bible dramas and mysteries were faithful to the Biblical text, while the Yiddish plays on Biblical themes—among them also *Akedat Yitzḥak*—were based mainly on the Midrash literature.
32. In fact, only on the basis of the first version which is, according to Schipper's correct view, closer to the original text than the others. Schipper, however, did not know that the same version is also found (along with three other *Akedat Yitzḥak* variants) in the anthology *No'ent Un Vayt*, Warsaw, 1914, 35–38.
33. The full title of this popular edition is: "*Meluchat Sha'ul Gam Akedat Yitzḥak.* Here is presented the entire war which David carried on with Goliath—all in rhymes. Also proper is the scene of the binding of Isaac with all of the facts. Added thereto are scenes from Abraham with Sarah, issued by J. B. Bloch."

is based on an older text. From this fragmentary text it may be conjectured that the oldest text consisted of a rather large *shpil* which embraced several Biblical episodes: the story of Sarah and Abimelech, the story of Sodom and Gomorrah, and the binding of Isaac. But because the play was overly long and its presentation on the stage would have required several hours, it was divided into three separate plays: (1) a play on Abraham and Sarah, (2) a Sodom and Gomorrah play, and (3) the binding of Isaac.[34] The Vilna version preserves only fragments of the first and the last plays. The play begins with a monologue of Abraham's in which he explains:

> I am Abraham the son of Terah . . .
> . . . .
> Nimrod wanted me to believe in his idols,
> But I exalted Almighty God . . .

Afterwards comes the scene between Abraham and the angel. Instead of God Himself, as in the Biblical text, here an angel figures. The angel declares to Abraham:

> My dear servant,
> What I shall tell, you should accept;
> You should leave your home . . .

Abraham agrees to fulfill the command:

> And also on the way I will praise You,
> And will exalt Your name.

In the subsequent scene, in which Abraham and Sarah are en route, Abraham advises Sarah:

---

34. The following interesting fact is worth noting: Traces of the Sodom and Gomorrah drama are preserved in a melodramatic version which was widespread in the Polish towns as late as the nineteenth century and is reprinted according to oral tradition in N. Prylucki's anthologies, II, 57–63. The text ends with the scene in which the angels order Lot and his household to leave the sinful cities. This play, however, was considered overly long in some places. Hence it was divided into two, and only the first half, entitled *Avrohom Ovinus Gebet*, which ends with the scene in which Abraham receives from the angel the promise that the city of Sodom will be spared if ten righteous men are found in it, was played (reprinted in the anthology *No'ent Un Vayt*, Warsaw, 1914, 46–48).

If you should be asked with whom you came traveling,
You shall say: With a brother born of the same father.

After this comes the scene in which Sarah is brought to
Abimelech, who is enchanted by her beauty. An angel at once
appears and warns Abimelech:

Listen, Abimelech, you have done wrong;
You have taken a woman away from her husband.

In the subsequent scene three angels come to Abraham and
tell Sarah that she will bear a child. Only after this does the
episode of the binding of Isaac commence. Apparently the
original text of the *Akedat Yitzḥak* began with a scene that
imitates the well-known introductory scene of the Book of Job.
In the Vilna version only the following short fragment of this
scene has remained:

The Speech of Satan:
Dear God, You consider Abraham an excellent man—
Yet he has not done everything You bade.

The Speech of the Angel:
Ye shall speak no evil of him,
For he did not depart from me.

This is followed by a scene in Abraham's house. First Ishmael speaks to himself, then he carries on a conversation with
Isaac. The conversation is based on a certain passage of the
Midrash[35] where it is related that Ishmael was very displeased
that Abraham's estate would go to Isaac, not himself. When
Ishmael boasts that he was the first to fulfill the commandment
of circumcision, Isaac replies:

Why do you boast . . .
When not God is in your mind
But winning the legacy.
If God should demand
That my father bring me as a burnt offering
I am ready . . .

35. It is naturally difficult to determine whether the reworker of the *Akedat Yitzḥak*
employed the midrashic material directly or whether he took it from the epic *Sefer
Ha-Yashar* and *Der Yidisher Shtam*.

Isaac's statement serves as a preparation for the next scene in which the angel commands Abraham to offer his son Isaac as a sacrifice. In the subsequent scene Abraham tells Sarah that he has come to her "to take counsel," for she is recognized as a valorous woman:

Now Isaac should be lead to the study-house of Shem and
    Eber,
So that he may know how to conduct himself in God's
    service.
As our son Isaac came to mature years,
I took this into my mind.

After the moving scene in which Sarah bids farewell to Isaac comes the scene on the way, at Mount Moriah. Isaac inquires of his father where the sacrifice is, and Abraham says: "God Blessed Be He has chosen you for a burnt offering." Isaac begs, just as in the epic *Der Yidisher Shtam:*[36]

And if you wish to offer me as a sacrifice,
Bring a little bone of mine to my mother.

The next scene is again in Abraham's house. Satan tells Sarah that her son Isaac has been slain, and Sarah falls down dead. Abraham and Isaac arrive. A scene of grief. Abraham chants his lament in which the verses are constructed according to the alphabet. In the closing scene Abraham purchases from Ephron a place in which to bury his dead. Ephron takes the money and says:

The money is with me,
The place is for you;
So bury your dead.

3. Biblical plays with the three kings—Saul, David, and Solomon—as central figures. The Biblical episodes which were worked up in the renowned *Shmuel-Bukh* and *Melokhim-Bukh* epics were subsequently, under the influence of the Bible dramas of the Reformation era, dramatically reworked. The celebrated Hans Sachs published a Biblical drama on King Saul. A contemporary of his, Wolfgang Schmelzels, composed

36. See above, p. 103ff.

a play under the long-winded title *Comödie von plint gebornen Sohn die schöns, tröstliche Historia von Jünklik David und den muts-villgen Golliat.* Magister Mathias Holzwart produced on the stage an enormously long play in ten acts, *Saul: ein schön neu Spiel von König Saul und dem Hirten David.* The play lasted all of two days, and about a hundred players and five hundred extras took part in it.[37]

Apparently such long *shpiln*, or plays, were also produced in Yiddish. The conjecture that one of these plays embraced the Biblical material of the *Shmuel-Bukh* and another that of the *Melokhim-Bukh* is more or less justified.[38] But since such long plays could be presented only on a properly organized theater stage by professional actors, they were divided into episodes. In this way separate plays were created: a "Hannah and Peninah play," a "David and Goliath play," an "Agag play," "The Reign of Saul," "The Wisdom of Solomon" (on King Solomon's clever judgment), a "Solomon and Ashmedai play," etc.

Of these pieces, only a version of an *Aktion* of "King David and Goliath" (Hanau, 1717) has been preserved in full. In this play a counsellor of Goliath plays the role of the "merry person," Hans Wurst. However, larger fragments of the above listed plays have also been preserved. Most important are two Vilna editions of the second half of the nineteenth century. One of these is the abovementioned edition of J.B. Bloch (1875) in which, along with *Akedat Yitzhak*, an older text of *Meluchat Sha'ul* (The Reign of Saul) is also reprinted.

The play begins, as is the fashion in almost all Yiddish folk plays and *Aktionen*, with the greeting of the clown:[39]

> Quieter and quieter, my dearest people,
> Let there be patience and quiet for a short time;
> The reign of King Saul will we present . . .

The play begins with the Goliath episode. The dialogues are carried on in a solemn, emotive tone. The mighty hero Goliath announces:

37. See Devrient, *op. cit.*, 73.
38. And this perhaps is the reason why the *Shmuel-Bukh* was not reprinted after 1612. It was far more interesting to see the material in dramatic reworking on the stage than to read the epic.
39. These greetings are identical with the introductory formulas with which the heralds or criers would appear in the Christian *Fastnacht* plays (for a discussion of this, see Schipper, *op. cit.*, II, Chapter 7; J. Shatsky, *Filologishe Shriftn*, II, 248–250).

I will fill my sword with their blood,
I will drive out all the Jews from their land,
Everything will be in my power;
I will not withdraw until the Jews bow down to me . . .

The Jews are in great terror, and Saul issues a command.

The speech of Saul:
Yes, I, Saul, Jewish king, have everything under my hand;
Jews and other peoples are in my power.
I command a proclamation: Freedom, freedom, freedom,
And whoever is loyal to the king . . .

He announces that he who vanquishes the great Goliath
"will have as his reward" the "only royal daughter who is very
beautiful":

He will sit with all the nobles,
With all the judges he will protect . . .

In the subsequent scene Saul asks his servant "what is happening with this command." The servant brings in "little David" and tells the king:

This is he who wishes to fight on the battlefield
With the renowned Goliath, the mighty hero.

Astonished, Saul looks at "little David" who undertakes to
do battle with such a mighty hero:

Young fellow, have you skill
With the bow and arrow . . . ?

"Little David" gives a long speech saying that he "needs no
gun and no sword." He puts his hope "in the Almighty God
very certainly":

God will assuredly be of help and power to me,
For the sake of His people Israel that is very precious to
   Him.

Then follows the scene with Goliath. The giant asks his
servant: "What is this tumult that is going on?" The latter

reports: "A knight from the Jews has come." When "little David" appears, Goliath breaks out in great wrath that they have sent as a battler against him, the great hero before whom the whole world trembles, such a "little Jew" whom he can crush "with a step of his foot." A long debate between Goliath and "little David" commences. Here there is a characteristic feature. Goliath, indeed, boasts that he can smite twenty such as David; nevertheless, the "little Jew" pleases him:

> O, how small you are,
> O how beautiful you are.

Goliath advises him: "Run away, young David." The same advice is also given David by Goliath's servant:

> You should not laugh, you should not mock,
> You should withdraw before the great man.

"Little David" declares: "I have no fear, even though I am small." He is certain that in battle one can prevail "not with human power" but "with the help of Almighty God." And he preaches to Goliath:

> If you would find the truth,
> You should serve the God of the Jews.

After the battle, which ends with Goliath's death, David calls out:

> O Goliath, you foolish hero,
> Your body will be buried on the open field!

The Goliath episode concludes with the triumphal ode of Saul's daughter:

> Saul asked: With what weaponry will you go?
> David answered: With the help of God alone.

The subsequent scenes deal with the later episodes of "the reign of Saul," telling how after the war of Saul with Amalek, the prophet Samuel informed Saul that God no longer wished him to be king over the people of Israel. Here ensues Saul's dirge or "song of sorrow" in which the king laments:

All kings reign for a long time,
But I, miserable Saul, have lost my kingdom.

The "song of sorrow" is put together according to the order of the alphabet. David's elegy on Saul's death is also composed on the same principle. With this elegy "The Reign of Saul" fragments end and the text of *Akedat Yitzḥak* begins. Further fragments of the cycle of plays that treat the *Shmuel-Bukh* text are to be found in another Vilna edition of 1868 printed at the press of Rabbi Abraham Isaac Dworsitz. This little book, which takes up thirty-two pages, bears the title *Ḥochmat Shelomoh Im Mamlechet Sha'ul*.[40] In the fragments belonging to "The Reign of Saul" *(Mamlechet Sha'ul)* are portrayed the last days of this "reign." It is before the battle with the powerful enemy Amalek. Saul feels that he will perish in the battle, for "God smites and is just." The "chief general of the army" comforts Saul. He assures him that King Saul need have no fear "before the pagans and should never do like the Swedes(?)." Saul inquires about a witch. The subsequent scene occurs with the witch at En-Dor. The witch summons up the shade of the prophet Samuel who tells Saul:

Today I am with you, and tomorrow you will be with me;
You will die, and David will inherit your kingdom.

The subsequent fragment already belongs to "The Reign of David." The herald announces: "David the king now comes to seat himself on God's throne. Trumpets sound and play before King David."

The aged David enters and gives a speech: "I am David, King of Israel." Soon Bathsheba enters and demands of the aged king that not Adonijah but her son Solomon "shall reign after David's years." Zadok the priest and Nathan the prophet enter, and David orders: "Let them proclaim: Forever live King Solomon!" The angel of death appears. David bids farewell to his family and dies. King Solomon gives a eulogy: "I have lost my father David."

The subsequent scene treats the episode of the two women

40. Before the dramatic fragments there are two poems. The first bears the title "The Beginning of the Story of Adam the First Man." This is a later reworking of the "Poem of Adam and Eve." The second poem celebrates the greatness of the fathers: "Abram, Abram was a godly man." Thereafter: "Isaac our father was a godly man." Further on there are stanzas which celebrate the "godly men"—Jacob, Moses, and Aaron.

and King Solomon's clever judgment. Then comes a scene from the *Ashmedai-Shpil.* Ashmedai manages to beguile the cleverest king, whom he "makes to go into exile" to the end of the world. The homeless king sings a dirge:

> Better for me not to have been born
> Than that I had been lost through Ashmedai.

This little book was reprinted three times (1870, 1872, 1878) at the same press. The text was published without any changes, but in the editions of 1872 and 1878[41] there is a scene not included in the edition of 1868. Before Saul appears to the witch at En-Dor the following scene occurs:

> Here comes the witch with her child;
> The witch says to her child.

The second half of this rather long scene is accompanied by music. The witch sings:

> The night, the night, is with us the best joy,
> And to us come all who have a sorrow.
> (Musicians: "The Night")

So after every subsequent speech of the witch, comes the notation—Musicians: "The Night." The scene with the witch and the child is undoubtedly under the influence of the corresponding scene in Joseph Tropplowitz's Hebrew drama *Meluchat Sha'ul,* which first appeared in 1794[42] and of which a prose Yiddish translation was published as early as 1801 by a certain Naftali Hirsch bar David under the title *Gedulat David U-Meluchat Sha'ul.*[43] In Tropplowitz also the witches sing a song in which every stanza concludes with the refrain:

> The night, the night, the night!
> The joy of our heart!

In Tropplowitz the witch's son Azmut (Azmoves) says of his mother:

---

41. We have not seen the edition of 1870.
42. The second edition was provided by Isaac Baer Levinsohn (in 1820).
43. We have utilized the Sudylkow edition of 1836.

My hatred of her has grown, strong as death;
What profit has she from all these magical tricks?
I fear, I fear she also will be killed
By the king's judges, like one of her friends.

In our folk-play "the child" declares:

I hate her for her witchcrafts,
Because of them, she is not at all true to me.
No matter how much she increases her witchcrafts,
She will ultimately be killed by the king.

To be sure, it is not entirely impossible that there was already a similar scene in the folk-play and that Tropplowitz utilized it in his drama. For the time being, this is difficult to establish, because the older texts of the Old-Yiddish *shpiln* were not preserved in full. Hence, one can merely conjecture where firmly established facts are lacking.

4. The Story of the Exodus from Egypt and *Moyshe-Rabeyne-Shpil.*—The rich legendary material that was created around the national hero Moses and is collected in the old Midrashim *Midrash Divrei Ha-Yamim Shel Mosheh, Midrash Petirat Mosheh,* and others[44] was also reworked in the Reformation era into dramatic *Aktionen* or perhaps into one large *Aktion.* Traces of these *Aktionen* were preserved in the later literature as a result of oral tradition. A late melodramatic reworking of the *Yetziat-Mitzrayim-Shpil* (Exodus from Egypt Play) is published in the collection *Fun No'ent un Vayt* (Warsaw, 1914, 49–58) and in N. Prylucki's collection (II, 84–96). According to a report of N. Shtif,[45] in 1876 there also appeared in Lemberg a printed edition of *Moyshe-Rabeyne-Shpil* in which the midrashic material of *Petirat Mosheh* is reworked in dramatic form. Another part of the great Moses epic was dramatically worked up in the play *Moyshe Mit Di Lukhes* (Moses With the Tablets).

44. These Midrashim were also translated in part into Yiddish.
45. *In Yidishe Filologye,* II–III, pp. 117–118, and according to personal communications.

CHAPTER THIRTEEN

Mystical Morality Books;
SOCIAL AND EDUCATIONAL CRITICISM

The strengthening of mystical tendencies—Mystical preachers—
Mystical morality books—Tzevi Hirsch Chotsh's "Taytsh Zohar,"
Naḥalat Tzevi—Apologies for Yiddish—Akiva Baer ben Joseph and
his *Abbir Yaakov* and *Maasei Adonai—Tikkunei Ha-Mo'adim* against
students of the *Gemara*—Solomon ben Simeon Wetzlar's *Ḥakirot Ha-
Lev*—Books of worldly content—"Till Eulenspiegel" and "Schildburger Geschichten" in Yiddish—Isaac Wetzlar and his *Libs-Brif*—
Benjamin Kroneburg and his practical handbooks—The *Dyhernfurther Tzaytung* and Abraham Moses Eidlitz' *Melechet Maḥashevet*—New
tendencies—Conclusion.

LL THE dra-
matic pieces
treated in the
previous chap-
ter were, first
of all, *shpiln*,
i.e., plays pro-
duced espe-
cially for the
stage. Where-
as in Italy
there were
even among
the rabbis and
scholars those
who, like Leo
de Modena,[1]
themselves
produced
plays and
were utterly devoted to the theater, in the German and Polish
communities the spiritual guides, the rabbis, were—without

1. See Vol. IV, pp. 127–28.

a single exception—quite hostile to the popular plays and theatrical presentations. Only because of the "miracle" of Purim could theatrical presentations have some existence—as *Purim-Shpiln*, tolerated amusement on the happy days when it is a religious duty to rejoice.

We noted in the previous volume that the Lurianic Kabbalah, which laid its stamp on the entire rabbinic world, gradually became the most important and influential factor in the spiritual life of the German-Jewish and, in even greater measure, of the Polish-Jewish community. All the fearful legends about "torments of the grave" and transmigration of the soul, about all kinds of evil spirits, demons, incantations, amulets, "names," and combinations of letters ruled boundlessly over the popular imagination. The fantastic and mystical obtained more concrete forms than the real and tangible. But the fantastic, the "yonder world," is, after all, merely the echo of melancholy reality. Ever greater grew the number of hostile powers, of belligerent church officials and urban crafts and guilds; and the popular imagination, veiled in mystical terror, created countless hosts of destroying angels, spoilers, and accusers, who lurk for men at every step of their life to lure them into the net of sin. Whenever a man allows himself to be led astray for a moment by the *sitra ahara* (other side), a grievous and merciless punishment awaits him. Ever darker and more melancholy became the narrow streets of the ghetto and, after the bloody deeds of Chmielnitzki's hosts and the failure of Shabbetai Tzevi's messianic movement, mystical elements obtained even more pathological forms. What the rabbis of previous generations did not manage to carry through—that the broad masses of the people should live according to the principle "Israel is not to rejoice like the nations"—was now, after the terrible troubles and persecutions which the Jewish community endured, successfully achieved by the Kabbalists of Rabbi Isaac Luria's school.

We have noted that in various centers there appeared from time to time exalted mystics such as Jehudah Ḥasid of Kalisch who admonished and summoned men to repent, for the day of redemption draws near. We have indicated[2] that in that era, at the threshold of the eighteenth century, there was an increase in the number of preachers and mystics, ardent disciples of the Lurianic Kabbalah, who sought in Luria's writings, which then circulated from hand to hand, the surest source of truth

2. Vol. VI.

and knowledge, and found in them the faithful guide over the confused ways of life. The ideas of the Lurianic Kabbalah were spread by these preachers in the form of *maasim nora'im*, or "dreadful tales," that were filled to overflowing with terrifying details about the "torment of the grave," rolling through tunnels to the Holy Land at the resurrection, the seven departments of hell, and enormous hosts of demons and destroying spirits. The preachers were not content merely with an "oral Torah," with sermons preached in the synagogues and study-houses; special books of moral instruction were also written which aimed, with the aid of these "dreadful tales," to awaken, in the common reader, fear of God and feelings of penitence. Such morality books were composed not only in Hebrew but also in Yiddish, so that they might penetrate into the broadest strata of the people. Tzevi Hirsch Koidonover, as we noted, himself published his *Kav Ha-Yashar* in the vernacular. Elijah Kohen's *Shevet Musar* was also soon translated into Yiddish (1726). There also appeared at that time especially in Yiddish a whole series of morality books permeated with the spirit of the Lurianic Kabbalah. The most popular among these was the "Taytsh Zohar," *Naḥalat Tzevi*, which the Kabbalist Tzevi Hirsch Chotsh of Cracow published in 1711.

Tzevi Hirsch Chotsh was a great Kabbalist and scholar. He wrote a long mystical commentary to *Tikkunei Zohar* (*Ḥemdat Tzevi*, 1706), but he acquired his reputation with *Naḥalat Tzevi*.[3] On the title-page of this work it is noted:

These words of moral instruction from the holy *Zohar* we translated, and we chose plain words to make the holy community drink the bubbling water of deep wells that are sweeter than honey and refined like pure gold. These wells were made by the godly *Tanna* Rabbi Simeon with his holy associates to enlighten the eyes of Jews who are united with God, and to proclaim the virtue of the Torah and its commandments and judgments which are just, and the virtues of those who repent and give to charity, and the levels of the souls that

---

3. In the Hebrew preface to *Naḥalat Tzevi* the author relates that his great-grandfather Abiezer Zelik, who was a rabbi and principal of a *yeshivah*, already occupied himself with a translation of the *Zohar* into Yiddish at the threshold of the seventeenth century (1601). Rabbi Zelik, however, died soon afterwards. His son, Rabbi Jose of Vienna, intended to publish his father's work, but he did not realize his wish because the "persecutions of 1648" soon began. The manuscript finally came into the hands of the author's great-grandson, Tzevi Hirsch. The latter, however, found it necessary to rework the material anew in a completely different fashion, and so from Rabbi Zelik's legacy was created *Naḥalat Tzevi*, the work of Tzevi Hirsch Chotsh.

are pure of transgressions, that are higher than the angels of heaven. And the punishment of the wicked men who are far from the fear of God, and who turn away from His Torah and whose heart is strengthened in this, is that they burn in the fiery flame of hell and their soul is thrown into the "hollow of the sling."

In the introduction the author deems it necessary to note that he wrote his work in order to bring the "end" near, for it is, after all, clear and certain that "redemption cannot come more quickly save through the *Zohar*, when it is studied by each one according to his comprehension and understanding."[4]

Here appears quite prominently a very characteristic feature which undoubtedly has a certain cultural-historical interest. We noted earlier that certain rabbinic circles were quite disturbed by the fact that, as a result of the efflorescence of the folk-literature, "literally the whole Torah and all of the laws" became easily accessible to the common people. These rabbis used to complain about the translation into the people's weekday language of such "holy books" in which very profound mysteries are concealed. The Kabbalists, however, issued forth decisively against this view. In opposition to the rabbis, they set themselves the task of familiarizing the masses with the esoteric lore and, above all, with the mystical world of the *Zohar*. Tzevi Hirsch Chotsh in fact appears quite forthrightly as a battler for the popular language. He emphasizes in his preface that the scholars also, those "familiar with the book," need not be ashamed of reading the *Zohar* in plain Yiddish, for the *Zohar* itself was also written in the ordinary folk-language of ancient generations: "In that land, where the language of the *Targum* is spoken, the *Zohar* is for everyone, even for the multitude, as in our land our *Leshon Ashkenaz* is available to all men; so let no one familiar with books think that it is a disgrace for him to read German books. The language of the *Zohar* there was their vernacular."

Like the *Zohar* itself, so the "Taytsh Zohar" is divided according to the Pentateuchal lections of the week. The central figure, the chief hero of the entire work, is the "godly" Rabbi Simeon ben Yoḥai, with his marvelous deeds and mystically ecstatic language. In it are portrayed with pedantic precision the seven palaces in which the righteous dwell with golden crowns on their heads.[5] The seven departments of hell[6] and the

4. We quote according to the Vilna edition, 1822.
5. *Ibid.*, 4–7.
6. *Ibid.*, 10.

seven gates that lead into heaven[7] are described in full detail. Certain passages of the Pentateuch are explained in a very remarkable, frequently quite unexpected fashion. The author of *Naḥalat Tzevi* adds in this connection: "There are many passages in the Torah of which people think that they are of no use, but we see that they are nothing but great mysteries." These explanations and translations are braided together with scores of marvelous mystical tales from the *Zohar*. To give the reader some notion of the style and spirit of Tzevi Hirsch Chotsh's work, which dominated the mentality of our grandparents for generations, we present here two short tales from *Naḥalat Tzevi*.

I

Rabbi Ḥiyya and Rabbi Jehudah were traveling and came to some very high mountains. There they found large bones that had lain there from the generation of the Flood. The length of one bone was three hundred paces. They were greatly astonished and said: So our sages said that the men of the generation of the Flood had no fear of any judgment and punishment, as the Biblical verse declares: "And they say to God: Depart from us; we have no desire for knowledge of Thy ways" (Job 21:14). What did they do? When water came up out of the abyss, they stopped up the well of the abyss with their feet. But the waters came out very hot, so that their feet were burned up by them. The *Tosefta* of the *Zohar* says: A voice from the voices above comes down. The voice breaks mountains and powerful crags, and it calls out every day to the wicked who have eyes and see not, have ears and hear not. With their transgressions they push away from themselves their holy soul, and for this reason they are not inscribed in the Book of Life. . . . For when a man sins he drives away the soul (*neshamah*) from himself, but when he purifies his spirit (*nefesh ruaḥ*) the soul rests among them. But the wicked—woe to them. When they depart from the world, they are handed over to the king of Gehinnom (Hell) whose name is Dumah. There they are consumed in burning fire and do not escape save on the Sabbath and on the New Moon . . . After the Sabbath or after the New Moon, a proclamation goes forth from the north and cries: Return, O wicked, to hell! Then many groups and classes of destroying angels assemble from all four sides to smite and afflict them, and to drive them again into the flaming fire of hell.[8]

7. *Ibid.*, 12.
8. *Ibid., Parashah* "Noaḥ."

II

Rabbi Jose began: "Thy people shall all be righteous; they shall inherit the land forever" (Isaiah 60:21). The Israelites are more worthy than all the nations, for the Holy One Blessed Be He calls them righteous. We have learned: There are eight thousand one hundred and twenty-five angels who are called *marei de-gadfin* (lords of wings). These angels go soaring over the whole world and hear everything that man says; as soon as the mouth utters speech, they receive it. As we have learned, there is nothing in the world that does not have a voice. The voice goes soaring into heaven, and the *marei de-gadfin* understand it. They hear it and bring it up on their wings before the judges on high, and these judge it for good or for evil. As the verse in Ecclesiastes (10:20) declares, "For a bird of the air shall carry the voice, and the winged creature will tell the matter."[9]

In close affinity with *Naḥalat Tzevi* is another work of that time. This is *Abbir Yaakov*[10] by the rabbi of Schnaitach, Akiva Baer ben Joseph (published in Sulzbach in 1700). This author had already in 1691 issued a collection of fifty tales and legends entitled *Maasei Adonai*.[11] The title-page announces: "Many wondrous miracles and stories from the *Gemara*, the *Zohar*, *Shalshelet Ha-Kabblah*, *Emek Ha-Melech* . . . and from other writers besides, men of truth, without falsehood; from Rabbi Simeon ben Yoḥai who made the *Zohar* and Rabbi Pineḥas his father-in-law, from his son Rabbi Eleazar, and many other Tannaim and rabbis; also from Rabbi Isaac Luria, may his memory be for a blessing, who lived not long ago." The most important place in these "wondrous miracles and stories" is occupied by the *anshei maaseh*, the Kabbalists and the mystics. To the major hero of the "esoteric wisdom," the godly Rabbi Simeon ben Yoḥai and his great wonders, Akiva Baer's other work, *Abbir Yaakov*, is devoted.

9. *Ibid., Parashah* "Lech Lecha".
10. "*Sefer Abbir Yaakov*: Composed by the great chieftain, the keen, distinguished, and marvelous scholar, the pious rabbi, our master Rabbi Akiva Baer, righteous teacher of Adath Yeshurun in the holy community of Schnaitach . . . And it is called *Abbir Yaakov*, for these are the letters of the name Rabbi Akiva." J. Meitlis, *op. cit.*, 41–42 conjectures that Akiva Baer also took part in the Frankfurt edition of the *Maaseh-Bukh* of 1703, in which the preface and twelve tales of his *Maasei Adonai* are reprinted before the text of the *Maaseh-Bukh*.
11. At the conclusion of several editions of *Maasei Adonai* are reprints of *Gzeyre Mimdinas Estraykh* and also the beginning of Abraham Ibn Ezra's *Iggeret Shabbat* under the title: "This document was sent by Rabbi Abraham Ibn Ezra, may the memory of the righteous be for blessing, to the children of the exile."

"Dear brethren, men and women, young men and elders," the author declares,

come and enjoy pleasures, run to this new book, and purchase it quickly. It is full of taste and grace. To read in it is very lovely. It is divided into *parashot*. Nothing is missing from it. It is much more beautiful than *Maasei Adonai* and the like. Let rich and poor buy it; scholars also should read it. Their hearts will certainly rejoice in it. Of the holy man Rabbi Simeon and his generation you will hear many wonders. You will certainly not wish to leave it even to eat. On the Sabbath, when people used to sleep, wife and husband should sit over it. You will obtain many new things. No scholar need be ashamed. Many mysteries will be revealed to you, many novellae of the Torah will you here learn, so that the Biblical verse may be fulfilled among us: "And the earth will be filled with knowledge, as the waters cover the sea."

As we see from the introduction, *Abbir Yaakov* is divided according to the weekly Pentateuchal lections. But it is not the Biblical text that is expounded there. The work treats only a single theme, which is also noted in the preface—the marvelous life-path of the godly man Rabbi Simeon ben Yoḥai. In it is described how the great man lay all of twelve years hidden in a cave together with his son Eleazar. There the profoundest mysteries were disclosed to him, and there was created the most marvelous book that is filled with brilliance and beauty —the holy *Zohar*. To Rabbi Simeon ben Yoḥai's father-in-law, Rabbi Pineḥas, the birds who soar over the waves of the sea bring the happy tidings that the godly man has already left his cave and appeared in the bright world. Legend after legend extends the imaginative thread of Simeon ben Yoḥai's marvelous and splendid life-path.

Thus, at that time, one work after another was produced with one definite purpose: to root in the consciousness of the people a deep feeling of enthusiasm for the creators of the "esoteric wisdom" and an unshakeable belief in the profound and holy secrets of the *Zohar*. These authors endeavored to strengthen in the common people the consciousness that, without the mysteries of the Kabbalah, one is quite incapable of grasping God's Torah. Not by accident does the author of *Abbir Yaakov* repeat that "no scholar need be ashamed" and that "scholars also should read it," for "many mysteries will be revealed to you, many novellae of the Torah will you here learn."

The Kabbalists who propagandized the mystical ideas of the *Zohar* and of the Lurianic Kabbalah in the tongue of the people went even further. There were among them also men who conducted in the popular language their battle against the scholars and rabbis who exult in their learning and expertise in the sea of the Talmud and devote themselves little to Kabbalah. The echo of Abraham Abulafia's wrathful words against the rabbis[12] are also heard in the folk-literature. Contemptuously the author of *Tikkunei Ha-Mo'adim*, Aryeh Leib Binswangen, declares that "not everything was dependent on the *Gemara* or *halachah* and *Tosafot.*" "Everyone," he says further, "thinks, as soon as he knows how to study a page of *Gemara*, that he is already a scholar, and so looks no more at any other book. But, my dear people, you must know that, when a man teaches us all *Gemarot* and *Tosafot* and has no knowledge in the science of the mysteries and the wisdom of the Kabbalah, he is, in comparison to those who do know the wisdom of the Kabbalah, like a child when he first begins to study."[13]

The propaganda for the wisdom of the Kabbalah among the masses of the people had considerable success. Even the quite ordinary reader lost his taste for the morality books written in simple, easy understandable language. He was much more impressed by books filled with mystical secrets and with barely comprehensible combinations of letters and divine "names." Characteristic in this respect is the fate of the morality book *Hakirot Ha-Lev* which was composed in 1715 by Solomon ben Simeon Wetzlar of Fürth.

A child of his time, Solomon Wetzlar was permeated with the ascetic world-view, but he was exceptional by virtue of the fact that the mystical world of ideas was alien to him and he was cool toward the Kabbalah with its mysteries. He greatly deplores the fact that "many morality books were printed in the holy language;" and they can "be of very little use to . . . such people as are not scholars . . . for these do not understand it, and it is necessary that the author himself always come to read it to them and to explain it, for they cannot help themselves in it and, unfortunately, consider it a disgrace to ask other people." In order, however, that no one should be able to say, " 'I do not understand anything of the holy tongue and cannot repent,' I have made this small book so that women and

---

12. See our *History*, Vol. III, pp. 38–39; Vol. V, p. 77.
13. We quote according to Schulmann, 78.

maidens may understand . . . Common people, too, may find consolation in it, and everyone may discover the remedy for his condition."

Even the titles of the chapters reflect quite clearly the ascetic spirit that dominates Wetzlar's morality book: "Chapter Ten speaks of the blindness of the children of the world." "Chapter Twelve speaks of how painfully the children of the world depart from the world." "Chapter Twenty-Eight declares: Revere not worldly honor; it is pure vanity of vanities when a man takes trouble to be praised by people." "Chapter Thirty-Eight: Do not laugh too much, else you spoil the game." "Chapter Forty-Five: A mortal should not be conceited." Wetzlar, however, does not wish to frighten the reader, to cast dread upon him with "fearful tales" about the grievous punishment that awaits the sinner in hell and about the hosts of destroying spirits that lie in wait for his body and soul. The author of *Ḥakirot Ha-Lev* embellishes his moral instruction with texts from the Bible and with parables and tales from actual daily life. These tales, which are written in simple, clear language, undoubtedly have a definite social-ethnographic interest. But precisely because Wetzlar's morality book, written in such a tender style, is free of mystical moods, it enjoyed no success.[14] It was not *Ḥakirot Ha-Lev* but *Kav Ha-Yashar* and *Naḥalat Tzevi* that ruled over the minds of those generations.

Nevertheless, it would be a mistake to think that the masses of Jewish readers at that time read only pious, mystically colored morality books and showed no interest in books of more worldly content. It must be stressed that even in the first half of the eighteenth century, in the era of greatest intellectual decline and strictest isolation, popular books of general content also found a definite, though limited, circle of readers in the Jewish quarter.

We noted previously[15] that in the sixteenth century a large number of popular German books were reprinted for Jewish readers in Hebrew letters, generally with quite insignificant changes. The following fact, however, is very interesting: one of the best loved and most popular German folk-books of the sixteenth century, a collection of anecdotes about the jester Till Eulenspiegel, was virtually unknown in the Jewish quarter. Handwritten copies of the German text in Hebrew letters

14. The work was first printed after the author's death in 1731.
15. See above, pp. 50–51.

alone have been preserved.[16] Only in the eighteenth century
did several editions of the *Vunderparlikh Und Seltzmi Histori Til
Aylin Shpigils* (Wonderful and Rare History of Till Eulenspiegel) appear.[17] Apparently it was only then that interest in this
popular book arose among Jewish readers. We observed previously[18] that, in consequence of the frequent persecutions and
intense competition that the German Jews experienced from
the Christian urban populace, these Jews were increasingly
pushed out of the cities and moved into the villages. This
process was most marked in the seventeenth century; at the
end of that century a considerable segment of German Jewry
already consisted of villagers living in the midst of peasants. It
was among these crude villagers who had settled in the vicinity
of the peasants, apparently, that the Till Eulenspiegel anecdotes, the unique product of the heavy peasant humor that was
directed chiefly against the city and the urban artisans, obtained great favor. Also popular among these readers was "The
Rare and Entertaining Stories of the Schildburger," anecdotes
about the German city of fools.[19] The villager took great delight in seeing city people ridiculed as clumsy fools.

Mystical ideas did, indeed, dominate the Jewish quarter, and
in it the firm belief prevailed that the wisdom of the Kabbalah
is the source of all the wisdoms and sciences in the world.
Actual life, however, constantly reminded Jews of needs and
requirements that could not be reconciled with Kabbalah and
mysticism; quite different kinds of knowledge were essential
for this life. In Poland, which was then in a condition of social
and economic decline, this was, for the time being, less noticeable. But the situation in Germany, especially in the Prussian
provinces, was very different. The industrial and economic
growth which was then marked in the north German cities had
a certain influence also on members of the Jewish community
with their civic disabilities. The more developed business con-
nections of these Jews broadened their world-view and their
circle of interests and made them feel more keenly the inferi-

16. The oldest copy of the Judeo-German *Till Eulenspiegel* is preserved in the Munich
    manuscript No. 100, completed in 1600 (See M. Erik, *Vegn Alt-Yidishn Roman*, 205).
17. Extracts of various editions of the Yiddish *Till Eulenspiegel* are given by M. Stein-
    schneider in *Serapeum*, 1848, 19–40; Avé-Lallemant, *Das deutsche Gaunertum*, Vol. III,
    485–6. M. Erik, *op. cit.*, indicates that the first Yiddish printed edition of *Till
    Eulenspiegel* appeared before 1721, the second in 1736.
18. See above, p. 289.
19. A chapter of the Judeo-German edition is given by Avé-Lallemant in his work
    cited above, Vol. II, pp. 477–484.

ority and backwardness of Jewish intellectual and economic
life.

Typical in this respect is Isaac Wetzlar's *Libs-Brif*, composed
in 1748–1749.[20] Born in the last decade of the seventeenth century, Isaac Wetzlar[21] studied until 1709 in the *yeshivah* of Prague
with the well-known Rabbi Abraham Broda. Later he lived as
a prominent householder in Tzele. As a businessman, Wetzlar
had dealings with officials, frequently visited Hamburg and
other cities, and had opportunity to observe closely the backward and abnormal conditions of the Jewish mode of life. This
moved him to write his morality book which he entitled *Libs-
Brif* (Love-Letters). What he means by this title Wetzlar explains at once in the preface. Here he asserts that he writes his
work "only out of inner, upright love from the bottom of his
heart for his dear brothers and sisters." Wetzlar makes the
same point a number of times in the work itself, for instance,
in Chapter Thirteen: "God is my witness that I write for the
sake of heaven and out of love for my brethren." With great
regret the author notes how rotten the foundation of Jewish
modes of earning a living are. "Having frequently considered
our miserable, grievous condition in our exile," Wetzlar laments, "I have experienced how, because of our many sins,
prosperity from trade declines, and with what difficulty and
trouble we must seek our livelihood. Most business dealing,
unfortunately, consists of swindlery." He repeats the same
thought in another place: "So also—God have pity upon it—
our livelihood is difficult, our trade swindlery, and our wealth,
unfortunately, very small."

The major cause of this decline is perceived by the author in
the bad education and lack of culture of the upper classes, who
keep the masses in slavery, both intellectually and economi-
cally.[22] The leaders of the community, the rabbis and scholars,
are responsible for the benighted situation in which the Jewish
quarter finds itself; it is they who keep the masses in ignorance
and darkness. The level of culture is so low that the masses
cannot even realize who bears the greatest responsibility for
their grievous condition. "But most of them, unfortunately, do
not know much more than do cattle who is responsible. The

20. This work has remained in manuscript and became known only thanks to the
    thorough report of Dr. Jacob Meitlis in *YIVO-Bleter*, II, 308–333.
21. Perhaps his father was Solomon Wetzlar of Fürth, the author of *Ḥakirot Ha-Lev*.
    See above, p. 348.
22. *YIVO-Bleter*, II, 217.

common man no longer has the ability to let his children continue to study. Our *parnassim* and political leaders realize still less that they should think of establishing a fund for the teaching of Torah, to come to the aid of the common man."[23] The author declares bitterly:

In the net are caught many leaders because of their pride and lordship, and they throw on the people a great fear that is not for the sake of God. And they enjoy great pleasures and do not help the people with the taxes, the burden of which they make light for themselves and heavy for others. . . . The congregation, the children of Abraham, Isaac, and Jacob, are crushed down and go naked and barefoot because of the officials who collect the taxes and the servants of the *Kahal* who rob them.

Isaac Wetzlar speaks with no less anger about the rabbis and scholars: "But now, by reason of our many sins, our holy Torah is unfortunately corrupted through many bad scholars, and the truth is hard to find. . . . By reason of our numerous sins, many people have multiplied in the present generation who, because of flattery or bribery, permit many things which are forbidden by the Torah." The rabbis and scholars, who ought to be true leaders but are not, bear, in Wetzlar's view, the entire responsibility for the lamentable condition of the Jewish masses. He tells of young scholars who immediately after their marriage, obtain a rabbinic post through money and as a result of influential patronage. "And it would be proper to write laments on this matter, and one of the most painful things is that such young rabbis, with their impudence and pride, mislead not only their brethren, whom they have blinded with money so that these have made them rabbis, but also good, common people, rich men, and even *parnassim* and leaders of the community and the country." Through such careerists, men who are truly pious and revere God are discredited among the people. "They are, by reason of our numerous sins, cut down through such bad young rabbis and other bad scholars such as are portrayed above; they bring respectable, honest men into contempt among the common people." If such careerist scholars study the *Shulḥan Aruch* or other codes, it is not for the sake of study but to profit therefrom, to be able to figure as an arbitrator or third party in a legal suit. In order for the side which they represent to prevail, they distort the

23. *Ibid.*, II, 318.

truth through all kinds of tortuous subtleties, so that the Torah judgment is no longer, as a matter of course, a Torah judgment and no longer a true judgment. How the people react to this, and how far the authority of these scholars has fallen there, is illustrated by the author with the following words: "By reason of our many sins, it has come to the point that, through such scholars, it is a public byword among common people: Our sacred Torah is very good; all rogues and thieves have it under their control and distort it as they wish."[24]

The author sees the root of the whole moral and social decline in the evil and barbaric mode of education. The unpedagogical system of learning among the German Jews, he asserts, brings it about that the children grow up to be crude vulgarians without elementary knowledge.

The project for reforming Jewish education proposed in the *Libs-Brif* is, however, very little distinguished from the educational programs put forward by the Maharal of Prague, Ephraim of Luntshitz, Shabbetai Bass, and others in their day.[25] Isaac Wetzlar also cites the method of study among the Sephardim, who give their children, first of all, thorough knowledge of the Hebrew language, teach them the Pentateuch first, then the Prophets, and finally the Mishnah. Only when the pupil is older and has been properly prepared, does he proceed to Gemara, *Tosafot*, etc. Like Shabbetai Bass and Moses Sertel, the author of the *Libs-Brif* also demands that the children begin to study "the grammar of the holy tongue" early, and as a textbook for Hebrew grammar he recommends Zalman Hanau's grammatical work.[26] Only in two points of Wetzlar's educational program is the influence of the rationalist enlightenment tendency, which had just become noticeable at that time in western Europe, felt. Wetzlar deliberately repeats that, when the child has obtained an elementary knowledge of Hebrew, he should begin to study the Mishnah, "instead of letting the children study *Ein Yaakov*."[27] The pious author of the *Libs-Brif* believes that *Ein Yaakov*, the aggadic and legendary part of the Talmud, is generally not suitable material for the common people, because the ignorant masses "consider all of *Ein Yaakov* plain truth."[28] He believes that the

---

24. Ibid., 319–320.
25. See our *History*, previous parts.
26. See our *History*, Vol. VI, pp. 149–150.
27. *YIVO-Bleter*, II, 329.
28. *Ibid.*, 318.

text of the Bible ought to be studied only according to its literal meaning, not by way of homiletic interpretation. Indeed, for this reason he also has a very negative attitude to the "women's Torah," the classic representative of the Midrash literature in Yiddish—*Tze'enah U-Re'enah*. He considers this work harmful because it does not present the correct meaning of the Torah. "Would it not be better," he argues, "that our women understood the written Torah, or at least that women and even ordinary householders, who could not study in their youth, should read the so-called German Bible that Rabbi Yekutiel translated into German rather than *Tze'enah U-Re'enah?*"[29]

Here we encounter the second original point of Wetzlar's program of education. He stresses that care should be taken not only for the education of sons but of daughters as well. The author of the *Libs-Brif* devotes a great deal of attention to the importance of educating the Jewish woman. He polemicizes against those scholars who do not properly understand the meaning of the Talmudic statement, "Anyone who teaches his daughter Torah, it is as if he taught her folly," and who, on this basis, do not permit Jewish girls to obtain a Jewish education. This, he argues, leads to the loss among the young women of every connection with Jewishness. Naturally, they turn to foreign languages and cultures, seeking in these satisfaction of their thirst for knowledge. The author notes: "It is, unfortunately, sincerely to be deplored that such bad scholars do not wish to teach the daughters of Israel the written Torah of Moses, and that they should thereby learn their holy mother tongue, Hebrew. On the other hand, they permit the daughters of Israel to study foreign languages—French, Italian." Thereby the Jewish women become estranged from Jewishness, whereas "among other nations, their women know our holy written Torah better than our women" (*ibid.,* 331).

The frequent persecutions in the neighboring and distant lands aroused in the Jewish merchants and their employees the desire to become familiar with the way of life of these lands, of the environment that was strange to them.[30] The extensive commerce in which they engaged demanded a certain minimum of basic knowledge which the old-fashioned Jewish elementary schools and *yeshivot* did not provide. Thus, precisely

29. On Yekutiel Blitz's translation of the Bible, see above, pp. 137ff.
30. It is characteristic that as early as the year 1746 *Robinson Crusoe* appeared in Yiddish (see *YIVO-Bleter,* III, p. 285).

in the middle of the eighteenth century, certain attempts were
made to provide, in the vernacular, these essential, practical,
positive items of information. Business required honorable exchange of correspondence and so various guides for letter-
writing with all kinds of model letters were printed. We read
in the preface to one such manual:[31] "Since I saw many letters
and none of them satisfied me, I again published this book and
many people asked me for it; therefore I undertook it. Many
things are well described in it. Hence, you should not spare
your money, but buy it quickly. I hope that soon thereafter you
will come running again." A certain Benjamin ben Zalman
Kroneburg who, in 1750, issued in the town of Neuwied on the
Rhine a medical handbook,[32] published two years later his
Kuriosen Antiquarius in which there are, as the author himself
notes, "all kinds of selected geographic and historical curiosi-
ties . . . translated into Yiddish for the first time, word for
word, from reliable authors." From the introduction to the
work[33] it is clear that the author intends, first of all, to provide
a geographical almanac about all the lands of the world for
those who are not in a position to undertake long journeys,
and, secondly—and this, for the author, is the most important
—to make it easier for the reader to learn the German language. "And chiefly," Kroneburg notes, "this little book is very
useful in order, through diligent reading, to master the High
German language thoroughly, as well as to master with applicable rules the correct spelling of the words." The same Kroneburg also made an attempt in the 1750's to issue a Yiddish
journal "Der Grosse Schau-Platz, Lust und lehrreiche auch
traurige und wunderliche Geschichten" (The Great Show
Place: Pleasant and Instructive, as well as Sorrowful and Wondrous Stories). It is difficult to say whether these "wondrous"
stories were belletristic material or geographical information

31. "*Leshon Paz* (Golden Language), printed in the holy community of Euchebach in
the new press which Seligmann Reis set up in "now [*attah*-1715] may might increase."
32. *Segullot Melachim Ha-Nikra Haus-Buch, oder medizinische Schatzkammer des Menschen
Nutzlichkeit.* Old-Yiddish literature has a considerable number of practical handbooks of medicine: *Derech Etz Hayyim* (1603); Issachar Teller's *Be'er Mayyim Hayyim*
(1657); Moses of Mezhirech's *Yerushat Mosheh* and *Yarim Mosheh* (1677); *Sefer Refuot,
Sefer Ha-Heshek,* and many others. For a discussion of the characteristics of popular
Yiddish medical literature, see Dr. Shatzky's article, "Sefer Ha-Heshek" in *YIVO-
Bleter,* IV, 223-235.
33. The introduction was reprinted by Dr. J. Shatsky in *YIVO-Bleter,* III, 406-407.

and descriptions of lands of a purely informative character. The single number of this journal that appeared has not been preserved.

Nothing came of Kroneburg's undertaking. On the other hand, fifteen years later, in December 1771, in the city of Dyhernfurth, there began to appear regularly on a twice weekly basis, every Tuesday and Friday, a newspaper under the title *Dyhernfurther Prifilegirte Tsaytung*. This paper was issued following the model of the first Yiddish periodical newspaper, *Kurantin*, which appeared in Amsterdam in the 1680's, also twice a week: Tuesday (under the title *Dinstagishi Kurantin*) and Friday (*Fraytagishi Kurantin*). The *Dyhernfurther Tsaytung*, which was intended for the merchant class, provided mainly informative material, political news, and Jewish chronicles of various lands. In one of the numbers that is preserved is given "a catalogue with prices of all kinds of Polish merchandise." At the end of each number is noted: "Single copies cost a silver groschen." The annual subscribers paid three Reichsthaler.[34]

Moses Zerah Eidlitz, a competent Talmudist and a close friend of Rabbi Jonathan Eybeschütz,[35] issued in 1775 a thick handbook of mathematics entitled *Melechet Maḥashevet* in Hebrew and Yiddish.[36] In the preface the author explains that "I have made this book *Melechet Maḥashevet* so that such people as cannot learn from the holy language may also find it useful." Eidlitz deems it necessary to emphasize in this connection that the only true wisdom is, indeed, our Torah; but such branches of science as mathematics are useful in practical life, and hence one must also have some knowledge of them.

Melechet Maḥashevet as well as the *Dyhernfurther Tsaytung* were written in a very *daytshmerish* or Germanized Yiddish. The influence of the new tendencies about which we have written at the end of the previous volume and of which we shall speak in later parts of our work, is already felt, and the bearers of these tendencies adopted an attitude of hatred and contempt for the popular language and its literature.

At the same time in the distant southern provinces of the moribund Polish kingdom, the powerful Hasidic movement, which based itself ideologically on the previously portrayed mystical tendencies and which gathered broad masses of the

---

34. See *ZHB*, V, 159; *ibid.*, VII, 24.
35. For biographical details on Eidlitz, see *Literaturblatt des Orients*, 1848, 140, 524–527.
36. After *Melechet Maḥashevet* two further parts (on geometry and astronomy) were to come. However, Eidlitz did not manage to write these.

people under its banner, developed. The *Aufklärer* of Berlin, who regarded with hostility everything that bore the stamp of the medieval ghetto, declared a bitter war against the "corrupted jargon" and endeavored to push it out as quickly as possible through the "language of the fatherland" (German). But the Hasidic movement, which addressed itself to the broad, democratic strata, strove to use the folk-language to the greatest extent possible as an instrument of propaganda. A new period with new demands begins in the history of Jewish literature. Of it we shall speak in the later volumes of our *History*.

BIBLIOGRAPHICAL NOTES

Old Yiddish Literature from Its Origins to the Haskalah Period

CHAPTER ONE

LANGUAGES AMONG JEWS; THE ORIGINS OF YIDDISH

The most important publications on the origins and early development of Yiddish up to 1958 are included in Uriel and Beatrice Weinreich, *Yiddish Language and Folklore: A Selective Bibliography for Research.*

Among works which the student will find of special value are: Y. Bin-Nun, "Ha-Ivrit Shebe-Yidish," *Leshonenu*, XVII (1941), 139ff; S. Birnbaum, "Jiddisch," *Encyclopedia Judaica*, IX (1932), cols. 112–127; idem, "Jiddische Sprache," *Jüdisches Lexikon*, III (1929), cols. 269–78; M. Erik (pseudonym for S. Merkin), *Di Geshikhte Fun Der Yidisher Literatur Fun Di Eltste Tsaytn Biz Der Haskole Tekufe* (1928); *For Max Weinreich on His Seventieth Birthday* (a collection of studies; 1964); Sol Liptzin, *A History of Yiddish Literature* (1972); Yudel Mark, "Yiddish Literature," in L. Finkelstein (ed.), *The Jews: Their History, Culture, and Religion*, Third Edition, New York (1966), Vol. II, 1191–1233; N.B. Minkoff, in collaboration with Juda A. Joffe, "Old Yiddish Literature," in *The Jewish People Past and Present*, New York (1952), Vol. III, 145–164; M. Pines, *Histoire de la littérature judeo-allemande* (1911); A.A. Roback, *The Story of Yiddish Literature* (1940); Zalman Rubashov (Shazar), "Yidishe *Geviyyot-Edut* in Di *She'elot U-Teshuvot* Fun Onhoyb XV. Bizn Sof XVIII. Yohrhundert," *Historishe Shriftn*, I (1929), 115–196; I. Schipper, "Kultur Geshikhtlikher Fun Der Eltster Yidisher Literatur," *YIVO-Bleter*, VIII

(1935), 44–60; Chone Shmeruk, "Yiddish Literature," *Encyclopedia Judaica* (1971), Vol. XVI, cols. 798–833; E. Schulmann, *Sefat Yehudit Ashkenazit Ye-Safrutah, 1500–1800* (1913); N. Shtif, *Die Eltere Yidishe Literatur* (1929); N. Susskind, "Batrakhtungen Vegn der Geshikhte Fun Yiddish," in *Juda A. Joffe-Bukh* (1958), 146–57; Max Weinreich, *Bilder Fun Der Yidisher Literatur-Geshikhte, Fun Die Onheybn Biz Mendele Moycher Sforim* (1928); idem, *Geshikhte Fun Der Yidisher Shprakh*, 2 vols. (1968); idem, "Ikerim in der Geshikhte Fun Yidish," *Yidishe Shprakh*, XIV (1954), 97–110; XV (1955), 12–19; idem, "Yidish, Knaanik, Slavik," in *For Roman Jakobson* (1956), 622–632; idem, "Yidishkayt and Yiddish," in *M.M. Kaplan Jubilee Volume* (1953), 481–514; Uriel Weinreich et al (eds.), *The Field of Yiddish* (a collection of studies, 1965–68); idem, *Ha-Ivrit Ha-Ashkenazit Veha-Ivrit Shebe-Yidish, Behinatan Ha-Ge'ografit* (1965; first published in *Leshonenu*, Vols. XXIV and XXV); idem, "Yiddish Language," *Encyclopedia Judaica* (1971), Vol. XVI, cols. 790–798.

CHAPTER TWO

BIBLE GLOSSARIES AND THE BEGINNINGS OF YIDDISH LITERATURE

On the beginnings of religious and secular literature in Yiddish, many of the works listed in the bibliography for Chapter One will be helpful.

On early Yiddish Bible glossaries, see W. Staerk and A. Leitzmann, *Die jüdisch-deutschen Bibelübersetzungen von den Anfangen biz zum Ausgang des XVIII. Jahrhunderts* (1923); S. Noble, *Khumesh-Taytsh: An Oysforshung Vegn Der Traditsie Fun Taytshen Khumesh in Di Khadorim* (1943); and Nehamah Leibowitz, *Die Übersetzungstechnik der jüdisch-deutschen Bibelübersetzungen des XV. und XVI. Jahrhunderts dargestellt an den Psalmen* (1931).

For early poetry, see M. Bassin, ed. *Antologye Finf Hundert Yohr Idishe Po'ezye* (1917); L. Fuks, *The Oldest Known Literary Documents of Yiddish Literature* (text, introduction, notes, and German translation; 1957); and S.M. Ginsburg and P.S. Marek (eds.), *Yevreiskiya Narodniya Pyesni v Rosii: Di Yidishe Folkslider in Rusland* (1901).

On Samuel Hogerlin's bilingual poem against gambling, see Isaac Rivkind, *Der Kamf Kegn Azart-Shpiln Bay Yidn* (New York, 1946), pp. 13–19 and Supplement I.

On Old-Yiddish love-songs and dance-songs, see Y.L. Cohen,

"Vi Alt Zaynen Unzere Libelider" and "Dos Yidishe Folkslid," in *Shtudies Vegn Yidisher Folksshafung* (1952). Texts of old songs and hymns are included in F. Rosenberg, "Über eine Sammlung detuscher Volks- und Gesellschaftsliedern in hebräischen Lettern," *Zeitschrift für die Geschichte der Juden in Deutschland,* II (1888), III (1889), and L. Löwenstein, "Jüdische und jüdisch-deutsche Lieder," in *Jubelschrift . . . I. Hildesheimer* (1890).

An important source-book of early Yiddish literature is Max Grünbaum's *Jüdsich-deutsche Chrestomathie* (1882).

For a bibliography of older printed Yiddish works, see M. Steinschneider, "Jüdisch-deutsche Literatur" in *Serapeum* (Leipzig, 1848–49; reprinted in Jerusalem, 1961).

CHAPTER THREE

ROMANCES AND EPICS

On Rabbi Anshel and his *Mirkevet Ha-Mishneh,* see J. Perles, *Beiträge zur Geschichte der hebräischen und aramäischen Studien* (1884), 33, 100, 117–19; J. Meisl, *Geschichte der Juden in Polen und Russland,* I (1921), 296; B. Szlosberg, "*Mirkevet Ha-Mishneh:* Der Eltster Yidisher Sprakh-Dokument," *YIVO-Bleter,* XIII (1938), 313–24; H.D. Friedberg, *Toledot Ha-Defus Ha-Ivri Be-Polanyah,* Second Edition (1950), Vol. I; and M. Weinreich, *Shtaplen Far Etiudn Tsu Der Yidisher Shprakhvisenshaft un Literatur-Geshikhte* (1923).

On the relation of early Yiddish prose to German prose, see A. Paucker, "Yiddish Versions of Early German Prose Novels," *Journal of Jewish Studies,* X (1959).

On the Hebrew Arthur-Romance (Ms. Codex Vat. Hebr. Urbino), see C. Leviant, *King Artus: A Hebrew Arthurian Romance of 1279* (Hebrew text with facing English translation, 1969). On the Arthur legends in Yiddish, see L. Landau, *Arthurian Legends or the Hebrew-German Rhymed Version of the Legend of King Arthur* (1912).

On Elijah Baḥur (Levita) and his works in Yiddish, see S. Buber, *Leben und Schriften des Elias Bachur, genannt Levita* (1856); M. Erik, *Vegn Alt-Yidishn Roman Un Novele* (1926); idem, *Geshikhte Fun Der Yidisher Literatur* (1928); N.B. Minkoff, *Eliye Bokher Un Zayn Bove-Bukh* (1950); J. Shatsky, *Eliye Bokher* (Yiddish, 1949; includes bibliography); M.A. Szulwas, *Ḥayyei Ha-Yehudim be-Italyah Bi-Tekufat Ha-Renaissance* (1955), 353, Index,

S.V. *Eliyah Baḥur;* G.E. Weil, *Elie Lévita: humaniste et massorète 1469–1549* (1963); M. Weinreich, *Bilder Fun Der Yidisher Literatur-Geshikhte* (1929), 149–91 and idem, *Shtaplen Far Etudien Tsu Der Yidisher Shprakhvisenshaft Un Literatur-Geshikhte* (1923), 72–86.

The first edition of the *Bove-Bukh*, published at Isny in Germany in 1541, was reprinted in facsimile, with an introduction, by Judah A. Joffe (1949) under the title *Eliye Bokher: Poetishe Shafungen In Yidish.*

CHAPTER FOUR

BIBLE TRANSLATIONS AND MIDRASHIM IN YIDDISH

For early poems in Yiddish, see M. Bassin (ed.) *Antologye Finf Hundert Yohr Idishe Po'ezye* (1917), and S.M. Ginsburg and P.S. Marek (eds.), *Yevreiskiya Narodniya Pyesni v Rosii: Di Yidishe Folkslider In Rusland* (1901).

On dance-songs and love-songs in Old Yiddish, see Y.L. Cohen, "Vi Alt Zaynen Unzere Libelider" and "Dos Yidishe Folkslid," in *Shtudies Vegn Yidisher Folksshaffung* (1952).

On early Yiddish versions of the Bible, see *Encyclopedia Judaica*, Vol. IV (1971), cols. 866–867.

On Joseph bar Yakar, see A.M. Habermann, in *Kiryat Sefer*, XXXI (1956), 483–500.

On Judeo-German reworkings of Midrashic material and on early epics about Biblical heroes, see P. Matenko and S. Sloan, "The Aqedath Jiṣḥaq" in *Two Studies in Yiddish Culture* (1968); Chone Shmeruk, "An Opgefunener Fragment Funem Alt-Yidishn Akeyde-Lid," in *Almanakh Fun Di Yidishe Shrayber In Yisroel* (1967); and L. Landau, "Der Yidisher Midrash Va-Yosha" *YIVO-Bleter*, III (1929). See also Shalom Spiegel, "Me-Aggadot Ha-Akedah" *Sefer Ha-Yovel Le-Chevod Aleksander Marx, Helek Ivri* (1950), 471–547 (translated into English by Judah Goldin under the title *The Last Trial: On The Legends and Folklore of the Command to Abraham to offer Isaac as a Sacrifice: The Akedah,* 1967), and M. Robinson, "Akedat Yitzḥak Be-Sifrut Ha-Ivrit," *Ha-Shiloaḥ,* XXV (5671) 208–13, 312–18.

Felix Falk published an edition of the *Shmuel-Bukh* in 1961 in two volumes, with an introduction and text-critical apparatus, under the title *Das Schemuelbuch des Mosche Esrim Wearba.*

On the *Shmuel-Bukh* and its author, see F. Delitzch, *Zur Ge-*

schichte der jüdischen Poesie (1836), 81; M. Erik, *Di Geshikhte fun der Yidisher Literatur* (1928), 79–81, 112–21; F. Falk, *Mélanges bibliographiques sur les livres de Samuel en strophes de Nibelungen* (1909); N.B. Minkoff, in *The Jewish People Past and Present*, III (1952), 146ff.; Z. Rubashov (Shazar), "R. Mosheh Esrim Ve-Arba," in *Zukunft*, XXXII (1927), 428–29; W. Staerk, "Zur Uberlieferungsgeschichte des jüdisch-deutschen Samuel-und Königsbuches," *MGWJ*, LXIII (1919); W. Staerk and A. Leitzmann, *Die jüdisch-deutschen Bibelübersetzungen von den Anfangen biz zum Ausgang des XVIII. Jahrbunderts* (1923); N. Susskind, "Shmuel-Bukh Problemen" in *For Max Weinreich on his Seventieth Birthday* (1964); M. Weinreich, "Dos Shmuel-Bukh," *Zukunft*, XXXII (1927), 278–88; and idem, *Bilder fun der Yidisher Literatur-Geshikhte* (1928).

A facsimile edition of the *editio princeps* of the *Melokhim-Bukh* (Augsburg, 1543) was published in 1965 by Lajb Fuks in two volumes under the title *Das Altjiddische Epos Melokîm-Bûk̲*. This work contains an introduction by Fuks, Hebrew and Aramaic sources, text-critical apparatus, and glossary. For reviews of the work, see J. Meitlis, "Alt-Yidishe Epishe Literatur," in *Zukunft*, LXXII (1967), 13–17, and Chone Shmeruk, "Di Naye Editsie Funem Alt-Yidishn Melokhim-Bukh," in *Di Goldene Keyt*, No. 59 (1967), 208ff.

On the *Melokhim-Bukh*, see M. Erik, *Di Geshikhte Fun Der Yidisher Literatur* (1928); N.B. Minkoff, in: *The Jewish People, Past and Present*, III (1952), 145ff; A.A. Roback, *The Story of Yiddish Literature* (1940); and W. Staerk and A. Leitzmann, *Die jüdisch-deutschen Bibelüberstezungen* (1923).

CHAPTER FIVE

POPULAR LITERATURE; *TZE'ENAH U-RE'ENAH*

On Jehudah Leib Bresch and the Cremona edition of the Pentateuch, see W. Staerk and A. Leitzmann, *Die judisch-deutschen Bibelübersetzungen* (1923), 114–5, 129–30, and E. Schulmann, *Sefat Yehudit-Ashkenazit Ve-Safrutah* (1913), 9f.

Other works dealing with Yiddish translations and paraphrases of the Pentateuch and other Biblical books are S. Noble, *Khumesh-Taytsh: An Oysforshung Vegn Der Traditsie Fun Taytshen Khumesh in Di Khadorim* (1943); S. Birnbaum, "Zeks Hundert Yor Tehillim Af Yidish," in *For Max Weinreich on his Seventieth Birthday: Studies in Jewish Languages, Literature, and*

Society (1964); and L. Landau, "A Hebrew-German Paraphrase of the Book of Esther" in *The Journal of English and Germanic Philology*, XVIII (1919).

On Isaac ben Aaron Prossnitz (Prosstitz), see H.D. Friedberg, *Toledot Ha-Defus Ha-Ivri Be-Polanyah*, 2nd ed. (1950), 5–25; M. Balaban, in *Soncino Blätter*, III (1929–30), 9–11, 47–48; and R.N.N. Rabbinovicz, *Ma'amar Al Hadpasat Ha-Talmud* (1877), 70–75.

On Isaac ben Samson Ha-Kohen and his *Taytsh-Khumesh*, see K. Lieben, *Gal Ed* (1856), No. 84 (Hebrew section); E. Schulmann, *Sefat Yehudit-Ashkenazit Ve-Safrutah* (1913), 10f.; and I.Z. Kahana, in *Arim Ve-Immahot Be-Yisrael*, 4 (1950), 262f.

Over two hundred editions of Jacob ben Isaac Ashkenazi's *Tze'enah U-Re'enah* have been published since the end of the sixteenth century. The Book of Genesis was translated into English by Paul I. Hershon (London, 1855), and the Book of Exodus by Norman C. Gore (New York, 1965). German translations of Genesis were published by S. Goldsmidt (in *Mitteilungen zur jüdischen Volkskunde*, Vienna, 1911–14) and by Bertha Pappenheim (Frankfort, 1930). On this work, which became so popular among the women in the Ashkenazic Jewish world, see M. Erik, *Di Geshikhte Fun Der Yidisher Literatur* (1928), 223–30; Ch. Shmeruk, "Di Mizrekh-Eyropeyishe Nuskho'es Fun Der *Tze'enah U-Re'enah* (1786–1850)," in *For Max Weinreich . . .* (1964); J. Prijs, *Die Basler hebräischen Drücke* (1964); and Ch. Lieberman in *Yidishe Shprakh*, XXVI (1966), 33–38, and XXIX (1969), 73–76.

CHAPTER SIX

MORALITY BOOKS

On the manuscript copy of *Seder Nashim*, see M. Weinreich, *Bilder* (1928), 149–50.

On Jonah ben Abraham Gerondi and his *Sefer Ha-Yirah*, see A.T. Schrock, *Rabbi Jonah ben Abraham of Gerona* (1968); A. Löwenthal, *Rabbi Jonah Gerundi und sein ethischer Kommentar zu den Proverbien* (1910), 3–36 (introduction); G. Scholem, in *Sefer Bialik* (1934), 141–55; and Bronznick, in *Hadorom*, XXVIII (1969), 238–42.

The anonymous Hebrew *Sefer Ha-Middot* (also entitled *Orehot Tzaddikim*), which was highly popular in its Yiddish version, was translated into English by S.J. Cohen under the title

The Ways of the Righteous (1969). On this work, see M. Güdemann, *Die Geschichte des Erziehungswesen und der Cultur der abendländischen Juden*, 3 (1888), 223ff.; J. Kaufman (Even Shemuel),
Rabbi Yom Tov Lipmann Mühlhausen (Hebrew, 1927); and M.
Weinreich, *Shtaplen* (1923).

For extracts from Abraham Ashkenazi's *Sam Ḥayyim* dealing
with the education of children, see S. Assaf, *Mekorot Le-Toledot
Ha-Ḥinnuch Be-Yisrael*, 2nd ed., 4 (1948). On the work, see I.
Zinberg, in *Filologishe Shriftn*, III, 177–180.

On Moses ben Ḥanokh Altschuler's *Brantshpigl*, see M.
Gaster, "The *Maasebuch* and the *Brantspiegel*," in *Jewish Studies
in Memory of George A. Kohut* (1935), 270–78; J.R. Marcus, "Etishe
Vantshpiglen," *YIVO-Bleter*, XXI (1943), 201–214; J. Prijs, *Die
Basler hebräischen Drücke* (1964), 283ff; M. Erik, *Geshikhte Fun Der
Yidisher Literatur* (1928), 287–99; and idem, *Tsaytshrift*, I, 173–180.

On Isaac ben Eliakum of Posen and his *Lev Tov*, see J. Fürst,
Bibliotheca Judaica, 2 (1863; reprinted 1960), 140f., and M. Erik,
Geshikhte Fun der Yidisher Literatur (1928), 294–301.

Erik also discusses most of the other authors of *musar*, or
morality, books treated in this chapter.

On the slanderous work of the apostate Samuel Friedrich
Brenz which moved Solomon Zalman ben Eliezer Ufenhausen
to write his *Yidisher Teryak*, see S. Krauss, "Zur Literatur der
Siddurim," in *Festschrift für Aron Freimann* (1935), 133–35. On the
Teryak, see N. Prylucki, in *YIVO-Bleter*, I (1931), 423, and M.
Erik, *Geshikhte* (1928).

CHAPTER SEVEN

FOLK-TALES; THE *MAASEH-BUKH*

The Arabic original of Rabbenu Nissim Ibn Shahin's *Ḥibbur
Yafeh Meha-Yeshuah*, Ferrara, 1557 (on which *Maasiyot Sheba-Talmud* [Constantinople, 1519] is based and of which *Ḥibbur Ha-
Maasiyot* [*ibid.*, 1519] is an anthology) was edited and published
by J. Obermann under the title *The Arabic Original of Ibn Shahin's Book of Comfort* (1933). A new Hebrew translation with
critical notes, was published by H.Z. Hirschberg in 1954.
Ḥibbur Yafeh is also included in Shrage Abramson, ed., *Ḥamis-
hah Sefarim Me-Et Rav Nissim Gaon* (1965). See also Abramson's
"Ha-Shem Ha-Ivri Shel Targum Sefer Ha-Maasiyot Le-Rav
Nissim Gaon," *Kiryat Sefer*, XLI (1965–66), 529–32.

On Nissim, see S.J. Rapoport, in *Bikkurei Ha-Ittim*, XII (1831), 56–83; S. Abramson, *Rav Nissim Ga'on* (1965); idem, in *Sinai*, LX (1967), 12–16; and A. Aptowitzer, in *Sinai*, XII (1943), 118f.

On the story of Meir the Ḥazzan, see I. Rivkind, "He'arot Le-Maaseh Akdamut," *Hadoar*, IX, No. 30, 507–509, and idem, "Di Historishe Alegorye Fun Rabbi Meir Sh-Tz," *YIVO-Bleter*, III (1929).

On the story of Beriah and Zimrah, see I. Schipper, "A Yidishe Libe-Roman Fun Mitlelter, Tsushtayern Tsu Der Geshikhte Vegn Dem Oyfkum Fun *Maaseh Beriah Ve-Zimrah*," *YIVO-Bleter*, XIII (1938), 232–245; M. Erik, in *Landau-Bukh*, 153–162; idem, *Vegn Alt-Yidishn Roman Un Novele* (1926), 147–172; and idem, *Geshikhte* (1928), 347–353.

The *Maaseh-Bukh* was translated into English by Moses Gaster under the title *Ma'aseh Book: Book of Jewish Tales and Legends* (2 vols., 1934). A German translation by Bertha Pappenheim appeared in 1929 under the title *Allerlei Geschichten*.

On this important work, see Jacob Meitlis' major study *Das Ma'asebuch, seine Entstehung und Quellengeschichte* (1933), which includes a list of the various editions; idem, *Ma'aseh in the Yiddish Ethical Literature* (1958); idem, *Di Shvokhim Fun Rabbi Shmuel Un Rabbi Yuda Khosid* (1961); M. Gaster, in *Jewish Studies in Memory of George Kohut* (1935), 270ff.; N.B. Minkoff, in *The Jewish People, Past and Present*, Vol. III (1952), 157f.; M. Erik, *Di Geshikhte Fun Der Yidisher Literatur* (1928), 353–64; I.Z. Zand, "A Linguistic Comparison of Five Versions of the Mayse-Bukh," in Uriel Weinreich, ed., *The Field of Yiddish*, Vol. II (1965); and I. Zinberg, "Vegn di Mekorim Fun Maaseh-Bukh," in *Literarishe Bleter*, 1927, No. 131.

For a fine review of Meitlis' *Das Ma'asebuçh*, see N. Susskind, in *YIVO-Bleter*, VI (1934), 157–65.

CHAPTER EIGHT

SIMḤAT HA-NEFESH; THE BATTLE FOR YIDDISH

J. Shatzky published a new edition of the second part of Elḥanan Kirchhan's *Simḥat Ha-Nefesh* in 1926. On the work, see his introduction, and N. Prylucki, in *YIVO-Bleter*, 222–227.

On the battler for Yiddish, Yeḥiel Michal Epstein, see S. Noble, "R. Yehiel Michal Epstein—A Dertzier Und Kemfer

Far Yidish in 17ten Yohrhundert," *YIVO-Bleter*, XXXV (1951), 121–138; Ch. Lieberman, in *YIVO-Bleter*, XXXVI (1952), 305–21; J. Freimann, in *Jahrbuch der jüdisch-literarischen Gesellschaft*, XV (1923), 37; M. Horovitz, *Avnei Zikkaron* (1901), 158; and B. Wachstein, in *Jahrbuch der jüdischen-literarischen Gesellschaft*, XVI (1924), 169–71.

On another noted protagonist and defender of Yiddish, Moses Frankfurter, see M. Horovitz, *Frankfurter Rabbinen*, 2 (1883), 74f., and I. Zinberg, "Di Ershte Yidishistn," *Moment* (1911), No. 26.

CHAPTER NINE

HISTORICAL AND TRAVEL LITERATURE; MEMOIRS AND *TEHINNOT*

On the Yiddish translation of Josippon, see M. Erik, *Di Geshikhte Fun Der Yidisher Literatur Fun Di Eltste Tsaytn Biz Der Haskole Tekufe* (1928), 373–375.

On the Yiddish versions of Solomon Ibn Verga's *Shevet Yehudah*, see M. Wiener's German introduction to *Shevet Yehudah* (1956), xv–xviii. See also Fritz (Yitzhak) Baer, *Untersuchungen über die Quellen und Komposition des Schebet Jehuda* (1923).

On Leib ben Ozer's chronicle *Bashraybung Fun Shabsay Tzvi*, see G. Scholem, *Sabbatai Ṣevi: The Mystical Messiah*, translated by R.J.Z. Werblowsky (1973), Index, s.v. Leyb b. Ozer.

The text of *Gzeyre Mimdinas Estraykh* was published by S. Krauss in *Historishe Shriftn*, II, 1937.

Menahem Mann Amelander's *She'erit Yisrael*, a supplement to the Yiddish translation of *Josippon*, was edited and translated into Hebrew, with an introduction, by H. Hominer under the title *Sefer She'erit Yisrael Ha-Shalem* (1964). Extracts from the work are contained in M. Grünbaum, *Jüdisch-deutsche Chrestomathie* (1892), 361–79.

J.A. Joffe has shown in his essay "Di Amsterdamer Tanakh Iberzetsung *Maggishei Minhah* Fun 1755(?)," *YIVO-Bleter*, XIV (1939), 229–250, that in the translation of the Bible published by Amelander in collaboration with his brother-in-law Eliezer Zussman Roedelsheim, only the Pentateuch translation is new. The translations of the Prophets and Hagiographa are a reprint of those in *Ha-Maggid*, by Jacob ben Isaac Ashkenazi of Yanov, the author of *Tze'enah U-Re'enah*.

Yitzḥak Ben-Zvi translated *Gelilot Eretz Yisrael*, with an introduction and notes, under the title *Iggeret Ha-Kodesh* (1953).

On *Megillat Shemuel*, see M. Erik, *Die Geshikhte Fun Der Yidisher Literatur* (1928), 419–420.

On *Megillat Eivah*, see I. Halpern, "Ḥibburei Rabbi Yom-Tov Lipmann Heller U-Ketavav," *Kiryat Sefer*, VII (1930–31), 140–148.

On the role of women as printers, publishers, and producers of Yiddish literature, see A.M. Habermann, *Nashim Ivriyyot Be-Tor Madpisot, Mesadderot, Motziot Le-Or Ve-Tomechot Be-Meḥabberim* (1933), and A. Yaari, *"Nashim Bi-Melechet Ha-Kodesh,"* in *Mehkerei Sefer* (1958), 280–281.

On Gele bat Moses bar Avraham Avinu, see A. Yaari, *Meḥkerei Sefer* (1958), 249–250, 262–263.

Extracts from *Meineket Rivkah* are included by S. Assaf in his *Mekorot Le-Toledot Ha-Ḥinnuch Be-Yisrael*, 2nd ed. (1948), Vol. IV, 45–46.

David Kaufmann first published the *Memoirs* of Glückel of Hameln in the original Yiddish, with an extensive introduction in German, in 1896. In 1910 Bertha Pappenheim published a complete German translation. An abbreviated Hebrew version, based on Kaufmann's edition, was published by A.Z. Rabinovitz in 1929.

An abbreviated translation into English, *The Memoirs of Glückel of Hameln*, was published by Marvin Lowenthal, with an introduction and notes (1931). J. Shatzky, in his review of Lowenthal's translation, *YIVO-Bleter*, VI (1934), 138–144, provides a bibliography on Glückel.

A complete English translation of the *Memoirs* was published by Beth Z. Abrahams under the title *The Life of Glückel of Hameln* (1962).

On Glückel, see N.B. Minkoff, *Glikl Hamil* (Yiddish, 1952), and Solomon Schechter, "The Memoirs of a Jewess of the Seventeenth Century," in his *Studies in Judaism*, Second Series (1908), 126–147.

On the *teḥinnah*-literature, see Solomon B. Freehof, "Devotional Literature in the Vernacular," *Yearbook* of the Central Conference of American Rabbis, XXXIII (1923). On Sarah Bas-Tovim, see S. Niger, *Bleter-Geshikhte Fun Der Yidisher Literatur* (1959), 83–85.

CHAPTER TEN

PARABLES AND MAXIMS; ELEGIES AND SOCIAL PORTRAITS

On the various Yiddish versions of *Meshal Ha-Kadmoni,* see A.M. Habermann, "Di Yidishe Oysgabes Fun *Meshal Ha-Kadmoni,*" *YIVO-Bleter,* XIII (1938), 95–105.

A facsimile reprint of Moses Wallich's *Sefer Meshalim* (Frankfurt, 1697) was published in Berlin in 1924. Two years later, in 1926, *Die Fabeln des Kuhbuches in Übertragung,* with a foreword by Aron Freimann, was published as a supplement to *Sefer Meshalim.* On the *Ku-Bukh,* see M. Erik, *Die Geshikhte Fun Der Yidisher Literatur.*

On *Tsukhtshpigl,* see A.A. Roback, "Yidish in der Harvarder Bibliotek," *Filologishe Shriftn,* II, 393–397.

On *Megillat Vintz,* see Erik, *Geshikhte,* 385–388. On a previously unknown edition (Hanau, 1733) of this poem, see L. Nemoy, "An Umbekante Oysgabe Fun *Megillat Vintz,*" *YIVO-Bleter* XXXIX (1955), 284–286.

Most of the Old-Yiddish historical poems are enumerated in chronological order by Moritz Steinschneider in his *Die Geschichtsliteratur der Juden* (1905). Examples of a considerable number of the texts are included, with annotations, in Max Weinreich's *Shtaplen* (1923; contains *Megillat Vintz*) and in his *Shturemvint* (1927).

On Jacob Tausk and his poem on the messianic pretender Shabbetai Tzevi, see Max Weinreich, *Bilder Fun Der Yidisher Literatur-Geshikhte* (1928), 219–52. See also G. Scholem, *Sabbatai Ṣevi: The Mystical Messiah* (1973), Index, s.v. Tausk, Jacob.

On Rebecca Tiktiner, see E. Schulmann, *Sefat Yehudit Ashkenazit Ve-Safrutah* (1913), 183–186.

On the popular Passover song "Ḥad Gadya," see Ch. Shmeruk, "The Earliest Aramaic and Jiddish Version of the Song of the Kid (Khad Gadje)," in Uriel Weinreich, ed., *The Field of Yiddish* (1954), 214–218. See also Y.L. Cohen, "Dos Yidishe Folkslid," in *Shtudies Vegn Yidisher Folksshafung* (1952), 16–18.

Di *Bashraybung Fun Ashkenaz un Polyak* was reprinted by M. Weinreich in *Filologishe Shriftn,* III, 540–551.

CHAPTER ELEVEN

THE BEGINNINGS OF DRAMA IN YIDDISH

The most valuable study of the origins and development of Yiddish drama remains I. Schipper, *Geshikhte Fun Yidisher Teater-Kunst Un Drama Fun Di Eltste Tsaytn Biz 1750* (three volumes, 1923–1928). Another important and comprehensive work is Bernard Gorin (Isaac Goido), *Di Geshikhte Fun Yidishn Teater* (two volumes, 1918).

On the medieval German Christian mystery plays, which exercised a certain influence on the rise of Yiddish drama, see R. Froning, *Das Drama des Mittelalters* (1891–92); O. Koischwitz, *Der Theaterherold im deutschen Schauspiel des Mittelalters und der Reformationszeit* (1924; reprinted 1967); E.E. Martin, ed., *Freiburger Passionspiele des XVI. Jahrhunderts* (1872); F.J. Mone, ed., *Schauspiele des Mittelalters* (1846); H. Reidt, *Das geistliche Schauspiel des Mittelalters in Deutschland* (1868); K. Weinhold, ed., *Weihnacht-Spiele und Lieder aus Süddeutschland und Schlesien* (1953); E. Wilken, *Geschichte der geistlichen Spiele in Deutschland* (1872); M.J. Rudwin, *A Historical and Bibliographical Survey of the German Religious Drama* (1924); O. Cargill, *Drama and Liturgy* (1930); and H.C. Gardiner, *Mysteries' End: An Investigation of the Last Days of the Medieval Religious Stage* (1946).

The first Hebrew Purim comedy *Tzaḥut Bediḥuta De-Kiddushin* was published by J. Schirmann (2nd ed., 1965; contains bibliography on the author, Jehudah Leone ben Isaac Sommo, pp. 173–176). On Sommo and his work, see A. Nicoll, *The Development of the Theatre* (5th ed., 1966, bibliography on p. 253); I. Gour, in *Bamah*, XXXI (1967), 14–25; and A. Holtz, in *Tarbitz*, XXXVI (1967).

On the German *Fastnacht*-plays, Biblical dramas, "English comedies," and *Staatsaktionen* of the Reformation and post-Reformation eras, which influenced the early Yiddish theater, see A. Cohn, *Shakespeare in Germany in the Sixteenth and Seventeenth Centuries: An Account of English actors in Germany and the Netherlands* (1965); R. Froning, ed., *Das Drama der Reformationszeit* (1895); F. Dietrich-Bader, *Wandlungen der dramatischen Bauform vom XVI. Jahrhundert bis zur Frühaufklärung* (1972); R. Genée, *Lehr- und Wanderjahre des deutschen Schauspiels vom Beginn der Reformation bis zur Mitte des XVIII. Jahrhunderts* (1882); R. Schwartz, *Esther im deutschen und neulateinischen Drama des Reformationszeitalter* (1898); A. Hauffen, ed., *Das Drama der klassischen*

Periode (1891); J. Mathes, *Die Entwicklung des bürgerlichen Dramas im XVIII. Yahrhundert* (1974).

CHAPTER TWELVE

AKHASHVEYROSH-PLAYS AND OTHER DRAMAS

On the Yiddish plays which came to be presented on the Purim festival as early as the middle of the sixteenth century see Ch. Shmeruk, "Purim-Shpil," *Encyclopedia Judaica*, XIII (1971), cols. 1396–1403.

The oldest surviving *Akhashveyrosh-Shpil*, dealing with the story of the Book of Esther, is a manuscript of 1697. It is discussed by B. Weinryb, "Zur Geschichte des ältern judisches Theaters (Über die Leipziger Ms. des Ahasveros-Esther-Spiels)," *MGWJ*, 1935, 415–424. The text of a similar *Akhashveyrosh-shpil*, printed at Frankfurt in 1708, is included in J.J. Schudt, *Jüdische Merckwürdigkeiten . . . Dritter Theil* (Frankfurt and Leipzig, 1714). Schudt also includes the text of a *Mechirat Yosef* play.

A collection of *Purim-shpiln* on various Biblical themes that were presented on the Yiddish stage in Europe from the eighteenth on into the twentieth centuries are to be found in N. Prylucki, ed., *Zamlbikher Far Yidishn Folklor*, I (1912) and II (1917).

On the *Akedat Yitzhak* play, see P. Matenko, "A Por Folkstimlekhe Tsugobn Tsu Der Akeyde-Literatur," *Yuda A. Joffe-Bukh* (1958), 284–286.

On the editions of the play *Gedulat David U-Meluchat Sha'ul*, see A. Yaari, "Hotza'ot Ha-Mahazeh 'Gedulat David U-Meluchat Sha'ul'," *Kiryat Sefer*, XII (1935–36), 384–388.

See also Ch. Shmeruk, "Di Moyshe Rabeynu Bashraybung," *Di Goldene Keyt*, No. 50 (1964).

CHAPTER THIRTEEN

MYSTICAL MORALITY BOOKS; SOCIAL AND EDUCATIONAL CRITICISM

A list of the various editions of Tzevi Hirsch Chotsh's "Taytsh Zohar," *Nahalat Tzevi*, is given by G. Scholem, *Bibliographia Kabbalistica* (1933), 209–210.

On Chotsh and his work, see M. Erik, *Di Geshikhte Fun Di Yidishe Literatur* (1928), 239–42; E. Milzahgi (Mehlsack), *Sefer*

Ravyah (1837), 276; D. Kahana, *Toledot Ha-Mekubbalim Ha-Shab-beta'im, Veha-Hasidim,* Vol. II (1914), 123–26; and E. Schulmann, *Sefat Yehudit Ashkenazit Ve-Safrutah* (1913), 38.

On Akiva Baer ben Joseph, the author of *Abbir Yaakov* and *Maasei Adonai,* see I.E. Benjacob, *Otzar Ha-Sefarim* (1880; reprinted 1956), 2, No. 22, 437, No. 12, 457, No. 69, and Moritz Steinschneider, *Catalogus Librorum Hebraeorum in Bibliotheca Bodleiana,* 3 vols. (1852–1860; reprinted 1964), 2612, No. 7210.

On Solomon Wetzlar and his *Hakirot Ha-Lev,* see Jehudah Elzet (pseud. of Rabbi Jehudah Leib Avida), "Mit 225 Yor Tsurik, A Mekhaber Fun A Muser Sefer—A Gewezener Aktyor," *Yidishe Folksshul In Johannesburg,* September, 1942.

L. Nemoy reports a previously unknown Yiddish version of "Till Eulenspiegel," which was published in Prague in 1735 and a copy of which is in the library of Yale University, in *YIVO-Bleter,* XXVII (1946), 198.

On Isaac Wetzlar and his *Libs-Brif,* see Isaac Rivkind, "Di Libs-Brif Un Zeyer Mekhaber," *Zukunft,* May, 1932, 306–309.

On the earliest "newspaper" in Yiddish, see J.S. da Silva Rosa, "Di Kurantin 1686–1687," in *Zamlbukh Likoved Dem 250 Yuvel Fun Der Yidisher Presse* (1937).

Glossary of Hebrew and Other Terms

Glossary of Hebrew and
Other Terms

Aggadah (or Haggadah): The non-legal part of the post-Biblical
Oral Torah, consisting of narratives, legends, parables,
allegories, poems, prayers, theological and philosophical
reflections, etc. Much of the Talmud is aggadic, and the
Midrash (see below) literature, developed over a period of
more than a millennium, consists almost entirely of Aggadah. The term *aggadah*, in a singular and restricted
sense, refers to a Talmudic story or legend.

Ashkenazim: Since the ninth century, a term applied to the
German Jews and their descendants, in contrast to the
Sephardim (see below). After the Crusades, many Ashkenazic Jews settled in eastern Europe and from there
migrated to western Europe and America. In recent centuries they have constituted the overwhelming majority
of the world Jewish population.

Baal Shem (in Hebrew, "master of the Name"): A title given
to persons believed capable of working miracles through
employing the divine Name. The title was not uncommon
in Eastern Europe in the seventeenth and eighteenth centuries, where it frequently implied a quack or impostor
who produced magical amulets, pronounced incantations,
etc.

Bakkashah (plural, Bakkashot): A Hebrew word meaning "supplication" and applied by the Sephardim to a kind of
hymn included especially in the liturgies of Rosh Ha-
Shanah and Yom Kippur.

Bar Mitzvah: The Hebrew words mean "one obliged to fulfill
the commandment," but the term is generally employed

to denote the ceremony marking the induction of a boy, when he has reached the age of thirteen, into the Jewish community and into adult observance of the commandments of the Torah.

Dayyan: A judge in a rabbinical court who is competent to decide on cases involving monetary matters and civil law, as well as questions of a religious or ritual character.

Derush: Homiletical interpretation of Scripture.

Etrog: A citron, one of the "four species" utilized on the festival of Sukkot, or Tabernacles, in the synagogue service.

Gemara: The second basic strand of the Talmud, consisting of a commentary on, and supplement to, the Mishnah (see Mishnah).

Gematria: A system of exegesis based on the interpretation of a word or words according to the numerical value of the constituent letters in the Hebrew alphabet.

Genizah: A depository for used and damaged sacred books, manuscripts, religious utensils, etc. The most widely known *genizah* was discovered in modern times in the synagogue of Fostat (Old Cairo), which was built in 882.

Golem (Hebrew, "shapeless mass"): An automaton, particularly one in human form, supposedly created supernaturally through magic, especially through the invocation of mysterious divine names.

Haggadah: When used in connection with the Pesaḥ or Passover festival, the narration of the story of the exodus from Egypt, recited in the home on the first night of Passover (outside of Israel, on the first two nights).

Halachah (in Hebrew, "law"; derived from the verb *halach*, "to go" or "to follow"): The legal part of Talmudic and later Jewish literature, in contrast to Aggadah or Haggadah, the non-legal elements. In the singular, *halachah* means "law" in an abstract sense or, alternatively, a specific rule or regulation; in the plural, *halachot* refers to collections of laws.

Hannukah (In Hebrew, "dedication"): An eight-day festival commemorating the victory of the Maccabees over Antiochus Ephiphanes in 165 B.C. and the subsequent rededication of the Temple in Jerusalem.

Haskalah: The movement for disseminating modern European culture among Jews from about 1750 to 1880. It advocated the modernization of Judaism, the westernization of traditional Jewish education, and the revival of the Hebrew language.

Haskamah (plural, Haskamot): Approbations or authorizations by respected rabbinic authorities, sometimes inserted in Hebrew books. The practice of inserting *haskamot* became particularly widespread after the synod of rabbis in Ferrara in 1554 decided that Hebrew books should obtain prior approval by Jewish authorities in order to prevent suppression or censorship by the officials of the Church. Later a *haskamah* was frequently solicited by the author of a book as testimony of his work's scholarly value and its orthodoxy.

Havdalah: The Hebrew term means "distinction" or "division" and refers to the ceremony marking the end of the Sabbath day and consisting of benedictions over wine, spices, and a special flaming candle.

Ḥazzan (plural, Ḥazzanim): In modern times, the precentor or leader of the synagogue service. In Talmudic times, he was an official charged with maintaining order and security and also the person who would officiate as precentor and reader of the Torah. In the Middle Ages, the *ḥazzan* was usually the only person in the congregation who knew the prayers or owned a prayer book.

Ḥeder: The Hebrew term means "room" and refers to a school for teaching children the fundamentals of Judaism. The ḥeder figured prominently in traditional Jewish education in Eastern Europe.

Hevlei Ha-Mashiah: (in English, "Pangs of the Messiah"): The woes and troubles, especially those inflicted on the Jewish people, that were expected to precede the advent of the Messiah.

Ḥiddushim (Hebrew, "novellae" or "new things"): Commentaries on the Talmud and subsequent works of rabbinic literature that seek to deduce new facts, principles, or interpretations from the implications of the text.

Ḥuppah: The term means "canopy" in Hebrew and refers to the canopy under which the marriage ceremony was traditionally held. The word is sometimes used to denote the wedding ceremony itself.

Kabbalah: The mystical religious movement in Judaism and/or its literature. The term Kabbalah, which means "tradition," came to be used by the mystics beginning in the twelfth century to signify the alleged continuity of their doctrine from ancient times.

Kahal: A Jewish congregation or community. In Eastern Europe the term denoted the organized Jewish community structure which had autonomous power and was officially charged with the responsibility for collecting taxation. It was abolished by the Russian government in the nineteenth century.

Kavvanah (plural, Kavvanot): In Hebrew, "devotion." The quality of devotion, intention, and spiritual concentration which, according to Jewish teaching, should accompany the fulfillment of religious commandments, especially prayer. *Kavvanah* was particularly stressed by the Kabbalists and the later Hasidim, in whose view prayers uttered with *kavvanah* have a direct influence on the supernal worlds. Many Kabbalists believed that *kavvanah* in prayer is effectuated by various combinations of the letters of the Ineffable Name, and such a combination itself came to be called a *kavvanah*.

Ketubah: The Hebrew word means "writing" and refers to the document setting forth the legal obligations of a bridegroom towards his bride.

Kiddush: A Hebrew term meaning "sanctification" and referring to a special ceremonial benediction recited on the Sabbath and festivals. The benediction consists of the ordinary blessing over wine or bread, and a blessing declaring the holiness of the particular occasion.

Kinah (plural, kinot): In Biblical and Talmudic times, adirge over the dead. Later the term came to be applied to a liturgical composition for the Ninth of Av dealing with the destruction of the Temple as well as with contemporary persecutions.

Lulav: The palm branch, one of the "four species" utilized on the festival of Sukkot, or Tabernacles, along with the etrog (see above), myrtle, and willow.

Maggid (plural, Maggidim): The title given to a popular preacher, especially by the Jews of Poland. These were frequently itinerants who travelled about preaching on both Sabbaths and weekdays and urging study of Torah and observance of the commandments.

Maḥzor (In Hebrew, "cycle"): A term commonly used to designate the Festival Prayer Book. At first the Maḥzor contained prayers for the whole year, including the daily and Sabbath services, but most Ashkenazic Maḥzorim now contain only the festival prayers.

Maskil (plural, maskilim): An adherent of Haskalah (see above).

Matzah (pl. Matzot): The unleavened bread prescribed by Jewish tradition for consumption during the Passover season as a memorial of the bread baked in haste by the Israelites departing from Egypt.

Megillah (plural, Megillot): The name for any of the five biblical books read on special occasions: the Song of Songs on Passover (read by the Sephardim also on Friday afternoons and the nights of the Passover *seder*); the Book of Ruth read on the festival of Shavuot; the Book of Lamentations, read on the Ninth of Av; Ecclesiastes, read on the festival of Sukkot, or Tabernacles (but not by the Sephardim); and the Book of Esther, read on Purim.

Meshummad: A Hebrew term referring to a convert to Christianity. The term is generally used in condemnatory fashion and implies disloyalty to, and apostasy from, Judaism.

Mezuzah (plural, Mezuzot): A parchment scroll placed in a container and affixed to the doorposts of rooms occupied by Jews, in fulfillment of an injunction in the sixth chapter of Deuteronomy.

Midrash (plural, Midrashim): The discovery of new meanings besides literal ones in the Bible. The term is also used to designate collections of such Scriptural exposition. The best-known of the Midrashim are the *Midrash Rabbah, Tanḥuma, Pesikta De-Rav Kahana, Pesikta Rabbati,* and *Yalkut Shimeoni.* In a singular and restricted sense, Midrash refers to an item of rabbinic exegesis.

Mishnah: The legal codification containing the core of the post-Biblical Oral Torah, compiled and edited by Rabbi Judah Ha-Nasi at the beginning of the third century C.E.

Mitzvah (plural, Mitzvot): A Hebrew term meaning "commandment," and referring to any precept of the Torah, positive or negative. According to the Talmud, there are 613 mitzvot in the Pentateuch, apart from other commandments ordained by the rabbis.

Oral Torah (or Oral Law): The body of interpretation and analysis of the written law of the Pentateuch created in post-exilic Judaism and handed down orally from generation to generation. The Oral Law consists of the Mishnah (see above) and the Gemara (see above), both of which were combined to form the Talmud (see below). Even after the redaction of the Talmud, the body of tradition contained in it continued to be known as the Oral Law because its roots were in an oral tradition.

Parashah (plural, Parashot): The Hebrew word meaning section, and signifying, in the synagogal reading of the Pentateuch, either the weekly portion (Sidrah; see below) or, more particularly, the smaller passages read to or by each person who is called to the reading of the Torah.

Parnass (from the Hebrew term *parnes,* meaning "to foster" or "to support"): A term used to designate the chief synagogue functionary. The *parnass* at first exercised both religious and administrative authority, but since the sixteenth century religious leadership has been the province of the rabbis. The office of parnass has generally been an elective one.

Paytan: A liturgical poet (see *piyyut*).

Pesaḥ: The festival, commonly referred to as Passover, which commemorates the exodus of the Israelites from Egypt.

Pilpul: In Talmudic and rabbinic literature, a clarification of a difficult point. Later the term came to denote a sharp dialectical distinction or, more generally, a certain type of Talmudic study emphasizing dialectical distinctions.

Piyyut (plural, Piyyutim): A Hebrew liturgical poem. The practice of writing such poems began in Palestine, probably around the fifth century C.E., and continued throughout the ages, enriching the Jewish Prayer Book. Perhaps the greatest of the medieval writers of *piyyutim* were Solomon Ibn Gabirol and Moses Ibn Ezra.

Purim (Hebrew, "lots"): A festival commemorating the saving of Persian Jewry through the efforts of Esther from the threat of destruction on the part of Haman, as recorded in the Biblical Book of Esther. Purim is observed on the fourteenth day of the Hebrew month of Adar.

Rosh Ha-Shanah (Hebrew, literally "head of the year"): The Jewish New Year, a holiday which inaugurates the Ten Days of Penitence culminating in the Day of Atonement or Yom Kippur (see below). It is regarded as a day of judgment for the entire world and for individuals when the fate of each man for the coming year is inscribed in the Book of Life.

Sanhedrin: A Hebrew word of Greek origin designating, in rabbinic literature, the assembly of seventy-one ordained scholars which served both as the supreme court and the legislature of Judaism in the Talmudic age. The Sanhedrin disappeared before the end of the fourth century C.E.

Seder (in Hebrew, "order"): The ritual dinner conducted in the Jewish home on the first night (and outside the State of Israel, the first two nights) of Pesaḥ. The story of the exodus from Egypt is recounted and a number of symbols related to it are included in the ritual.

Seliḥah (plural, Selihot): The term means "penitential prayer," and refers to a special type of *piyyut* (see above), begging mercy and pardon for sins and transgressions.

Sephardim: The term applied to the Jews of Spain (in Hebrew, Sepharad) and afterwards to their descendants, no matter where they lived. The term Sephardim is applied particularly to the Jews exiled from Spain in 1492 who settled all along the North African coast and throughout the Ottoman empire.

Shavuot (in Hebrew, "weeks"): The last of the three Biblical pilgrim festivals, originally marking the wheat harvest, but after the destruction of the Temple commemorating especially the Covenant between God and Israel and the giving of the Torah on Mount Sinai.

Shechinah: A term used to imply the presence of God in the world, in the midst of Israel, or with individuals. In contrast to the principle of divine transcendence, *Shechinah* represents the principle of divine immanence.

Shema: A Hebrew word meaning "hear" and beginning the fundamental confession of faith in Judaism: "Hear O Israel, the Lord our God, the Lord is One" (Deuteronomy 6:4). The confession is pronounced both in the evening and morning service and also before going to sleep at night. The Shema is also recited by, or in behalf of, a Jew on the point of death.

Shemoneh Esreh: The chief prayer, consisting of eighteen benedictions, in the Jewish liturgy.

Shofar: The horn of a ram sounded on Rosh Ha-Shanah, or the New Year, as well as on other solemn occasions, e.g., the ceremony of excommunication or at a time of epidemic or famine.

Shulḥan Aruch: The abbreviated code of rabbinic jurisprudence, written by Joseph Karo in the sixteenth century, which became the authoritative code of Jewish law and is still recognized as such by Orthodox Judaism.

Siddur (Hebrew, "order"): Among Ashkenazic Jews, the volume that contains the statutory daily prayers.

Sidra[h] (plural, Sidrot): A Hebrew word meaning "order" or "arrangement," and signifying a section of the Pentateuch prescribed for reading in the synagogue on a particular Sabbath. There are fifty-four *sidrot*, permitting the reading of the entire Pentateuch in the course of one year.

Sukkot: The Hebrew term means "tabernacles" and refers to the autumn pilgrim festival. The eighth day, called Shemini Atzeret, is, strictly speaking, a separate holiday. In Israel the eighth day is combined with Simḥat Torah, the day devoted to rejoicing over the Torah, but in the diaspora Simḥat Torah is the ninth and last day of the festival of Sukkot.

Tallit: The prayer shawl worn by adult males (among orthodox Jews usually only by married males) during the morning prayers.

Talmud: The title applied to the two great compilations, distinguished as the Babylonian Talmud and the Palestinian Talmud, in which the records of academic discussion and of judicial administration of post-Biblical Jewish law are assembled. Both Talmuds also contain Aggadah or non-legal material.

Tanna (plural, Tannaim): Any of the teachers mentioned in the Mishnah, or in literature contemporaneous with the Mishnah, and living during the first two centuries C.E.

Targum (plural, Targumim): The Aramaic translation of the Bible. There are three Targumim to the Pentateuch: Targum Onkelos, Targum Jonathan, and Targum Yerushalmi.

Tefillin: Two black leather boxes, fastened to leather straps, worn on the arm and head by an adult male Jew, especially during the weekday morning prayer. The boxes contain portions of the Pentateuch written on parchment.

Teḥinnah (plural, Teḥinnot): Private devotions recited by the individual as a supplement to the standard congregational liturgy. Devotional books in Yiddish, intended for women, also came to be known as teḥinnot.

Torah: In its narrowest meaning, the Pentateuch. Torah is also known in Judaism as the Written Law. In its broader meaning, Torah comprises as well the Oral Law, the traditional exposition of the Pentateuch and its commandments developed in the late Biblical and post-Biblical ages. In its widest meaning Torah signifies every exposition of both the Written and the Oral Law, including all of Talmudic literature and its commentaries. The term is sometimes used also to designate the scroll of the Pentateuch read in the synagogue service.

Tosafists: The French and German scholars of the twelfth to the fourteenth centuries who produced critical and explanatory notes on the Talmud.

Tosafot (Hebrew, "addenda"): Critical and explanatory notes on the Talmud by Jewish scholars in France and Germany during the twelfth to fourteenth centuries. Among the most famous of the Tosafists are Rabbenu Tam, Rabbi Samuel ben Meir, and Rabbi Isaac of Dampiere.

Tosefta: A supplement to the Mishnah (see above). The one version that has survived has six Orders, with the same names as those of the Mishnah, and its treatises correspond to all but four of the treatises of the Mishnah.

Tzaddik: In Hebrew, the term means "a righteous man." It is a title given to a person renowned for faith and piety. The concept of the tzaddik became especially important in the Hasidic movement of the eighteenth century, in which the tzaddik was regarded as endowed with extraordinary powers and capable of serving as an intermediary between God and man.

Wissenschaft des Judentums, die: (German for "the science of Judaism): The modern type of scientific and critical exploration of Jewish history, literature, and religion, initially developed in Germany in the first half of the nineteenth century.

Yeshivah (plural, Yeshivot): A traditional Jewish school devoted primarily to the study of the Talmud (see above), and rabbinic literature.

Yom Kippur: Hebrew, "Day of Atonement." A solemn fast day observed on the tenth day of the Hebrew month Tishri and serving as the culmination of the Ten Days of Penitence. It is a day on which the individual is to cleanse himself from sin and to beg for the forgiveness of God through confession, prayer, and atonement.

Yotzer (plural, Yotzerot): A term generally denoting a hymn preceeding the Shema (see above) and more broadly all the special *piyyutim* (see above) added to the blessings of the Shema on the Sabbath and festivals.

Zohar: The chief work of the Spanish Kabbalah (see above) traditionally ascribed to the Tanna Simeon ben Yoḥai (second century) but probably written by the Spanish Kabbalist Moses de Leon at the end of the thirteenth century.

Index

Index

Milḥamah Ve-Shalom), 333n, 334n.

Geiger, Abraham, 14, 178n.

Geistliche Schauspiele und kirkliche Kunst (Weber), 307n.

Gele (young typesetter; daughter of Moses ben Abraham Avinu), 242.

Gelilot Eretz Yisrael (or Derech Ha-Kodesh, by Gershon ben Eliezer Edels), 236–237.

Gerondi, Jonah, 21, 143, 145.

Gershom, Rabbenu, 12.

Gesammelte Schriften (Leopold Zunz), 14n, 236n.

Geschichte der deutschen Schauspielkunst, Die (Eduard Devrient), 311n, 315n.

Geschichte der Juden, Die (Heinrich Graetz), 8n, 312n.

Geschichte der Juden in Rom, Die (Vogelstein and Rieger), 20n.

Geschichte der Juden in Schlesien, Die (Marcus Brann), 18n.

Geschichte des Erziehungswesens und der Kultur der abendländischen Juden, Die (M. Güdemann), 149, 151n.

Geschichtsliteratur der Juden, Die (Moritz Steinschneider), 232n.

Geshikhte Fun Der Yidisher Literatur, Di (Max Erik), 52n, 67n, 106n, 108n, 149n, 176n, 181n, 186n, 205n.

Geshikhte Fun Der Yidisher Teater-Kunst Un Drame, Di (Ignacy Schipper), 51n, 292n, 323.

Gezerat Kehillah Kedoshah Pozna, 278.

Ginsburg, S.M., 91.

Ginzberg, Louis, 178n.

Ginzburg, Mordecai, 254.

Glückel of Hameln, 125, 241ff.

Golden Ass (Apuleius), 184, 189n.

Goliath (Biblical), 112, 316, 335n, 339, 340, 341.

Gordon, J.L., 125.

Gottesdienstlichen Vorträge der Juden, Die (Leopold Zunz), 14n, 15, 18, 103n, 110n.

Graetz-Festschrift (ed., Perles), 20n.

Graetz, Heinrich, 8n, 14, 312n.

Graziano, Eliezer, 310.

Gregory, Johann, 320.

"Grosse Schau-Platz, Lust und lehrreich auch traurige und wunderliche Geschichten, Der" (journal, ed. by Benjamin ben Zalman Kroneburg), 359.

Grünbaum, Max, 17n, 30n, 33n, 97n, 109n, 121n, 127, 142n, 145n, 157, 166n, 170, 186.

Güdemann, Moritz, 20n, 124, 136n, 149, 151, 193n.

Guide for the Perplexed (Maimonides), 164.

Guta bat R. Nathan, 23n

Gutenberg, Johann, 46, 48, 121, 149.

Gzeyre Mimdinas Estraykh, 232n, 350n.

Hagar (Biblical), 7.

Haggadah (Passover), 8, 20, 34, 49, 294.

Haggadah Shel Shavuot (Midrash Aseret Ha-Dibberot), 102, 107, 174, 188n.

Haggadot Ketu'ot, 178n.

Ḥakirot Ha-Lev (Solomon ben Simeon Wetzlar), 352–353, 355n.

Halevi, Abraham ben Eliezer, 312n.

Halevi, Jehudah, 16, 27, 187.

Halevi, Meir, 232n.

Halom Mordecai (medieval Midrash), 107.

Haman (Biblical), 274n, 316, 320, 321, 322, 324, 325, 327, 328, 329, 322.

Hanau, Samson, 247n.

Hanau, Simeon of Frankfurt, 221.

Hanau, Solomon Zalman, 231, 357.

"Haninah, Tale of Rabbi," 189ff.

Hannah (Biblical), 31, 111, 112, 258.

Hannover, Nathan Nata, 231, 250, 251.

Hans Sachs ausgewählte dramatische Werke, 312n.

Hans Wurst. See Pickelhering.

Harkavy, A., 44n, 149, 150, 170n, 175n.

Hasid, Jehudah of Kalisch (and Shedletz), 346.

Haupt- und Staatsaktion, 315, 316, 321, 322.

Hauptmann, Gerhart, 212n.

Hayyei Olam, 145ff.

Ḥayyim of Hameln, 243, 244.

Ḥayyim Abraham of Mogilev, 333n.

Ḥayyim ben Nathan of Prague, 222, 230.

Helin, Elḥanan bar Abraham, 275.

Heller, Yom-Tov, 240, 241n.

Helwig, H., 197n.

Ḥemdat Tzevi (Tzevi Hirsch Chotsh), 347.

Herod, 167.

Hessen, Julius Isidorovich, 76n.

Hibbur Yafeh Meha-Yeshuah (Rabbenu Nissim), 175, 188.

Hildebrant, 87, 88, 121.

Ḥiyya, Rabbi, 349.

Hipsher Khotonu, Ayn, 313.

Ḥochmat Nashim (Yeḥiel Ha-Kohen of Anoscrivi), 217, 218n.

Ḥochmat Shelomoh Im Mamlechet Sha'ul, 342.

Hogerlin, Samuel ben Moses, 39.

Holophernes (Apocrypha), 316.

Holzwart, Magister Mathias, 339.

Homer, 304.

Horowitz, Isaiah, 219n.

Horowitz, Sheftel, 136, 159.

Ḥovot Ha-Levavot (Baḥya Ibn Pakuda), 212, 223.

Humboldt, Wilhelm von, 15.

Hutten, Ulrich von, 46.

Index